Judging W. T. Cosgrave

Judging

W.T.
COSGRAVE

THE FOUNDATION OF THE IRISH STATE

MICHAEL LAFFAN

ROYAL IRISH ACADEMY

Judging W.T. Cosgrave

First published 2014

by Prism
Prism is an imprint of the Royal Irish Academy
19 Dawson Street
Dublin 2
www.ria.ie

The author and publisher are grateful to the following for permission to reproduce documents, photographs and illustrations in this book: Liam Cosgrave; British Pathé; the Bureau of Military History; Chicago History Museum; Corbis; Cork City and County Archives; Dublin Diocesan Archives; the ESB Archive; Colm Gallagher; Gallery Oldham; George Mason University Special Collections and Archives; Getty Images; Mark Humphrys; the Irish Architectural Archive; the Irish Film Institute; the Irish Visual Artists' Rights Organisation; the family of Seán Keating; the Board of the National Archives of Ireland, the National Archives, London; the Board of the National Library of Ireland; Punch Magazine Ltd; the RTÉ Stills Archive; the Royal Mint; John Stafford-Langan; the Board of Trinity College Dublin; UCD Archives, School of History and Archives; John Weedy; and the Wolfsonian Florida International University.

During the production process some documents, photographs and illustrations have been retouched or tinted for aesthetic purposes. Every effort has been made to trace the copyright holders of these items and to ensure the accuracy of their captions. See Photo Credits.

Text copyright © 2014 Michael Laffan

ISBN 978-1-908996-39-8

British Library Cataloguing in Publication Data. A CIP catalogue record for this book is available from the British Library.

Editor: Helena King
Design: Fidelma Slattery
Index: Aisling Flood

Printed in Spain by Ganboa

10 9 8 7 6 5 4 3 2 1

To Elizabeth, David, Angela and Maura

CONTENTS

PAUL·HENRY

PREFACE

The suggestion that I might write a biography of W.T. Cosgrave, and that I would have access to his surviving papers, has resulted in a project that involved several years of research. It has provided challenges and it has provoked occasional frustration, but it has been an overwhelmingly stimulating and satisfying experience. I have struggled with faded microfilm and with Cosgrave's difficult handwriting; I have ploughed through vast files and have found insights and evidence in unlikely places; and I have benefitted from the kindness and expertise of others. I appreciate their assistance deeply, and it is a pleasure to acknowledge those who have helped me.

Above all I am grateful to Liam Cosgrave, who urged me to undertake this biography, who lent me his father's papers and who was a source of constant information and encouragement, but who never tried to influence or control what I wrote.

The book has been supported and published by the Royal Irish Academy, and I would like to express my appreciation to Nicholas Canny and Luke Drury, the Academy presidents who commissioned it. Patrick F. Wallace, an Academy member, acted as a facilitator. Ruth Hegarty has been a patient, supportive and creative editor, and she made helpful comments on an early draft. Alice Butler, the research assistant on the project, acquired much of the illustrative material. Helena King has copy-edited the volume, and Fidelma Slattery has designed it. I am most appreciative of their work, which has resulted in a handsome production.

I am particularly indebted to my old friends Ciaran Brady and Tom Garvin, who read a draft of the book with great care, made many constructive proposals, and saved me from solecism and error. The two anonymous readers for the RIA have also made numerous informed and thoughtful suggestions. Additional material has been added to the text since the draft encountered by these four readers; they bear no responsibility for any mistakes that remain. Frank Bouchier-Hayes was exceptionally generous in sharing his vast fund of information.

Librarians and archivists have given me invaluable help—in particular the enormously knowledgeable Mary Broderick of the National Library in Dublin and Paul Ryan of the Killaloe Diocesan Archive in Ennis. Their assistance has gone far beyond the call of duty.

I am also indebted to Seamus Helferty, Kate Manning and Orna Somerville of UCD Archives, who have been friendly and helpful as always; Julia Barrett, Anne Conway and Monica Cullinan of the UCD Library; Mary Clark of the Dublin City Library; Catriona Crowe, Aideen Ireland and Patrick Sarsfield of the National Archives; Lisa Dolan of the Military Archives; Noelle Dowling of the Dublin Diocesan Archives; Marie Léoutre and Gerry Long of the National Library; Aisling Lockhart of the Manuscripts and Archives Research Room, Trinity College; and Brian McGee of Cork City and County Archives.

Others have assisted me in various ways, and I am grateful to Gary Agnew, Johnny Bambury, Frank Barry, Joe Brady, Maurice Bric, the late Patrick Buckley, the late Jim Cantwell, John Coolahan, Peter Costello, Ian d'Alton, David Dickson, Tom Dunne, Lindsey Earner-Byrne, Bryan Fanning, Diarmaid Ferriter, Colm Gallagher, Patrick Geoghegan, Daire Hogan, Edward James, Finola Kennedy, Michael Kennedy, Dympna Kiernan, Felix Larkin, Charles Lysaght, Bill McCormack, Deirdre McMahon, Robert Marshall, Ciara Meehan, Conor Mulvagh, Brian Murphy, Will Murphy, Úna Newell, Willie Nolan, Éimear O'Connor, John O'Dowd, Eamon O'Flaherty, Cormac Ó Gráda, Clare O'Halloran, Eunan O'Halpin, Mary O'Hegarty, Margaret Ó hÓgartaigh, Susannah Riordan, Paul Rouse and Mary Ruane.

Previous pages:
Detail from *Irish Fun*, May 1922, p. 4, caricature of Cosgrave.

Detail from cover of *Dublin Opinion*, Holiday Issue, August 1935, vol.14, no.162; from back left: John Marcus O'Sullivan; James Ryan (examining horse); Patrick McGilligan (waving); Frank Aiken; Eamon de Valera and Seán T. O'Kelly; Cosgrave; Seán McEntee (collecting money); Alfie Byrne shaking the hoof of Cosgrave's horse; and Eoin O'Duffy in the distance on his own merry-go-round.

Pencil sketch of Cosgrave by Paul Henry, late 1922/early 1923.

Opposite: 'We got him out to put him in', Sinn Féin election poster for Cosgrave, 1918.

WE

TO

GOT

PUT

HIM

HIM

OUT

IN

G

VOTE FOR

COSGRAVE,

A FELON OF OUR LAND.

Issued for the Candidate, William T. Cosgrave, by his Authorised Election Agent, M. J. Crotty, and printed at the Gaelic Press, 30 Upper Liffey Street, Dublin.

'the art and science
of nation-building'

- THE PRESIDENT -

Opening image: Cosgrave and his
son Míceál at the inauguration of the
Ardnacrusha hydro-electric station
on the River Shannon, July 1929.

THE beginnings were prosaic. There were no celebrations, no bands played, and no crowds sang in the streets. The Irish Free State, the end product of the Irish revolution, was inaugurated in a subdued and businesslike manner. On 6 December 1922 members of the Irish parliament took an oath of fidelity to King George V, as was required by the treaty with Britain that had been signed exactly a year earlier, and they elected a head of government. The new 'president of the executive council', W.T. Cosgrave, informed Governor-General Tim Healy of his election by the Dáil and he received the three-word reply 'I appoint you'.[1] Cosgrave then nominated his cabinet. Apart from journalists, no members of the public were present. Newspapers described the proceedings as decorous and dull, without pomp or panoply and 'devoid of spectacular interest'.[2]

There were good reasons for this lack of ceremony. The creation of the new Irish state was bitterly controversial, and Cosgrave's government was, from the outset, fighting for its existence against opponents determined to destroy it. Ruthless provocation was soon followed by ruthless retaliation. The French consul in Dublin began his report to Paris on 9 December by declaring that the Free State had been born in blood.[3] The circumstances could hardly have been less auspicious.

Yet the structure that was completed in December 1922 proved resilient and enduring; a stable and democratic political system took root after the storms of insurrection, guerrilla conflict and civil war. Much of the credit for this achievement lies with the man who led the government throughout its early years, but after he retired from public life he remained for decades one of the forgotten figures of Irish history.

Cosgrave did not deserve such neglect. He headed the first fully independent Irish administration, and he presided over a slow but steady expansion of the freedom provided by the Anglo-Irish Treaty of 1921. He led the victorious side in a brutal civil war, and once the fighting had ended he ruled with moderation and humanity. Although sometimes authoritarian he was nonetheless a committed democrat in a period when many newly-independent states lapsed into dictatorship. His party won three successive general elections, and with a single exception (in Luxembourg) his was the longest unbroken term of office of any democratic head of government in Europe between the wars. During his decade in power there were five changes of prime minister in Britain and ten in France. For most of the time he presided with little apparent effort over a talented cabinet, some of whose members had more dominant personalities or who outshone him intellectually. In this respect he resembles three successful

British prime ministers during his lifetime, Henry Campbell-Bannerman, Stanley Baldwin and Clement Attlee. To draw another foreign parallel, he might bear comparison with the US president Harry Truman, of whom little was expected when he succeeded the dominant and charismatic Franklin D. Roosevelt but who later proved himself in office.

According to one observer Cosgrave was 'greater as a party leader, as a master of men than as a statesman'.[4] Other commentators have seen him as more a statesman than a party leader, and he frequently gave the impression of being bored by the mechanics of politics. He failed to appreciate the importance of creating a strong, disciplined party, and he despised populism—even if at times he felt obliged to make distasteful concessions to his supporters. He saw himself as the people's servant, but not their slave.[5] His commitment to the Cumann na nGaedheal party was more dutiful than enthusiastic; he was seen to be above party politics, and he often acted as if he were.[6] When he lost an election, against opponents who had been his wartime enemies less than a decade earlier, he accepted his defeat gracefully and moved to opposition. He was not successful in this role—to lose five general elections in a row is a melancholy record—but he minimised the impact and consequences of his party's brief, disastrous flirtation with paramilitary extremism. At the end of his life he established a pattern of dignified retirement that has been followed by most of his successors.

Cosgrave had what has been described as a 'constitutionalist' mentality, which emphasised the need for a state to provide social order, to uphold the rule of law and to protect individuals from the assaults of others.[7] He tried hard, but with only limited results, to inculcate a sense of moral responsibility and a respect for authority in a people who for centuries had regarded 'the government' as an alien and hostile force—often with good reason. He saw the aim of independence as being to improve their conditions and to make them more self-reliant. He believed strongly, almost passionately, in 'the gradual education of the people by experience of political life and by the inculcation of proper standards of political conduct by all those in a position of influence'.[8] He was a man of austere integrity, he did his best to practise what he preached, and subsequent generations have had cause to regret the limits of his impact and influence. One of Cosgrave's characteristics was a no-nonsense practicality, and he possessed 'an admirable tendency to distinguish between willingness to promise and capacity to deliver'.[9]

Like many others, he began his career as a reformer and grew more conservative with age. He was a man of his time who represented its strengths and weaknesses. By the standards of later generations his concept of the state was narrow, and he assumed that a government 'can do little more than create conditions favourable for industrial development and after that the initiative must be left in most cases…to those who undertake the immediate responsibility of establishing new industries'.[10] He is often seen as representing the cultural and economic values of the 1920s, values that have long been out of fashion. John Maynard Keynes went even further and described him as 'a nineteenth century liberal'.[11] But he governed at a time of intermittent worldwide economic depression, and he was obliged to manoeuvre within the financial constraints imposed by a destructive civil war. He had good reason to be concerned with the cautious and conscientious management of a fragile state that had still to prove its viability.

He had no strong feelings about systems of government: 'I don't care what form it is so long as it is free, independent, authoritative, and the Sovereign Government of the people, and that it will be respected'.[12] Although an Irish nationalist he was not anti-British, and he saw the Anglo-Irish Treaty as marking a fresh start in the relations between the two islands. 'With the British Government and the British people our peace is made'.[13] Towards the end of his political career he regretted that 'hatred of England has been a cloak for inefficiency, incompetence, uselessness in the hard work or in the art and science of nation-building'.[14]

THE MAN AND THE OFFICE

Cosgrave has been widely belittled. Irish writer Francis Hackett portrayed him in terms of bland and cute mediocrity, of ferocity covered by smugness.[15] William O'Brien the old home ruler disparaged him as 'an unknown spirit-grocer', while his namesake William O'Brien the trade union leader viewed Cosgrave somewhat more charitably as being 'reasonably able, not just a soldier pitchforked by accident into politics'.[16] The British prime minister Ramsay MacDonald dismissed him as a weak man who would fight hard if driven into a corner.[17] On the other hand, the Canadian prime minister Mackenzie King described him as unassuming but brave as a lion, and he concluded 'I have the greatest admiration for him'.[18] Winston Churchill, who had encountered Cosgrave in different roles, portrayed him as

> a quiet, potent figure…a chief of higher quality than any who had yet appeared. To the courage of Collins he added the matter-of-fact fidelity of Griffith and a knowledge of practical administration and state policy all his own.[19]

A shrewd literary critic who had observed him in action saw him as 'the perfect exemplar, in that period, of the ordinary man suddenly elevated to high office, who had the inborn moral character that is required for rule'.[20]

Cosgrave was a small man, quiet and humorous, with light blue eyes, a quizzical expression, stooped shoulders, a neatly trimmed moustache and sandy-coloured hair that turned silver with age. He was described as having a thoroughly conservative face (but with hair standing up straight on his head, *à la Pompadour*), and as looking like the general manager of a railway company.[21] His frail health was often a source of comment and concern, yet he lived to the age of 85. He was not an instinctive politician or rebel, and his background was not that which might be expected to produce a national leader: for twenty years he had managed his family's public house in Dublin. He lived comfortably throughout his political life and he dressed formally, wearing bowler hats long after they had gone out of fashion. But he never lost the common touch. He was sociable and popular, he could be a forceful public speaker, and he viewed himself as a down-to-earth, no-nonsense businessman who was impatient with inefficiency and who wanted to get things done. He believed in meritocracy. He was described as having 'the rare and enviable knack of administering reproof in a fashion that serves as a stimulus'.[22] At the end of his career he remarked that it had always been his wish to hear other people's views, while reserving judgment.[23]

Among Cosgrave's most striking features were his cheerfulness and his ability to entertain others. Tim Healy described him as shy but jolly.[24] A party colleague remarked of him that he was 'a man with a sense of humour, with the wit and smartness of repartee that is typical of Dublin. One cannot fall out with him'. Years later the same man found him 'affable, friendly, genial as always'.[25] Over the decades many who knew or met him enjoyed his company.

He was exceptionally devout. It was a source of comfort to him that he received permission to maintain a private oratory in his house.[26] He worried about a lost set of rosary beads and he was grateful when it was replaced by another that had been blessed by the archbishop of Westminster.[27] He performed traditional Catholic devotions such as visiting seven churches on Holy Thursday.[28] His friend Oliver St John Gogarty, whose wit and teasing he relished, joked that Cosgrave's piety had greatly embarrassed the pope.[29] His opinions reflected, perhaps in an extreme form, the sentiments of his own time, but on occasion they can appear fulsome to later generations. For example, he described the pope as 'the Vicar of Christ, the Apostle of Peace, the Holy One of God', and he saw the arrival of the papal nuncio as 'a day of days, a year of years, a century of centuries'.[30] But his deep Catholic faith did not prevent him from enjoying excellent relations with those who held other beliefs. For example, in his last term of office his vice-president was Ernest Blythe, a member of the Church of Ireland.

He was well-read in Irish history but, like many other people, he approached the past in a practical and even utilitarian manner. He believed that the real value of historical study was not sentimental reverence but 'the stern lessons to be learned from the successes and failures of past generations and from the knowledge accumulated throughout the ages in which those successes and failures have occurred.'[31] The word 'stern' may be significant.

Cosgrave was the first to admit that he achieved his pre-eminence in large part by chance, and he described having reached the position of president as 'a pure accident'.[32] He was elected to Dublin Corporation for the first time when he was aged 28. He was appointed to a cabinet position (in what soon became an 'underground' government) ten years later, but during the interval he had participated in a rebellion, had been sentenced to death and had spent two years in jail. More obvious potential leaders of an independent Irish state, such as Seán MacDermott or Thomas Ashe, were killed after the Easter Rising. Eamon de Valera, under whose presidency Cosgrave had served effectively for nearly three years between 1919 and 1922, went into opposition when the Dáil rejected him after its approval of the Anglo-Irish Treaty. The two leading figures in the pro-treaty government, Michael Collins and Arthur Griffith, died young and unexpectedly, within months of negotiating independence and before the establishment of the Irish Free State. So, when Collins was killed Cosgrave was the right man in the right place, with the right experience; and he succeeded to a position that neither he nor others could have envisaged.

He was modest, and even when in power he was not solemn or pompous when describing his position. In 1923 he was asked about the office that he held, and he began the ensuing dialogue as follows:

> 'some people say President of Dáil Eireann, some people say President of the Executive Council, some people say President of the Irish Free State and other people say Uactaran [*sic*]. The generally accepted term is President.'
>
> Q. 'President of what?'
>
> A. 'That is the point.'[33]

Others might have been more conscious of their status.

He was aware of the impression that lucidity was not one of his strengths, and he envied Lord Birkenhead who, he claimed, could 'say in a sentence what I'd require a page to say'.[34] (He often asked colleagues to draft his speeches, and he even sought advice from the chief justice.[35]) It may seem unlikely that he would confide in his political opponents, but the Northern Irish prime minister, James Craig, quoted him as confessing 'I've been pushed into this. I'm not a leader of men!' Thomas Johnson, the leader of the Labour Party, recorded Cosgrave's reflection that someone 'not of the old Dail group' would probably have to become head of government before there would be any settled peace between supporters and opponents of the treaty. His preferred candidate was the philosopher and historian John Marcus O'Sullivan, who was then minister for Education.[36] In a more frivolous mood he sent a letter of congratulation to Count John McCormack when he learned of an American newspaper report that the tenor might be elected president of the Irish Free State.[37]

But his presidential title was soon abolished, his party atrophied and it was re-born with a different name. Many of his objectives and achievements were either swept away by his successor or lost their relevance to a rapidly changing world. His long years in opposition were frustrating, and for the last 22 years of his life his retirement from public affairs was complete.

Over the decades since his death W.T. Cosgrave has generally been viewed with a vague respect, but his achievements have lacked an appropriate examination and recognition. In terms of his posthumous reputation he was unfortunate that his decade in power was sandwiched between the leadership of two of the most dominant figures in modern Irish history, Michael Collins and Eamon de Valera—each of whom has inspired at least a dozen books about his life or aspects of his career. Cosgrave has been the subject of one short biography and one study in which he is linked with his son Liam, who served as leader of the Fine Gael party from 1965 to 1977 and as taoiseach from 1973 to 1977.[38] He had no interest in justifying his record and he contributed to his own neglect by leaving few papers behind him—in contrast to contemporaries such as de Valera and Richard Mulcahy.[39]

This book has been able to benefit from a long perspective, from a wide range of secondary works and from sources that were not available to earlier researchers. It is an attempt to fill a gap and to pull Cosgrave back from the margins of history. Its aim is to assess his achievements and to examine the career of a man who, despite failures and lost opportunities, was remarkably successful in the 'big things'. Judged by the standards of his time, but also those of later generations whose values have often differed from his own, he was one of the most significant figures who shaped twentieth-century Ireland.

PRESIDENT COSGRAVE,
the Irish Free State leader, in the bosom of his family.

Montage of four stills from the film 'Ireland 1922', showing Cosgrave relaxing with his family.

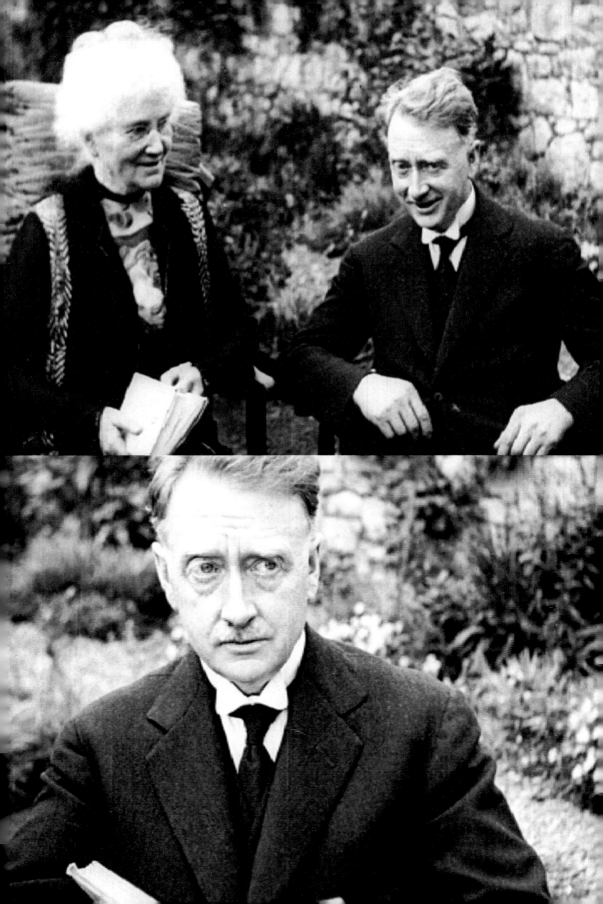

Cosgrave in the garden of his home in
Templeogue, Dublin, early 1920s,
holding his son Liam on his shoulders.

Opposite: Page from Liam de Róiste's
diary, written in Cork, 25 October
1922, describing Cosgrave.

connected with the enactment this evening. Pádraig
O'Máille and myself spoke entirely in Irish, and
McGoldrick, of Donegal, also spoke partly in Irish.
Quietly as this act was passed, it does mark
another step on in the way of orderly procedure for
the setting up of the State organisation and makes the
position of the Irregulars still more untenable.

Hogan, minister of agriculture, still twits me,
but with somewhat better spirit this evening, as one
"crying for the sugarstick you cannot get." I retorted
that expressing one's opinion is not "crying" and that
we were all "crying", by propaganda to the world,
up to the time of the Truce. Desmond Fitzgerald was
near at the time; he was Director of Propaganda in
the old Dáil; and he acknowledged it was "crying"
then, that we were exhibiting our "sores" to the world.

Cosgrave is a man with a sense of humour,
with the wit and smartness of repartee that is
typical of Dublin. One cannot fall out with him.
and he, too, was genial this evening.   There

Cosgrave (seated, second from left) between Lord Birkenhead and future British prime minister Winston Churchill; official photograph of premiers and delegates to the 1926 Imperial Conference, in the garden at Downing Street, London, 1 October 1926. Kevin O'Higgins is fourth from left, second row; Desmond FitzGerald second from right, second row; Diarmuid O'Hegarty, government secretary, fourth from left, back row.

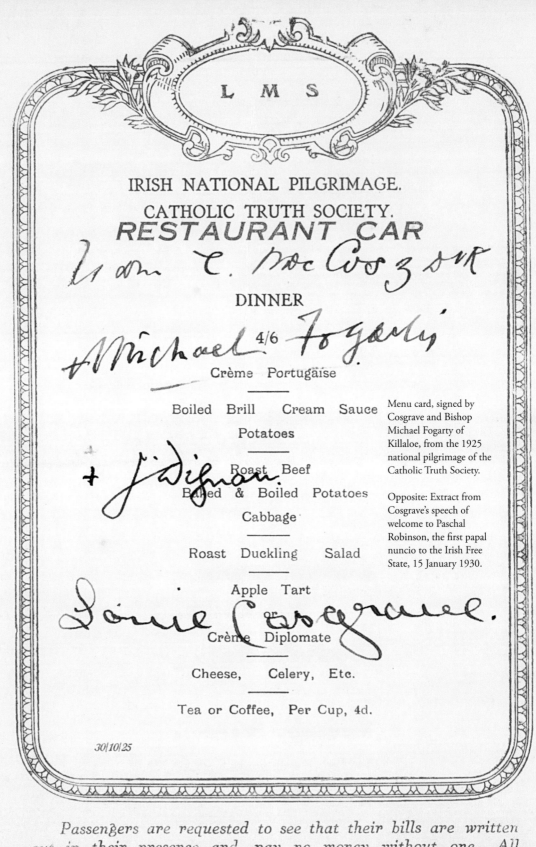

L M S

IRISH NATIONAL PILGRIMAGE.
CATHOLIC TRUTH SOCIETY.
RESTAURANT CAR

Liam T. MacCósgair

DINNER

+ Michael 4/6 *Fogarty*

Crème Portugaise

Boiled Brill   Cream Sauce

Potatoes

+ J. Dignan.

Roast Beef

Baked & Boiled Potatoes

Cabbage

Roast Duckling   Salad

Apple Tart

Liam Cosgrave.

Crème Diplomate

Cheese,   Celery,   Etc.

Tea or Coffee,   Per Cup, 4d.

30/10/25

Menu card, signed by Cosgrave and Bishop Michael Fogarty of Killaloe, from the 1925 national pilgrimage of the Catholic Truth Society.

Opposite: Extract from Cosgrave's speech of welcome to Paschal Robinson, the first papal nuncio to the Irish Free State, 15 January 1930.

Passengers are requested to see that their bills are written out in their presence and pay no money without one. All observations and complaints should be sent to Arthur Towle, Controller, L.M.S. Hotel Services, St. Pancras, N.W. 1.

It is a day of days, a year of years, a century of centuries,
and I thank the great God that the lot has fallen to me to be
the instrument through which the people of Ireland ~~and the~~
~~millions of our race all over the world~~ extend a welcome to the
first Ambassador of the Vatican State to an Irish Government.
The moment is full of the solemnity of a nation's ritual and we
cannot but feel that the spirits of all the great men who have
gone before us and who have built up our nation are joining with
us today in our welcome to our guest.

CEAD FAILTE ROMHAT.   Patrick and Paladius would join with
us. They brought the light of christianity to our pagan ancestors
in the fifth century. They sowed the seeds of a monasticism re-
nowned for its austerity, learning and holiness. And their zeal
brought forth Columbcille and Columbanus and their disciples who
helped to
evangelised the Europe of the early middle-ages. From the fifth
to the ninth century Irish missionaries carried light and learning to all the countries of the Continent. They went to France
and down the Rhine to Switzerland. They went to the Danube and
the Elbe. They established schools in Carinthia, Saxony,
Thuringia, Salzburg, and Bavaria. They pushed their hard way
across the Alps and Fiesole, Lucca, Naples, even Rome itself
received the fruits of their labour. All these men of our
nation would surely join with us tonight in saying CEAD FAILTE
ROMHAT.

Cosgrave and Bishop Fogarty at
the funeral of the nuncio, Paschal
Robinson, 31 August 1948.

Cosgrave and Ernest Blythe on a tour of inspection to the Carlow
sugar beet processing factory, 1926.

Cosgrave in a group with the crew of the *Bremen* aircraft, which
completed the first non-stop transatlantic flight, from Baldonnel in
Dublin to Greenly Island, Canada, in April 1928. Among the group are
Richard Mulcahy; Eamonn Duggan; Desmond FitzGerald; Patrick
Hogan; Captain Hermann Köhl; Fionán Lynch; Cosgrave; Major James
Fitzmaurice; James Fitzgerald-Kenney; and John Marcus O'Sullivan.

Cosgrave and the other members of Trinity College Dublin's
Edmund Burke bi-centenary committee (1928). From left to right;
Rupert Edward Cecil Lee Guinness, second Lord Iveagh; Edward J.
Gwynn, Provost of Trinity; Cosgrave; Frederick Edwin Smith (or
Galloper Smith), first Earl Birkenhead; and James Henry Mussen
Campbell, first Baron Glenavy and first chairman of the Senate.

Cosgrave with Hugh Kennedy (to his right), Eoin
MacNeill and Bryan MacSwiney (both behind, to his
left), along with members of other delegations,
including King George V, arriving in Geneva for the
fourth Assembly of the League of Nations, 1923.

'A good steady boy'

- BECOMING A POLITICIAN, 1880–1913 -

Opening image: Newspaper reproduction
of a photograph of Cosgrave as a young
boy; the only surviving image of Cosgrave
in the first twenty years of his life.

W . T . Cosgrave was a Dubliner who lived for almost 40 years close to the old medieval heart of the city. He was always proud of Dublin and he studied its history, buildings and people.[1] But like most of the capital's inhabitants his roots lay in the countryside. His maternal family, the Nixons, came from Prosperous in north Co. Kildare. Bridget Nixon was the seventh of eight children; as a girl she and her sisters went to the United States, but she soon returned to Ireland, where she met and married Thomas Cosgrave. His ancestors came originally from Co. Wexford, and one of them was hanged during the 1798 Rebellion after a massacre at Carnew. Subsequently, the family moved to Castledermot in south Kildare, where Thomas was born.

Bridget and Thomas married in 1877, and in that same year they moved to Dublin and purchased a public house and grocer's shop at 174 James's Street—in an area dominated by one of the most powerful and successful of Irish manufacturers, Guinness's brewery. They had six children in rapid succession; the second of these was William Thomas, born on 6 June 1880. He had an older brother, Patrick, and four younger siblings, Thomas, May, Philip and finally Joseph (who died in infancy). Such a family size was common at the time. The business must have prospered, for in 1884 Thomas bought another property on nearby Emmet Road, and in the following year he purchased 162 James's Street, a building which until then had been owned by a rival spirit dealer and which was situated only a few doors away from the family's public house.[2] This rapid progress indicates a man of exceptional ability. Thomas was active in local politics and he was a member of the Poor Law Guardians, who were responsible for managing the South Dublin Union and other bodies.

Then disaster struck: Thomas Cosgrave died suddenly in July 1888, at the age of 33. Bridget carried on the family business, and three years later in September 1891 she married Thomas Burke, who was manager of the public house at 174 James's Street. Two children were born of her second marriage, Joan and Frank—who was always called Gobban. Mrs Cosgrave was listed as the owner of the two properties on James's Street until after her remarriage, and then for many years her second husband replaced her in the records. She was admired as a refined woman of strong character, and she died in 1934 at the age of 78. A family friend, Moira Lysaght, remembered Thomas Burke as a pleasant but bombastic man, very different from his stepchildren who must have been irritated by his banter.[3] W.T. Cosgrave's older brother Patrick (the only one of his siblings to marry) died in 1920, his younger brothers Thomas and Philip in 1910 and 1923 respectively, and Gobban was killed in the Easter Rising. His sisters were musically talented; May was a pianist while Joan was a concert singer, and for years they ran the Leinster School of Music. Both survived him.

When he retired from public life Cosgrave remarked that he wrote no diary and that his records were negligible.[4] In 1923, during the civil war, anti-treaty forces burned down his house and destroyed all its contents, with the result that there is almost no record of his early decades. One photograph of his early years survives, taken when he was a young boy; otherwise his childhood, adolescence and early adulthood are virtually unknown. Trivial details, such as the fact that when he was a boy he was taken to visit the Institute for Male Deaf Mutes in the Dublin suburb of Cabra, stand out because of their rarity.[5] In middle age he described himself as having been well-bred and well-reared, and having been taught to behave himself in public and in private.[6]

As children, he and his siblings spent their holidays with their maternal grandparents who lived beside the Grand Canal at Landenstown in Co. Kildare, where his grandfather worked as a steward for the Digby family.[7] Throughout his life he loved horses, an interest that may have begun when as a boy of eight he visited his paternal grandfather in Castledermot. His stepfather kept a horse in the yard at James's Street, and William's favourite childhood recreation was watching games of polo in Phoenix Park. He has been described as riding in the park 'with his golden hair flying in the wind'.[8] As a young man he owned a horse; he hunted with the Kildares and the Meaths in then-rural areas such as Lucan and Clondalkin, and he would ride gently from James's Street down the Naas Road to Palmerstown in Co. Kildare to take part in hunts.[9] Most participants were British army officers, farmers or members of the gentry, so someone with Cosgrave's background would have been an anomalous figure. But it seems clear that business prospered and that the family lived comfortably.

Young William was educated by the Christian Brothers. At first he went to school in James's Street only a few minutes' walk from the family home, and then from January 1891 to January 1895 he attended the O'Brien Institute in Marino—where his older brother Patrick had preceded him the previous September. January was a normal month for enrolment, and many of his classmates entered at the same time. The institute was a boarding school that had been opened by the Christian Brothers three years earlier, and it was situated beyond what was then the city boundary. It was and is a large, imposing neo-Gothic building, and since 1982 it has served as the training centre for the Dublin Fire Brigade.

In 1913 a letter from the trustees' solicitors to the revenue authorities described the purposes of the institute as 'the maintenance, support and education of orphan boys in destitute circumstances', but in practice the students came from varied backgrounds. On the same page of the school's register on which William Cosgrave's admission is entered, the occupations listed for other boys' fathers include those of sea captain, pig buyer, postman, builder and contractor, dealer in pictures, musician and medical doctor.[10] The Christian Brothers emphasised the cult of the saints, and their textbooks were infused with a Catholic ethos. Their range was narrow; they included extensive biographical lessons and sketches relating to Irish history, but they contained little or no geographical or cultural information about countries outside Ireland.[11] In the O'Brien Institute, classes were given in reading, arithmetic, science, commerce, religion, physical education and (depending on the availability of sufficient funds) Irish. The school day began with mass, at 7a.m. in summer and 7.30a.m. in winter. Cosgrave remarked that one of the few prizes to have come his way at school was a biography of the Young Irelander and home ruler John Martin.[12] He retained happy memories of his schooldays, he kept in contact with the Institute and in his later years he made frequent contributions to benefit its students.[13]

When he retired as leader of his party in 1944 a former schoolmate reminisced to him in a letter about an incident that had taken place half a century earlier. Cosgrave, who was either a captain or a monitor in the O'Brien Institute, was walking in from the playing field beside some other boys when—to his embarrassment—one of the Christian Brothers remarked of him 'there goes the future Lord Mayor of Dublin'. The writer continued appropriately, 'you went much further'.[14] William Cosgrave's formal education ended when he left the Institute at the age of 14½, a normal pattern at the time. The overall assessment of his schooldays was that he was 'a good steady boy'—a verdict that was not incompatible with being a future lord mayor. Steadiness would remain one of his striking characteristics. (In the school record, teachers' comments on his classmates ranged from 'excellent', through 'lifeless' and 'not bad but wild', to 'a good boy—but stupid'.)[15] It is clear that he received a sound basic education, and throughout his life he remained an avid reader. He amassed a substantial library. Long afterwards Professor Michael Hayes wrote of Arthur Griffith and other Sinn Féiners who left school at a comparatively early age that the surroundings of Dublin in their manhood gave them something like the equivalent of a university education.[16] In this group he might have included Cosgrave, who was born less than a decade after Griffith.

After leaving school Cosgrave worked as a cashier, and as a shorthand and typing clerk in a dairy engineering firm, before he joined the family business.[17] He often used shorthand in later life. He read newspapers about Irish and international affairs. He was proficient in mathematics, and towards the end of his career he told the Dáil: 'I need never read figures. I need only hear or see them and they satisfy me and I do not boast about the way I got my information or education in these matters. It happens to be a facility'.[18] He used this skill to good advantage, and according to family lore he helped to turn around the fortunes of the pub. In 1909 the ownership of 174 James's Street, hitherto listed in his stepfather's name only, was altered to include William and his sister May. (William's name was removed in 1921, when he was on the run.)[19] Before his marriage, Cosgrave lived in an upper back room above his mother's licensed house, from which he could look out at the Royal Hospital and Phoenix Park; he acted as the manager; and he was paid a salary.[20] More than half a century later Moira Lysaght remembered vividly how he entertained an audience in the family dining room.

> In deep studied tones he held us spellbound recounting a ghost story about 'the headless coach' which words and rolling delivery still ring in my ears. In the background the step father Tom, impatient at the length of the recital, kept on muttering—'Will the bloody fellow ever shut up?'[21]

In the 1901 census the family was recorded as being accompanied by a servant, a grocer's assistant who, like Cosgrave's stepfather Thomas Burke, came from Co. Tipperary. Perhaps optimistically, all the adults were described as being able to speak Irish as well as English. Ten years later, the 1911 census revealed some changes; most notably, all the names were now recorded in Irish (although his stepfather, the head of family, signed the form in English). Cosgrave's uncle Patrick (his father's brother) lived in the house, and his own younger brother Philip had moved to the family's other property on the street, No. 162, which was also occupied by his maternal aunt. Virtually no information survives concerning his life during these years.

In Ireland public houses were traditional venues of local activity, the principal centre of male working-class recreation. It was estimated that in the mid-1870s, about the time that Cosgrave's father opened his business, between a quarter and a half of the Dublin population frequented public houses on Sunday afternoons. 'Organisations as varied as trade unions, young men's societies, and fenian circles all held meetings in pubs'.[22] A successful manager had to be a popular and/or respected figure, and throughout his life Cosgrave was always an affable man who could display firmness on occasion. An authority on Dublin pubs has remarked that only 'a man of genial temper can keep a tavern or an inn. It is a job that calls for patience, tact, understanding, wide interests and that love of mankind in its bright or sorry aspects which these qualities imply'.[23] Cosgrave possessed such characteristics. Long afterwards he accepted that some licensed houses were dens of vice, but he also argued that apprentices in pubs could learn 'great lessons in Christian charity, in kindness, in humanity, and in many of the other virtues…there is brought home to young boys some of the realities of life that are very useful to them'.[24] It was obvious that he spoke from experience. His activities in helping his mother and stepfather to manage the pub must have given him a wide circle of acquaintances and a familiarity with the problems of his neighbourhood, thereby facilitating his entry into local politics.

Such a progression was common at the time. In 1903 Arthur Griffith pointed out that 29 of the 80 members of Dublin Corporation were publicans, ex-publicans or people otherwise directly connected with the liquor trade; in 1910 nineteen councillors were publicans/grocers, and they came a close second to the largest occupational group, merchants, who numbered twenty-one.[25] Publicans were a powerful force in John Redmond's home rule party, and it is significant that, despite his family background, Cosgrave moved in a different and more radical direction. It is possible that, in common with many others, he had been influenced by the centenary commemorations of the 1798 rebellion—particularly because of his ancestor's execution.

His earliest recorded expression of political views was in 1900, when Queen Victoria made her first visit to Ireland for 39 years. Her tour was designed to arouse support for the unpopular Boer War and it provoked numerous protests. One of these took the form of a letter from the nineteen-year-old Cosgrave to the *Irish Daily Independent* in which (prophetically in light of his future political career) he criticised Dublin Corporation's plan to present the queen with an address of welcome. Most of his letter was in a traditional nationalist style. He claimed that the British had replaced fire and sword by 'over-taxation, coercion, and famine', and that the Great Famine was largely the result of the British government's denial of assistance at a time when 'one of the most despotic oligarchies that ever disgraced Christendom feasted upon the fat of the land'. He revealed a publican's professional concerns in his complaint that duties imposed by Gladstone had resulted in the closure of 70 Irish distilleries.

He also pointed out that a subsequent additional tax of six pence per gallon of whiskey was too small for the retailer to pass on to the consumer, thus frustrating the possibility of reducing sales.[26]

Like many other Irish nationalists Cosgrave was influenced by Griffith's writings, and in later years he reminisced about having attended the first annual convention of Sinn Féin (which was then called the National Council) in November 1905. A list of over one-hundred people who were present at this meeting included the names of figures such as P.H. Pearse and Oliver St John Gogarty; Cosgrave probably appears as 'U. Ua Cosgar, Dublin'.[27] Ua Cosgair was the Irish form of his name that would be used in the census return some years later. There is no record of his having any political involvement in the course of the following months, and when a Sinn Féin branch was formed in his electoral ward of Usher's Quay in March 1907 he was not among the nine people who comprised its officers and committee. By the end of that year, however, he was one of several members who spoke on the party's policy. Soon afterwards he became treasurer, and he proposed one of his colleagues as a candidate for election to Dublin Corporation.[28] He rose rapidly through the ranks and within a few months he had been elected branch chairman.[29] Some of its meetings took place in 'the rooms' of the family's public house.[30]

THE CORPORATION

In January 1909 Cosgrave ran for election to the corporation in Usher's Quay ward, a sprawling area in the south-west of the city with (in 1911) a population of 25,793. Only two of the fifteen wards had more inhabitants. He saw himself as the candidate of 'a self-supporting, self-reliant people',[31] and in this he remained consistent for decades to come. In the course of his campaign he portrayed himself as being outspoken in his opinions on the needs and rights of the working class, and as having the endorsement of every labour body in the ward. An ex-president of the Trades Council, John Farren, urged all trade unionists to vote for Cosgrave, and some of his former schoolmates rallied round. He was described as a supporter of the Gaelic League. Councillor Denis Healy, who was elected as a Sinn Féin representative for Usher's Quay a year earlier, claimed that Cosgrave had been urged to stand for election on previous occasions because he had a prior claim to the nomination, but that he had declined.[32] (Healy later became a political opponent and regretted having introduced Cosgrave to public life.[33])

His margin of victory was narrow and he won by 1,122 votes to 1,045, a mere 77 more than his home rule opponent. He was one of five Sinn Féin candidates who were elected to the corporation in 1909, while another four were defeated.[34] Cosgrave joined senior colleagues such as Alderman Tom Kelly and Seán T. O'Kelly as one of a small group of radical members in a body dominated by the home rule party. He would subsequently be returned unopposed in 1912 and 1915 at the end of two three-year terms

In the past Sinn Féin had denounced the influence of publicans in Dublin politics, and it claimed that 'the temperance cause has ever had in us its warmest advocates'. But in the 1909 municipal election campaign, when the party's newspaper drew attention to the large number of its opponents who owned public houses, it felt obliged to single out Cosgrave as 'one of the few men in his business who has always placed the National interests above trade considerations'.[35] He was an oddity within the Sinn Féin party. He was not a member of the publicans' professional body, the Licensed Grocers and Vintners Protection Association. In January 1909 the association's minutes recorded its congratulations to two of its members who had been elected, and who thereby 'increased the strength of the Trade in the Corporation by two votes'.[36] Cosgrave's election did not belong to this category and he was not mentioned.

His first intervention in the corporation, a speech supporting Tom Kelly for the office of lord mayor, was described as 'brief'.[37] This was to prove characteristic, and throughout his long political career Cosgrave preferred to speak concisely, eschewing the verbiage associated with many Irish politicians. He soon made his mark; within a few months of his election he, along with five others, was 'named' by the mayor as being responsible for outrageous behaviour at the previous corporation meeting—which had involved councillors pummelling each other as they rolled on the floor.[38] He was conscientious, and he attended meetings more diligently than almost all his colleagues; in 1911 only five other members had a better record.[39] In 1914 he was present at 32 of the 33 general meetings. Following custom he rotated from one committee to another, and thereby he acquired expertise in public health, city distress, waterworks, cleansing and supplies and housing. He chaired committee meetings and intervened regularly in discussions and debates, but he and his Sinn Féin colleagues were usually in a minority. In 1915 his abilities were recognised when he was elected to chair the most important of the corporation's committees: estates and finance.

As a councillor Cosgrave involved himself in local activities; for example, he was elected chairman of a bazaar and fête to help clear off the debts of James's Street church.[40] He addressed meetings in his own ward and in other parts of Dublin.[41] He was a member of the Dublin Industrial Development Association and the Co. Dublin GAA committee.[42] He became his party's spokesman on some national issues, such as its refusal to be associated with a vote of sympathy on the death of Edward VII, and shortly afterwards he was one of a number of speakers at a protest meeting who objected to an expression of loyalty to the new king, George V.[43]

Cosgrave soon acquired a reputation for his concern about the poor, and he became familiar with their problems; one of Dublin's two main centres of poverty was located next to the ward that he represented.[44] Tom Kelly wrote at the time about a charitable institution close to the Cosgraves' house where hundreds of poor women lay on the ground with only rough blankets to cover them.[45] Not long before, streets in area had borne revealing names, such as 'Pigtown Lane, 'Cut-Throat Lane' and 'Murdering Lane'. In the 1911 census the Usher's Quay ward was recorded as having 1,308 one-room tenement dwellings—of the city's total of 21,133.[46] Two years later a report stated that 60,000 people in Dublin needed re-housing as a matter of urgency. Over 1,500 tenements, containing 22,700 people, were 'unfit for human habitation and incapable of being rendered fit for human habitation'; 20,000 families lived in one-roomed tenements, and one building was occupied by 98 people.[47]

In March 1910 Cosgrave proposed that the corporation should donate £100 to its public health committee 'for the housing of poor consumptives', but the motion was narrowly defeated.[48] In 1912 he suggested that it should establish a housing committee (a body that would soon be dominated by his colleague Kelly, himself a famous crusader on behalf of Dublin's impoverished citizens). By 1916 Cosgrave was known to the unionist William Wylie as a member of the corporation who was always ready to help the poor of the city.[49] Three years later, Cosgrave wrote to Griffith (by then the acting president of the Dáil government) quoting a British-appointed engineering expert to the effect that the Easter Rising might not have taken place if the people of Dublin had been better housed.[50]

The Sinn Féin councillors worked hard to effect reforms and they attempted to force owners to keep tenements in repair. They encountered hostility from their home rule opponents on the corporation, several of whom were slum landlords. They also tried to ensure that meetings would be held in the evenings, so that councillors who worked at 'day jobs' (unlike publicans, who were busier in the evenings) would be able to attend. He and his colleagues voted against a petition by the corporation that women should be entitled to vote in parliamentary elections, but they did so because approving the petition would constitute recognition of 'Westminster'; they supported the wording of the resolution in so far as it sought to remove discrimination against women.[51]

Sinn Féin representatives on the corporation lobbied for Irish to be made a compulsory subject for admission to the new National University, and on occasion Cosgrave spoke in Irish at corporation meetings—as in seconding the proposal to confer the freedom of the city on Kuno Meyer and Peadar Ó Laoire.[52] Subsequently, he denounced the withdrawal of Meyer's honorary citizenship.[53] He also advocated the use of Irish-manufactured goods and materials, and he argued that when making appointments the corporation should give preference to people of Irish birth and residence.[54]

Sinn Féiners tried to reduce unnecessary costs and to audit the salary and allowances voted to the lord mayor. Cosgrave objected to the pattern whereby from 1908 onwards the mayor was voted an extravagant salary of £3,688 during his first year in office.[55] This was over nine times the annual amount that MPs received after 1911, when they were first paid for their services, and it was almost 50% greater than Cosgrave's own salary of £2,500 (after a period of high inflation) when he became head of the national government. He and others fought regularly, almost ritually, against the home rule group on the corporation in an effort to reduce this sum paid to the lord mayor—with intermittent success. (Cosgrave's dissatisfaction was to culminate much later, in 1924, when the government that he headed abolished the corporation.)

Cosgrave was prepared to take issue with his party's establishment. In September 1911 Griffith's newspaper *Sinn Féin* published a letter from 'Boyesen of Kollund' (one of the editor's many *noms de plume*), complaining that Dublin was threatened with starvation by irresponsible fomenters of 'sympathetic' strikes, and that the police and army should act as strike-breakers. Cosgrave wrote to Jim Larkin's *The Irish Worker* declaring bluntly that no member of Sinn Féin in Dublin or elsewhere approved of such sentiments.[56]

Some months later, in January 1912, he proposed the creation of a committee of inquiry that would investigate the grievances of employees in the public and private services—with the aim of preventing strikes by removing their causes. He pointed out that the condition of wage-earners in towns and cities had not improved, in comparison with that of farmers and farm labourers. He continued:

there are long hours and scanty remuneration in many large concerns; there are under-paid girls in large catering establishments,
and abuses to be remedied in the treatment of nurses in some of
our large hospitals, not to speak of the most urgent need for better
housing for the poor.

He suggested that such committees of inquiry should include Irish people who
had lived abroad. They would, he argued, be more likely to have a fair con-
ception of the wage-earner's just status than those who viewed the matter 'from
a merely traditional standpoint'.[57]

DUBLIN DISPUTES

Cosgrave became involved in the long-running controversy that began when
Hugh Lane offered to the city of Dublin his valuable collection of paintings—
including masterpieces by Degas, Manet and Monet—on condition that the
corporation would provide a suitable gallery to house them. Lane's ideas for a
gallery became increasingly exorbitant, and ultimately he insisted that the paintings should be installed in a building that would span the Liffey, on the site of
the present Metal Bridge, and that the gallery should be designed by his friend
Edwin Lutyens. His generosity was accompanied by arrogance, and his cause
was not helped when W.B. Yeats entered the fray, powerfully but tactlessly dis-
paraging 'Paudeen' and 'Biddy', and (in a later poem) those who 'add the
ha'pence to the pence / And prayer to shivering prayer'. Populists and philistines
exploited such easy targets. Opposition soon grew, and among the project's
most vehement critics was one of Ireland's leading capitalists, William Martin
Murphy. There were good arguments against Lane's ideas in their final form; as
has been pointed out, apart from the risk from sparks from steamboats passing
underneath, 'visitors would hardly be unaffected by the exhalations from the
river; one could imagine the emptying of the gallery with each receding tide'.[58]

From the beginning Cosgrave supported the plan for a new Gallery of
Modern Art, but like many others he seems to have become uneasy at Lane's in-
transigence and he was concerned at the extent to which ratepayers would be
levied to fund the gallery. In March 1913 he supported the bridge site, but by
June his enthusiasm had lessened and he voted for further discussion, particularly of the costs involved.[59] Subsequently he proposed that the employment of
a particular architect should not be a condition of the gift, and that no plan
should be considered if it excluded competition from Irish architects. Although

there should be no objection to a design from Lutyens, Cosgrave was anxious that 'native Irish genius' should not be ignored. His proposal was defeated on a tied vote.[60] At the decisive meeting he seconded a motion that expressed gratitude to Lane but declared that the site he had chosen was 'expensive, unpopular, and highly impracticable', and requested him not to insist on it. Instead, the corporation should select another site and invite designs for a building.[61] This motion was passed. Lane withdrew his offer, and the end result appeared to be that 'through the Corporation's pusillanimity, Murphy's enmity and Lane's arrogance, the pictures were lost to Dublin'.[62]

Its refusal to support Lane's proposal has always been viewed as an indictment of the pre-war Dublin Corporation, but controversies over the Lane pictures continued, and Cosgrave maintained his support for the principle of the gallery (although not for the details that Lane had demanded). After the Easter Rising, W.B. Yeats wrote to Lady Gregory regretting that 'Cosgrave, who I saw a few months ago in connection with the Municipal Gallery project and found our best supporter, has got many years' imprisonment'.[63] Long afterwards, when he was head of an independent Irish government, Cosgrave was able to strengthen the city's case for acquiring the Lane pictures and, in quite a different context, he was also able to make amends to Lutyens.[64]

At the same time that a small group of people quarrelled over the fate of artistic masterpieces, the city of Dublin was convulsed by one of pre-war Europe's most intense and protracted battles between rich and poor, between employer and employee. Headed by Murphy, the employers' federation took the initiative in its long-running feud with Jim Larkin's Transport Union, and the result was the great lock-out of 1913–14. John Redmond's Parliamentary Party was dismayed by the eruption of social conflict at a time when it wished all nationalists to be united in the struggle for home rule, but Sinn Féin was divided and therefore unable to capitalise on its opponent's embarrassment. Griffith denounced Larkin and his methods with characteristic intemperance, but at a corporation meeting Cosgrave voted for a public inquiry into police brutality during the lock-out (400 people had been injured in the course of the previous two days) and for the demand that the peace of the city could best be served by withdrawing extra police and military from the streets. He took a moderate, cautious stand, opposing the measures taken by the police and saying that the sanctity of human life must be preserved; 'no man had a right to take the life that God gave'. That was the issue on which they should all be united.[65] (Circumstances would change, and—like other Irish nationalists, and like millions of people throughout Europe—Cosgrave soon became reconciled to the idea and the reality of taking life.)

After his unopposed re-election to the corporation in 1912 he remained active in its affairs, maintaining his concern with working-class housing, and in five of the seven years between 1915 and 1921 he chaired the estates and finance committee. This was a significant tribute at a time when he belonged to a small minority on a corporation that continued to be dominated by members of the Parliamentary Party. His position may have made him more cautious in financial matters, more concerned with the details of revenue and expenditure; for example, he was among those who voted against increasing the minimum wage of the corporation's labourers and who supported an amendment whereby the motion should instead be referred to his committee for a report on the costs involved.[66] This might be seen as foreshadowing his concern when he was head of government with balancing budgets and avoiding debts. Another feature of his later career already noticeable at this point is that despite his growing prominence in Dublin Corporation, Cosgrave was not a member of Sinn Féin's nineteen-strong body of officers and executive.[67] Throughout his life he appeared to be uninterested in the details of party politics; he viewed them simply as a means of achieving practical results.

Long before the social and artistic controversies that erupted in 1913, Sinn Féin had begun to decline. Redmond and his home rule party held the parliamentary balance of power in Westminster in the years after 1910, and their fortunes revived when some form of a devolved government in Dublin was seen to be inevitable. Irish nationalists gradually lost their tolerance for radical alternatives that appeared to be futile or irrelevant. Sinn Féin's membership on the corporation dwindled to a small core, and as its rank and file members drifted away the party was obliged to merge branches in its Dublin stronghold.[68] In 1914 a hostile writer sneered that some years earlier 'there were Sinn Feiners looking for seats; that is a thing of the past evidently'.[69] Cosgrave's political career might seem to have reached a dead-end. He had become an effective, respected and experienced member of the corporation, but he belonged to a party that appeared to have no future. This may be one reason for the change of direction he had already begun to take.

View of Thomas Street, Dublin, as it was in 1891; Cosgrave lived in nearby James's Street.

Following pages: Pages from the Roll Book of the O'Brien Institute, Marino, showing Cosgrave's enrolment in January 1891; he attended school there until 1895.

No.	Date of Admission			Pupil's Name	Date of Birth			Residence	Occupation of Parents	The Last School (if any) attended by Pupil
	Day	Month	Year		Day	Month	Year			
94	30	9	89	Michael John Graham 92/1	8	7	80	Drumcondra Road, 48	Solicitor	N.S.
95	30	8	90	Henry Tate Allingham 93/1	22	2	80	Red Cross, Rathdrum	Merchant's Clerk	P.S.
6	30	8	90	Leo Connolly 94/1	16	8	80	Parsonstown, King's Co.	Auctioneer	N.S.
7	30	8	90	Edward Patrick Fagan 95/1	1	2	80	Nelson Street, 19	Merchant's Clerk	C.B.S
8	30	8	90	Robert Hayden 96/1	1	12	79	Foyle Terrace, Fairview	Accountant	C.S.
9	26	8	90	William Griffith Morris 98/1	11	11	79	Upper Rutland St. 38	Sea Captain	C.B.S
100	28	8	90	Edward Kearney 99/1	4	2	79	Phibsborough Avenue, 7	Printer	N.S
1	28	8	90	Patrick Jos. Cosgrave 100/1	11	4	79	James' Street, 174	Grocer & Spirit Merc.t	C.B.S
2	30	8	90	James E. P. Whelan 97/1	12	4	81	Merville Avenue, 3	Corn Merchant	N.S.
3	1	9	90	Richard Doyle 101/1	20	9	81	Monkstown Avenue, 3	Butcher	N.S
4	1	9	90	Michael O'Brien Keon 102/1	29	3	78	St. Alphonsus' Road, 8	Commission Agent	C.B.
5	3	9	90	William Dalton 103/1	20	1	79	Athassel Abbey Co. Tip.y	Farmer	N.S
6	4	9	90	Joseph Gilbert Phelan 104/1	3	7	78	Upper Gardiner St. 48	Postman in N. York	C.B.S
7	12	9	90	Martin Patrick Maher 105	5	7	79	Bray	Grocer	N.S
8	10	1	91	David O'Dwyer 107/102	25	8	80	Anne Street, Wexford, 3.	Draper & Buyer	None
9	12	1	91	John Flood 108/2	17	5	79	Ballyglunin, Co. Galway	Medical Doctor	N.S
110	13	1	91	Charles Brady 109/2	24	10	81	North Strand, 138	Builder & Contractor	C.B.
1	13	1	91	William Redmond 110/2	24	10	80	1 St. Ignatius R. 1, Drumcon.	Sea Captain	N.S
2	13	1	91	William Cosgrave 111/2	6	6	80	James' Street, 174	Grocer & Spirit Merc.	C.B.
3	13	1	91	John McNally 112/2	30	5	81	Seafort Ave. 43. Sandym.t	Marshall in H.C.f Admir.	N.S
4	13	1	91	Thompson Neill 113/2	6	7	81	Upper Gloucester St. 5	Shop-Assistant	N.S
5	14	1	91	Patrick Carroll 114/2	5	1	82	Belvidere Road, 20	Commercial Buyer	N.S
6	14	1	91	Christopher Kerrigan 115/2	10	11	81	Drumcondra Road, 142	Clerk in Post Office	N.S.
7	14	1	91	Michael Russell 116/2	24	1	78	Sarsfield Quay, 13	Sea Captain	C.B.
8	15	1	91	John Dunne 117/2	30	7	77	Newbridge Ave. 29, Sandym.t	Tea Merchant	P.S.
9	15	1	91	Thomas Haughton 118/2	19	12	81	Great Brunswick St. 178	Musician	Non
120	21	1	91	Edward Anthony 119/2	11	2	79	Meath Road, Bray	Dealer in Pictures	N.
1	23	1	91	Martin Lynam 120/2	16	9	80	Whitehall, Eyrecourt, Co. Gal.	Farmer	N.
2	27	1	91	Thomas Curran 121/2	9	2	79	Innisfallen Parade, 24	Wine Merchant	C.B
3	24	8	91	Edward Daly 122/2	26	6	80	High Street, 27	Pig Buyer	C.B
4	24	8	91	John Reddy 123/2	31	10	80	S.H. Home, Drumcondra	Merchant	N.

HIGHEST STANDARD	\multicolumn{6}{SUCCESSIVE STANDARDS}						S. KENSINGTON EX.	INTERMEDIATE EX.	DATE OF LEAVING			NOTES OF CHARACTER AND CONDUCT.
	I.	II.	III.	IV.	V.	VI.			Day	Month	Year	
0	30·9 / 89	14·6 / 92	11·9 / 93	3–2 / 94	2·5 / 94	28·2 / 95, c/1						A quiet, good boy
2	"	"	30·8 / 90	11·9 / 93	3·2 / 94	2·5 / 94, c			✓ 1	7	95	A good boy. Went to Arm
1	"	30·8 / 90	11·9 / 93	14·10 / 90	28·1 / 95	9·3 / 96, c/1			✓ 31	1	96	A very good boy
2	"	"	30·8 / 90	2·9 / 90					✓ 1	7	96	A very good boy
1	"	30·8 / 90	14·10 / 92						✓ 30	12	90	Good but dull
0	26·8 / 90	17·4 / 91	10·6 / 92	11·9 / 93	2·5 / 94	23/ε²			✓ 12	8	93	Exceedingly dull
2	"	"	28·8 / 90	14·3 / 91	17·5 / 92				✓ 8	7	94	Good but dark boy
1	"	28·8 / 90	12·10 / 91	4·6 / 92	11·9 / 93	2·5 / 94, c/1·23/ε²			✓ 28	8	93	A good quiet boy
2	"	"	30·8 / 90	11·9 / 93	3·2 / 94	2·5 / 94, c			✓ 21	5	94	A good boy, not smart
0	1·9 / 80	11·9 / 93	3·2 / 94	2·5 / 94	28·2 / 95	9·3 / 96, D/VI			✓ 1	8	95	A good, quiet boy.
	"	"	1·9 / 90	6·7 / 92	11·9 / 93	23/ε²			✓ 1	7	97	A very good boy.
1	"	3·9 / 90	4·5 / 91	6·7 / 92	11·9 / 93	2·5 / 94, 5/1·23/ε²			✓ 1	10	93	Good & Industrious
2	"	"	4·9 / 90	15·3 / 91	12·10 / 92				✓ 10	12	94	A quiet, lifeless boy
✓	"	12·9 / 90	11·9 / 93	2·5 / 94	28·2 / 95	c			✓ 1	4	93	A good boy & industrious
0	10·1 / 91	11·9 / 93	10·12 / 93	2·5 / 94	28·2 / 95				✓ 1	7	95	A good little boy
2	"	"	12·1 / 91	14·5 / 92	11·9 / 93	5/1·23/ε²			✓ 23	8	96	A good boy with little in h
0	13·1 / 91	6·10 / 91	17·5 / 92	11·9 / 93	3·2 / 94	2·5 / 94, 5/2·23/ε²			✓ 8	1	94	A good smart boy
0	13·1 / 91	6·10 / 92	11·9 / 93	3·2 / 74	2·5 / 94				✓ 25	8	94	Not bad but wild
	13·1 / 91	6·11 / 91	7·8 / 92	6·2 / 93	11·9 / 93	2·5 / 93, 5/1·23/ε²			✓ 22	1	95	A good boy- but stupid
	13·1 / 91	11·9 / 93	10·12 / 93	3·2 / 94	2·5 / 95	9·3 / 96, 5/2·D/VI			✓ 27	1	95	A good steady boy.
	"	13·1 / 90	11·9 / 93	3·2 / 94	2·5 / 94	28·2 / 95, D/V			✓ 1	7	97	A good boy- Mechanical T
	14·1 / 91	6·11 / 92	14·9 / 93	3·2 / 74	2·5 / 94	2·4 / 97, D/2·VI			✓ 1	7	97	A very good little boy
	14·1 / 91	4·7 / 92	11·9 / 93						✓ 1	7	97	A smart good boy
	"	14·1 / 91	12·11 / 91	6·7 / 92	11·9 / 93				✓ 1	7	94	Good boy- Delicate
	"	15·1 / 91	14·9 / 91						✓ 8	1	94	A very good boy.
	15·1 / 91	11·9 / 93	10·12 / 93	3·2 / 94	2·5 / 94				✓ 26	10	91	Fair but not diligent
	"	21·1 / 91	6·9 / 92	11·9 / 93	2·5 / 94	23/ε⁵			✓ 1	8	95	A very good boy.
	23·1 / 91	14·11 / 91	6·9 / 92	11·9 / 93	3·2 / 94	2·5 / 94, c/1·5/2·23/ε²			✓ 17	9	94	A good diligent boy.
	"	"	27·1 / 91	11·9 / 93					✓ 28	10	96	An excellent boy.
	24·8 / 91	14·4 / 91	6·9 / 92	11·9 / 93	3·2 / 94	2·5 / 94, 5/2			✓ 28	3	94	Not diligent at Study
	"	24·9 / 91	11·9 / 93				5/1·23/ε²			✓ 23	5	95	A good talented boy.
									✓ 21	6	94	Died of Consumption

THE EDITOR DAILY INDEPENDENT.

Dublin, March 11, 1900.

Dear Sir—It was with feelings of the deepest disgust that I read of the intention of the Corporation to present an address to Her Majesty. I should like to be informed what are the reasons which prompt such an undertaking.

It is stated on good authority that she is in no way responsible for the political conduct of her Ministers. It should be remembered that within three years of Her Majesty's accession to the throne the population of Ireland was 9 millions. Now it is only 4½ millions. The industries and factories of Ireland were numerous in 1837, and the country, generally speaking, in a flourishing condition. Those are now few and far between, and the once prosperity of the country has long since been scattered to the four winds. One of the then most flourishing industries, whisky distilling, was decimated by the duty imposed on it by Mr. Gladstone, directly after which memorable epoch 70 distilleries closed down, as Mr. T. M. Healy, M.P., told the House of Commons. There has since been an additional tax of 6d. per gallon put upon whisky, an amount too small for the retailer to charge the consumer, thus frustrating the possibility which such a course could possibly have in decreasing the sale of it.

Famine occurred in 1847, famine so indelibly sunken in the people's minds as to have it known by the appellation of "Black '47." The havoc wrought by this famine was mainly due to the want of help denied by the Government, when hundreds of thousands of impoverished Irishmen died by the roadside, whilst one of the most despotic oligarchies that ever disgraced Christendom feasted upon the fat of the land; for it has been proved that during the famine the exports of Ireland to England were more than sufficient to feed the hungry population.

Since '47 there has not been a famine of such a severe character. Nevertheless, although I can only speak of quite a recent date, there have been few years in which it was not necessary to raise subscriptions to feed and supply the necessaries of life to a starving peasantry.

Coercion Acts have been passed in the "Longest Reign," which were all, and had to be, signed by the occupant of the monarchical chair.

Perhaps the situation was best described by the Very Rev Father Kavanagh in his recent lecture, when he said "that every evil which human malignity could possibly inflict upon us was ruthlessly piled on, and at the same time we were made beggars at the doors of those who robbed us."

What has Her Majesty done to alleviate our sufferings during her long reign? How has she shown that she took any interest in our welfare? Her occasional £5 to Irish charities, etc., once so seemingly popular with her, has now almost vanished.

Her Majesty "is" sympathetic, to judge from her recent despatch to General Buller, and also from the fact that in future Irish soldiers will wear the national emblem on St. Patrick's Day. Fortunately Her Majesty's sympathy is of a cheap kind.

During the long reign the hitherto weapons of English monarchs in Ireland were left aside—i.e., fire and sword—and for them substituted over-taxation, coercion, and famine, and, as the direct result of these, forced emigration. Those evils, which might be said to illustrate the intellectual advancement of Her Majesty's Ministers, were the means used by her Governments in Ireland to accomplish that which was begun centuries before, and which, notwithstanding all attempts to bring to a "successful" finish, is still undone—viz., the extermination of the Irish race.—I am, sir, yours, etc.,

W. T. COSGRAVE.

Letter by Cosgrave protesting against the visit of Queen Victoria to Ireland in 1900, published in the *Irish Daily Independent*, 12 March.

Opposite: Political cartoon published in *The Lepracaun* magazine, August 1911, p. 209, noting that some members of Dublin Corporation were at the time owners of tenements in the north inner-city area.

Following pages: Political cartoon published in *The Lepracaun*, July 1909, p. 41, depicting a meeting of the Dublin Municipal Council in the Mansion House, Dawson Street, 4 June, which had to adjourn when fighting broke out among the councillors. Cosgrave, a member of the council, is recognisable in the centre of the drawing.

Dublin's Insanitary Monster.

The Congress of the Royal Institute of Public Health, which opens in Dublin on August 15, includes in its programme a series of papers on the Housing Problem. It is to be hoped that a visit to the Dublin slums— largely the property of members of the Dublin Corporation, who weep crocodile tears over the lot of the poor while they are robbing them—will not be omitted.

God sends his creatures light and air
And water open to the skies.
Man locks him in a stifling lair
And wonders why his brother dies.

THE DAWSON
AND SCHOOL OF

"Extraordinary scenes, culminating in physical violence, were enacted at an adjour presided. After several blows had been struck by Sinn Feiners and Nationalists, and p adjournment to next Monday was, so far as could be understood, carried."—" Irish Indepe

Thrice is he armed that hath his quarrel just
But ten times he who gets his blow in fust.

REET ACADEMY
YSICAL CULTURE.

of the Dublin Municipal Council yesterday in the Mansion House, at which the Lord Mayor
had reigned in the Oak Room for over half-an-hour, the meeting broke up in disorder. An
5th, 1909.

Sketch of the design by Edwin Lutyens for a Gallery of
Modern Art, proposed to house the Hugh Lane collection;
Lane wanted the gallery to span the River Liffey.

'Guilty. Death by being shot'.

Opening image: Cosgrave speaking
at a rally in College Green, 1923.

COSGRAVE remained active in the corporation after the outbreak of the First World War, but

he also followed a widespread pattern by engaging in paramilitary activities, by marching, drilling and preparing for combat.

Like most Irish nationalists he was dismayed by the apparent success of the opposition to home rule, manifest in the fact that a unionist private army was able to rule in Ulster with the acquiescence of the state.[1] He played a prominent role in a public meeting at the Rotunda in Dublin in April 1914 that was convened as a protest against the threat of partition, and he joined Arthur Griffith, Roger Casement and others in a group whose function was to make proposals to 'the Ulster people'. (However, he opposed Griffith's suggestion that, as a compromise, meetings of the Irish parliament should alternate between the capital and Belfast; this might have been too great a concession for such a loyal Dubliner to make).[2]

The Ulster unionists had seized the political initiative by their armed challenge to the Liberal government's policy of home rule, and in establishing the Ulster Volunteer Force they began the process of militarising Irish society. They captured the imagination of their nationalist enemies, and the formation of the Irish Volunteers in November 1913 was a 'copycat' response to and an imitation of the Ulster Volunteers. Together with his Sinn Féin colleagues on the corporation Tom Kelly and Seán T. O'Kelly, Cosgrave attended the inaugural meeting of the Irish Volunteers in the Rotunda.[3] He had never been a member of the Irish Republican Brotherhood (IRB); like many Catholics he disapproved of secret oath-bound societies. He had turned down an invitation to join the IRB in 1910 and he would avoid any connection with it in 1916.[4] But he would seem to have lost hope of achieving independence by peaceful means, as he welcomed the formation of a nationalist armed force of volunteers, and he promptly enlisted in its ranks.

He became a lieutenant in B Company of the 4th Battalion under the command of Eamonn Ceannt, a fellow-member of the Sinn Féin party. He took part in the Howth gun-running of July 1914, and later he reminisced about loading so many rifles into a taxi that he had difficulty in keeping the door closed.[5] The guns were stored carefully until the Easter Rising.

Although he had no involvement in planning the rebellion Cosgrave was aware of the preparations to bring it about; he knew what he needed to know. Ceannt did not try to keep his intentions secret from many members of his battalion, one of whom later remarked that ten or twelve weeks before the rising Ceannt had told 'a crowd of us' what to expect.[6] Cosgrave was not informed about the plans directly by his commander, but he was given a broad hint. Long afterwards he recalled a conversation during which Thomas MacDonagh had spoken to him of an insurrection that would take place within the next month or two. He responded that this would be little short of madness; a rebel force would lack men and munitions. When asked would his views change in the event of a German naval victory and a large-scale importation of arms, he replied that this would alter the situation completely, but that the Volunteers alone would not be capable of a sustained conflict.[7]

On Good Friday, two days before the rising was due to begin, Cosgrave delivered a message from Ceannt to John Styles, the battalion dispatch rider. This consisted of an order to transfer ammunition to a grocer's shop facing the South Dublin Union.[8] The description matches that of the family's public house. On the same day Cosgrave sent and received other dispatches.[9] He ordered that two days' supply of emergency rations should be distributed to his unit and—significantly—that the men should go to confession.[10] The postponement of the manoeuvres, and therefore of the rising, allowed him to attend a concert on Easter Sunday at which his sister Joan sang *The West's Awake* and *The Minstrel Boy*. But with William, Philip and Gobban all planning to take arms, his stepfather was sufficiently well-informed to warn friends on Sunday morning 'be careful tomorrow and don't go out'.[11]

It was probably because of his awareness that he might be involved in a rebellion, and might in consequence be imprisoned or killed, that Cosgrave made an unusual suggestion in a letter to the *Irish Independent* little more than five weeks before the insurrection was due to begin. He offered to resign his seat on the corporation and to request that William Martin Murphy should be co-opted in his place—provided that Murphy would undertake to do all in his power to secure adequate housing for Usher's Quay ward in particular and for Dublin City in general. He was confident 'that the Council would do so, and that the Finance Committee would also elect him chairman'.[12] The letter reveals both Cosgrave's continuing concern with housing and his readiness to think in terms of 'business' rather than politics. It also indicates a change in his priorities, which would no longer be dominated by civic matters but would instead be focused on the achievement of national independence.

THE SOUTH DUBLIN UNION

Moira Lysaght recorded that on Sunday evening, 23 April, Gobban spoke briefly with his brother when he returned from informing Volunteer units that the rising would take place on Easter Monday, a day later than planned.[13] According to Cosgrave's own subsequent account he did not receive any official communication about the mobilisation on Monday, and he speculated that this might have been because IRB circles were suspicious of non-members. When he heard from his two brothers that they had been mobilised he cycled to his battalion headquarters in Kimmage—and found that it was empty. He was told where to go, and he then joined the rest of the battalion at Dolphin's Barn.[14] A small group of 120 men tried to occupy the vast and sprawling South Dublin Union (now St James's Hospital), which covered twenty hectares. 'This walled community was the country's biggest poorhouse, with 3,000 destitute inmates, its own churches, stores, refectories, and two hospitals with full medical staff.'[15] The rebels also manned three nearby outposts—Watkins's Brewery and two distilleries, Roe's and Jameson's. These positions placed them close to Richmond army barracks and the Royal Hospital, which served as the military headquarters in Ireland—and from which, as it turned out, British soldiers could machine-gun the defenders in the union. Their positions also enabled the rebels to threaten but not disrupt British movements from Kingsbridge (Heuston) Station.[16] In terms of its situation the battalion's main position in the South Dublin Union was well-chosen—although it was heartless in terms of the impact on the principal victims of the fighting, the union's unfortunate and vulnerable inhabitants.

Cosgrave had an advantage over most other members of the garrison: because his family's home was nearby he was familiar with the union's buildings and topography. The wardmaster in charge of the main dining hall on Easter Monday knew him and Ceannt personally.[17] Cosgrave was also able to exploit his good relations with a next-door neighbour who passed food and messages over his garden wall while the fighting was in progress.[18] He, Ceannt and Cathal Brugha discussed their plans, and it was at Cosgrave's suggestion that the rebels used the night nurses' home as their main defensive position; it was the strongest building in the complex and it was relatively easy to defend.[19] The assistant matron was informed that a group of Volunteers 'went straight over to the Nurses' Home and occupied it. They were headed, I understand, by Cosgrave'. She also remarked that throughout Easter Week the bakers in the union supplied bread to both the rebels and the British forces, as well as to many others in the vicinity.[20] The outlying Marrowbone Lane garrison was able to capture a bread-van, and also some passing cattle.[21]

Heavy fighting broke out between the rebels and the attacking British forces, and patients, nurses and other staff were terrified when their hospital was turned into a battlefield. Some of them were killed. A British officer described how his troops advanced through a convent where nuns were praying, and then through wards occupied by screaming patients.[22] Members of the garrison were helped by an inmate of the union who provided them with a ladder, and by a nun who opened a gate.[23] Cosgrave was seen running from one building to another under heavy fire.[24] His brother Gobban was shot dead by a sniper. Brugha was one of the most prominent and courageous of the defenders of the garrison, and later he remarked that he would never forget Cosgrave's 'extreme kindness' towards him after he had been gravely wounded.[25] By late Monday night the British had occupied all the buildings at the back of the institution while the Volunteers held those at the front, overlooking James's Street. This stalemate lasted for another six days. Subsequently, Cosgrave recalled that after he had been released from jail one of the commanders of the attacking British troops complimented him on the garrison's defenders, as they had fought against great odds.[26] Throughout the week his mother could hear the continuous sound of gunfire from her house across the street, all the while aware that three of her sons were involved in the battle.[27]

On Sunday, 30 April, the seventh day of the rising, Thomas MacDonagh arrived under a flag of truce to inform the garrison of Pearse's order that they should lay down their arms. Reluctantly, Ceannt agreed to surrender. That evening he and Cosgrave accompanied the British commander, General Lowe, to the rebel outpost in Marrowbone Lane and they confirmed that the insurrection was over.[28] As the garrison filed out into James's Street Cosgrave did not look up at his mother and sisters who waved at him from the window of their house.[29] When the prisoners were gathered together in Richmond Barracks he walked up and down with John MacBride, whom he had helped to secure a post in the corporation some years earlier. William O'Brien the trade union leader sat on a box nearby, and as they passed him Cosgrave said with a smile 'I imagine it will be a long time before we again discuss housing policy together'.[30]

LIFE SENTENCE

The surrender was followed by courts-martial. Many of the prisoners were tried in rapid succession by three British army officers, who acted as judges, and provision was made for a prosecuting counsel, although not for a defence. These trials were held in secret, without any legal justification, and the proceedings were perfunctory.[31] Cosgrave was among those court-martialled, and he was fortunate to have had an offer of assistance from John Ronayne, a barrister who had been one of his companions in B Company and who was also a friend of his sister May. In the course of their conversation Cosgrave denied the charge of a connection with Germany, although he accepted responsibility for having been in arms. He was advised that if he wanted to shorten his sentence he should say nothing during the trial.[32] William Wylie, the prosecutor, knew of Cosgrave's reputation on Dublin Corporation and warned him of the seriousness of his position. According to Wylie's record, which was written 25 years later, Cosgrave said that he had never heard of the rebellion until he was in the middle of it. This is at odds with the other evidence, however, and Wylie's account is unreliable in some of its details.[33]

On 4 May Cosgrave was tried and accused of taking part 'in an armed rebellion and in the waging of war against his Majesty the King…with the intention and for the purpose of assisting the enemy'. He pleaded not guilty, arguing that the charge of assisting the enemy was 'baseless unsustained and utterly unfounded…I never had any communication direct or indirect with the enemy. The sword which I carried was simply an ornament'. He was able to call two formidable character witnesses: the current mayor of Dublin James Gallagher and his immediate predecessor, Lorcan Sherlock. Both men praised Cosgrave generously, describing him as innately a gentleman; as the best type of citizen; as a man who, while holding strong views, was tolerant towards those who differed from him; and as a member of the corporation who had been elected chairman of the estates and finance committee, by those who disagreed with him politically, 'because of his great ability'.[34]

As in the case of several other prisoners, Wylie went beyond his prosecutor's brief in Cosgrave's court-martial. Since there was no-one else to do the job he also conducted the defence and he interrogated the character witnesses. He later reflected that although this was a rather strange procedure no-one had thought so at the time. Evidence was produced that Cosgrave had surrendered, but not that he had been in rebellion. He noted that while the members of the court-martial were pleasant and polite, their knowledge of law was most elementary, and that on several occasions the prosecutor had to insist on prisoners' rights.[35] His trial lasted between ten and fifteen minutes. The verdict and sentence were 'Guilty. Death by being shot'.

According to Wylie's retrospective account, after the court-martial the presiding officer, General Blackader, asked him privately 'is this a decent man, and was he in your opinion rushed into this?' Wylie answered yes, and Blackader decided to recommend a reprieve.[36] General Maxwell, the British commander-in-chief, accepted this advice and Cosgrave was sentenced to penal servitude for life.[37] His brother Philip had also fought in Ceannt's battalion, in the Marrowbone Lane outpost, and he shared the same fate: a death sentence, commuted to one of life imprisonment. This was not unusual. While relatively junior figures were executed in the immediate aftermath of the surrender (and Cosgrave's trial took place at an early stage, when prisoners were shot with less compunction than would be the case a few days later), some important leaders were tried only after a long delay. James Connolly and Seán MacDermott were the last to be executed, and Maxwell described them—quite reasonably, from his point of view—as 'the worst of the lot'.[38] He came under intense pressure to limit the number of people killed; he became more discriminating, and 75 of the 90 death sentences issued were commuted to terms of imprisonment. Eamon de Valera believed that he and Thomas Ashe, both prominent figures in the rebellion, would have been shot if they had been tried earlier.[39] But Ceannt was executed, as was another member of his battalion, Con Colbert. So too was John MacBride. Cosgrave listened as MacBride was summoned from the cell next to his own in Kilmainham Jail and was then shot in the prison yard. He thought that his turn would come next, and he waited for a rap on the door.[40]

Having spent two days in Kilmainham after his death penalty was commuted to a life sentence, he was held in Mountjoy Jail for five days before being transferred to Portland, in Dorset; finally in December he was moved to Lewes Jail in Sussex. On the way to Portland he was allowed to read newspapers, and he derived some comfort from John Dillon's speech in the House of Commons, in the course of which he praised the rebels' courage during the insurrection and denounced the repressive measures taken by the British in its aftermath.[41] J.J. Walsh, one of Cosgrave's future government colleagues, was in a neighbouring cell in Portland. Many years later Walsh remembered scrubbing floors, sewing mail-bags, enduring the 'cruel hardships' of convict food, and also the deathly silence. But there were some compensations; prisoners could read books on subjects ranging from the classics through history, modern languages and religion to astronomy.[42] Another of Cosgrave's colleagues, Gerald Doyle, recalled that every week they were allowed to borrow a book from the library; they lived on a diet of porridge, bread, soup, potatoes and cabbage; and they worked at making sacks, mail-bags and coal-bags for the navy.[43] A third (who was later a political opponent), claimed long afterwards that Cosgrave stopped a protest in the prison.[44]

Conditions improved when they were moved to Lewes, where their companions included senior rebels such as de Valera and Ashe, and also Eoin MacNeill, an Early Irish historian who had been chief of staff of the Irish Volunteers and who had tried to prevent the rebellion (but without informing the British). Cosgrave was one of the 'cleaners' who swept the paths and yards. A fellow-prisoner recalled him as 'very distant'—a rare if not unique reaction.[45] Cosgrave was not on the committee that organised the prisoners' activities, nor was he among the 25 who opposed the idea of contesting the South Longford by-election in spring 1917.[46] (The election was subsequently won, very narrowly, by one of the Lewes inmates, Joe McGuinness.)

On MacNeill's release from prison he described their conditions. The food was 'almost uniformly middling' and in general 'repulsive to persons of delicate appetite', while the work consisted of weaving hearthrugs on a loom, making floor brushes, and digging in the garden. 'Sewing bags is one of the most monotonous tasks imaginable.' Artificial lighting was bad and at times reading was impossible, but the prison was clean, and with one or two exceptions the warders behaved quite humanely. He taught Irish language and history to his fellow-prisoners. In recounting their activities MacNeill remarked that 'Cosgrave is as much interested in the housing of the working classes as if he were at home in Dublin'.[47]

In the prisoners' absence Irish public opinion changed dramatically, and one example of the new national mood was the support provided by Cosgrave's colleagues in Dublin Corporation. In January 1917 they co-opted him and other jailed members who had become disqualified from holding seats on the grounds of their long absence and lack of attendance at council meetings.[48] In supporting Cosgrave's co-option, Laurence O'Neill, the mayor, described him in extravagant terms as 'the embodiment of everything that was gracious and good'.[49]

WIDER HORIZONS

The rebels were released in June 1917, so Cosgrave's 'life sentence' had amounted to little more than a year in jail. They returned to a joyous welcome in Ireland. Eamon de Valera was promptly elected MP for East Clare, and almost immediately afterwards Cosgrave was chosen to run for the next vacant seat, in Kilkenny. No contest had taken place in that constituency for 22 years.

The county's police inspector reported that political feeling was running very high and that Sinn Féin propaganda was being spread by the many party leaders who arrived in the city. 'All the young people are rampant Sinn Feiners, but the older and representative citizens keep aloof from it'.[50] Even before the election campaign began the British authorities suppressed the regional newspaper the *Kilkenny People*, whose editor was chairman of the Sinn Féin club.[51] As Cosgrave moved around the constituency he was accompanied by groups of

Irish Volunteers and his supporters marched in procession, preceded by bands and banners. In one of his speeches he told the audience that they were being asked why they demanded a republic. His answer was that the British broke treaties, and Ireland would have no more agreements with Britain but would stand for complete and absolute separation.[52] In theory, Sinn Féin's aim was still to achieve a dual monarchy, but he was one of the party's members who had already fought under the republican flag in Easter Week. Thus he had less difficulty than many of his colleagues in adapting to more radical circumstances and policies—even if he displayed no signs of 'ideological' commitment to a republican form of government. In another speech he complained that the Parliamentary Party had acquiesced in partition and had done nothing to protect Irish industry.[53]

Kilkenny City was the smallest constituency in the country, with less than one-tenth the population of East Belfast at the opposite extreme, and the poll was correspondingly low: Cosgrave won by 772 votes to 392. His expenses were listed as £209, compared with a mere £8 for his home rule opponent, John Magennis.[54] In his victory speech he declared that in the course of the campaign the Irish people had shown a self-restraint that was typical of them, and in subsequent years he would continue to advocate self-restraint (even if he might not always regard it as a national characteristic). His defeated rival, a former mayor of the city, complained of gross terrorism and intimidation.[55]

Until the rebellion Cosgrave's world had been Dublin-centred, and his political career was characterised by a deep immersion in local battles.[56] In prison his horizons had widened to embrace people and problems from other parts of Ireland, and this pattern continued after his election for Kilkenny. He began to become a national figure.

In September 1917 he and two colleagues paid a visit to Tim Healy, the veteran parliamentarian. Healy described them as 'all jailbirds!! I must say I found them very reasonable and pleasant fellows', and he reported that 'they took my counsel or preachments very well'.[57] Shortly afterwards Thomas Ashe went on hunger-strike in a demand for 'political prisoner' status and died as a result of medical incompetence during an attempt to force-feed him. There were fears that his funeral would be an occasion for violent protest, but Cosgrave helped to avoid a bloody confrontation. He contacted Edmund Eyre, the city treasurer, who arranged with the British commander that his troops would remain in their barracks during the funeral, which subsequently passed off peacefully. The funeral was a triumph of organisation by the Irish Volunteers. Accompanied by

Michael Collins, who was at that point still little-known, Cosgrave returned to Healy's house and asked him to interrogate witnesses at the inquest. They made it clear that they wanted the British government to be held responsible for Ashe's death.[58] Healy performed the task brilliantly, provoking the opposing counsel to abuse him as 'a disgrace to the Bar'.[59]

While Cosgrave had been in Portland Jail his mother received cheques from the Irish National Aid and Volunteer Dependants Fund (INA-VDF), the charitable body that cared for the interests of those who were imprisoned or had suffered otherwise as a result of their association with the Easter Rising. After his release he returned the money on the ground that 'there are cases of much greater losses than mine'. But some months later he wrote to the society again, explaining that circumstances had changed during the interval; he requested a loan of £100, most or all of which he expected to return in six or seven months' time. His brother Philip sent a similar letter. The association's minutes of 11 December 1917 recorded that 'it was unanimously decided to grant £150 each' and the secretary was instructed to inform the brothers when sending the money that 'there should be no question of repaying same'.[60] It may be a mere coincidence that a month earlier, when there were rumours of a new insurrection, detectives were able to report reassuring news to Dublin Castle. Cosgrave and his brother were seen walking in the Crumlin area, immaculately dressed and wearing chamois gloves, and not looking as if they were about to take part in a rebellion.[61] They might have spent heavily and have been in need of money.

Like de Valera and many others who had fought during Easter Week, Cosgrave put the military phase of his life behind him once he returned to Ireland in 1917; there was no chance of a successful rising in the near future, and they believed that Irish public opinion could be channelled and exploited in peaceful ways. (Radicals such as Brugha and Collins, however, retained their commitment to military measures.) Cosgrave never returned to the family business.[62] For the rest of his career he devoted himself to politics and administration, and for a while he showed signs of reverting to some of the views characteristic of the 'non-violent' Sinn Féin party before the rising. He claimed that in demanding independence he and his colleagues followed Parnell, and he declared that 'Grattan had won legislative independence by Sinn Fein methods'.[63] He resumed his activities in the familiar world of Dublin Corporation, where he continued to be a conscientious member; he attended 34 of the 37 meetings that were held between his release and his re-arrest. At the end of 1917 he and all the other councillors voted in favour of proportional representation (PR) in parliamentary elections.[64] Griffith's Sinn Féin party had already supported PR, but Cosgrave would later come to dislike the system.

In two articles written towards the end of the year he took issue with critics of the corporation's housing policy. He argued that although slums must be eradicated, people did not wish to live in the suburbs; instead, accommodation must be provided in the city. 'The applications for cottages in the city quadruple the applications for cottages on the outskirts'.[65] (Nonetheless, there would be a drift towards suburbanisation during his period of office.)

At the Sinn Féin convention in October 1917 the party abandoned its policy of a dual monarchy and committed itself to the objective of securing an Irish republic. De Valera was elected president in succession to Griffith. In one of his interventions at the convention Cosgrave declared that the constituent assembly, which was expected to meet after the next general election, would be the sovereign assembly of Ireland and that no-one should have a right to limit its activities.[66] On this issue he would prove to be consistent. He was elected one of the honorary treasurers of Sinn Féin—achieving a higher vote than the other joint treasurer, the well-known Laurence Ginnell. The figures were 537 votes to 491.

Despite his long-standing membership of the party this was one of the few offices that he held. Although he was a respected figure and an effective speaker, throughout his career he regarded political activity less as a valuable or stimulating activity in itself than as a necessary means to other ends. He would later (too late) come to see this as a serious weakness. Because he was one of Sinn Féin's four MPs he was in demand at public meetings, and in the course of the next few months he addressed numerous gatherings in subsequent by-election campaigns and at party rallies.

During the 1917 convention he had disagreed sharply with Brugha's proposal for a national insurance scheme, seeing it as bureaucratic and as likely to result in 'another method of stamp-licking and another horde of officials'. He suggested in vain that the matter might be postponed.[67] Yet in the course of the next few months he began implementing such a plan, although on a personal rather than on a national scale, and he became joint manager of an insurance firm (he left the partnership within a few years.[68]) By June 1918 an advertisement in the press for 'Wm. T. Cosgrave & Jos. MacDonagh', insurance brokers, was accompanied by the message that 'our business has not been interrupted in any way'.[69] This reassurance was necessary, since by then both Cosgrave and MacDonagh were interned in England.

When the British government decided belatedly to impose conscription on Ireland in spring 1918, to help repel a major German offensive, and when Irish nationalists prepared to resist this measure, William O'Brien kept de Valera and Cosgrave informed of trade union activity.[70] But both the recently elected MPs were among the 73 Sinn Féin leaders who were arrested in May 1918 for being involved in the so-called German Plot—whereby Sinn Féin leaders were alleged, implausibly, to be in collusion with Germany. The arrests were a retaliatory move by the British government after the threat of a mass rebellion forced it to abandon its plans for conscription. Soon afterwards Cosgrave was reported to be seriously ill and later he contracted influenza.[71] He recovered and spent ten months in prison in Gloucester and Reading jails. His fellow-prisoner and business partner Joseph MacDonagh reported that 'Cosgrave, though not of a robust constitution, is pretty well', and he was sufficiently healthy to engage in push-up competitions with fellow-prisoners.[72] He was described as appreciating his treatment in prison, although it was noted that he suffered from nervous dyspepsia and had been put on a special diet.[73]

Cosgrave wrote to Dublin describing 'normal' prison preoccupations, such as the theft of a thousand cigarettes that had been sent to him. He tried to protect the interests of the clients of his insurance business, and he arranged a meeting in jail with his solicitor.[74] To a colleague he wrote that life in Reading was not congenial but he and the other internees were making the most of it, and he had benefitted from their circumstances; 'you get to know men better & for that alone it has had good results'. He shared the widespread but unrealistically high hopes of Woodrow Wilson's influence in European affairs.[75]

As had been the case a year earlier in Lewes Jail, Cosgrave remained preoccupied with civic and corporation matters during his time in Gloucester and Reading. In July 1918 he warned of a possible coal shortage during the following winter and he advised the mayor of Dublin to acquire supplies of timber and turf; he suggested that a colleague might discuss the question of communal kitchens; and (returning to an old theme) he urged that 'we've got to do two things—build outside the centre area & have slum clearances…like cancer you must cut it out'.[76]

Cosgrave and the others incarcerated as part of the 'German Plot' were detained without trial until after the end of the war, and while still in prison he was returned unopposed as MP for North Kilkenny in the general election of December 1918. His old city constituency, which, with its tiny electorate, was almost a rotten borough, was merged with the surrounding countryside. Sinn

Féin won 73 of the 105 Irish parliamentary seats, but like most of his newly-elected or re-elected colleagues Cosgrave was still interned when their companions who were at liberty convened the new Irish parliament, the Dáil, in January 1919. Leading figures in the Dáil subsequently presided over a political and administrative campaign against British rule, a counterpart to the military struggle waged by some units of the Irish Republican Army (the new name of the Irish Volunteers).

All the prisoners were released in March 1919 and Cosgrave was one of the first to return to Ireland. Collins noted that he and Laurence Ginnell looked rather well, 'considering everything'.[77] Shortly afterwards the minutes of the INA-VDF recorded that Cosgrave had returned a cheque for over £500 (a substantial sum at the time), covering amounts sent to members of his family while he had been imprisoned. He said that two items to the value of £150 each had been devoted to non-personal matters. The committee decided that while it could accept a refund of £300 it would send Cosgrave the balance of more than £200.[78] As had been the case with his offer in July 1917 to hand back any money that had been provided to his mother by the INA-VDF, such an attitude was exceptional among beneficiaries of the committee's largesse.

Then his life changed. On 24 June 1919 Cosgrave, a 39-year-old bachelor, married Louisa Flanagan in the Pro-Cathedral in Dublin. They had met some years earlier on a pilgrimage to Lough Derg and they lived close to one another. Their son Liam remembered Louisa as a mild, quiet and sociable woman who, like her husband, had a sense of humour.[79] Louisa's father, Michael Flanagan, was a self-made man who prospered as a market gardener and who bought extensive property in the greater Dublin area.[80] He farmed almost 1000 acres (400 hectares) and he was able to reassure one of his sons that there was no need for him to take up a profession; the family had enough land and property to ensure the young man's future.[81] Flanagan also represented Usher's Quay ward on Dublin Corporation, although as a member of the rival Parliamentary Party. The family was well-known in Dublin circles, and Cosgrave's new brother-in-law 'Bird Flanagan' was a character notorious for his pranks and escapades—such as riding his horse into the Gresham Hotel. He had acquired his nickname by attending a fancy dress ball dressed as a bird, and when he failed to win a prize he mounted the platform, 'laid an egg', and threw it at the judge.[82]

On his marriage Cosgrave moved from his family's premises on James's Street to Beechpark, a large and comfortable house in Templeogue, to the south-west of the city, that was given to his wife by her father. It was described subsequently as a 'rambling Georgian mansion'.[83] The house was situated far beyond what was then the city boundary, and Cosgrave remarked years later 'I am a Dublin citizen born and reared, although I live in the county'.[84] With interruptions between 1920 and 1924, caused by political and military conflict, it remained his home for the rest of his long life. He and his wife enjoyed a happy marriage for the next 40 years; their two sons Liam and Míceál were born in 1920 and 1922, respectively. Liam followed in his father's footsteps, by becoming leader of the Fine Gael party and then taoiseach from 1973 to 1977, while Míceál maintained the family's interest in bloodstock by studying veterinary science.

LOCAL GOVERNMENT

Following the precedent established after his first term of imprisonment, Cosgrave resumed his work in Dublin Corporation in 1919, and he continued to act as chairman of its estates and finance committee. When the Dáil convened in April 1919 its president, de Valera, appointed him minister for Local Government in the new 'rebel' Irish cabinet. This was an appropriate post for someone with Cosgrave's long and varied experience of municipal administration. He held the office under changing circumstances until September 1922, first in the 'underground' Dáil government, then with greater freedom of action after the truce of July 1921, and finally in Collins's provisional government. These national responsibilities ensured that his rate of attendance at corporation meetings declined significantly during 1920.

The initial phase of the department of Local Government has been described as a year and a half of indolence,[85] but for at least its first year of existence it had virtually no money and there was little that it could do. Cosgrave carried out tasks such as negotiating the purchase of a new building for the Dáil's offices.[86] Ultimately, however, his department proved to be—second only to Collins's Ministry of Finance—the most important branch of the 'underground' Irish administration. A few months before the truce of July 1921 de Valera declared that the two big problems facing the Dáil were the military struggle against the British and the control of local government.[87]

One of Sinn Féin's distinctive characteristics had been its concern not only with the nation but also with the state. From 1905 onwards its policy had been to establish a rival parliament, government and bureaucracy in Ireland that would render British rule superfluous and would ultimately displace it. (Perhaps this could be seen as an unconscious Irish variant or adaptation of the Marxist idea of 'the withering away of the state'.) A principal feature of the Irish struggle against the British between 1919 and 1921 was the control of Irish local administration exercised by the Dáil government and its bureaucracy. Cosgrave's department was central to this programme of creating a counter-state.

A takeover of local government was made possible by Sinn Féin's victory in the long-delayed regional elections. They were held in two stages; those for urban councils and corporations took place in January 1920, and those for county councils and other rural authorities in June. In an effort to block the party's advance the British introduced a variant of PR (a system that, despite its tainted origins, was retained after independence), yet the results were nonetheless decisive. In the cities and towns Sinn Féin's vote *did* decline in relative terms, compared with its sweeping victory in the parliamentary elections a mere thirteen months earlier. Nonetheless, the party and its allies won a comfortable majority in all the urban districts of nationalist Ireland. Most corporations delayed any significant action until after the second, 'rural', round of elections in June, and instead confined themselves to anti-British gestures. (These could prove embarrassing, and some months later the Dáil cabinet decided to stop the councils from passing foolish resolutions.[88]) The Local Government Department was reluctant to take any drastic steps for fear that these might provoke the British authorities into postponing the summer elections.

In January 1920 Sinn Féin secured a majority in Dublin Corporation, winning 42 out of 80 seats. Although Cosgrave was now MP for North Kilkenny he remained active in Dublin affairs. He topped the poll in Usher's Quay ward, obtaining 2,033 votes to 1,059 for the next in line, his Sinn Féin colleague (and fellow-member of Ceannt's battalion) Joe McGrath; Cosgrave came second only to Tom Kelly in terms of votes for Sinn Féin candidates in Dublin.[89] Thereby he rose from the level of councillor to that of alderman—and in this role he succeeded his own father-in-law, the home ruler Michael Flanagan.

Cosgrave also faced a demand that he should become the city's mayor. Despite the forecast that had been made during his schooldays he did not seek the post; he believed that it should go to Kelly, who had been the first leader of the Sinn Féin faction on the corporation, and whom Cosgrave had already proposed for the office on two different occasions.[90] A group felt that only someone who had been a 'participant' in 1916 would be suitable for the post, but Kelly's long service in the corporation was reinforced by a new badge of honour: his recent arrest by the British authorities. He was elected unanimously.[91] Although Cosgrave chaired the Sinn Féin group in the corporation, by declining the position of mayor he faced fewer distractions as he concentrated on national affairs. It was characteristic of him that he enjoyed good relations with William O'Brien of the Labour Party.[92]

The Dáil cabinet directed him to prepare a report 'showing definitely the results of taking a stand' against Dublin Castle's Local Government Board,[93] but before this exercise could be completed he was jailed for the third and last time in March 1920. He had played an active part in securing Sinn Féin's 15:1 victory in a by-election in his ward of Usher's Quay and he was arrested the day after the result was announced.[94] Military parties had searched for him in his former residence in James's Street, and it was said that he had been warned not to stay in Templeogue on the night of his arrest but that he did so because his wife was ill.[95] He was described as looking pale and fatigued, 'in anything but robust health'.[96] He was imprisoned in Wormwood Scrubs in London, but through the intervention of Laurence O'Neill, the mayor of Dublin, he was released on parole a month later because his wife was seriously ill after the birth of their son Liam. He gave a clear understanding that he would not engage in politics.[97] Other prisoners were released in similar circumstances. The parole was extended to enable Cosgrave to have a hernia operation in Dublin, and during this time the Irish prisoners in the 'Scrubs' went on hunger strike. They were subsequently freed.

When Cosgrave's parole expired he presented himself once more at the prison and was offered a further extension of his parole, but he refused to accept the condition that he should continue to take no part in politics; he argued that the authorities should either release him unconditionally or imprison him. The deputy governor of the prison did not want to follow this latter course, and after further discussions he was set free.[98] Some weeks later he was elected chairman of the General Council of County Councils.[99] He had spent a total of almost two years in jail since the Easter Rising.

CONFRONTATION

Sinn Féin's sweeping victory in the rural elections in June 1920 was followed by a struggle between the British and Irish governments to control the country's local administration. During Cosgrave's absence, at first in jail and subsequently in hospital, his deputy Kevin O'Higgins had organised a conference on local government. In the course of this meeting O'Higgins warned against a premature break with the Local Government Board—and a resulting loss of revenue.

Responsibility for any such financial constraints should lie with their opponents. As expected, the British took the initiative; they declared that loans and grants would be issued to local authorities only if they allowed their books to be audited by the Local Government Board. The consequent withdrawal of grants resulted in an annual loss of more than £1,500,000.

In June 1920 the Dáil formed a commission to investigate the possibility of running local government without British grants, and to examine what economies might be necessary. Three months later Cosgrave outlined the commission's proposals. All local bodies were to sever their connections with the British system and were to recognise the authority of the Dáil's Local Government Department, which would recruit staff to carry out the work hitherto conducted by the British-controlled bureaucracy. Cuts would be required because of the withdrawal of central support, and savings would be made through rationalisation and through curtailing services—such as reducing payments on road works, child welfare schemes and the treatment of tuberculosis and venereal disease. Workhouses would be closed or amalgamated, and some patients in asylums would be sent home.

Cosgrave requested a significant increase in the size of his department and the substantial annual sum of £23,000 to cover 33 appointments. Collins, as minister for Finance, rejected this, but he agreed to a figure of £5,000 to cover the department's expenses for the next three months. After a long debate and after making some amendments (such as accepting Seán MacEntee's proposal that child welfare be deleted from the list of areas where economies should be made) the Dáil approved Cosgrave's proposals.[100]

The vast majority of councils obeyed this decree, although some of them were dilatory or obstructive in their response to other instructions (for example, the order that they should dismiss banks as their treasurers). In a similar fashion the councils' own directives were often ignored lower down the chain of command. O'Higgins complained that in Meath only two of eighteen collectors were obeying the county council's instructions regarding the collection and disposal of rates.[101]

The Dáil was banned in September 1919 and its government was forced to go underground. The Department of Local Government went 'on the run' and it was obliged to be mobile. Its offices were moved from one location in Dublin to another, from Harcourt Street to Clare Street, then to Parnell Square, O'Connell Street and finally Wicklow Street, where it masqueraded as a company providing advice on taxation. Many years later one of Cosgrave's officials wrote to him that it was 'probably the happiest period of our lives'.[102] He and O'Higgins carried out tasks, such as drafting letters, which would normally be the responsibility of officials.[103] Communications with other Dáil departments and with local authorities were conducted by sending messages to Cosgrave at his 'other' address (chairman of the corporation's estates and finance committee), or else by using messengers, envelopes within envelopes and a series of covering addresses (often of sympathetic business firms). It was necessary to inform one county council what was meant by a covering address: 'it was not intended that letters should be sent to the "Minister for Local Government, C/O etc."'[104] Collins ran a singularly efficient department, and one of his officials, Seán McGrath, visited government offices periodically and handed them enough cash to carry on their activities. He was known as 'the walking bank'.[105] Cosgrave wrote later that he had joined the cabinet very much on the side of Brugha, with whom he had been associated for a long time, but he was soon attracted by what he saw as the genius, ability and greatness of Collins.[106]

The Local Government Department struggled hard to retain the services of rate-collectors, many of whom were dubious about switching from one master to another. By August 1921 the department employed a total of twenty inspectors and some auditors.[107] These officials travelled around the country attending meetings of the county and district councils, they established regular contact between Dublin and the county councils, and they tried to improve local administration by speeding up rate collection and completing balance sheets. Cosgrave and O'Higgins held monthly meetings with their inspectors.[108] They all operated under extraordinary difficulties; files were seized, offices were burned and several of the office staff, rate collectors and auditors were arrested.

By now substantial amounts of money were available, thanks to the loan organised by Collins in Ireland and to the funds that de Valera raised during his lengthy tour of the United States. At the beginning of 1921 the Dáil approved Cosgrave's request for an allocation of £100,000 in loans to the local authorities—although only in areas where three-quarters of the rates had been collected.[109] (A year earlier, in vastly different financial circumstances, the cabinet had approved the department's application for the sum of £10 to use as petty cash.[110])

Whenever possible Cosgrave waged war on localism, and he tried to impose national rather than regional priorities on county councils and other bodies. 'In general, the Sinn Féiners wished to clean up what were seen, with some accuracy, as local Tammany Halls',[111] and Cosgrave was committed to this long-standing objective. Sectional pressures should be resisted in the national interest. In retirement he wrote that some people saw independence 'as a means to divide up the wealth of the State rather than a God-given opportunity to expand the wealth of the State'.[112] He planned to rationalise the structure of local government, with which he had been familiar for more than a decade, but he encountered entrenched resistance to the amalgamation of poor law unions—including 'very considerable opposition' from some of his Dáil colleagues.[113] The department was warned that 'Tipperary is very obstinate when it believes it is being ruled from Clonmel' and that the county's policy was to eschew the question of amalgamation.[114] In carrying out this agenda he was almost a decade ahead of the United Kingdom government.[115] He warned that his department was 'determined to rid the ratepayers of the burden of maintaining a number of expensive institutions' throughout the country.[116] The abolition of boards of guardians was essential to his programme, and he insisted that the Dáil should establish new institutions in place of the poor law unions to remove the taint of pauperism.

Cosgrave rejected the idea of doles for the unemployed and he hoped to get rid of the 'workhouse citizen', a class that he believed had developed as a result of the poor law. He saw the workhouses as uneconomic, as demoralising to their supposed beneficiaries and as a burden on society. One of his communications to local authorities began bluntly 'the workhouse is an evil institution', and he described its inhabitants as 'a peculiar race…people who had got no sense of civic pride or sense of civic responsibility'.[117] He believed strongly that the 'workhouse mentality' blunted and stultified the character and will-power of its victims. In the long term he wished to transform the system, to make the Irish people more self-confident and self-reliant—a hallowed objective of the Sinn Féin party; but in the short term he felt that some workhouse residents would have better prospects if they cut their links with the society that had failed them and started afresh in a more stimulating environment.

One letter illustrates his views with particular clarity. Cosgrave wrote to his colleague Austin Stack, the minister for Home Affairs, that people reared in the workhouse 'are no great acquisition to the community and they have no ideas whatever of civic responsibilities…it would be a decided gain if they all took it into their heads to emigrate. When they go abroad they are thrown on their own responsibilities and have to work whether they like it or not'. At first reading this might seem to be an unfeeling letter, but it must be set against the background both of the Dáil government's prohibition of emigration and of the details of the particular case. The Dublin Board of Guardians had proposed to send a girl to Canada, and Cosgrave expressed concern that no information had been provided about her age, whether she had any prospects in Canada, or whether she had any relatives there.[118]

Efficiency and economy would be complemented by integrity, and corruption was to be stamped out at local level. One county council was overruled when it limited employment of road-workers to Sinn Féiners and Volunteers; this violated the Dáil decree banning religious or political tests for public service positions, and it would enforce a kind of lip service to the republic.[119] During the Sinn Féin convention in 1917 Cosgrave had urged that Dublin Corporation's pattern of competitive examinations should be adopted more widely.[120] Posts were to be filled by the best-qualified candidates wherever possible, even in circumstances where the department was 'on the run'. Examinations were held to fill vacancies for offices such as county council secretaries—to the dismay and rage of worthies and bullies who felt entitled to control appointments in their neighbourhoods. Cosgrave claimed that candidates who had passed such tests were accepted by the county councils.[121]

Shortly afterwards the cabinet directed him to form an external examining board for local government positions.[122] But however admirable this policy might be, in practice it could create difficulties. Advertisements were placed in the newspapers inviting applications for the post of auditor, detailing the requirements but without disclosing the name of the employer. An examination was conducted in the offices of Dublin Corporation, and only the successful candidates were informed of the nature of the work. One of these, Frank Barnard, was delighted to be told that he had obtained first place, but initially he declined the offer when its full nature was revealed to him.[123]

Cosgrave boasted that his department avoided extravagance, and that in general it ensured greater efficiency than at any time since the passing of the Local Government Act in 1898.[124] But he and his colleagues encountered a range of problems, both internal and external. For example, when the British government stopped all payments due to Dublin Corporation he persuaded politically hostile banks to buy corporation stock.[125] He attached great importance to this agreement. On one occasion the corporation acted behind his back, by altering a report submitted by the estates and finance committee that he had chaired, and thereby committing itself to expenditure at odds with his agreement with the Bank of Ireland. He wrote to its governor deploring this decision.[126] The bank's directors seem to have been impressed by the Dáil and corporation representatives and to have felt that 'it made more sense to subsidise a rebel administration than see the capital descend into chaos'.[127]

In a report to the Dáil Cosgrave noted that hostility to rate collectors was practically universal throughout the country.[128] He complained to O'Higgins that certain members of the IRA in Co. Galway were involved in this resistance and asked him to draft a very strong letter on the matter; the message duly described such conduct as stupid, short-sighted and flagrantly unpatriotic.[129] Opposition persisted, however, and the IRA commander in mid-Clare warned that if his brigade's nominee for rate collector were not accepted, anyone else who attempted to collect rates would be shot.[130] Two weeks later O'Higgins reported to Cosgrave that the condition of rate collectors was 'pretty sound everywhere except in Clare and Leitrim. In Clare it is very bad; in Leitrim it is desperate'. This latter description seems not to have been an exaggeration. The inspector reported an 'irreconcilable anti-rate attitude', and he was obliged to defend himself by firing over the heads of a crowd. It was recommended that the cabinet should 'sanction the sending of an expedition of forty active, intelligent men with orders to collect the outstanding rates'.[131]

Cosgrave intervened in other areas outside the responsibility of his department. The Dáil government was anxious to lessen the impact of labour disputes and of class conflict in general, seeing them as distractions from the struggle against British rule. He was instructed by the cabinet to arrange arbitration in a dispute between public bodies and their employees.[132] He tried to mediate in labour conflicts, and in October 1920 he made heroic efforts to resolve a dispute in the building trade. One Sunday he called three times to meet the secretary of the Plasterers Society, and the following day he visited the man in his office to discuss hourly rates of pay (higher in Belfast than in Dublin). He then held meetings with the mayor of Dublin and with William O'Brien the trade unionist, and he wrote various letters. All this was to no avail and the dispute continued.[133] Cosgrave also provided a scheme for coping with a milk shortage.[134] He was one of four TDs (Dáil deputies) who went to the ceremonial removal of Terence MacSwiney's coffin from Brixton Jail to Southwark Cathedral after his death on hunger strike.[135] He expressed disquiet when the Dáil debated Brugha's proposal that all TDs and Volunteers, as well as people belonging to various other categories, should swear allegiance to the republic and to the Dáil. He had conscientious scruples about taking an oath unless it was absolutely necessary—and he believed that any military organisation in the country should be under the control of the Dáil.[136] Once the Anglo-Irish treaty was signed in 1921 this issue would dominate Irish public life, and Cosgrave would feel obliged to defend and impose his beliefs.

He made one highly improbable and unworldly proposal: that an upper house should be added to the (unicameral) Dáil. This would take the form of a 'Theological Board' that would decide whether any legislation proposed by the Dáil would be 'contrary to Faith and Morals'. He also suggested that in return for a guarantee that the Dáil would not make laws at odds with Catholic teaching, the pope might recognise it as a body entitled to legislate for Ireland. Joking that the letter had been mislaid for 900 years, the cabinet secretary warned that the scheme would not work and 'might lead to very grave trouble. Besides for the Dail to admit that there existed a necessity for such a check on their legislation would, I think, be a fatal error'. De Valera agreed.[137]

Lying low

The efforts and achievements of Cosgrave's department took place against a background of increasing harassment and intimidation, at local as well as at national level. On the day that the Dáil was suppressed his house was one of several that was searched by crown forces.[138] His stepfather was arrested. Cosgrave had a price on his head of £3,500—the same reward as for Stack, but a lesser sum than would be paid for the arrest of the military leaders of the independence struggle, Brugha, Collins and Richard Mulcahy.

One of Cosgrave's colleagues remarked of him later that as a Dubliner and a long-serving member of the corporation 'he was known personally to perhaps one hundred times as many people as any of the rest of us'.[139] In November 1920, after the killings on Bloody Sunday and the arrest of Griffith (who in de Valera's absence in America was the acting president of the Dáil and its government), he realised that someone had informed on him. He went on the run. An Oblate priest collected him in Dublin and drove him to the order's monastery in Glencree in Co. Wicklow, where he remained for some time. He shaved his moustache; he was called 'Brother Doyle'; and his real identity was known to only two members of the community. It is said that he left the monastery on one occasion during this period, for a meeting with Collins.[140]

There has been disagreement about how long Cosgrave stayed in Glencree, and estimates range from one month to three, but it seems to have been for about six weeks. He wrote a memorandum on 22 November, and a cabinet minute indicates that shortly afterwards he was either present or presumed to be contactable; he and others were directed to draft a report.[141] Subsequently, O'Higgins signed letters in his role as assistant local government minister, and notices were sent with messages such as 'Mr. Cosgrave is not available at the moment'.[142] By early January 1921 he was once more engaged in official correspondence—with county councils and with de Valera, who had recently returned from his American tour. But Cosgrave's absence meant that he was unfamiliar with some details of government discussions, and de Valera complained that one of his memoranda had missed the whole point of a cabinet decision (relating to a sum of £100,000 that would be lent to the councils). He was advised to consult with O'Higgins.[143] More than a decade later de Valera accused Cosgrave of having run away to England in late 1920; he rejected this claim as untrue and absolutely without foundation.[144] His sojourn in Glencree reflected common sense rather than any lack of moral fibre—which he had already displayed in 1916.[145] After his return to Dublin he stayed in a house in Clontarf.[146]

His clerical cover may, however, have been suspected. In December 1920 Mark Sturgis, a Dublin Castle official, quoted the belief that Cosgrave was dressed as a priest or a monk and that, like other wanted men, he walked about the city almost daily.[147] He wore disguises, and accounts varied as to their effectiveness. A French journalist remembered that his hair had been coloured a blazing red. A colleague recorded that on 9 January, at the first cabinet meeting after de Valera's return from America, 'when he entered the room all of us thought for a moment a stranger had thrust his way in. His hair and moustache were dyed black or dark brown, and his appearance was therefore very substantially altered'.[148] Another recollection gives a different impression. On one occasion in late May 1921 he left his office in Wicklow Street ('Greene and Lloyd, consulting engineers'), disguised to his own satisfaction and that of his staff—until, in the hallway leading to the street, a loitering beggar accosted him with the words 'spare a copper, Mr Cosgrave'.[149]

His apprehensions were well-founded. In raids on his family's house and in Drumcondra British forces made inquiries about him, and later his stepfather's premises in James's Street were searched.[150] British forces disrupted a meeting of the corporation in May 1921 at a time when Cosgrave acted as mayor; it was assumed that they had expected him to be present and that their objective was to arrest him.[151] Sturgis recorded an objection that had been made to the idea of a truce: 'under it Cosgrave for instance would expect to come home unmolested to visit his wife'.[152] The British authorities' determination to arrest him must be seen as a tribute to his importance and effectiveness.

Although some members of the government (most notably Collins) took daring risks, Cosgrave's caution was not unusual. No meetings of the Dáil were held for four months between September 1920 and January 1921, and it was suggested that the only way in which a TD might express his opinions was to write to the newspapers.[153] No meetings of the Sinn Féin party's standing committee took place for almost four months, between 14 October 1920 and 10 February 1921. Another member of the Dáil, Liam de Róiste from Cork, later took an even more drastic refuge than Cosgrave; he hid in a mental asylum.[154]

Cosgrave's deputy, Kevin O'Higgins, also lay low after Bloody Sunday; he stayed in his fiancée's family's house for some weeks, and a priest even warned him not to go to mass.[155] But he was a less well-known and less-recognisable figure, and he remained at his post for much of the time that Cosgrave was away. The contrast between their responses to British repression may have worsened the frosty relationship between the two men. After Cosgrave had returned to his department in January 1921 and had made a report to the Dáil, O'Higgins disagreed publicly with the 'rosy' situation described by his minister.[156] He also wrote to the government secretary referring to 'the disappearance of Mr. Cosgrave'.[157] Two months later he announced to the Dáil that there was some difference between him and Cosgrave over the seizure of money from debtors.[158]

In private he was far more scathing. He sent a series of condescending and sometimes bilious letters to his fiancée, in the course of which he mocked and disparaged his minister. He wrote:

> he really gives very little attendance—messing about to Corporation meetings etc.—and then when he does blow in he'll take up some business at random, give some wholly outlandish ruling on it and blow out again most complacently, feeling that he has saved the State sufficiently for one day…One comfort is that he's most amenable—if you point out anything to him with moderate emphasis he'll swallow it with enthusiasm and crow, like a hen after laying, over the fine thing he has done…the man is only fitted to drive his wife about the countryside in a smart pony and trap and return the salutes of the peasantry with the proper mixture of graciousness and bonhomie. His Corporation reputation is the kingship of the one-eyed man amongst the blind.[159]

He even referred to 'my jumped-up quitter of a senior partner'.[160] Allowance should be made for O'Higgins's notoriously virulent tongue and pen, and possibly also for any temptation he may have felt to show off when writing to his fiancée.

Despite the tensions between the two men, their characters and skills complemented each other, and Cosgrave was experienced and emollient while O'Higgins was efficient but acerbic. (He has also been described as unrealistic and intolerant in some of the demands he made of councils and officials.[161]) Another letter indicates a warmer and more self-critical aspect of O'Higgins's character and of their relationship. He wrote:

> Whenever there's an abusive letter to be written C. says 'here H., you're a cross-grained divil, you'd better deal with this fellow—and for God's sake work off some of your spleen on him, instead of on me!' Poor old C.—but he knows I love him—unofficially'.[162]

The two men remained in harness together for the next seven years.

But others too were critical, and de Valera rebuked both Cosgrave and O'Higgins because circulars were carelessly worded.[163] Collins made sharp comments about the department. He complained angrily to de Valera about an uncharacteristic mistake it had made, by sending a Sinn Féin party notice from its office. (The president responded that his fundamental point was unquestionable, but that the judgment was too harsh).[164] On another occasion he urged de Valera to tell Cosgrave 'not to be so fussy'.[165] Collins has been described as a 'truly awful' cabinet colleague who engaged in ongoing persecution of the departments of Local Government and Propaganda.[166] His impatience was spread far more widely, however, and in January 1921 he deplored the fact that only two departments, Agriculture and Trade, had submitted their estimates. He described one action of Brugha's as not gentlemanly or dignified and—damningly—'above all it is not organisation'.[167]

Despite occasional criticisms, it was generally recognised both at the time and subsequently that between 1919 and 1921 the Department of Local Government was faced with exceptional opportunities and responsibilities. Under the joint leadership of Cosgrave and O'Higgins it proved not merely that the Dáil's government could administer a complex system with considerable efficiency in challenging circumstances, but also that it could carry out long-overdue reforms neglected under Dublin Castle rule.

The military and political conflict continued throughout the first half of 1921, but during these months the British government began implementing a two-stage plan to 'solve' the Irish question. The island was partitioned into two new units of six and twenty-six counties, each of which would have its own home rule parliament and government subordinate to Westminster. Elections for the assemblies in both parts of Ireland were held in May 1921, and the underground Irish government decided to use them to create a new, second Dáil. In theory, the system of PR was extended from local to national elections, but in practice every seat for the southern Irish parliament was uncontested. As a result, and following the pattern of 1918, Cosgrave was returned unchallenged to his Dáil seat for the constituency of North Kilkenny.

Only when the interests of Ulster unionists had been fully satisfied by the details of this new measure did Lloyd George's cabinet turn its attention to a settlement with Irish nationalists.[168] The British authorities in Dublin wanted to meet de Valera and they asked the American consul, J.J. Dunant, to act as intermediary. He approached a judge in the Sinn Féin courts, Patrick Moylett, who sought the assistance of Cosgrave (then using the alias McDermott, and with an office in the Alexandra Hotel), who in turn passed the message to de Valera and the cabinet. Subsequently, on 28 May, Cosgrave and four others escorted Moylett almost as far as the gates of Dublin Castle, where he met the influential assistant under-secretary Andy Cope and was told that the British intended to evacuate southern Ireland. Moylett reported the good news back to Cosgrave.[169] Six weeks later a truce came into effect. People celebrated in the streets, 'bonfires blazed all night' and old people took their furniture out of their homes to sit in comfort around the flames.[170]

De Valera, accompanied by Griffith, Austin Stack, Robert Barton and Count Plunkett, went to London to meet Lloyd George. On his return he informed his cabinet of proposals made by the British, which went far beyond any previous offer to Irish nationalists and amounted to dominion status with some qualifications; violence had extracted concessions where political methods had failed. According to a memorandum written by Stack two years later, 'MacNeill and Cosgrave did not give themselves away one bit'.[171]

The two leaders carried on an extensive correspondence, which concluded with an agreement to hold a conference in October. Once more, Cosgrave was not a member of an Irish 'inner cabinet' that discussed strategy and tactics for the forthcoming negotiations; the members were de Valera, Collins, Griffith,

Cathal Brugha, Richard Mulcahy, Eoin MacNeill and the government secretary Diarmuid O'Hegarty.[172] A feature of Cosgrave's early career was the number of bodies or groups to which he did *not* belong. According to claims made decades later by one of his friends, he had proposed to the cabinet that de Valera should lead the delegation to negotiate with the British.[173] The minutes of this discussion, which consist of a mere twelve lines, do not record any objection. It was decided that Cosgrave and Joe McGrath would travel to Britain with the Irish reply on finalising the details for the October conference, but in the event McGrath was accompanied by Harry Boland.[174]

When the membership of the Irish delegation to the conference was repeated in the Dáil Cosgrave took a firm stand. He argued publicly that de Valera should form part of the delegation because he had extraordinary experience in negotiations. In a famous image he declared that 'this was a team they were sending over and they were leaving their ablest player in reserve. The reserve would have to be used some time or other, and...now was the time'. He secured little support, and even his own deputy, Kevin O'Higgins, felt that de Valera should remain in Dublin. Collins too believed that de Valera should go to London, and he told the Dáil that he would much prefer not to have been chosen as a member of the delegation.[175] The reasons for de Valera's decision not to attend the negotiations have been debated ever since. It is likely that he intended the negotiations to be no more than the overture to the main performance, which he planned to deliver, with the result that he would be able to conclude the talks personally at the eleventh hour.[176] If so, the delegation's main function was to be used and then discarded.

In August 1921 de Valera shuffled his cabinet, removing some of its most radical members—and in the process relegating its only female member, Countess Markievicz. Almost six decades would pass before another woman headed a government department in Dublin. Cosgrave retained his ministry, a sign that any complaints made by Collins and O'Higgins were not allowed to outweigh the department's achievements under his leadership. Three members of the new cabinet (Griffith, Collins and Barton) would be in the delegation to London, while four would remain in Dublin (de Valera, Brugha, Stack and Cosgrave). De Valera sent a divided team to London and initially he failed to provide it with instructions on one of the principal aspects of the negotiations: the Irish policy on Ulster.[177] The 'rump' cabinet in Dublin, accompanied by Cosgrave's deputy, O'Higgins, met regularly to discuss reports from the delegation during the conference discussions in London. When de Valera and Brugha were absent from Dublin at the end of November, inspecting army units in the west, the president asked the delegates in London to communicate with Stack; nonetheless (and perhaps revealingly) Griffith sent a dispatch to Cosgrave, who promptly delivered it to Stack.[178]

After the truce had come into effect in summer 1921, the Dáil administrative machinery could operate with few inhibitions, and it succeeded in consolidating its control over most of the country. Cosgrave was able to concentrate on departmental matters, without the disruptions of recent years. He announced new reforms: rates were to be reduced; the old poor law unions were to be abolished; and each county should replace them with one 'home' and one well-equipped hospital. He hoped to eliminate bureaucracy and inefficiency, so that 'a far greater proportion of the money collected for the benefit of the poor will reach those for whom it was intended than was hitherto the case'. In Co. Galway, for example, ten workhouses and the county infirmary were closed in 1921, and the Galway city workhouse was adapted to accommodate a new county hospital.[179] The cabinet also directed Cosgrave to investigate the accuracy of the franchise lists.[180] He was concerned that a government subsidy to railways should not be used to make a profit for others.[181] He made speeches. He told an audience in Kilkenny that Ireland had a civilisation and a respect for law and order 'long before Hanoverians contemplated landing in England', and in Dublin he hoped that a war-weary world would realise that there was another war to be undertaken: for the relief of the suffering and afflicted poor.[182]

All this was of secondary importance. In autumn 1921 most people's attention was focused on developments in London, but Cosgrave played no part in the treaty negotiations; he was excluded from the delegation in October, just as he had been from the team that accompanied de Valera to meet Lloyd George in July.[183] He was still outside the 'inner circle'.

Photograph of the members of B Company, 4th Battalion of the Irish Volunteers, commanded by Eamonn Ceannt, following the surrender of the South Dublin Union and Marrowbone Lane garrisons on 30 April 1916; Cosgrave was a lieutenant in Ceannt's garrison.

PROSECUTION.

1st. WITNESS - Major J.A. ARMSTRONG, Enniskillen Fusiliers, being duly sworn, states :-

I was on duty at Patricks Park on the 30th of April last. The British troops were fired on in the morning. Later on in the day I saw Mr. McDonna passing to and fro under a flag of truce. A surrender was arranged. About 5 p.m. on that day two armed bodies of men surrendered. The laying down of arms took place in 2 streets one at right angles to the other. The accused was one of those bodies of men, he was in uniform and armed. I had a list of the names of all the men who surrendered made. In the list the name of accused appears as Lieutenant. He was subsequently removed to Richmond Barracks.

CROSS-EXAMINED.

I made a list of the men who were armed and a list of men who were unarmed (produced and shewn to the accused).

The list of the unarmed men was taken before any of the men were disarmed. The list of the armed men was taken after the men were disarmed.

The list of the unarmed was made on the same side of the street the men halted at when they came in. They were afterwards marched across the street to the other side and a list of the whole party then taken. The unarmed list was taken by an Officer the armed list was taken by Officers N.C.O. men detailed by me.

Pages from the transcript of Cosgrave's court-martial and details of his sentence, following his participation in the 1916 Rising.

2nd WITNESS - CONSTABLE JOHN WHEELAN 37a, Dublin
Metropolitan Police, being sworn, states :-

I was on duty at Cork Street on the 24th April
last, The Irish volunteers formed up in Emerald Square
near there. I saw the accused coming down Cork Street,
he was leading a body of volunteers in uniform.

CROSS-EXAMINED.

The accused was at the head of the body of
volunteers.

DEFENCE.

The accused in his defence states :-

The charge which is made regarding the intention
of assisting the enemy is baseless unsustained and
utterly unfounded. That I never had any communication
direct or indirect with the enemy. The sword which I
carried was simply an ornament.

The accused calls evidence as to character.

1st WITNESS - JAMES MICHAEL GALLAGHER, LORD MAYOR of DUBLIN,
sworn states :-

I have known the accused for a number of years, He
has been a member of the Dublin Corporation for 9 years.
He was chairman of the Finance Committee and held it
for two years an exceptional length of time, it is
usually held for one year only, during the time he has
held the office he has always acted in a straightforward
and proper manner. I know him to be a very good citizen
and of exceptional ability.

SCHEDULE.

DATED 4th MAY 1916.

Not more than 6 names to be entered on one form.	Name of Alleged Offender.	Offence charged	Plea	Finding, and if convicted sentence. (b)	How dealt with by Commanding Officer.
Not more than 6 names to be entered on one form.	35 William Cosgrave.	Did an act to wit did take part in an armed rebellion and in the waging of war against His Majesty the King such act being of such a nature as to be calculated to be prejudicial to the Defence of the Realm and being done with the intention and for the purpose of assisting the enemy.	Not Guilty.	Guilty.Death by being shot.	Confirmed but I commut the sentence to Penal Servitude for life.

(a) If the name of the person charged is unknown, he may be described as unknown, with such additions as will identify him.

(b) Recommendation to mercy to be inserted in this column.

J.G. MAXWELL
Convening Officer.

C.J. BLACKADER Brig. General
President.

Promulgated this sixth day of May 1916.

H. ANDERSON Capt.
3/The Royal Irish

Kilmainham Goal,
Dublin.

Cosgrave's notes on events at the South Dublin Union between Easter Sunday and Easter Thursday 1916 (including injuries and fatalities), on the surrender of the garrison and on his court-martial; documents submitted as part of his application for a military pension.

(32)

Inspection Summary - April 1916. with O.C
4th Battalion

Easter Monday 1916
Led Battalion Companies to S. D. U.
James Street. midday.
Comdt Ceannt. Vice - Comdt Brugha
Capt French-mullen. Capt. S. Irvine
and Capt. Mac Carthy following.
Casualties -
Fatal - Volunteers. Owens. McDonnell &
Quinn - (Easter Monday)
Frank (Robban Burke) Tuesday. (Easter)
Wounded. Easter monday Vol S. Mac Carthy.
Ill. Vol Fogarty.
                           Willie
Capt Irvine - Lee C. Corrigan Vol Dorney
Captured on Easter Monday.
Capt. Mac Carthy returned - Easter Wednesday
       (according to Times - Sinn Fein Reb.)
Wounded Comdt Brugha. Easter Thursday.
+ Capt French-mullen - date escaped my
recollection -
Rank + duty of Vice - Comdt. fell
to me - the Sole Surviving Commissioned
Officer - neth Comdt Ceannt.
            L. E. Mac Cosgrave

EXPLANATORY NOTES   PAGE 7.

6.   Low Sunday 1916.   Very Rev. Fr. Augustine and Albert O.S.F.C.
arrived with Comdt. McDonagh about midday, bringing word of
the surrender.   Capt. Rotherham [B.A] who was known to me came
at 3 p.m. to conduct garrison to Bridge Street.   Comdt.
Ceannt Connor and I flanked him to Barrowbone Lane whwere the
garrison joined us.   British personnel took down the names -
noting those unarmed.   Having laid down arms - were marched
to Richmond Barracks - 2nd Lt. M E. Wylie [B.A]   one of the
Guards.

7.   Preliminary investigation next day -   On Tuesday
Field General Court Martial.   Wylie prosecuted.   Charged
(from recollection) In arms against His Majesty at Jacob's
Bishop Street} Peter Street which occasioned casualties
amongst His Majesty's troops - in treasonable contact with
Germany - Policeman Walsh gave evidence that I led the
volunteers from Emerald Square.   No change was made in the
description of our location.   On release from British
custody in 1917   Miss M Crummins Cammins who was acquainted with
Capt. Rothersham, told me he had been directed to tender
evidence at our Court Martial.   He refused saying "he met
those men yesterday, he had not known them before; he was not
in position to identify them".

8.   Found guilty - Sentence - Death.   Commuted to prison sentence
for life.
                                        É. Ó. ноеС

WILLIAM T. COSGRAVE,
CANDIDATE FOR KILKENNY.

Cosgrave election postcard, 1917.

Photograph of Sinn Féin members ahead of the 1917 by-election in Kilkenny. Standing, left to right: Dan McCarthy; Darrell Figgis; Rev. Dr Browne, Maynooth; Alderman Tom Kelly; Austin Stack; Eamon de Valera; Seán Milroy. Seated, left to right: Laurence Ginnell; Countess Markievicz; Cosgrave; Alice Ginnell.

THE COMIC SIDE.

"Our opponents have won by intimidation"—**Magennis** (would-be M.E.P.) at Kilkenny, after the declaration of the election result.

'The comic side', political cartoon published in *Irish Fun*, October 1917, showing the outcome of the by-election in Kilkenny in which Cosgrave won his first seat.

Opposite: Cosgrave's notes relating to the death and funeral of Thomas Ashe in 1917 (part of his military pension application).

EXPLANATORY NOTES PAGE 3

Autumn 1917. VICEComdt. T. Ashe died, after forcible feeding
~where he had been~ in Mountjoy on hunger strike. Dr. R. F. Hayes and I had
consultations with Counsel (T. M. Healy and P. Lynch) Lord
Mayor O'Neill was refused facilities for the lying in State
of ~Comdt~ Ashe in the City Hall. Arising out of a
discussion with me Mr. E. W. Eyre City Treasurer went
over to the Castle to talk over the matter with the
Commander-in-Chief. General Sir Bryan Mahon C.-i.C made
an inspection of the guard and directiong alternative
~~posts~~ ~~beats~~ for the sentries - solved the difficulty. As
General Mulcahy was on his way escorting the coffin,
with a Volunteer Guard, bloodshed was inevitable but for
Mr. Eyres intervention with Sir Bryan Mahon (they were
old friends). On the formation of the Senate in 1922 Mr.
Eyre and Sir Bryan Mahon were nominated by me to be
Senators.

Many years afterwards General Sir Bryan Mahon (Senator)
informed me that he was instructed to prevent any parade
by volunteers at the funeral of ~Comdt.~ Ashe. He took
the opposite course - in defiance of instructions - confin
-ed troops to Barracks on the Sunday and everything went
off peaceably.

His nurse during his last illness at my request got him to
dictate the story of these incidents, which she wrote down
Unfortunately the paper is mislaid.

Apart from my own testimony the principal witnesses in
these ~~witnesses~~ incidents have passed from human jurisdiction and
now wait Archangel Gabriel's trumpet.

                                        E. T. McC.

Letter written by Cosgrave to Henry Dixon,
1 January 1919, while interned in Reading
along with other Sinn Féin members
following their arrest in May 1918.

Jan 1st 1919.

My Dear Dixon. Your letters
are always welcome even
though they are difficult
to diagnose. I'm not a star
at writing but seldom fail
to make out what I write, after
some effort. We have had a
few patients since Xmas
Hurley Daly MacDonagh.
Former is not fit yet. Daly is
convalescent: & MacD is alright.
Thornton sprained his foot; this
not the best place in the
world for such a complaint.
Fahey is in great humour
working like a Trojan. Gives
an hour everyday at Irish.
& plenty of help as well at
other times. It is not a congenial
life but Thank God we are

making the most of it & I have
benefitted by it so far. You get to
know men better & for that alone
it has had four results. We
are living in great times
& much depends upon the
success of the Wilson philosophy.
He may not do all he expects
but his entry into European
matters lifts the plane of
statesmanship to a great
height. Cole has not been out
for a number of weeks. He's got
old & I wish Gwinnel were out of
this. I fear confinement in
these two cases & in Hurleys
also. Give my tenderest remembrances
to the Lynch family & your sisters
& everyone in your own family
circle & with a hundred thousand
good wishes to everyone of the
heaven. Believe me
                    Yrs
                    W J Cashen

Copy. Secret & Pressing 2/15115/1 A.2.

Headquarters. Dublin District.

On 24th inst. I handed to your G.S.O.2.
warrants for W.T. COSGRAVE and
29/3/20 expected
26/3/20
JOSEPH McDONAGH.

Will you please report as soon as practicable the
date of execution.

H. Toppin
Lt. Col.
A.A.G.S.
for M.G.A.

G.H.D. 201
26/8/1920

Note relating to arrest warrants executed for Cosgrave and Joseph 'McDonagh' in March 1920 by GHQ, Dublin District.

Entry in ledger from Wormwood Scrubs prison, London, dated 19 June 1920, indicating that Cosgrave had returned to the prison at the end of his period of parole and had been released.

52628
33.

H.M. Prison - WORMWOOD SCRUBS | 29th June 1920

MEMORANDUM.

3937 W. P. Cosgrave,
Irish Internee on parole

The above named surrendered this
morning. He was given a Railway
warrant to Dublin - and his private
property.

Governor

Photograph of Cosgrave disguised as 'Brother Doyle', when he took refuge with the Oblate fathers in Glencree, late 1920.

Photograph of Alderman Michael Flanagan, father of Cosgrave's
wife Louisa Flanagan, with his grandchildren Liam and Míceál
Cosgrave, taken at a garden party in the Cosgraves' home in 1925;
Colonel J.J. 'Ginger' O'Connell in the background.

Opposite: Extract from a letter by Kevin O'Higgins to his fiancée,
Brigid Cole, 1920–1, showing the difficult relationship he had
with Cosgrave.

tate that too flatly to the little sweetheart when she was going
'own because there was just an outside chance. Fact is,
olly, (I hope I say it in charity) things is wuss 'stead of
etter with C. back — he really gives very little attendance —
issing about to corporation meetings etc — and then when
e does blow in he'll take up some business at random,
ive some wholly outlandish ruling on it and blow out
goin most complacently, feeling that he has saved the state
ufficiently for one day. So that my attendance now has
he positive side of getting through work and the negative
ide of stopping old C. from doing things hopelessly reactionary
ne comfort is that he's most amenable — if you point out
nything to him with moderate emphasis he'll swallow it
ith enthusiasm and crow, like a hen after laying, over the
fine thing he has done. I fear me there's acid in this, but
ord, it's true, tragically true — the man is only fitted to
rive his wife about the countryside in a smart pony and
rap and return the salutes of the peasantry with the proper
ixture of graciousness and bonhomie. His corporation
eputation is the kingship of the one-eyed man amongst the
lind. Did I tell you he was giving me Spud as sec. to the C. —
he only thing he has shown any firmness about — I told him
traight what I thought of Spud and he said I must be
istaken and that he considered him "a very fine and an
xtremely able fellow." Help! This is rotten shop, child, but
I wanted you to glimpse why it was not on the cards to
et away just now. Of course to leave definitely and
inally would be different but while a man is on a job

grip on himself, and he got through his days' work supported by the thought that when it was through he would set down the outpouring of his lonely old heart to his little one — and that if she smiled at its bulk it would be a tender little smile born of the thought that it was the only pleasure in her boy's day and he was making the most of it. What a time we'll have when my Bird comes back to me — all the pent up love and gossip of a big long fortnight — and how I'm going to down the next few days — three! — without writing to my darling I'm hanged if I know. I can see the moth eaten getting an L of a time during these few days — wouldn't be surprised if he brings me before a Diet Court for language calculated to lead to a breach of the peace. Whenever there's an abusive letter to be written C. says "here H., you're a cross-grained divil, you better deal with this fellow — and for God's sake work off some of your spleen on him, instead of on me!". Poor old C. — but he knows I love him — unofficially. I wonder did I notice the old boss's name amongst recent resignations of the magistracy — had it all he was nearly going down with the ship, doing the Casabianca stunt, however, one mustn't bustle people, just give grace time to work — and it was really the sacerdotes that prevailed on him to hang on so long. Oh these sacerdotes! when will they learn, when a thing is right, man, an animal that walks on his hind legs and turns his face to the skies, should not be ashamed to stand for it — that it is the people who stand against it that should hang their heads for shame, and the people who well knowing that it is right "pass by on the other side" like the levite — the meanest character in the Bible — meaner than Judas, meaner than Pontius Pilate — who poor man, if he did wash his hands, at least had the courage to speak his mind. But — let it pass, they're coming round now — with the Protestants. Sure, we're respectable now, isn't old Christy Dalks of Dundrum a posthumous Republican. They're discovering belatedly that a Republican is not necessarily a man who "saucers" his tea or eats peas with his knife — it's just dawning

Letter from Diarmuid O'Hegarty to Eamon de Valera, 24 February 1921, regarding Cosgrave's proposal for a Theological Board.

Opposite: Extract from another letter by O'Higgins to Brigid Cole, 1920–1, showing a warmer side of his relationship with Cosgrave.

Following pages: Photograph of Cosgrave and Eamon de Valera meeting Irish-Americans (possibly in Dublin, May 1919), in an effort to secure international and American recognition for the Irish republic. Standing: Cosgrave, Eamon de Valera and Governor Edward Dunne of Illinois. Seated: Michael J Ryan (Friends of Irish Freedom, New York), Frank P. Walsh (later American chairman of the Irish Press fund raising committee) and unknown.

24th. February, 1921.

To:
The President.

A Chara,

The attached letter from Mr. Cosgrave which reached me on Saturday last was unfortunately mislaid for a few days and I have only just discovered it. Judging from the date on the letter it would seem to have been mislaid for 900 years, but this is not so.

The suggestion contained in it is that there should be a sort of "Upper House"" to the Dail consisting of a Theological Board which would decide whether any enactments of the Dail were contrary to Faith and Morals or not.

There is also a suggestion that a guarantee be given to the Holy Father that the Dail will not make laws contrary to the teachings of the Church, in return for which the Holy Father will be asked to recognise the Dail as a body entitled to legislate for Ireland.

I am afraid that in practice the Theological Board would not work and might lead to very grave trouble. Besides for the Dail to admit that there existed a necessity for such a check on their legislation would, I think, be a fatal error.

Mise, le meas

Runaidhe na hAireachta.

'We are the custodians
of the rights of the people'.

Opening image: Cosgrave raising
the flag on the roof of City Hall,
Dublin, January 1922

AFTER almost eight weeks of negotiations the delegates returned to Dublin at the beginning of December and brought with them a draft treaty proposed by the British. The full cabinet of seven members debated it at length. Cosgrave remarked shortly afterwards that towards the end of this meeting he had informed his colleagues he could not take the oath of allegiance to the king contained in the draft. The extensive minutes do not record his intervention, but they make it clear that the cabinet's decision to reject the British version of the oath of allegiance was unanimous.[1] (Some weeks later, O'Higgins told the Dáil that in October he and Cosgrave had decided they would not recommend any settlement 'involving allegiance to the King of England.'[2]) Cosgrave is mentioned only as one of the majority who voted in favour of the delegates meeting the Northern Irish prime minister, James Craig, if they believed this to be necessary.[3]

Griffith and his colleagues went back for a final round of negotiations in Downing Street, during which they wrote to de Valera and Cosgrave giving details of the discussions.[4] On 6 December they signed a treaty that was significantly changed from the draft rejected by the cabinet only three days earlier. In particular, the oath of allegiance to the king was replaced by an oath of allegiance to the constitution of the new Irish Free State and a separate oath of fidelity to the king.

Cosgrave kept his cards close to his chest, and he remained silent on the subject of the treaty until the 'rump' cabinet of four members met after the terms had been published. De Valera rejected the agreement and wished to dismiss the three ministers who had signed it, but Cosgrave argued that the delegates should be given the opportunity to explain their action. According to de Valera's later account, this was the first indication that Cosgrave disagreed with him; caution was necessary.[5] If Cosgrave had acquiesced in the president's proposal it is probable that de Valera would have used his majority in the cabinet (four members present, as opposed to three who were absent) to sack and replace Griffith, Collins and Barton, and a new cabinet would have rejected the treaty. In that case it is virtually certain that the Dáil would not have had any influence on the treaty—no more than it had been able to influence the exchanges that led to the opening of formal negotiations in October.[6]

It is also likely that de Valera still viewed Cosgrave as an ally and that he agreed to postpone the decision for one day in order to keep him on side. This delay bought time for the treaty, allowed public opinion to consolidate behind it before any cabinet split was revealed, and enabled those who supported the agreement to outvote and outmanoeuvre the militants.[7]

At a lengthy meeting of the full seven-man cabinet on 8 December 1921 the three ministers who had signed the treaty gave it their support (although Barton soon changed his mind), and three of the four who had remained in Dublin (de Valera, Brugha and Stack) opposed it. Erskine Childers, who had acted as secretary to the Irish delegation in London, was present at the discussion and he noted in his diary that after other members had expressed their opinions 'all hung on Cosgrave's vote'.[8] His was the crucial 'swing' vote, and he sided with the delegates who had negotiated the agreement. Afterwards he described his support of the treaty as 'the one big event in the whole of my life'.[9] The then mayor of Dublin, Laurence O'Neill, later maintained that Cosgrave had agonised over what he should do and that he was reluctant to side against de Valera, who 'stood by me when others wanted me turned down'.[10] This decision seems to have caught de Valera off guard, for until then the two men had been closely associated. Their offices in the Mansion House, used by the government, were near one another—the president's in the drawing room and the minister's in the billiard room—and it has been claimed that Cosgrave used to call to de Valera's office and accompany him to lunch.[11] He said later that de Valera 'thought he had me "in his pocket"'.[12]

Over many years Cosgrave had been influenced by Griffith's ideas, and although (like numerous others) he had suffered from the lash of Collins's tongue, the energy and efficiency displayed by the minister for Finance commanded his respect. Yet it would have been completely in character if Cosgrave had not been guided by personalities, if he did not make his decision on the basis of a choice between 'Dev' and 'Mick', but if he judged the agreement on what he regarded as its merits. He fought for a republic in 1916, but for almost a decade before the rising he had been a member of the Sinn Féin party that had sought a dual monarchy—a system that was now provided by the treaty. Above all, he was a pragmatist.

With the cabinet split almost equally attention moved to the Dáil, which proceeded to discuss the treaty in private and in public over a period of more than three weeks. In the public debates Cosgrave's interventions were characterised by wit, and also by a meticulous attention to detail and procedure. He was unusual if not unique in amusing his audience, and he was probably justified in his concluding belief that the Dáil was in a better mood at the end of his principal speech than it had been at the beginning.[13] One chapter of a book on the debates published a few months later was titled 'Alderman Cosgrave's Humour'. In this work he was described as a model of precision, a lover of order in debate and a provider of delightful comic relief. He was a debater who hurled back his opponents' arguments and who possessed the self-composure of an after-dinner speaker.[14] Another journalist wrote that he spoke for almost an hour and kept the Dáil in fits of laughter for most of the time. He also seemed to be one of the few deputies acquainted with the rules of debate.[15]

On the issue of the oath to the king, he distinguished carefully between the significance of the words 'faithfulness' and 'allegiance', and (significantly?) he cited a doctor of divinity who explained that one can be faithful to an equal; he argued, accurately as things turned out, that 'in this commonwealth or association each of the members is equal'. He made effective use of Childers's distinction between Canada's theoretical subordination and its practical independence. He made gentle fun of de Valera when he referred to the best colleges playing foreign games and added that the president (who had played rugby in Rockwell) would bear him out on that point. He teased those who objected to the title 'Free State', claiming 'I believe we are responsible for the name ourselves, but now that the English Government has agreed to give it to us we don't like it'. He disparaged Cathal Brugha, saying that he was interested only in shooting and that 'except for war he is not worth a damn for anything else'. Later he provoked laughter by describing Brugha (the minister for Defence) as 'the Minister for War'. He argued that Ireland's economic circumstances would not justify a resumption of the struggle against Britain. 'Here in the capital of Ireland there are something like 20,000 families living in single-room tenement dwellings, and are these the people you are going to ask to fight for you? It is not fair, I submit.' He forecast, wrongly, that the treaty 'gives us an opportunity of capturing the Northern Unionists'. And he was one of the few speakers to look to the outside world, by hoping that it might 'even be possible from the influence that would be exercised by the Irish Free State to effect improvements in these down-trodden nationalities such as Egypt and India'.[16]

Later he dismissed de Valera's attempt to be re-elected president, ridiculing the idea that the minority in the Dáil should take over the government of the country.[17] He made numerous procedural points. In the private debates he contributed relatively little, though he welcomed the efforts of a group of deputies from both sides who attempted to reach an agreement.[18]

Like other supporters of the treaty he could take comfort in the knowledge that his stand was widely popular. His own electorate was strongly in favour of the settlement, and the Sinn Féin constituency executive in North Kilkenny endorsed it unanimously.[19]

The treaty faced powerful opposition, principally because of the oath to the king and because a section of the army was reluctant to acknowledge civilian

authority. Some radicals were prepared to accept nothing short of an unam-
biguous British defeat; they hoped for renewed combat and did their best to
bring it about. Partition was not then the important issue that it became in
later years.[20] There was also resentment in some quarters at what was seen as a
settlement dictated by the British under the threat of 'immediate and terrible
war'. A section of Irish nationalists seemed not to appreciate that the break-
down of a military truce normally results in the resumption of conflict, and
that if the two sides did not reach an agreement the likely result would be a
return to war—possibly a 'terrible war'. Such people felt that while the Irish
were free to act as they chose, their enemy had no right to defend its perceived
national interests. But the British were in a stronger position and therefore had
less to lose, so they emphasised the logical consequences of failure to conclude
(and later to implement) a settlement. Opponents of the treaty should not have
been surprised or outraged by this, as many professed to be.

Before the negotiations began Lloyd George had made it clear that the new
Irish state would not be a republic; in the circumstances of the time that would
have amounted to a British surrender. Therefore, the Irish government and the
delegates in London had not tried to achieve this objective. Nevertheless, once
the treaty was signed many of its critics demanded and even fought for a republic that they had not sought until then. (When some of them gained power
in 1932, however, they were careful not to implement this policy they had advocated in opposition.)

After long and often bitter debates, on 7 January 1922 the Dáil approved
the treaty by 64 votes to 57. De Valera resigned the presidency but ran for re-
election, and on this occasion he was defeated by a mere two votes. The
majority then elected Griffith in his place, and only Collins and Cosgrave retained their former offices when the new president announced his cabinet.

THE PROVISIONAL GOVERNMENT

The British still refused to recognise the Dáil, which they saw as a republican assembly. According to article 17 of the treaty they would hand over the power
they exercised in the area of the future Free State to a provisional government established by the 'members of Parliament elected [in May 1921] for constituencies
in Southern Ireland'. In theory this parliament was the second Dáil, with the ex-
clusion of those members representing constituencies in the new political entity
of Northern Ireland. But because of a boycott by opponents of the treaty, it consisted in practice only of pro-treaty Sinn Féiners, reinforced by four independent

unionists elected for Trinity College. The new provisional government would have limited powers of legislation. The Dáil continued to meet, and its government remained in existence, although its power diminished steadily. Confusingly, for the next eight months there were two pro-treaty cabinets in Dublin, one recognised by some members of the Irish opposition and the other by the British. Griffith headed the first of these, the Dáil administration, but it was Collins who took over as chairman of the provisional government.

Long afterwards Cosgrave reminisced about an incident that took place on 14 January 1922, the day when members elected to the 'southern parliament' were to meet and choose a government. Griffith complained that Collins had refused to allow the gathering take place because the British would not release some prisoners, and he asked for Cosgrave's opinion. Cosgrave answered that until then the British were dealing with a political party. 'After this meeting they deal with a Government'. Collins took the point and announced immediately 'Call the meeting'.[21] The MPs convened for a total of one hour before dispersing, and they never met again. During this time they chose a provisional government, which in turn elected Collins its chairman, and he then appointed his colleagues to their offices. Cosgrave held the position of minister for Local Government in both pro-treaty administrations. He was a senior, experienced figure and a safe pair of hands.

Two days later Collins, accompanied by his ministers, took ceremonial possession of Dublin Castle from the last of the British viceroys, Viscount FitzAlan. Cosgrave met his counterpart Henry Robinson, who headed the rival Local Government Board—and who would subsequently be of great assistance to him.[22] One of those representing the outgoing regime was William Wylie, who had prosecuted many of the rebels in 1916 and was now a judge and privy councillor. Cosgrave raised the flag at the City Hall, the centre of Dublin's civic administration.[23]

A large majority of Irish people welcomed this transfer of power; most of the country had obtained a vastly greater degree of independence than could have been imagined a few years earlier. Supporters of the treaty believed that they needed to build on the gains that had already been achieved. A hostile minority, which was particularly numerous and influential in the army, remained dissatisfied and unreconciled.

The aftermath of the Easter Rising had seen a bloody purge of radical Irish leaders. The treaty split provoked a second, bloodless purge, and senior ministers such as de Valera, Brugha and Stack went into opposition. Together with Griffith and Collins, Cosgrave was now one of only three survivors in office of de Valera's original cabinet of eight members that had been approved by the Dáil in April 1919. Compared with de Valera, Griffith and Collins he was a relatively unknown figure, yet the events of recent months, combined with those of the tragic months to come, would force him to emerge from the shadows that had been cast by other men. Even as late as the formation of the two new pro-treaty administrations in January, many people—and probably Cosgrave most of all—would have been astonished by the idea that before the end of 1922 he would become the leader of an independent Irish state.

His relations with O'Higgins continued to be strained, and while he was absent for three weeks through illness his former deputy (by now minister for Economic Affairs) complained to the cabinet that Cosgrave had wanted to reduce rates rather than spend money on housing and road works. Whether or not he was influenced by this complaint, soon afterwards Cosgrave secured the cabinet's agreement that an even larger sum should be made available for the relief of unemployment to those county councils that had submitted approved schemes.[24] The souring of his friendship with de Valera as a result of the treaty split is indicated by his rebuke in January to the former president that 'you are so touchy'—although he added that he did not wish to cause offence.[25] This solicitude soon vanished, and their relationship became poisonous. He remained on good terms with Collins who, accompanied by Oliver St John Gogarty, used to drive out to Cosgrave's house, relax over tea, joke, and tease their host.[26]

As minister for Local Government Cosgrave had a wide range of responsibilities. These included rebuilding areas damaged or destroyed during the Anglo-Irish War and finding quarters for the new parliament. He was assigned practical tasks, such as installing telephones for the provisional government in the City Hall, inspecting the new Government Buildings on Merrion Street and compiling a new electoral register.[27] He tried to provide work for the unemployed and he met labour delegations. His department attempted to restore a normal pattern of local administration after the disruption caused by the recent conflict, but its efforts to resume the collection of rates were hampered by raids and robberies carried out by opponents of the treaty. In April 1922 he took over the structure and staff of his old opponent, Dublin Castle's Local Government Board, and the merger of this 'enemy' body with his own Dáil department was predictably difficult. Yet he was soon able to announce that Local Government 'has shown a very much larger amount of work done for the last three months than in all its previous existence'.[28]

His department distributed relief—particularly food—to impoverished areas along the west coast; in May he warned that the economic distress had approached the level of famine in counties such as Donegal, Galway and Kerry; and he pointed out that certain districts suffered from unemployment because of the withdrawal of British troops.[29] He constituted a new section of his department to assist refugees from anti-Catholic violence in Northern Ireland.[30]

In June Cosgrave wrote to Archbishop Edward Byrne of Dublin expressing concern about the plight of unmarried mothers. He suggested that Byrne might form a committee to unify and assist the efforts of the existing religious and charitable associations in the diocese, and that the Local Government Department could provide a 50% grant. The committee could review cases that were dealt with in Dublin and find out what additional help might be proposed.[31] In mid-July Frank Duff, the founder of the Legion of Mary, met Cosgrave and asked him to help women who wanted to escape from prostitution. Within two days he provided a house on Harcourt Street, free of rent and taxes, and a cheque for £50 ('real money in those days').[32]

Long before the truce Cosgrave had been able to begin implementing some of the policies that he had advocated in Dublin Corporation; in June 1919 he had outlined measures to provide working-class accommodation.[33] One of the provisional government's early decisions was to allocate £1,000,000 for housing.[34] Even after the outbreak of open civil war, Cosgrave retained his concern with the problem; while fighting was still taking place in Dublin he organised a committee to improve the city's food supply and to assist those who were compelled to leave their homes.[35] (A year later when he spoke on the familiar topic of housing he compared himself to an old war-horse who neighs and snorts when it smells battle.[36]) He encouraged the new Dublin housing architect and others to inspect Dutch construction methods.[37] He intervened on other social issues.

He continued to hold his old ministry in the Dáil administration, headed by Griffith, and he chaired this cabinet in the president's absence. At least in theory his responsibilities extended beyond Local Government, and on 16 January 1922 Collins announced that Cosgrave would be associated with him in the Finance Department.[38] It is unclear to what extent this decision was implemented.

Cosgrave had been a member of Sinn Féin from its earliest days, but as a cabinet minister he was excluded *ex-officio* from the party's leadership after 1919. He was a man of government and administration, often impatient with the demands of politics. He would later describe the Dáil as a time-absorber; he contrasted its debates unfavourably to the preparatory work carried out before its meetings, and to the construction of an efficient government machine.[39] In 1922, however, he revelled in parliamentary contests with opponents of the treaty. During the spring and early summer he intervened frequently in debates in the Dáil, often vigorously and sometimes aggressively, stressing the need to follow procedures, showing impatience ('what is the use of talking rubbish?'), claiming that republicans wished 'to postpone the issue; they are afraid to meet the people', and dismissing their arguments as 'twaddle' and 'chaff'.[40] Time and again he made clear his commitment to democracy.

He watched in dismay as republicans continued to undermine the treaty and as they ignored even Griffith's administration. The most extreme among them were anxious to resume the war against Britain and seemed prepared to establish a military dictatorship. He was frustrated by their defiance of the Dáil and of public opinion, and he asked whether a majority had any rights.

> Is there to be government by majority or is there to be government by autocracy? It is not a question of whether one thing is worth a Civil war or not. It is a question of whether the people have a right to elect a Government.

He insisted that the people were entitled to express their views; they 'are sovereign, deriving their power and their authority from God'.[41] He reminded deputies that

> it is not this Dáil who are the government of this country. It is the people, and from the people you derive whatever authority you have got, and not an inch more.[42]

In a similar fashion he rejected the belief of a military elite that it, and not the mass of the civilian population, represented the country. He claimed later that he had decided at the end of June (after the outbreak of widespread fighting) that he would not make any further effort to meet the republicans.[43]

THE TREATY ELECTION

In May 1922 Collins and de Valera negotiated a pact in advance of the forthcoming general election. They agreed that the two factions in the Sinn Féin party would form a united 'panel' and that each side would nominate only as many candidates as it already held seats in the Dáil. Other parties would be free to participate, in contrast to the situation in May 1921, when no-one had wished or dared to challenge Sinn Féin. Opponents of the treaty did their best to prevent candidates from other parties running, not wanting such outside in-tervention in a family feud; Cosgrave said later that the election was neither free nor fair.[44] The pact laid down that the two factions of the party would form a coalition government after the election. Some of Collins's colleagues were ap-palled by what they saw as an anti-democratic conspiracy that would violate the treaty, but the pact was almost certainly the only means of dissuading republi-can extremists from preventing an election taking place—which they could easily have done. Cosgrave had already noted that no party, or even the Dáil itself, had the power or authority to ensure that members would be returned un-opposed. He also pointed out that to assign different responsibilities to the Dáil and the Free State would inevitably result in friction.[45]

At meetings with Irish ministers in London on 26–7 May, Winston Churchill (who, as colonial secretary, was responsible for dealings with south-ern Ireland) expressed his outrage at Collins's action in agreeing an election pact with de Valera and denounced it as a betrayal of the treaty. He was advised that Cosgrave should accompany Collins to the next meeting with the British, since the minister for Local Government was in charge of organising the election. Cosgrave duly went to London, and he and Griffith argued vigorously that the poll should take place on schedule. He explained to Lloyd George and Churchill how the republicans had already disrupted the election campaign, but he claimed that conditions had improved since the signature of the pact. He expected that 80% of the voters would support the treaty (the actual figure proved to be 78%), but that that the workings of PR would necessitate a 'non-party' government. He was wildly wrong when he expressed the opinion that 'in the second or third Parliament the two chief parties would be the Farmers' Union and Labour'.[46] It was claimed that after this meeting had ended he calmed Churchill by expressing concern about his recovery from a fall in a recent game of polo.[47] Subsequently he, Griffith and Collins observed a debate in the House of Commons—to which they had all been elected as abstention-ist MPs in 1917–18.[48] This was his only visit to London between the signature of the treaty and Collins's death, although colleagues such as O'Higgins met British ministers frequently.

Cosgrave argued that the two sides in the Dáil should solve the 'mess' they had created.[49] He defended the pact as being necessary in the circumstances, but his commitment to it appears to have been half-hearted. Months later he de-scribed the agreement as having been made under duress, with the aim of ensuring peace and an election, and he claimed that it secured 'maximum ad-vantages for the political anti treaty section'.[50] He probably shared the views of

Griffith and other pro-treaty leaders who felt frustrated by what they saw as Collins's excessive willingness to appease his old republican comrades. He complained that the election campaign had lost much of its fire because of the pact.[51] He argued that once voting had taken place the pattern of dual administration, whereby Griffith headed one pro-treaty government and Collins another, should be brought to an end.[52] *The Irish Times* queried this proposal. 'For the purposes of the Treaty that authority surely must be the Provisional Government. For the purposes of the Collins–de Valera pact it must be Dail Eireann, otherwise why a Coalition Government?'[53] A post-election coalition with de Valera does not seem to have held any attractions for Cosgrave. He denounced the republicans' intimidation of non-Sinn Féin candidates, and he insisted that there should be no counterpart to attacks on Catholics in Northern Ireland: 'we must let it be known that here in the South we can give an example of civilisation and Christianity'.[54] This was probably a reference to the murder by republicans of Protestants in Cork and elsewhere.

In June 1922 the electorate was aware that to reject the treaty would end the truce with Britain, with the probable consequence of renewed warfare. Within the limits placed on its freedom of choice by republican threats and violence, it voted decisively for compromise and for peace. When they were offered an alternative, electors systematically rejected panel candidates who opposed the treaty and not those who supported it.[55] But as well as routing the anti-treaty republicans, the electors also favoured 'third party' candidates who had no association with the recent war—or the threat of a new war. These candidates gained more first preference votes than either faction of Sinn Féin.[56]

It was therefore not surprising that in the Carlow-Kilkenny constituency Cosgrave came second to the Labour candidate, Patrick Gaffney. There was a gap of almost 4,000 between the first preference votes each man received, but nonetheless Cosgrave had a surplus over the 'quota', and his pro-treaty Sinn Féin colleague was also elected. In Carlow-Kilkenny, 85.6% of the votes were cast for the four candidates who supported the treaty; the republicans lost both their seats, to Gaffney and to Denis Gorey, the leader of the Farmers' Party. Gorey had been attacked by republicans in an unsuccessful attempt to force his withdrawal from the campaign. Although Gaffney initially supported the treaty he later refused to take the oath of fidelity to the king and abstained from the Dáil.[57] Cosgrave's own second preference votes divided 93% in favour of the remaining pro-treaty candidate and only 7% for the republican.[58] His constituents shared his convictions.

Speeches and votes were soon followed by gunfire and bloodshed. By now elements on both sides were reconciled to the probability of civil war, and within two weeks of the election the long-simmering conflict boiled over. The government was frustrated by challenges to its authority; it was under pressure from Lloyd George and Churchill; and it was anxious to prevent the republicans from carrying out their aim of attacking Northern Ireland, re-igniting the war against the British and destroying the treaty. On 28 June Collins's forces besieged the anti-treaty garrison in the Four Courts.[59] Fighting in Dublin lasted for several days, and elsewhere for almost eleven months. When ministers met Archbishop Byrne and others who sought a cease-fire, Cosgrave's intervention enabled the discussion to proceed amicably, but fruitlessly.[60] As early as 1 July, however, he told a deputation that the government would accept nothing less than unconditional surrender. The cabinet approved this statement.[61]

By August government troops had won the 'conventional' war and the republicans (called 'irregulars' by their opponents) resorted to guerrilla tactics, using against their former colleagues the methods they had previously employed against the British. Collins devoted his energies to winning the war and he appointed himself commander-in-chief of the army.[62] (A year later, with the benefit of hindsight, this action was seen as laying the foundation of civilian control of the armed forces.[63]) He had already announced that he 'would act as minister of Defence for the present' in place of Richard Mulcahy, who held that office in Griffith's Dáil government.[64] Collins transferred the day-to-day leadership of the provisional government to Cosgrave, who in terms of service was the senior member of his cabinet and who was not involved in military operations—as were several other ministers. He was a natural choice.

But no-one doubted where ultimate power lay. When the cabinet held its first meeting after Cosgrave's appointment as acting chairman, Collins took charge and promptly gave orders. He sent his colleagues directives such as 'In dealing with these papers please see that they are kept intact'.[65] The cabinet minutes contain remarks such as 'the Commander-in-Chief should be consulted'; 'the Commander-in-Chief should be asked to consider the advisability of having a Notice issued to that effect'; and 'the Commander-in-Chief advised, and it was decided, that Parliament should be again prorogued'.[66] He 'announced' to the cabinet, as a *fait accompli,* the appointment of a 'War Council of Three' consisting of himself, Mulcahy and Eoin O'Duffy (all IRB men, which may have been significant).[67] Later, he wrote to his government colleagues that 'I spoke to Mr. Cosgrave last night on this matter and I think that the decision will be reconsidered to-day'.[68] In his absence the cabinet expressed its concern at not being sent reports on the military situation.[69]

It has been claimed that in effect Collins became a dictator.[70] His actions in the last weeks of his life were undoubtedly high-handed and autocratic, but in wartime there is nothing unusual in heads of government arrogating to themselves exceptional powers. Such patterns have not always endured after the restoration of peace. It was hardly surprising that soldiers should play a leading role in the cabinet after several years of violence and in the context of renewed conflict. Initially, the military was independent of the government, or at least of its civilian members—whose control was established only slowly and incrementally. In April 1923 the attorney-general Hugh Kennedy wrote that:

> the army has never been definitely constituted…its organisation and powers, the direction and control of its policy, the mode and authority of its appointments, have been assumed by the Army itself…[the] Army Council was in truth and in fact constituted in the first instance in the Army itself…It seemed as if a slow nursing process was ahead before civil authority could be openly asserted over the Army.[71]

Griffith was the most prominent civilian in the pro-treaty leadership, but he was ill during the summer of 1922 and on 12 August he died suddenly of a stroke. Shaken by this news, and aware that members of the government were on a list of people who were liable to be shot by republicans, Cosgrave composed a memorandum or testament that contained clear evidence of some of his attitudes and beliefs.

> [The republicans] are irresponsible and must not be allowed to cow or awe the people of Ireland. Even if the members of the Government are shot and die others will be found to take their places. None of us could be indispensible…Genl. Collins is one of the greatest men Ireland has produced. A statesman and a soldier—and there are others also in the Government and the Army. My place will be easily filled…Hard times are coming, but they—the people of Ireland—will endure, but they must prevail against any minority seeking to order their will or their life save under the laws which the people's representatives pass. I willingly forgive those who think I should be shot and those who take part

in such shooting and I ask forgiveness of all those I have offended…I ask for obedience to the Parliament of the Irish Nation,
and may God in His infinite mercy forgive me my sins and
pardon my shortcomings.[72]

As the fighting continued some treaty supporters or neutral figures peeled off.
George Gavan Duffy, the minister for Foreign Affairs in the provisional government, resigned in July in protest at the abolition of the Dáil courts, and he
wrote to Collins complaining that since his departure and that of other ministers, 'the remnant of the Cabinet has been dominated by a spirit of narrowness
and intolerance'.[73]

The government did not have to face the embarrassment of parliamentary
criticism or control. When faced with a demand that the second Dáil should be
reconvened Cosgrave responded by announcing that its functions had come to an
end on 30 June—the date on which it had been scheduled to hold a final meeting.

The Sovereign Assembly of Ireland is now the Parliament elected
in June last, whose authority the irregulars have flouted. The
present military action undertaken by the Government is necessary to enforce obedience to Parliament…peace must be firmly
established on the basis of the supremacy of the elected
Government of the Irish people.[74]

Yet Collins was determined not to convene this 'sovereign assembly'; he would
fight and win the war before he became answerable to a parliament. He would
be responsible merely to his (reasonable and well-founded) interpretation of
the electorate's vote. Convocation of the Dáil was postponed on five separate
occasions during the summer of 1922.[75] Discussions were held about when it
should be summoned, and the Labour Party threatened to resign its seats if this
were not done. Collins asked for a copy of the Dáil's agenda, and the cabinet
planned to decide the matter at its meeting on 22 August, but in the meantime
Collins wrote from Cork on 21 August that it was 'wise to postpone the Dail
meeting as already suggested'.[76] When the cabinet met it acquiesced in his
advice or direction, and the minutes do not record any discussion of the question.[77] Cosgrave seemed uneasy when he was sent a draft proclamation that
deferred once more the convocation of the Dáil, and he wrote 'the supremacy
of Parliament open to some criticism. It may be alleged that the Govt & Army
are closing the mouths of Parliament'.[78]

That evening, the 22nd, Collins was killed in an ambush at Béal na Bláth in west Cork, and when the news reached Dublin Cosgrave chaired a lengthy emergency meeting of civilian and military leaders that began at 4 a.m.[79] Two days later his cabinet colleagues formally and unanimously elected him as chairman.[80] Once more, he was the obvious choice. Apart from Eoin MacNeill, he was the oldest member of the cabinet; he had the most extensive political and administrative experience; he was a civilian at a time when the government was trying to impose democratic, majority rule on soldiers; and he was a reassuring, unifying figure. (Later it was claimed that O'Higgins had initially favoured Mulcahy—an irony, in view of their later conflicts—and that MacNeill had also been encouraged to assume the office.[81]) Whether Collins would have welcomed Cosgrave as his successor, as distinct from his deputy, cannot be known. He might have preferred someone more in his own image, but his colleagues decided otherwise.

He had been an incomplete convert to the principles of majority rule and civilian control of the army. Particularly in his policy towards Northern Ireland he had behaved more like a warlord than the head of a civilian government;[82] his private deals with the anti-treaty IRA and his attempts to undermine the Belfast government were carried out behind the backs of his colleagues. Those days were over, and there was a decisive change under Cosgrave.

One of the government's first actions after Collins's death was to end his policy of procrastination and to summon the Dáil for early September.[83] Another sign of a move towards 'normal' government was the agreement that all cabinet decisions should be unanimous and strictly confidential; the principle of collective responsibility was established.[84] Some months later J.J. Walsh, the postmaster general, was rebuked for making a unilateral pronouncement, and the cabinet decided that if he did not correct a statement made in the press the government would issue an official repudiation.[85] On the other hand Mulcahy was treated more gently. He was not formally reprimanded for holding a private meeting with de Valera, thereby defying the government's decision against negotiating with opponents of the treaty while the civil war continued.[86] The cabinet minutes on this particular issue recorded that 'certain Ministers had been associated without the knowledge or sanction of the Cabinet with negotiations for peace with the Irregulars, and it was decided that the Ministers concerned should be asked to submit a report on the matter'.[87] No further action was taken, but the incident increased suspicions of the military in the minds of some civilians.

The new government also brought to an end the futile and expensive pattern of paying Northern Irish teachers not to recognise the Belfast administration, and ultimately this decision left many of them out-of-pocket.[88] More generally, it abandoned Collins's policy of de-stabilising Northern Ireland. During the June election campaign Cosgrave had spoken against taking action with regard to Ulster.[89] The new approach had already been outlined two weeks before Collins's death when Ernest Blythe, then assistant minister for Home Affairs, claimed that the government's Northern policy 'has been really, though not ostensibly, dictated by the Irregulars'. He argued that military or economic pressure against the Belfast government would not bring about reunification, while a peaceful policy had at least some chance of protecting northern Catholics.[90] (Blythe was a Protestant and had the advantage of having lived in Co. Down during the unionists' campaign against home rule; he appreciated the extent of their hostility towards the prospect of rule from Dublin.) At a meeting on 11 October Cosgrave told a delegation of northern nationalists that his government took 'very strong action' against people who refused to give it their allegiance, and that if he were to discourage them from giving their allegiance to Craig's administration he would provide a weapon that could be used by his enemies in both the north and the south.[91]

When the third Dáil finally met, on 9 September 1922, Cosgrave was elected its president. His programme was clear:

> We insist upon the people's rights. We are the custodians of the rights of the people and we shall not hesitate to shoulder them…We want peace with England on the terms agreed to by the country.[92]

Without delay he implemented the policy he had advocated some months earlier and he announced that the two pro-treaty governments would be merged. (Long before this the Dáil administration led by Griffith had become little more than a fiction, its ministers attended meetings of the provisional government, and its cabinet had not met since April.) The Dáil accepted his decision without protest, and with virtually no comment.[93] The government was now answerable to a parliament; the process of democratisation was gaining ground. Cosgrave followed Collins's example by doubling his role of chairman of the provisional government with that of minister for Finance, and he retained control of that department until September 1923. His annual salary as a minister had been £960, and now as head of government he received

£2,500—a sum seven times greater than a TD's salary and about forty times greater than the average agricultural wage.[94] The figure would not be increased until 1947.

His priorities were to implement the treaty, enact a constitution, assert the authority and supremacy of parliament, restore order, suppress crimes and hasten the work of reconstruction.[95] His cabinet consisted of seven ministers, with four others beyond the inner circle, theoretically appointed by the Dáil rather than by the president, who functioned as 'externs'.[96] (The government abandoned this unsuccessful experiment in 1927, when the constitution was amended and the cabinet was expanded to include all the ministers.) The provisional government now had a minister for Defence (Mulcahy, who had held that post in Griffith's Dáil administration), so the difficult process of bringing the army under the cabinet's control gained momentum.

Cosgrave soon grew into his new role. A British journalist reported that when he had held a relatively minor position in the first Dáil he was criticised for a flippant style more suitable to the Dublin Corporation than to a national assembly. Responsibility had sobered and strengthened him. Although he had no pretension to oratorical brilliance he spoke weightily and confidently in the Dáil; 'he has thrown off some of his initial reserve'.[97] Liam de Róiste saw him, with his common sense and humour, as being a reaction against the posturing and the heroic moods of recent years.[98]

For their safety, ministers and their families were obliged to live in Government Buildings, which were protected by sandbags and barbed wire. At times they slept on the floor.[99] During the conflict with the British the Dáil cabinet was a government on the run; now Cosgrave and his colleagues were a government under siege. At least during the civil war there were good reasons why they might have developed a 'bunker mentality'.[100] As the struggle continued, month after month, they met constantly—often two or three times a day. In one week (21–28 September) the cabinet held eleven meetings, and Cosgrave remarked later that during his first year in office he worked fourteen hours a day.[101] He faced constant pressures, and on one occasion he wrote that he had begun preparing headings for Hugh Kennedy, the government's law officer, to edit in a message he wished to send to Churchill but he found 'that my time is so cut up that it useless to try & do such work'.[102] Republicans even hoped to kidnap him.[103]

The government sought and secured the support of the Catholic hierarchy, which condemned the republicans' campaign in forceful terms:

they have deliberately set out to make our motherland, as far as they could, a heap of ruins. They have wrecked Ireland from end to end…They have caused more damage to Ireland in three months than could be laid to the charge of British rule in so many decades.[104]

Many priests were intemperate or even obsessive in their attacks on anti-treaty soldiers—who were sometimes denied the sacraments.[105]

The republicans were embittered but undeterred by such assaults, and they tried to defeat the treaty by ruining the country's infrastructure. Their campaign of destruction continued long after they had any serious hope of military victory. Their commander, Liam Lynch, wrote that 'a hundred bridges blown up was just as effective a blow…as a hundred barracks blown up', and Cosgrave would later claim that 3,000 bridges had been damaged or destroyed.[106] After the formation of a senate in December, its members (together with unionists) were favourite targets. Between January 1922 and April 1923 about 200 'big houses' were burned, almost three times more than in the War of Independence. In response to a directive from Lynch, 37 houses belonging to senators were razed.[107] As well as stamping out cultural and religious diversity, this campaign formed a pattern that Cosgrave described as the 'driving of the wealthy classes out of the country with a consequent loss in the revenue'.[108] Unionist former landlords held substantial assets as a result of the land acts, and it was in the national interest to ensure that they would remain in the state; their money would benefit independent Ireland. But many of them fled. Even allowing for the impact of the Great War and for the departure of British troops, there was a significant fall in the Protestant population of the Free State between 1911 and 1926, from 10.4% to 7.4%.

PRISONERS AND EXECUTIONS

Initially there were widespread concerns about what was perceived as the government's inexperience and restraint. After Collins's death a British intelligence officer reported the opinion that Cosgrave, 'though a capable and sincere man, would not be able to carry through by himself the task of establishment of order, and it was becoming increasingly difficult to see where new leaders were to be found'. Soon afterwards one of his colleagues repeated the message: the Irish people were depressed and were not satisfied that Collins's successor was a sufficiently strong man to carry through the government's programme.[109]

Yeats worried along similar lines: 'I have met some of the ministers who more and more seem too sober to meet the wildness of these enemies; and every-where one notices a drift towards Conservatism, perhaps towards Autocracy'.[110] (Another observer remarked in Collins's lifetime that the government intended to rule in an authoritarian fashion for the immediate future, but a month later, when the Dáil finally met, he noticed a lack of direction at the top—perhaps due partly to Cosgrave's desire not to appear autocratic.[111]) Alfred Blanche, the French consul in Dublin and a committed opponent of the government, re-ported that its members lacked the necessary experience and capacity, and that power seemed to be concentrated increasingly in a military and police junta.[112] The imprisoned republican leader Rory O'Connor was confident that 'Cosgrave can be easily scared to clear out'.[113] He underestimated his opponent; the president stayed put, and two months later a cabinet meeting under his chairmanship ensured that O'Connor would be shot by a firing squad.

Within a few months those who doubted the government's resolve had less cause for concern, and supporters of the treaty showed that, as well as acting firmly and decisively, they could match and even surpass the ferocity of their enemies. Both sides carried out atrocities.

In an effort to avoid bloodshed and to maintain army unity, Collins had been prepared to make concessions before his patience snapped and he ordered the attack on the Four Courts on 28 June. Cosgrave saw no need to revive those concessions once widespread hostilities had broken out. It was now too late; after the election 'we are not entitled to barter terms with those people'.[114] He felt that a compromise might be conceivable in the event of a 'drawn' conclu-sion, but the pro-treaty forces were winning the war. 'The Government cannot leave indefinitely open their willingness to temper Justice with Mercy'.[115] He be-lieved that 'the more we try to placate them the weaker they think we are'.[116]

A Public Safety Bill came into effect in October 1922. It established mili-tary courts that could impose death sentences for the possession of arms and for attacking government forces. In Cosgrave's words this action was intended 'to show that there is a Government prepared to take the responsibility of govern-ing'. He continued 'although I have always objected to a death penalty, there is no other way I know of in which ordered conditions can be restored in this country'.[117] Offers of pardon and amnesty met with no response from the republicans, and he declared that 'we are not going to treat rebels as prisoners of war'.[118] He did not share Collins's loyalty and forbearance towards old comrades-in-arms.

Executions began in November, commencing with a group of young men from Cosgrave's own parish in James's Street. A prominent later victim was Erskine Childers, who had been captured with a gun in his possession. He was one of several republicans whose actions Cosgrave had criticised in the Dáil more than ten weeks earlier.[119] He inspired a particular dislike among his opponents, and some of them would have shed no tears at his death. After Childers was shot, the president explained in the Dáil that

> the people responsible for bringing these unfortunate dupes to their doom must take the responsibility for their action…Are we to let off the intellectual—those people who have money at their back and who have the opportunity of defending themselves—are they to get everything, and is there to be another law for the unfortunate dupes of these very people?[120]

This execution could be seen as a warning to other prominent republicans that their lives were not safe—and an even grimmer warning would soon follow. It has been described as the act whereby 'the treatyites' commitment to an uncompromising counter-revolution was crystallised'.[121] It could more plausibly be seen as an expression of the government's belief that the achievement of an independent Irish state represented the victory of the revolution, and that this victory must be consolidated—however harshly, or even brutally—against enemies who were determined to endanger or undermine it.

Following the execution of Childers, Liam Lynch then listed fourteen categories of people who were to be shot on sight—including all the Dáil deputies who had voted for the Public Safety Bill, certain senators and judges and hostile journalists. A week later one TD (who had not even voted for the bill) was killed and another wounded. Several deputies fled from Dublin, but Cosgrave ensured that they came back and he spoke with them individually.[122] The government's response to this attack dismayed both its friends and its enemies: on 8 December four members of the republican executive, all of whom had been imprisoned since the beginning of the war, were taken from their cells and shot. They were punished for actions they had not committed. Among them was Rory O'Connor, the commander of the Four Courts garrison, who had been the most vocal opponent of the people's right to decide their own fate.

Cosgrave declared bluntly 'terror meets terror', and the unionist *Irish Times* pointed out that this action 'eclipses in sudden and tragic severity the sternest measures of the British Crown'.[123] Thomas Johnson, the leader of the Labour

Party, declared in the Dáil 'I am almost forced to say you have killed the new State at its birth'.[124] Archbishop Byrne drafted a letter to Cosgrave expressing his dismay that the four men had been shot as a reprisal; 'the policy of reprisals seems to me to be not only unwise but entirely unjustifiable from the moral point of view. That one man should be punished for another's crime seems to me to be absolutely unjust'. He feared that this policy was bound to alienate many of the government's friends.[125] Other bishops were privately dismayed by the execution of prisoners and by the criminal activity of some of the pro-treaty forces, but they made no public protest.[126]

Many years later Blythe remarked that the executions were never discussed again by the cabinet and he did not 'think that anyone except Mr. Cosgrave himself was much troubled about the matter'. (Cosgrave deplored the official use of the word 'reprisal';[127] it was certainly foolish to use a term that was associated with the Black and Tans.) Whether or not the president was troubled, some months later he claimed that the executions 'have had a remarkable effect. It is a sad thing to say, but it is nevertheless the case'.[128] This tragic, severe retaliation succeeded in its objective; although both sides continued to wage war, sometimes in a savage fashion, the republicans were shaken by the government's action and they did not kill any more Dáil deputies while the conflict lasted.[129]

Almost 70 more republicans were executed in the course of the next five months. Two ministers in particular, O'Higgins and Hogan, demanded firmness in combating what they saw as the forces of anarchy.[130] Blythe subsequently recollected, with characteristic bluntness, that the government had 'got over the various types of sentimentality and softness and regard for what might be called rebel tradition which had heretofore prevented us from discharging our full duty as independent Irish rulers'.[131]

Cosgrave displayed no such sentimentality or softness. In January 1923 he proposed that every man caught in arms should be shot. He complained that executions had been confined to Dublin, Kildare and Kilkenny, leading to the conclusion that the rest of the country was peaceful. Commanders 'who are neglecting their duty in this respect might as well be losing battles'.[132] He told Mulcahy that the exercise of clemency 'can only be of use when the irregulars crave it'.[133]

Some time later he defended the executions in a letter to Byrne:

> if there were a reasonable inference or deduction that Peace were likely to result we would certainly stop these extreme measures...The situation had to some extent an appearance of returning to the Jan–June period of last year [1922], which of course would

be fatal. Captured correspondence shows that pressure is felt in most areas now, and that the more it is exercised the greater the peace desire is developed. A real peace can only come from good military results, & we feel it would be much better that they would be beaten in the field which they selected.[134]

The Irish conflict, with a death toll of less than 2,000, was no more than a minor skirmish compared with the slaughter of the American Civil War. Allowing for the great difference in scale, there is nonetheless a parallel between the Free State government's policy of executing some of its prisoners and the relentless devastation with which Sherman broke the back of the Confederacy in his march through Georgia. In both cases it was clear to almost everyone that only one side could win, but it was also felt that only harsh measures could bring a swift end to the war. In both cases these harsh measures wore down the enemy's resistance.

The Irish government now faced the problem of what to do with 10,000 captured anti-treaty soldiers, and it approached the British to see whether they might make available St Helena in the South Atlantic, where Napoleon had died. Nothing came of this idea, and one argument used against it was that the Irish prisoners might overpower their guards and take over the island.[135] In April, Cosgrave wrote again to Byrne that 'the demands, the propaganda & the general demeanour of prisoners indicate that stern methods only can bring them to their senses'.[136] By the middle of that month seven members of de Valera's underground 'cabinet' were in jail.[137]

The president and his colleagues had no hesitation in rejecting the Vatican's clumsy attempt at mediation through Monsignor Luzio, who spent several weeks in Ireland just as the republican campaign was on the point of collapse. Much of the emissary's time was spent in meeting and corresponding with opponents of the treaty. His encounter with Cosgrave was not a success and the president refused to discuss political matters with him.[138] The cabinet decided to inform Pope Pius XI that Luzio was 'endeavouring to interfere in the domestic affairs of the country' and that his action was 'an encouragement to the Forces of disorder and anarchy operating against the Government and the people'.[139]

Cosgrave denounced the republicans as 'the very dregs of society'; they were murderers who burst water-mains and roasted children.[140] Towards the end of the war he criticised their 'anarchic and spasmodic crime directed against public and private property—a peculiar form of revenge on the Irish people and their homesteads for their courage and sanity'.[141] He regarded de Valera with particular loathing and contempt; like other supporters of the treaty he was inclined to blame the former president for the civil war.[142] (He cited a newspaper report in which de Valera was quoted, already three months before fighting broke out, as saying that only by civil war could the country gain independence. Cosgrave concluded that if the report were correct it showed an absolute bankruptcy of statesmanship on the anti-treaty side.[143]) He almost certainly had de Valera in mind when, at Griffith's funeral, he referred to 'those magicians of political metaphysics who say one thing and mean another', and also when he wrote some time later that the people 'must be free to dispense with politicians who may have rendered good service but whose period of usefulness has for some time been eclipsed'.[144] From his standpoint this was unduly optimistic. He asked of the republicans 'why don't they pitch de Valera to the devil?...There is nothing in the fellow.'[145] (The feeling was reciprocated; de Valera described Cosgrave as 'a ninny'.[146]) One of his government colleagues, Patrick Hogan, referred to de Valera as 'a criminal lunatic'.[147]

The president was more tolerant or charitable in other cases. On a Sunday morning he was asked to issue a parole to his old corporation colleague Seán T. O'Kelly, and in the absence of a secretary he personally typed a copy of the form that prisoners seeking release were required to sign.[148] But such gestures did not alter his basic attitude, and after the war he still viewed members of the new, third Sinn Féin party as anti-democratic, as political apostates and as comprising 'all orders of society who have a grudge against the great mass of the people'. They took what they wanted—people's lives, cars, money, food and property.[149]

Cosgrave's hard-line stance coincided with that of cabinet colleagues,[150] but it was also consistent with his views before he became chairman of the provisional government. Despite his mild manner his approach was unyielding, and he was determined that there would be no compromise, no 'armed truce'.[151] In an interview towards the end of the conflict he declared bluntly 'I am not going to hesitate if the country is to live and if we have to exterminate ten thousand Republicans, the three millions of our people is bigger than this ten thousand'.[152] He must have found it reassuring that the government's aim was to enforce and carry out 'the Law of God' in Ireland.[153] In Reading Jail in 1918 his fellow-prisoners were reported to have given him the nicknames 'Gentle Willie' and 'Holy Willie'.[154] There was little sign of gentleness now.

The Free State constitution had been drafted before the June 1922 elections. Following negotiations with the British on the text of the document, the draft was published on polling day (too late to influence many voters); it was subsequently modified and ratified by the Dáil in a series of meetings that lasted over a month. Cosgrave had little involvement with its details, although he had interrogated a member of the drafting committee about the provisions setting out the form that the executive would take.[155] Later when he was head of government he defended the constitution forcefully, praising its 'democratic feeling and sense' and declaring proudly that 'from beginning to end [it] is certainly the most democratic Constitution in any country in the world at the present'.[156] He intervened from time to time in the debates, mainly to make explanatory points, but it was O'Higgins who carried the burden of securing its passage through the Dáil. One authority described the 1922 constitution as embodying 'the most revolutionary constitutional project in the history of the two islands since the instruments of government of the Cromwellian period'; it was permeated by an intense democratic radicalism; a republican *leitmotif* ran through it; and the king appeared almost as the permanent president of an Irish republic.[157] It began with a declaration of fundamental rights, modelled on recent Continental European examples—although this would later be virtually swept away by the supreme court.[158] The Dáil was to be elected by the PR system, and much British parliamentary procedure was adopted. Provision was made for referenda, and for the people to 'initiate' legislation; if 75,000 electors signed a petition the proposal must either be enacted or be made the subject of a referendum. In conformity with the treaty, the king was written into the constitution. When Gavan Duffy, a signatory of the treaty, complained that the king was mentioned nine times in the constitution, and that this was nine times too often, Cosgrave's retort was characteristically sharp and forceful: 'If you left him out of your own document, we need not have put him in at all'.[159]

While admitting that in theory a republic was the highest form of government,[160] in practice (like his colleagues) he seems to have become a committed defender of what had originally been accepted as a compromise settlement. At the end of 1922 he declared 'Not one single iota of the Treaty will I waive in any discussion or conference or public statement'.[161] Members of the Free State government seem to have abandoned the view of Collins and many others that the treaty was no more than a stage on the road towards a fuller degree of independence. As early as 1923 Cosgrave was asked whether the government had represented the treaty as a stepping-stone, and whether the Free State might evolve from dominion status to a republic. He replied that from his recollection of his own statements 'I accepted it on the face of it'; the Free State was greater than a republic in every respect.[162] (This was indisputable in the sense that the Free State government, unlike the abstract 'republic', exercised real power.) The most extreme example of these sentiments was Blythe's silly boast that 'If I could turn the Free State into a Republic to-morrow, I would not lift a finger to do it, and, what is more, I would work with all my might against it'.[163] Those whose acceptance of the treaty had been influenced by Collins's 'stepping stone' interpretation came to have more in common with the anti-treaty side.[164]

Having fought so hard and having sacrificed so much to defend the treaty, government ministers regarded it as an end rather than as a means towards unqualified sovereignty, and they believed that dominion status gave them sufficient independence to achieve their objectives. They shared the view of the British colonial secretary J.H. Thomas who wrote in June 1924 that 'the Treaty which we have kept and shall keep is not a stepping stone to be kicked aside at the first convenient moment'.[165]

There was some justice in Seán MacEntee's taunt that the government had deliberately turned its back on the arguments and principles that had animated Griffith and Collins, and also in the complaint that when the republicans waged civil war they 'tended to drive the Government into the arms of the ex-unionists and tame nationalists'.[166] The war converted 'the conditional, pragmatic and at times lukewarm support for the Treaty into something of an article of faith'.[167] These patterns allowed the Free State government's enemies to play the 'green card', and they would make supporters of the treaty vulnerable in the 1930s when—ironically—de Valera implemented Collins's programme and eliminated the settlement's remaining unwelcome aspects.

As in the past, the British connection remained the great dividing issue in Irish politics. 'The initiative, in the sense of the dynamic for change…rested with the opponents of the treaty, just as it had rested with the opponents of the union in the nineteenth century.'[168] But there was no counter-revolution in or after 1922, no attempt to undo the changes that had come about, to turn back the clock or to limit the degree of independence that had been achieved. Cosgrave's governments did not share Fianna Fáil's determination to revise the treaty, but they *were* determined to honour it, maintain it and exploit its potential.

The Irish Free State was formally established in December 1922, a year to the day after the treaty had been signed, and one minor consequence was that the cabinet was now called 'the executive council' and Cosgrave became 'president of the executive council'. This remained the designation of the head of government until 1937.

He was magnanimous, and he appointed his critical colleague O'Higgins as minister for Home Affairs, a position later to be re-titled minister for Justice, and as his vice-president. Ability was rewarded. Just as Cosgrave was now the only survivor in office of de Valera's cabinet of 1921–22, so the relegation of Eamonn Duggan to the level of parliamentary secretary meant that the government no longer contained a signatory of the treaty. This matched the pattern in Britain, although several British signatories returned to office two years later. Tim Healy, the brilliant, bitter and divisive anti-Parnellite, became governor-general, after overtures had been made to him by Cosgrave and by O'Higgins (who was his nephew).[169] The new British prime minister, Andrew Bonar Law, objected that Healy drank too much whisky at night, but this proved not to be an insuperable obstacle.[170] From the very beginning Cosgrave was determined to ensure that the king's representative would not exercise any more power than was laid down by the treaty.[171]

On 6 December the president appointed half of the members of the first senate, and he went to great lengths to ensure that unionists were over-represented. Yeats was the most distinguished of his nominees. Twenty-four of the sixty members of that first senate were non-Catholics, and its chairman, Lord Glenavy, had been a prominent unionist opponent of home rule. Throughout Cosgrave's term of office, however, he regarded the senate with little interest or respect. Long afterwards he was quoted as saying that the two disappointments of the new regime were the senate and PR;[172] he had some responsibility for the first of these.

Cosgrave suffered personally as a result of the civil war. His uncle was murdered in September 1922, in what may have been an 'ordinary' robbery but may have been a political attack. The president viewed it as the latter, and almost a decade later he referred to 'the people who slaughtered my uncle'.[173] Some months later, in January 1923, his family house was burned down by opponents of the treaty. All its contents, including valuable historical documents, were destroyed. The whole family moved for a while to a bungalow in a barracks in the Curragh. Cosgrave claimed to have rejected suggestions that other houses should be burned in retaliation.[174] His wife was later offered compensation of £4,748 for re-building the house.[175] The Cosgraves were only two of numerous victims of such attacks during the civil war; many people were killed or bereaved, many others lost their jobs, and many beautiful houses were burned. As a result of the republicans' campaign of devastation as they sought to overthrow the treaty Ireland became a poorer and uglier country.

In May 1923 the anti-treaty forces laid down their guns and the civil war came to an end. Six months later conditions were described as 'normal' in thirteen of the twenty-six counties.[176] But Cosgrave and his colleagues insisted that republican prisoners should forswear further violence, and he was unyielding when some of them went on hunger strike. He rejected pressure from his friend Archbishop Byrne to modify his policy, and he insisted that they would be released only when they promised not to take arms once more against the government. He believed that every minister would prefer to leave public life than to give way.

> I should be sorry to see or hear of any deaths from a hunger-strike, but as between deaths from hunger strike & release—if I have any responsibility whatever—I should say on no account should a single man be released save when the ordinary machinery of the State operates to secure it...I am myself perfectly satisfied that generosity or mercy is thrown away on these people and that the change which they claim has taken place is a change of necessity—not conviction or any sense of wrong doing.[177]

He claimed that republicans wanted access to their weapons 'any time they took it into their heads to interview a bank manager'.[178] But eventually all the interned republicans were freed. The government consolidated its position by refusing to give way to the hunger strikers, and its policy has been judged as ungenerous but amply justified by circumstances and events.[179] Opponents of the treaty were encouraged to participate in the political life of the Free State, and even one of the most unforgiving among them, C.S. Andrews, conceded that the government's policy was 'less vindictive than might have been expected'.[180]

Republican violence continued for years, and on one night in November 1926 the IRA attacked twelve police barracks across the country. At times the army and police responded brutally—to the dismay of ministers such as Cosgrave and O'Higgins. It is said that on one occasion Cosgrave demanded an explanation of a fatal shooting in Dublin and was taken aback to learn that the authorities had nothing to hide. His response was 'splendid...In that case we'll have an enquiry'.[181] All too often, both sides had much to hide. The civil war crippled and poisoned the independent Irish state; it inaugurated a bitter ice age that froze Irish politics for generations.[182]

Opposite: Cabinet minute, 3 December 1921; decision to reject proposal for an oath of allegiance to the king in the Anglo-Irish Treaty, and for the treaty delegation to meet Sir James Craig if necessary.

3rd. Dec. 1921.

3. (a) Delegation to return & say that Cabinet wont accept Oath of Allegiance if not amended & to face the consequences, assuming that England will declare war.

(b) Decided unanimously that present Oath of Allegiance could not be subscribed to.

(c) Mr. Griffith to inform Mr. Lloyd George that the document could not be signed, & to state that it is now a matter for the Dáil, & to try & put the blame on Ulster.

4. On a majority vote it was decided that the Delegation be empowered to meet Sir James Craig if they should think necessary The following voted for & against:
For: Pres., L.A., Fin., Econ. & Loc. Gov.
Against: Def. & H.A.

8th Decr. 1921.

1. Following a discussion of the terms of the Treaty the following members declared in favour of recommending it to the Dáil : —

A. Griffith, M. Collins, R. Barton, ~~Barton~~ & W. Cosgrave, & K.O'Higgins (no vote

Mr. Griffith would recommend doc-ument on basis of its merits — the remaining members on basis of signature.

Cabinet minute, 8 December 1921; decision by majority of cabinet members, including Cosgrave, to recommend to the Dáil the Anglo-Irish Treaty as signed by the delegation on 6 December; and decision by full cabinet to summon the Dáil in public session on 14 December.

The following declared against recommending Treaty to Dáil: President, Cathal Brugha & A. Stack

2. The Pres. to issue a statement to the press defining his position & that of the Mins. of H.A. & Def.

3. A Public Session of Dáil to be summ for Wed. 14th Dec. at 11. a.m. Mansion Ho Ministers to remain in charge of thei Depts. in meantime.

G.D. said he had ~~signed~~ because he was
told all must sign & recommend

. . . . . .

3 p.m.

Page from diary of Erskine Childers, secretary to the
Irish treaty delegation in London, indicating that
Cosgrave's was the decisive vote on the treaty in the
cabinet meeting of 8 December 1921.

A.G. said that he would have gone to
Dublin but for the ~~recommendation~~
undertaking to submit draft
to Cabinet.

E.C. said he did not regret : No choice
E.D. " " " " " "

A.G. said he stood over document.

B.C.B. said he did too but he was
intimidated & had to declare
war on his own behalf.

M.C. said he did the same (!)

(My notes end at this point
and of the long discussion which
followed I remember only certain
salient points, not in their correct
order of time.)
Cabinet asked their opinions in
turn. Cathal & Austin against
Treaty Bdn, A.G. & M.C. for it – all
hung on Cosgrave's vote, the gave
it for treaty. K. O'Higgins also
spoke but could not vote. Said
Treaty should never have been signed
but being signed should be
supported

O'Higgins, Griffith and Cosgrave arriving at Earlsfort Terrace
in Dublin for the Dáil debates on the treaty, 1921–2.

British troops leaving Dublin by boat; 'Dublin Castle "surrenders" to Sinn Féin Provisional Government'; Cosgrave leaves the Castle after Collins's provisional government took possession, January 1922.

IRISH FREE STATE

DUBLIN CASTLE

symbol and citadel
of British Rule in
Ireland for centuries
"surrenders" to Sinn Fein
Provisional Government.

Pathé Gazette.

THE IRISH FREE STATE BROUGHT INTO BEING: "A NEW ERA" BEGUN.

Photographs by Sport and General and C.N.

"WE WANT THE OLD DIFFERENCES BETWEEN IRISHMEN TO BE BANISHED FOR EVER": PRESIDENT GRIFFITH (FIFTH FROM LEFT, IN FRONT) AND OTHER ELECTED MEMBERS OF THE SOUTHERN PARLIAMENT WHO RATIFIED THE TREATY.

"WE ARE STARTING ON A NEW ERA": THE RATIFICATION OF THE ANGLO-IRISH TREATY BY THE SOUTHERN PARLIAMENT AND THE FORMATION OF A PROVISIONAL IRISH GOVERNMENT, IN THE OAK ROOM OF THE MANSION HOUSE, DUBLIN.

The Irish Free State was called into existence on January 15, in the Mansion House, Dublin, at a meeting of 65 elected Members of the Southern Parliament, convened by President Griffith as Chairman of the Irish Delegation of Plenipotentiaries. Mr. de Valera and his party were absent, so there was no opposition, and the proceedings were brief and businesslike. The Anglo-Irish Treaty was unanimously approved, and a Provisional Government was appointed consisting of Messrs. Michael Collins, W. Cosgrave, E. J. Duggan, P. Hogan, F. Lynch, J. McGrath, J. MacNeill, and K. O'Higgins. President Griffith said: " We are starting on a new era, and we want the old differences that existed between sections of Irishmen to be banished for ever." His words drew a cordial response from Professor W. E. Thrift on behalf of the four members for Trinity College. In the front row of the upper photograph (from left to right, beginning with the second figure) are seen: Messrs. J. MacNeill, F. Lynch, Michael Collins, Arthur Griffith, W. Cosgrave, Kevin O'Higgins, E. J. Duggan, and Desmond Fitzgerald. In the right foreground (standing with left hand in pocket) is Mr. J. McGrath. In the lower photograph the Chairman (on the right) is Alderman Liam de Roiste. On the front bench (to the left) are : (left to right) Messrs. Cosgrave, Duggan, Griffith, and Lynch. Mr. Michael Collins was on the front cross bench facing the Chairman.

Michael Collins with Joseph McGrath, Sean McGarry, Pádraig
Ó Máille, and Cosgrave at a pro-treaty meeting in College Green,
Dublin, 1 March 1922.

Opposite: 'The Irish Free State brought into being', from *Illustrated
London News*, 21 January 1922, p. 72.

CAREY COLLINS - GO DOWN ON YOUR B____ KNEES WITHOUT ANY MORE D___D FUSS
SWEAR ALLEGIANCE TO KING GEORGE AND HIS HEIRS.

FAKER FITZGERALD - DON'T LISTEN TO DEVALERA. I COULD TELL YOU A LOT ABOUT
GREAT GREAT GRANDMOTHER AND SPANISH GOLD.

THE BISHOP - TAKE ANY OATH MY CHILD THAT WILL GET YOU OUT OF YOUR
DIFFICULTIES.

COMIC COSGRAVE - IT WAS AN AWFUL MOKE TALKING ABOUT FREEDOM, YOU KNOW.

Anti-treaty cartoon attributed to Constance Markievicz, showing
Hibernia, with her arms chained behind her back. Collins holds a
gun to her head. Behind him are a bishop and Cosgrave in pierrot
costume.

Opposite: Pro-treaty election poster, 'You can get to the Republic for
All Ireland'.

YOU CAN GET TO THE REPUBLIC
—————FOR ALL IRELAND—————

Through the safe and sure road of the Treaty

or

YOU CAN TRY ANOTHER ROUND

Through the Alphabet of Miseries

Auxiliaries	Jails	Spies
Black and Tans.	Knoutings	Threats
Commandeerings	Licence	Usurpation
Deaths.	Murders	Vandalism
Executions	Nerve Strain	Wails
Ferocities	Oppression	
Gallows	Persecution	X The final horrors
Harassings	Questionings	Y which words
Internments	Raids	Z cannot describe.

to get

(perhaps)

DOCUMENT No. 2
(or others in later series)

Which way should a
Sane Man or Woman Go ?

NATIONAL
EXTERMINATION

Support the Treaty Candidates.

rish Labour, Irish Paper a d Iri:h Ink.

Facts for Voters

'Facts for Voters', Anti-treaty election poster, 1922.

1—The Anglo-Irish Articles of Agreement were signed in London behind the backs and against the express orders of the Dail Cabinet.

2—In July, De Valera and the Dail rejected the Dominion Home Rule which Collins and Griffith accepted in December.

3—All the disunion in the Country is caused by the broken pledges of Griffith and Collins.

4—That disunion will be increased if the Irish people back up the pledge breakers.

5—The I.R.A. are pledged to maintain and defend the Republic, and the Republic alone.

6—Every town and village in Ireland will be another Limerick if Collins tries to introduce his new army and police.

7—The new Free State army and police may be used as Smuts' army is used in South Africa to-day to suppress the Independence Movement.

8—If Griffith and Collins win the Elections the worst kind of war—namely, civil war—will destroy the country.

9—If De Valera wins there will never be another shot fired in Ireland.

10—When De Valera and the Dail rejected Dominion Home Rule in July, England did not declare War.

11—When the Irish people elect Republicans, a new Treaty will be signed that will bring true peace.

THEREFORE, EVERY VOTE FOR THE FREE STATE IS A

VOTE for WAR

Dáil Éireann.

Dictated
25

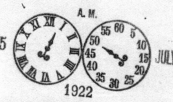

1922

24th July, 1922

Commander-in-Chief,
Michael Collins

Private & Confidential

Dear Mick,

      I am very sorry to say that I have had
to resign. Since you and other Ministers left,
the remnant of the Cabinet has been dominated by
a spirit of narrowness and intolerance that has
made it daily harder to cooperate. As you know,
I am loyally with the Government on the War itself,
but on most of the other important issues that
arise I have found myself nearly always in a ma
minority of one.

      To-day we had the last straw, when the
Cabinet solemnly decided against recognising the
undoubted jurisdiction of our Judges (whether
Courts are sitting or not) to deal with Habeas
Corpus cases. That to my mind is the limit
and absolutely indefensible, as well as being
foolish and unnecessary from the practical point
of view and putting the Government hopelessly
in the wrong.

      Incidentally, the attitude taken is all
the worse in view of the fact that the old corrupt
gang of Judges is still in control at the Kings'
Inns, so that anyone with a genuine case for Habeas
Corpus will now have no Court, worthy of popular
confidence, to go to.

        Always yours,

         Seosamh Gabhán Ó Dubhthaigh

P.S.   I am sending a similar note to Dick.

Letter from George Gavan Duffy (the minister for Foreign Affairs in the
provisional government) to Michael Collins, 24 July 1922, explaining his
resignation from the cabinet.

A Free State armoured car, with 'The Big Fella' painted on the front, drives through the gates of Portobello (now Cathal Brugha) Barracks, Rathmines, Dublin, 17 May 1922.

RIALTAS SEALADACH NA HÉIREANN
(IRISH PROVISIONAL GOVERNMENT)

AIREACHT UM RIALTAS ÁITIÚIL
(Ministry of Local Government),

SRÁID MHUIRBHTHEAN UACH
(Upper Merrion Street),

BAILE ÁTHA CLIATH.

Reference No.

L.G.

Now under the shadow of a great national
calamity the death of President Arthur Griffith
comes the news that members of the
Government are on a list to be shot. This is
misguided "patriotism" on the part of those who
have been unequal to the shock of war. The people
who so act are irresponsible & must not be
allowed to cow or awe the people of Ireland.
Even if the members of the Government are shot
& die others will be found to take their places.
None of us could be indispensable. The country
has not yet discovered the true worth of our
successors. The people must discover them. I believe
Genl Collins is one of the greatest men Ireland
has produced, a statesman & a soldier. and there
are others and in the Govt & the army. My place will be easily filled.
I am sorry for my people, my wife & children
my mother & family — They all suffered during
the late war. & did not grumble. others suffered
too & did not grumble. They all did not suffer in
vain. Hard times are coming. but they - the
people of Ireland will endure. but they must
prevail against any minority seeking to order
their will or their life save under the laws which
the people's representatives pass. I willingly forgive
those who think I should be shot and those who take
part in such shooting. and I ask forgiveness of
all those I have offended. I thank all who helped
me & all those whose help any work in which I was
engaged would have been valueless. I thank all who
pray or for me & helped me whom in life it was not
possible to even thank. I thank the archbishops & all
his priests & all my colleagues & friends &
acquaintances. & if it can do any good I ask
those who are in arms against the Government
to consider if it be not possible to come to agree.
ment with the nation. No member of the Government wishes to continue any war on any section
I ask for obedience to the Parliament of the Irish
nation. & may God in his infinite mercy forgive me
my sins & pardon my shortcomings.

Liam T. Mac Cosgair

12.8.22.

IRISH PROVISIONAL GOVERNMENT

Minister of Local Government,
Upper Merrion Street,
Baile Atha Cliath.

Testament by Cosgrave (handwritten and transcribed) following Griffith's death, expressing his commitment to democracy and forgiving those whom he suspected might wish to kill him and others in the provisional government.

Now under the shadow of the great national calamity, the death of President Arthur Griffith comes the news that members of the Government are on the list to be shot. This is misguided patriotism on the part of those who have been unequal to the shock of war. The people who so act are irresponsible and must not be allowed to cow or awe the people of Ireland. Even if the members of the Government are shot and that others will be found to take their places. None of us could be indispensible. The country has not yet discovered the true worth of our successors, The people must discover them, I believe Genl. Collins is one of the greatest men Ireland has produced. A states man and a soldier - and there are others also in the Government and the Army. My place will be easily filled. I am sorry for my people, my wife and children, my mother and family. They all suffered during the late War, and did not grumble - others suffered too and did not grumble They all did not suffer in vain. Hard times are coming, but they - the people of Ireland - will endure, but they must prevail against any minority seeking to order their will or their life save under the laws which the people's representatives pass. I willingly forgive those who think I should be shot and those who take part in such shooting and I ask forgiveness of all those I have offended. I thank all who helped me and without whose help any work in which I was engaged would have been valueless. I thank all who prayed for me and helped me whom in life it was not possible to even thank. I thank the Archbishop and all his priests and all my colleagues and friends and acquaintances, and if it can do any good I ask those who are in arms against the Government to consider if it be not possible to come to agreement with the nation. No member of the Government wishes to continue any war on any section. I ask for obedience to the Parliament of the Irish Nation, and may God in His infinite mercy forgive me my sins and pardon my shortcomings.

12.8.22

(Sd.) LIAM T. MAC COSGAIR.

Alfie Byrne, Cosgrave, Collins and Darrell Figgis at Glasnevin
Cemetery, Dublin, for the funeral of Arthur Griffith.

Opposite: Provisional government cabinet minute, 18 August 1922,
decision to prorogue the Dáil on the advice of Michael Collins.

(a) Appointment of Committee:

A Committee consisting of the following:-

> Mr. Hogan
> Mr. Blythe
> Mr. Hayes

was appointed to consider the various matters requiring settlement and adjustment in connection with the new Parliament, and it was decided that the Law Officer should submit a memorandum on the subject for their information.

(b) Prorogation of Parliament:

The question of the further prorogation of Parliament was discussed.

The Commander-in-Chief advised, and it was decided, that Parliament should be again prorogued.

He stated that this was the opinion of the Army and that the situation which had caused the previous prorogation still existed. If, however, matters improved in the meantime he would communicate with the Government, when the decision to prorogue could, if necessary, be reconsidered.

The Law Officer advised that, even if prorogued for a fortnight, the meeting could be accelerated.

CIVIC GUARD COMMISSION:

Following a discussion on the report of the Civic Guard Commission, the following proposals were provisionally approved:-

1. That the report should be communicated confidentially to Commissioner Staines.

2. That Mr. Staines should then resign on the ground that he is a public representative and as such should not hold office in the Civic Guard.

P.G.97.

MEETING OF THE PROVISIONAL GOVERNMENT
HELD ON THE 23rd AUGUST, 1922. 4.p.m.

ATTENDANCE.

There were present Messrs Cosgrave, Hogan, Walsh, Major General McGrath, and Commandant General O'Higgins.

Messrs Fitzgerald, Blythe, Hayes, Kennedy, O'Shiel, General Mulcahy, Commandant General O'Sullivan, Commandant General O'Hegarty, Commandant O'Reilly, Commandant T. Cullen and Dr. Hayes were also in attendance.

DEATH OF COMMANDER-IN-CHIEF.

The tragic death of the Commander-in-Chief from wounds received in an ambush at Bealnablath, Co. Cork, shortly after 7 p.m. on Tuesday the 22nd instant, was announced.

Arrangements for the embalming of the body, and for its removal from Cork were discussed and approved.

THE MEETING THEN ADJOURNED.

----------oOo--------

L. T. Mac Cosgair

Provisional government cabinet minute, 23 August 1922, 4 a.m.,
noting the death of Collins and signed by Cosgrave.

Wire from Winston Churchill to Cope, 24 August 1922, suggesting
how to proceed in dealings with the provisional government
following the deaths of Griffith and Collins.

From Mr Churchill to Mr Cope.

My preceding message is a textual
communication to Cosgrave and the Provisional Government. The following is for your own guidance.

The danger to be avoided is a sloppy
accommodation with a quasi-repentant De Valera. It may
well be that he will take advantage of the present
situation to try to get back from the position of a
hunted rebel to that of a political negotiator. You
should do enerything in your power to frustrate this.
The Provisional Government cannot do better than stand
firm on the declarations of Collins and Cosgrave of
August 4th. These are being telegraphed to you for
greater surety. The surrender of the rebels or rebel
leaders would of course be all to the good, but it
ought not to be in any circumstances followed by the
immediate reappearance of these men defeated in the
field as Members of the Assembly. Having appealed to
the sword and having been defeated, they are out of
politics for the time being and ought to be rigorously

Cosgrave speaking at Collins's graveside, 28 August 1922.

24th (P) INFANTRY BRIGADE WEEKLY INTELLIGENCE SUMMARY
FOR WEEK ENDING 26th AUGUST, 1922.

Confidential British intelligence report (1st page) for week of 26 August 1922, noting the likely effect of Collins's death and Cosgrave's efforts to impose order on the country.

C.R. 2/202.

The tragic death of MICHAEL COLLINS, following so closely on that of ARTHUR GRIFFITH, will probably have one of two effects, it will either cause the army and the Nation to lose its temper and take really drastic action against the rebels or it will dishearten them to a dangerous degree. For the moment the indications are thatthe second alternative is supervening. P.G. Officers at NORTH WALL on the night of the arrival of the late GENERAL COLLINS' body were badly despondent and their remarks noticeably lacked anymention of determination to avenge his death. A reliable civilian said that he knew of a woman formerly of strong Republican sympathies who now openly advicated the resumption of control by H.M. Government and he himself that people of the middle and professional classes were tired of the unsettled conditions, that they would support the Free State wholeheartedly as long as it could carry on but that when and if it collapsed they would implore the English to come back. He said that ALDERMAN COSGROVE, though a capable and sincere man, would not be able to carry through by himself the task of establishment of order, and it was becoming increasingly difficult to see where new leaders were to be found. These remarks are the more significant as they were made by a man who has hitherto and in the blackest times been firmly confident of the Free State.

"Voice of Labour" makes the following comment on the death of COLLINS :-
"Following upon the death of ARTHUR GRIFFITH, the death of MICHAEL COLLINS will strike a heavy blow not only at the P.G. but at the LONDON Treaty itself, and maybe, at the whole Irish National movement."

The meeting of the Irish Parliamant has again been postponed until 9th September. In view of the deaths of GRIFFITHS and COLLINS it is not probable that the Labour Members will carry out their threat to resign if Parliament did not meet on or before the 26th August.

MILITARY:

The Military situation in DUBLIN remains unchanged, There has been somewhat less firing at night, though P.G. Patrols on foot and in Motor Vehicles have been active. To judge by the bearing and turnout of parties on duty at funerals, the discipline of the P.G. /pro Troops is improving, but it is likely that a/portion of these parties are picked men always detailed for such parties. A member of the P.G Guard at NORTH WALL EXTENTION recently had a rifle whose barrel was choked with dirt and although he had several months service appeared to have no idea what a pull-through was.

by
Recruiting is still being carried out on/the P.G. Forces, and a number of the latest recruits are of a very poor class and physique some being mere boys.

WEEKLY
DUBLIN DISTRICT/INTELLIGENCE SUMMARY No. 176.
FOR WEEK ENDING 2/9/22.

POLITICAL.

The Labour Party having satisfied themselves that the Post-poned meeting of Dail will now be held on Sept. 9th have not re-signed and now the country awaits the assembly of all parties with interest. Efforts will be made to allow all T.D's to be present, whatever their political views, but the proceedings are not expected to run smoothly. The main question to be raised will be the contihuance or not of the present civil strife and the Government

(OVER)

CABINET DECISIONS.

It was decided that all decisions of the Cabinet should be regarded as unanimous, and should be treated as strictly confidential.

Provisional government cabinet minute, 26 August 1922, introducing the principle of collective cabinet responsibility.

NEW DAIL - SPEAKER AND DEPUTY SPEAKER.

(a) Speaker and Deputy Speaker.

Professor Michael Hayes and Mr. Liam de Roiste were selected as suitable for appointment as Speaker and Deputy Speaker, respectively, of the new Dail.

(b) Constitution.

It was decided that the Government should regard as vital the clauses dealing with External Relations, the Senate and matters relating to Justice, and that no alteration in any of these clauses could be permitted.

(c) Standing Orders.

Mr. Blythe mentioned that he had completed the revision of the draft Standing Orders for the new Dail.
It was decided that they should be referred to Mr. O'Shiel for consideration.

(d) Adult Suffrage.

It was decided that Adult Suffrage would form the subject of a resolution to be submitted, at the earliest opportunity, to the new Parliament.

(e) Land Legislation.

It was decided that this matter could not be dealt with until after the passing of the Constitution.

NORTH EAST ULSTER.

It was decided that copies of the memoranda prepared by Mr. Blythe and Professor Hayes, relative to the policy to be adopted with regard to North East Ulster, should be circulated to Ministers.

ARMY.

(a) Strength.

The Commander-in-Chief referred to the fact that an Army of a total strength of 35,000, including Volunteer Reserves, had been approved, and stated that it was proposed to maintain it at at least this strength until conditions in the country should be returned to normal.
This was approved.

P. (contd.)	At no time has there come any sane proposal from their so-called leaders. You have mentioned some names. All I have to say is that your information and mine does not tally. I have documentary evidence about some of the people you have mentioned. I don't want to name them. You are either wrongly informed or these men did not write the truth. In another case I have specific information to the effect that the man was sick of it from his own brother, and I have written proof on the other side criticising his men. So I have made up my mind you cannot depend upon them. There is one voice for Deasy and another for me. In other words, they are only Military men whose business is to deceive you.
B.	I think they are prepared to deal with the matter themselves.
P.	Why don't they pitch De Valera to the devil?
B.	They are not in a position to do so. If they could meet.
P.	We did it, and I am sure it was harder then that it is now for them. There is nothing in the fellow.
H.	They are not following him but their own leaders and these leaders are taking advice from him - Rutledge, Derrick, etc.
P.	Take Rutledge, I remember his speech. He said he was against the Treaty but that if rejection of the Treaty meant chaos he was prepared to accept the Treaty.
B.	Would you not give us an idea if we give a guarantee that the other side are willing to accept how far you are prepared to go?
P.	I am not a free agent in this business. I made certain statements, and these were accepted by the Dail and I am only the agent of the Dail. As far as we are concerned I believe that any honourable understanding that can be reached we are prepared to everything possible to reach that honourable understanding but we cannot take any risks. I dare not. I do not know whether you understand the situation or not, but the end of last June I made up my mind definitely I was not going to make any further effort to meet the Republicans. We had stretched every possible point and every point so stretched put us further away from the North. The one thing I want is a united Ireland. Every inch we go to meet these fellows in the South means going further away from the North. A bad peace in the South means absolute partition in the North for many a generation perhaps.
B.	The North will not come in while the fighting is going on down here.
P.	No. They will not. But the most ideal solution would be to give these Irregulars a damn good hammering

Transcribed page from a conversation between Cosgrave ('P.') and two 'neutral IRA' members in February 1923; the remarks relate to his refusal to compromise with republicans in the ongoing civil war and his commitment to a united Ireland.

8864] 9884/2770 200 pads 8/21 6520 G & S 194

T.S. 148.

POST OFFICE TELEGRAPHS.

TELEGRAM RECEIVED IN THE IRISH OFFICE.

45630

Date 1 Sep 13 SEP 22 192

Handed in at _____ at _____ . Received here at 8.30p

From Martin   To Curtis

Dublin Monday night Stop Mr Cosgrave
rose in the Dail at half past three this
afternoon to make a full statement of the
new Governments policy in response to the
wish of the House Stop In the old Dail
when he held only a minor administrative
position his style used to be criticised for
a certain flippancy more suitable to the Dublin
Corporation where he won his spurs than to
a National assembly but today all that was
changed Stop Responsibility — a more heavy and
sudden responsibility than has ever before in
history been thrown on one Irish leaders
shoulders — has sobered and strengthened him
Stop Though Mr Cosgrave has no pretensions
to oratorical brilliance he spoke weightily and
confidently. Sometimes discarding his manuscript
and letting his indignation have full vent in
a sarcastic emphasis of some particularly
outrageous deed of De Valeras followers Stop
The House listened sympathetically in tense

and shot.   And, in Italy, Mussolini, the
Fascist leader, now Premier, has been given
powers of a dictator.

A statement of Cosgrave's appears in the
papers to-day.   Cosgrave, more even than
others, shows the reaction from the high posturings
and heroic moods of the last few years.   Hence,
some people would probably regard what he
says as almost flippant, and as shallow.   He
has, however, plain commonsense, and humour.
He thinks the Irregulars will intensify their
terrorism during "the next ten days" – he means
until Dec. 6th, when the Rialtas shall co longer
be "Provisional"; but after that there is likely to
be a collapse on their part.   Certainly the situation
seems much quieter in Cork and the South :
Irregular activities have grown less and many
captures have been effected by the National forces.

Some public boards are passing resolutions on

...ions. Yet, the majorities on the boards are opposed to the Irregulars and are pro-Treaty. It is right they should not favour executions; it shows that the spirit of "Kill, Kill" is not their spirit: yet, they have not condemned the killings on the irregular side, as strongly as they might. It is idle to hide the truth that there is a feeling of terror of "unknown gunmen"; and a lack of moral courage among many public men.

The English terrorist regime has left its mark in many ways upon the people; on every one of us, I believe.

Dia D'ár mbeannicad.

Samain 30. Diardaoin. Meádón Oidce. Cosmo Hotel, ...nthampton Row, London. In London once more. Its ...ghts and scenes and some at least of its ways are ...w familiar to me. Sharkey arrived here before me ...is morning. The crossing to Fishguard last night was ...easant. Firstly we hied to a Bank to get a ...tter of Credit. The introductions from our Cork

Pages from Liam de Róiste's diary, 29 November 1922, describing Cosgrave's sense of how the civil war was likely to unfold in the run-up to the establishment of the Irish Free State.

C O P Y.

MEMO. BY PRESIDENT.

Those on whose behalf the writer of the proposals now put forward challenged that right by force of arms and it is not possible to re-open the discussion of terms on the basis of the maximum offer – made for the purpose of preventing bloodshed and making for stabilisation in the country.

The Government faced with the difficulty of building up a new State had to deal with those who disputed representative Government by force. That force is now triumphant and while the Government is willing to restore order by the most peaceful means and is desirous of affording every possible facility to those who are willing to abide by the authority which they have just challenged by armed force – the Government will not subject any public service of the State to the decision of a Commission composed of two fifths of those now in arms against the State.

The Government cannot, therefore, accept the proposals put forward. These terms might be the subject of consideration in a case when it was evident that only a "drawn" conclusion could be looked for and might in fact be supposed to be in sight. Such is not the case. The result is already in sight in a very different way. The Government cannot leave indefinitely open their willingness to temper Justice with Mercy.

These proposals are objectionable from this point of view that loyalty is promised on conditions. No person has a right to take up such an attitude who has any patriotism.

I have given careful consideration to the proposals put before me by .... I should think that it would have been clearly understood that the position had materially altered since June last. If I dwell for a short period on the terms which were then in contemplation it is only because the proposals put before me have a preface which indicates a return to reason on the part of the person putting them forward. The period at which these terms were likely to form the basis of an agreement was one in which the Provisional Government could legitimately father such an agreement and the electorate would have had an opportunity of approving of rejecting them had they been so agreed to by both parties. Members of the Provisional Government then went before the people and laid it down that any and all armed forces in the country were to be under the control and subject to Parliament.

Memo by Cosgrave, December 1922, stating that although the government was willing to restore order in as peaceful a manner as possible, it was not willing, indefinitely, to 'temper justice with mercy'.

Opposite: 'Sabotage in Ireland: a campaign of train-wrecking and arson', *Illustrated London News*, 20 January 1923, page showing incidents from the republican campaign during the civil war, including Cosgrave's burnt-out home.

SABOTAGE IN IRELAND: A CAMPAIGN OF TRAIN-WRECKING AND ARSON.

PHOTOGRAPHS BY KEYSTONE VIEW COMPANY, L.N.A., AND TOPICAL.

ONE OF 42 DERAILMENTS IN SIX MONTHS: A TRAIN OVERTURNED BY IRISH REBELS BETWEEN DUNDALK AND INISHKEEN.

BLOWN UP BY A LAND MINE AFTER THE GARRISON HAD BEEN ORDERED OUT: THE CIVIC GUARD BARRACKS AT RATHFARNHAM.

PRESIDENT COSGRAVE'S HOUSE BURNT DOWN, WITH A VALUABLE COLLECTION OF BOOKS AND HISTORIC LETTERS: IRISH C.I.D. MEN IN CHARGE AT BEECH PARK.

THE FIRST ATTACK ON THE NEW IRISH POLICE: MEMBERS OF THE CIVIC GUARD WHOSE BARRACKS AT RATHFARNHAM WERE DESTROYED BY REBELS.

CLOSELY GUARDED BY HIS STAFF ARMED WITH RIFLES AND REVOLVERS: PRESIDENT COSGRAVE IN THE RUINS OF HIS HOUSE NEAR RATHFARNHAM.

AFTER A COLLISION BETWEEN A PASSENGER TRAIN AND A GOODS ENGINE DERAILED BY REBELS NEAR CLONTARF: A WRECKED COMPARTMENT.

Since the end of last June the Irish rebels have committed numerous outrages on the Great Southern and Western Railway in the South of Ireland, which is not only a line of communication of Free State troops, but is one of the chief means of transport to supply the country with food. Within six months and a week the rebels have wrecked the permanent way in 375 different places, have derailed 42 engines, and have damaged 258 bridges, 83 signal-cabins, and 13 other buildings. A typical outrage was the derailment of a goods train at Killester, Co. Dublin, on January 6. The whole train toppled over, and a passenger train ran into some wreckage, with the result that the sides were torn out of several carriages and seven passengers were injured. On the 11th the Civic Guard barracks at Rathfarnham, Co. Dublin, were blown up by a land mine, after the garrison of five men had been ordered out. This was the first attack on the new Civic Guard, an unarmed police force which has replaced the R.I.C. At 7 a.m. on January 13 President Cosgrave's country house, Beech Park, near Rathfarnham, was set on fire, and burnt down. Valuable books and furniture and historic Sinn Fein letters were destroyed. President Cosgrave arrived under heavy escort at 9 a.m., by which time the roof had collapsed. Once, it may be recalled, he was arrested there by Crown forces, who searched the house.

Cosgrave and O'Higgins, accompanied by Seán Milroy, Eamonn Duggan and J.J. Walsh, taking the salute of Free State soldiers outside Government Buildings, Dublin, *c.* 1922.

'Good government is a lot to ask
from a relatively poor country
& from a people so long divorced
from any respect for order'.

- BUILDING THE FREE STATE, 1923–7 -

Opening image: Cosgrave speaking
at the cenotaph commemorating
Griffith and Collins on the lawn of
Leinster House, 22 August 1926.

EVEN while the civil war was in progress Cosgrave and his colleagues prepared for a peaceful future, and they carried out 'normal' activities, such as deciding where the new parliament should meet. Eventually they chose Leinster House in preference to the Royal Hospital in Kilmainham. (Tim Healy, the governor-general, would have preferred his own residence, formerly the Vice-Regal Lodge, subsequently Áras an Uachtaráin, but then known popularly as 'Uncle Tim's Cabin'.[1]) The government struggled to collect taxes, and it dealt severely with a postal strike; pickets were arrested and the army intimidated strikers with armoured cars and rifle fire.[2] It engaged in long-term planning, discussing issues such as the border with Northern Ireland and the state's application for membership of the League of Nations. Early in 1923 Cosgrave and his ministers formed a new party, Cumann na nGaedheal, to provide themselves with a political machine. Taking the name of an organisation founded by Griffith in 1900, they were happy to leave the title of their former party to their enemies. In effect, this party became the successor of the pro-treaty wing of the united Sinn Féin.[3] Over the years it was joined by former Redmondites and even former unionists, and it proved to be a coalition of various interests held together only by their support of the treaty and of the state.

A general election was held in August 1923, three months after the civil war came to an end, and for the first time in modern Irish history every constituency was contested. This was also the first election fought on a universal adult suffrage; unlike the situation in 1918 and 1922, women now had equal voting rights with men. In this respect the Free State was years ahead of the United Kingdom, let alone countries such as France, where women were enfranchised only in 1944, and Switzerland, where they acquired the vote in stages between 1959 and 1971.

The government campaigned on a 'safety first' programme, associating itself with Ireland's independence and democracy, and its attitude was summed up as being 'hit me now and the Free State in my arms'.[4] In contrast to the election of 1922, when the old Sinn Féin party was split, now Labour was weakened by internal divisions. It was also placed at a disadvantage in an election dominated by voters' attitudes towards political rather than social questions. The principal issues in the campaign were the treaty and the civil war. The new anti-treaty Sinn Féin party was associated with the republicans' conduct of the war, and many of its activists were interned. On the other hand, in certain areas of the country opponents of the treaty resumed their practice of intimidation; as one example, only seven of the 128 Protestants in Durrus, West Cork, cast their ballots in August 1923.[5]

De Valera had been on the run for a year, and the government incurred much criticism when he was arrested while addressing a crowd at an election rally in Ennis. Some people saw him as a martyr in the cause of free speech. But it could be argued that the decision to detain him was taken for his own safety; he had promised that he would speak in Ennis and had claimed that nothing but a bullet would stop him.[6] Bullets might have been provided. Extremist supporters of the government carried out private acts of vengeance against republicans, several of whom were murdered, and if de Valera had been killed the image of the Free State would have been gravely tarnished. A few months later, in a private letter, Cosgrave expressed concern about de Valera's safety if he were to be released.[7]

In some respects Cumann na nGaedheal's management of the election campaign was casual. A mere ten days before the country went to the polls Cosgrave invited Alfred O'Rahilly, the registrar of University College Cork, to stand as a candidate.[8] (O'Rahilly agreed and he won a seat, but he soon became disillusioned and resigned.) The party relied on the social and economic 'establishment', and afterwards Cosgrave wrote that it owed its success to the loyal support of people in 'high and important positions throughout the country'.[9] Cosgrave himself was an effective speaker at public rallies. Boosted by his Easter Week record and subsequent death sentence, he enjoyed forcing republican hecklers to admit that they had never fired a gun in their lives. On one occasion during the campaign when women harangued him he denounced 'their degradation, their infamy, their falsehood'; on another he told them that they should either have their rosaries in their hands or be at home knitting.[10] (As a member of the pre-war Sinn Féin party and of Dublin Corporation he had a limited experience —unlike most of his colleagues—of working with female politicians. Nonetheless, he seems to have shared the widespread male exasperation with the extremism shown by the women in the Dáil at the time of the treaty split.) He acquired attention, or notoriety, by flying from Ennis to Carlow, from one election meeting to another.[11] This trip required four air corps planes to fly four passengers, and since the occasion was a political rather than a state function their use must be seen as an inappropriate use of government property. However, such behaviour was out of character.

The result of the 1923 election was not a humiliating defeat of the republicans, as had been widely expected. Cumann na nGaedheal won 63 seats, abstentionist Sinn Féin an unexpectedly high total of 44, Labour (the official opposition) only 14, Farmers 15, and 'others' 17. Despite the republicans' campaign of destruction during the civil war, hostility to the treaty had grown—doubtless encouraged by the brutal actions of some government soldiers. Cumann na nGaedheal's share of the vote rose by a mere 0.5%, while Sinn Féin's increased by a formidable 6%. Liam de Róiste, a supporter of the treaty, was right when he remarked 'the Cosgrave Government is not loved'.[12] It was in a theoretical minority of 27, but the republicans' abstention turned this into an actual majority of 17. In effect, it was only Sinn Féin's folly in refusing to enter the Dáil that allowed Cumann na nGaedheal to rule alone and without serious challenge for the next four years. Labour, led by Thomas Johnson, formed the opposition. But the election result encouraged many republicans to appreciate that the Free State *was* a democracy, and that they could hope to achieve power by peaceful means.

Cosgrave headed the poll in his constituency, and with the exception of the 1938 election he would continue to do so for the rest of his career. He won twenty times more first preference votes than Patrick Gaffney, the Labour candidate who had been more popular than him in 1922 but who had since broken with his party and who ran as an independent in 1923. Gaffney's share of the first preference votes fell from 35% to 2%.

A PRESIDENT'S ROUTINE

Cosgrave soon settled in to his role as head of government. He was a formidable parliamentarian who spoke in a 'staccato, quick-firing style'.[13] An English journalist observed Dáil debates during the civil war, and when he wrote his memoirs almost half a century later he recalled 'the laughing, fighting voice of Cosgrave'.[14] Another visitor to Ireland described his performance in debates as precise and courteous, he was 'the magician conjuring away the tempests', while a third saw him as being 'far more liberal in disposition than might be supposed by the freedom with which he hurls "Toe-rags!" and "Ould cods!" and "Hardchaws!" at his critics when in the throes of public oratory'.[15] A friendly observer, the independent TD Bryan Cooper, wrote of him as follows.

> At first sight he looks colourless. His face is pale; the shock of hair that gives it character is of a neutral hue, between flaxen and grey, and the tiny moustache that shades his lip is barely visible. He is a small man, and when he speaks in reply to a question in the Dail his voice is so low that it is barely audible…Something— maybe an interjection, maybe a question—rouses him. The challenge is accepted. The hair bristles for combat, and he seems

to grow taller. His voice becomes louder, and the sentences rattle out, short and crisp, as the report of a machine gun. There is no doubt as to the words now, no doubt as to their meaning. And that meaning is always the same. 'We are a free people and responsible for our actions,' he has said, and responsibility is the keynote of every utterance he has made. No camouflage, no appeals to sentiment, no threats or intimidation will induce him to abdicate one particle of his responsibility...If he is, as unquestionably he is, sometimes unduly sensitive to criticism, and unwilling to make concessions in minor matters, it is precisely because he idealises his duty.[16]

Some years later Cosgrave was described as being the happiest man in the Dáil, quietly and consistently good-humoured. He knew everyone; he was interested in everything from horse-racing to roller-skating, and he was forgetful of his high office. 'There is no man in the Dáil who handles figures with the same dexterous precision that he does...As a theorist, he has many superiors in the House, but as a realist he has none.'[17]

In debates he disconcerted opposition deputies who

would snap at the flies dangled so tantalisingly before them to find themselves a moment later with a hook fast in their gills to their own amazement and to the amusement of the House in general which, without distinction of party, appreciates a leader who can be trusted to show sport.[18]

One of his statements on unemployment relief was described as 'less a speech in the orthodox sense than a Socratic dialogue with interruptions of various parties'.[19] Seán MacEntee, not intending to be complimentary, told the Dáil 'if there is one thing in which the President shines more than another it is in debating strategy'.[20] Cosgrave was happy to praise the speeches of his political opponents.[21] It has been claimed that one of them, Seán Lemass, modelled his own style of debating in the Dáil on that of Cosgrave.[22] In turn, the president respected Johnson as a responsible opposition leader, a man who might be called on some day to form a government of his own. (Johnson later complained that ministers' 'fulsome patronising praise' of his conduct in the Dáil damaged his chances of election in 1927.)[23]

In the Dáil, Cosgrave maintained the conscientious habits he had shown as a member of Dublin Corporation, and he claimed that in 1926 he had voted in 84 of 89 divisions.[24] He made speeches and intervened in debates more often than any other twentieth-century Irish head of government, perhaps because his early years in power were marked by frequent crises. The number of days on which he answered questions was close to the average.[25] But the Dáil did not take up much of its deputies' time; it met on only 110 days in 1925, and by 1928 the figure had dropped to 87. Attendance at debates was often poor.

The president worked long hours. A meeting with one delegation was originally scheduled for 8 a.m., and eventually it took place at 9 p.m.[26] When it proved possible, Cosgrave followed the usual practice of the time by going home for lunch and then returning to work. He normally ate his evening meal sitting at his desk. In 1925 it was estimated that his daily journeys between his house in Templeogue and his office, at thirty miles a day (presumably allowing for lunch breaks), totalled 10,000 miles annually. He calculated that his official Lancia car had covered 44,000 miles in the course of the previous year, much of which was accounted for by travels around the country.[27]

In general his style of doing business was casual and informal; for example, on a Sunday morning he visited Defence Minister Richard Mulcahy's office for a brief conversation, and he habitually offered cigarettes to those who called to see him.[28] He was modest and even self-deprecating. At Michael Collins's funeral, even though he was then the chairman of the provisional government, he was content to walk in the second row, behind relatively minor figures such as J.J. Walsh, the postmaster general. His geniality and humour were commented upon widely. One of his political opponents, examining the physiognomies of Irish politicians, declared that 'Willie Cosgrave shows wit'.[29] When he and two members of his cabinet arrived in London in 1923 they were seen as 'extraordinarily cheerful and jocular'; and even die-hard imperialists could not help liking him.[30] The censorious Sean O'Casey conceded Cosgrave's joviality, good humour and erring humanity, and concluded that he was warmer-natured than de Valera.[31]

He was stern on matters of principle, and when necessary he could be firm with colleagues. Despite his deep respect for and dependence on Hugh Kennedy, Cosgrave sent him a sharp reproof when it emerged in late April 1924 that the attorney-general's department was responsible for half of the numerous delays in replying to communications from the Colonial Office in London; on one occasion seventeen reminders had been sent. He said that he expected to see a considerable improvement in the course of the following week and that he would monitor the situation. (Kennedy rejected the indictment as 'far from fair'.)[32] Cosgrave insisted that the minister for External Affairs, Desmond

FitzGerald, should supply the cabinet with a summary of the arguments relating to the Geneva Protocol, a doomed plan for preventing international aggression.[33] And he criticised Blythe's procrastination as minister for Finance in regularising an appointment to be made in the Department of External Affairs, warning him on two occasions that he should follow instructions.[34]

Like his contemporaries Calvin Coolidge in the United States and Stanley Baldwin in Britain, Cosgrave wanted a return to 'normalcy', an escape from the novelties, uncertainties and dangers that characterised the world of the 1920s. Like them he wished to reduce the role of the state, which had expanded massively during the Great War. (By 1925, governments collected and spent in the region of 20–25% of national income, about double the share they took before the war.[35]) It was noted that in one of his speeches he concentrated more on what the people ought to do than on what the government could do.[36]

His relative indifference to politics continued, and when the pro-treaty Cumann na nGaedheal party was formed he did not take office as its president; he had more important responsibilities. Eoin MacNeill occupied this position until he resigned from the cabinet in 1925 because of his role in the Boundary Commission, and J.J. Walsh succeeded him. Cosgrave was a rare visitor to meetings of the party executive. Cumann na nGaedheal was neglected by most of its leading figures, who chose (or felt obliged) to concentrate on their departmental duties. Mulcahy was the principal exception. This pattern was partly a consequence of the fact that the government had existed before the party was formed, and ministers accordingly felt little loyalty or gratitude towards it. It was amateurish in many respects, and it failed to attract much commitment. Already in November 1924 Blythe described it as 'a snarling organisation', and an item on the agenda of one meeting was 'the decay of the Party'.[37]

The previous year it was suggested that Kevin O'Higgins appeared to be the government's chief spokesman, 'and what he predicts one is inclined to accept as settled governmental policy'.[38] The president could be scathing in dealing with those whom he saw as unhelpful critics, but he was not a divisive figure, and provided that his position was unchallenged he seemed prepared to allow his deputy play a prominent public role. Despite O'Higgins's general unpopularity (he was described as having a harsh, caustic wit that burnt everything it touched, and Mulcahy complained that he 'suffers from manners'[39]) his influence in the government grew steadily between 1924 and 1927. At least in public Cosgrave appeared to be unperturbed, however uneasy he may have felt in private.

Except on important matters or on questions of principle, he guided his cabinet with a loose rein, and in contrast to de Valera he was *primus inter pares*, a chairman rather than a chief.[40] In July 1923 the cabinet minutes recorded that Cosgrave was outvoted and that a decision was taken to delete sub-sections from the Civic Guard Bill, 'the President dissenting'.[41] He was happy to delegate responsibilities, both to governmental colleagues and to civil servants whom he trusted. For example, while he was briefly minister for Finance he gave his full support to Joseph Brennan, the departmental secretary.[42] And although (or because?) Brennan had greater respect for Cosgrave than for his own minister (now Blythe), he was prepared to defy him; he disallowed payment for a second car bought for the president's *aide-de-camp*, and Cosgrave had to pay the expense out of his own pocket.[43]

In the mid-1920s the pro-treaty leadership was dominated by former lawyers (O'Higgins, Patrick Hogan and Patrick McGilligan) and professors from University College, Dublin (MacNeill, John Marcus O'Sullivan, Michael Hayes and—again—McGilligan).[44] As students, the three lawyers had all belonged to the same Economics class in UCD.[45] Hogan, who in addition to being a fellow student was also a close friend of O'Higgins, had also studied History there, and two of the History professors, MacNeill and O'Sullivan, became his ministerial colleagues. They would soon be joined in cabinet by John A. Costello, another student contemporary. They were a close-knit group, and almost all of them came from comfortable backgrounds. In 1924 Hugh Kennedy, an eminent figure in his (somewhat earlier) days as a UCD student, had moved from being attorney-general to chief justice. He had not even been a member of the pre-treaty Sinn Féin, although he had made anonymous financial contributions to the party.[46] Cosgrave was an 'odd man out' in his cabinet, and few of his colleagues had played prominent roles in the revolution.

Mulcahy, another outsider, muttered retrospectively about the 'Ballsbridge' complex that operated against him.[47] Mulcahy was a dogged and conscientious minister, Walsh bombastic, and MacNeill aloof. Blythe was dogmatic and in-different towards—even contemptuous of—public opinion. FitzGerald was a marginal figure, while O'Higgins, Hogan and McGilligan were all men with sharp minds and sharp tongues. As a group they were not inclined to pander to the electorate. Among his colleagues, Cosgrave enjoyed particularly good re-lations with Kennedy, O'Sullivan and Joe McGrath (who had fought beside his brother Philip in Marrowbone Lane in 1916), and also with Hayes, who served as *ceann comhairle* or speaker of the Dáil.

Under the Free State constitution a minister was appointed for the lifetime of a Dáil, with the result that between general elections the president could not remove his colleagues. Cosgrave was recorded as claiming that 'the Constitution gave me no opportunity of getting rid of any Minister except by the resignation of the President'.[48] In practice, however, McGrath (Industry and Commerce), Mulcahy (Defence), MacNeill (Education) and Walsh (Posts and Telegraphs) all resigned their ministries in unhappy circumstances. Long afterwards Mulcahy referred to the 'disintegration' of Cosgrave's cabinet.[49] A pattern of his governments was to tolerate disagreement on some important issues—particularly from Walsh who, unlike his colleagues, opposed free trade and believed in protection for Irish industries. Another was the supremacy of the Department of Finance, which was facilitated by the fact that until September 1923 its minister was also head of government.[50] This was not a recipe for dynamism. Cosgrave's administrations might have achieved more if they had been led in a more decisive fashion. On the other hand, the quarrels between ministers that characterised the early 1920s might have encouraged him to adopt a consensual approach in later years.

Austerity

The Cumann na nGaedheal government ruled in hard times. There had been widespread—and often naïve—expectations for a better life after independence, but hopes for major changes were either restrained or abandoned because of the circumstances in which the new administration found itself. Ireland suffered from the world-wide post-war depression that began in late 1920. Agricultural prices collapsed. As a result of partition the Free State had virtually no manufacturing sector, and 30% of its modest industrial output was represented by brewing.[51] The civil war and its consequences imposed a heavy financial burden on the state, which in 1923–4 had a debt of £26 million. A debilitating 37% of its revenue was spent on defence and on compensation for the enormous damage resulting from the recent conflict. Had Ireland remained a part of the United Kingdom, at no time between the late 1920s and the late 1950s would Irish living standards have been lower than they actually were.[52] As Cosgrave explained to British ministers, the system of administration inherited by the Free State was one 'suited to the needs of a country of much greater financial resources'.[53] He admitted privately that 'our administration is now more costly and less efficient than it was in the British occupation period'.[54]

The cabinet responded to these circumstances with what was the normal policy at the time: financial stringency. In Britain, for example, government policy was characterised by rigid economy; the Geddes Report of 1922, which was a response to national debt and heavy expenditure during the First World War, led to drastic cuts in government expenditure. These were accompanied by a reduction in income tax.[55] 'A budget balanced at the lowest possible level of expenditure was a conventional mark of a self-reliant national personality'.[56] Even during the time of the provisional government Cosgrave had worried about inflation 'with all its corresponding evils', and he referred to Continental European examples.[57] Germany's disastrous experience in 1923 soon provided a clear lesson and warning. He believed that the Irish people were relatively better off than those of bigger and richer countries crushed by the weight of their national debts.[58] Any such debts were to be avoided; the Irish cabinet rejected demands for additional spending, and the result was austerity, even parsimony.

The president and his government were determined that the new state would behave responsibly and would thereby disprove taunts that the Irish were a feckless people, incapable of running their own affairs. In late 1922 Cosgrave remarked that the government must show it could 'deliver the goods'.[59] He and his ministers felt obliged to combat the widespread presumption that peaceful stability could be combined with 'the laxer financial disciplines of rebellion and unrest'.[60] Budgets would be balanced; public expenditure would be controlled; and there would be no irresponsible borrowing.

The caution that Cosgrave had displayed as chairman of Dublin Corporation's estates and finance committee was now applied on a much grander scale to the Irish Free State. He agreed with George O'Brien, the professor of Economics in UCD who was consulted frequently by the government, that an unbalanced budget was the first step in a rake's progress.[61] He had no patience with people who failed to share his understanding of the harsh realities of Irish life, and he told a party meeting that those 'who denounced the policy of Balancing the Budget did not know the first thing of what they were talking about. Income and Expenditure must balance'.[62]

The government's attitude was paternalistic; it felt that the people could not be trusted to act in their own long-term interests, and that it was often obliged to be cruel in order to be kind. The prevailing economic doctrines, combined with the post-civil war conditions facing government ministers and their advisers, seemed—rightly or wrongly—to offer few alternatives. With the exception of Walsh, there is no evidence of disagreement on these matters. But some of Cosgrave's ministers were gratuitously harsh in their public comments, and they seemed to associate concern or compassion with weakness.

Hardship was spread widely, if unevenly. Civil servants were paid less than their counterparts in Britain, or than their Dublin Castle predecessors. The poor and the vulnerable suffered far more. The pension for the blind was cut and, notoriously, in 1924 the old age pension was reduced by 10%. This was a miscalculation that entered Irish political folklore, an action that would be associated with the Cumann na nGaedheal government for decades to come. But at the time it made financial sense. As a proportion of average industrial earnings the Irish old age pension was one of the more generous in Europe,[63] and pensions were an exceptionally heavy burden because of Ireland's demographic structure. Before independence, about £3 million in pensions payments had been transferred annually from the United Kingdom exchequer to what became the Irish Free State, and as early as May 1922 Cosgrave argued that the burden of such an expenditure on the new government would be excessive.[64] It amounted to over one-sixth of normal government expenditure in 1922–3. He had already expressed unease that some people receiving state pensions lived in fairly comfortable houses, supported by their relatives.[65] (In 1928 the pension was largely restored to its earlier rate but, unsurprisingly, this move attracted little attention.)

The taxation system was regressive. Income tax had never produced much revenue in Ireland, and to prevent potentially fugitive capital seeping out of the country the government ensured that the Free State's rate of income tax was lower than that of the United Kingdom. In compensation, indirect taxes such as customs and excise were increased, and they amounted to between 60% and 70% of the state's revenue. The consequence was a growth in income inequality, and most of the people were penalised while the upper and middle classes escaped relatively lightly.[66] This was at odds with many revolutionaries' earlier beliefs and expectations, even if it suited some wealthy Cumann na nGaedheal supporters.

The government was constrained by the continuing economic dominance of the United Kingdom, which was the Free State's most convenient and profitable market. In 1926 trade with the UK accounted for 75.7% of its imports and 96.3% of its exports.[67] Most ministers and their advisers inclined instinctively towards free trade. Griffith had been a passionate advocate of protection and it was one of the basic principles of his Sinn Féin party, to which Cosgrave had belonged for so long. After independence, however, the government gave priority to the interests of agriculture, where Ireland had a comparative advantage. The relevant minister, Patrick Hogan, pointed out that agricultural products accounted for 75% of national exports, and much attention was devoted to keeping farming production costs as low as possible—even if this had negative consequences in other areas. Such a policy ruled out widespread tariffs, which might have benefitted industry, because they would raise the price of imports and might provoke retaliation against Irish agricultural exports.[68] Cosgrave shared these views. He believed not only that agriculture was 'the basic industry of the country, but the agricultural population constitutes the foundation and the source of our racial stock'.[69]

Even if these economic policies bore the marks of being grounded in economic theory, they also happened to suit most Cumann na nGaedheal voters; the party drew much of its core electoral support from the urban middle class and the more substantial farmers.[70] The government was courted by the propertied classes and it returned their embrace.

Nevertheless, Cosgrave insisted that the state could not continue to purchase beyond its means, and therefore he accepted that some tariffs were necessary in light of Ireland's adverse trade balance.[71] He declared that 'our policy is frankly a protectionist policy, but we have no intention of imposing indiscriminate tariffs'.[72] Free-trade policies were modified, although only to a moderate extent before the end of the decade, and products such as clothing, furniture and confectionary benefitted from protection. By 1931 the government felt that it had to follow the example of other countries, and duties of 50% were imposed on a wide range of imports.

The government's policies have been much criticised, as in the judgment that economic retrenchment 'became a form of ideological compensation for the retreat from the inspirational policies that had led the national revolution'.[73] But there were economic as well as ideological reasons for the severity of the Cumann na nGaedheal government's economic policy.

Gradually, the financial impact of the civil war receded and it became possible to devote more money to 'normal' activities. For example, the annual defence budget fell from £11 million in 1923–4 to £2 million in 1926–7, while between 1923–4 and 1927–8 the proportion of expenditure on education rose from 11.7% to 14.5%.[74] As time went on, more money could also be devoted to areas such as agriculture, health, social services and the railway system.[75]

Cosgrave believed in hard work and self-discipline, both by individuals and by the nation as a whole. After his retirement, one of his former cabinet colleagues praised his creation of a sense of civic responsibility.[76] He hoped, optimistically and wrongly, that Ireland was 'turning from politics in the old sense to economics'; *The Irish Times* claimed that his government envisaged the country's true welfare in 'butter and eggs and a pound of cheese'.[77] In one speech he dealt with the Shannon electrification scheme, the improvement of grass-lands, dairy herds, milk yields, butter production, and the marketing of eggs.[78] Thereby, he linked a costly and imaginative investment in the national infra-structure to Ireland's traditional agricultural products. He often deplored the Free State's poverty, and he declared that 'you will not get the country to move forward unless it is prosperous'.[79] But prosperity in itself was not sufficient, and looking at the experience of other countries he concluded that their industrial and commercial progress provided a basis for artistic and cultural develop-ment.[80] Cosgrave rejected the urge to 'get rich quick', and he argued that it was the duty of every citizen to contribute his quota, to live within his means and to support home-made goods.[81]

Independent Ireland inherited a tradition of alienation from government, combined with an equally ingrained tradition of passive dependence on state aid.[82] Cosgrave wanted to break this pattern. He believed that the state should not simply dispense largesse; people should pay something for the advantages that, he believed, they derived from the achievement of independence. He was wary of 'pledging the credit of the Nation for a single particular service—for which only those who benefit by that service are concerned—at the cost of the people'.[83] He believed strongly that it was not part of ministers' duties 'to supply soft jobs'.[84] He told Cumann na nGaedheal members that the purpose of the party was to ensure

> an ordered society, hard work, constant endeavour, a definite settled policy of reconstruction and rehabilitation, recruitment to the public service on the basis of merit; efficient, upright, eco-nomic public service, greater national economy day by day, year by year; balanced budgets, a national revival of Irish culture; the maintenance of peace.[85]

This programme has been described, like Cumann na nGaedheal's policy more generally, as reading like a Protestant assault on Catholic sensibility; it was dis-passionate, temperate, reasoned and cool; it invoked none of the sentiment or emotion that had accompanied so much of modern Irish political history.[86]

Cosgrave and many other prominent figures in Cumann na nGaedheal saw themselves as modernisers who challenged self-indulgent and destructive na-tional characteristics. He appealed to people's heads but not to their hearts, and as Yeats wrote in 'Parnell's Funeral', he failed to satisfy the land's imagination. The cabinet was down-to-earth and undemonstrative; it was more concerned with the substance than with the forms of liberty.[87] Its members have been described as 'unenthusiastic and rather authoritarian democrats, who combined within their minds an almost hysterical acceptance of electoral democracy and a rather bossy paternalism'; as 'intellectually severe and brusque martinets'; and as austere, prickly men who 'attempted to do their duty with a fine disregard for sentimentality'.[88] At national level their achievements were intimately linked with Fianna Fáil's later political successes;[89] their policies played into the hands of their enemies.

Efficiency

The achievements were substantial. Despite its limited financial resources, Cosgrave's administration initiated a major legislative programme, bringing about significant changes in the way in which Ireland was administered. Between December 1922 and August 1923 forty-seven acts were passed.[90]

One early success was the 1923 Land Act. Already, 70% of Irish land had passed to the ownership of tenant farmers and, not surprisingly, resolving ownership of the remaining 30% posed the greatest problems. During the civil war numerous acts of violence had been carried out for agrarian rather than political reasons. Hogan informed Cosgrave that house-burning had become a regular pattern, and that shooting land commission officials had come to be regarded as a normal and legitimate activity. Many grievances would be impossible to solve, since the Free State had about 1,500,000 landless men and only 30,000 holdings available for them.[91]

Perhaps inevitably in the circumstances the government decided on a conservative measure, and the minister exploited the potential divisions between tenant farmers, labourers and smallholders.[92] The precedents of earlier acts were followed: there would be no gains for labourers and for 'non-inheriting' farmers' children. Some of those who already held land became owners, and those without land received nothing. Landlords were obliged to accept compulsory purchase, but otherwise they were well treated; the patterns established under British rule were maintained after the revolution. But the expense of implementing the Land Act was enormous, and Hogan estimated that the completion of land purchase would cost the state £30 million. This would constrain the government's expenditure in other areas of social policy.[93] The new Land Commission had the power to carry out the compulsory acquisition and redistribution of land; 'it became the principal agent of social engineering in modern Ireland', and it impacted positively or negatively on the vast majority of farmers in the state.[94] From 1923 to 1932 the commission acquired and divided 330,800 acres (134,000 hectares) between nearly 17,000 beneficiaries.[95] Cosgrave referred to an area in the Maam valley in Connemara—hitherto used almost entirely for sheep grazing—where it was hoped that 50 families might be provided with holdings large enough for them to live in 'frugal comfort'.[96] (This term was later made famous by de Valera and became associated with him.) Some reforms of Irish agriculture were controversial, and the government provoked resentment by its efforts to raise standards in the breeding of cattle, sheep and pigs, to improve the quality of eggs and butter, to extend the practice of pasteurisation, and to enhance the appearance of Irish products.

In quite a different area, one of the Cosgrave administration's most remarkable triumphs was to create an unarmed and depoliticised police force that soon won widespread public acceptance. Perhaps most impressively of all, this break with the pattern of British rule in regard to policing was initiated during the civil war. The new civic guards commanded by Eoin O'Duffy kept out of the fighting, and although they encountered some resistance they were usually welcomed at local level. The government was inundated with requests from communities throughout the country that guards should be dispatched to them as quickly as possible.[97] The members of the new force were less numerous and less expensive than the old Royal Irish Constabulary, or than the new police forces in Northern Ireland. The separate Dublin Metropolitan Police force was amalgamated with the civic guards in 1925.

In January 1922 it was announced that the crown courts were to continue in operation until the establishment of the Free State, and the revolutionary Dáil courts were soon suppressed in an insensitive manner after one of their judges challenged the provisional government. The Dáil courts had been one of the most striking administrative/political achievements of the revolution, but the minister for Justice, Kevin O'Higgins dismissed them ungraciously as channels of corruption and abuse.[98]

A new judicial structure was established. In a letter that was drafted by the attorney-general, Hugh Kennedy, Cosgrave announced the government's intention 'to construct a system of judiciary and an administration of law and justice according to the dictates of our own needs and after a pattern of our own designing'.[99] Cumbersome, expensive and amateurish procedures were replaced by a more logical and professional network of district, circuit, high and supreme courts, reinforced by a new court of criminal appeal.[100] Independent

Ireland would retain the English common law tradition, but relics of British rule such as the resident magistrate ('civil servant and chief constable—forever at the bidding of government'[101]) were swept away. The new district justices would be representative of the communities among whom they worked.[102]

Cosgrave lacked his usual sureness of touch when he tried unsuccessfully to limit judicial independence in the Courts of Justice Bill—thereby provoking intense resistance during debates on the bill in the Dáil and Senate. Critics argued that the government should not be allowed to regulate matters such as judicial dress, titles, court rules, or age of retirement. In his handling of this issue the president has been described as 'rather hysterical' and as acting out of character.[103] More positively, he appointed his formidable attorney-general Hugh Kennedy as chief justice, or president of the supreme court, arguing that 'it would be a clean start'.[104] In making judicial appointments, Cosgrave was described as displaying indifference to barristers' political opinions.[105] A clean start *was* made in many respects, even if the changes were less radical than Kennedy had hoped.[106] Cosgrave's declared aim was 'law well within the purse limits of the citizen, and there will be absolute and implicit confidence in every institution'.[107] The first of these objectives, at least, was not realised.

Women were allowed to exempt themselves from jury service, and subsequently O'Higgins introduced a bill that would exclude them—on the ground that as most were unwilling to serve, calling them to do so resulted in unnecessary administrative expense. His proposal was criticised sharply. Thomas Johnson argued that privileges and obligations should be equal, and he pointed out that men would also like to be relieved of the duty. The bill was amended so that women could apply for inclusion on the jury register.[108]

The Ministers and Secretaries Act (1924) eliminated a clumsy and antiquated system inherited from the British, replacing an 'informal, casual and poorly supervised collection of boards [with] a centralised and ruthlessly driven State machine'.[109] The civil service was reorganised into a hierarchical system of departments under the control of the Department of Finance and answerable to politicians. It created the sort of structure that the British had tried and failed to build in Ireland.[110] Cosgrave made only minor comments as the bill was drafted, but he was satisfied with the result.[111] He believed that from the point of view of the state this act was next in importance to the constitution, and the report on which it was based has been described as an example of 'the speed and vigour with which the most far reaching administrative reforms were prosecuted' in the first years after independence.[112]

The government was obsessive in upholding its belief in probity.[113] Cosgrave was noted for his personal integrity, and this was reflected when he wrote that ministers should not hold directorships; he felt very strongly about the matter, and he wanted it discussed by the cabinet.[114] Before the truce he had argued for a code to prevent jobbery in local authorities, and as early as November 1922 the cabinet agreed to his proposal that a Civil Service Commission should be established.[115] This measure followed the British model and, together with the creation of a Local Appointments Commission, it did much to eliminate time-honoured patterns of canvassing and nepotism. Cosgrave argued that the new system deprived local authorities of patronage and the ability to appoint people who were not the best qualified, while it allowed 'the poor man's son' to secure appointment by merit alone.[116] (When Fianna Fáil came to power the responsible minister, Seán T. O'Kelly, waged war on the latter body and it was obliged to make some concessions, but it survived.[117])

Local government was reformed and rationalised. The new Free State ministers believed in strong, centralised administration, and they showed no hesitation in dismissing subordinate bodies that they viewed as inefficient, obstructive or corrupt. Between 1923 and 1931 they dissolved a total of 36 local authorities, including several county councils and Dublin and Cork corporations. Cases were reported of electorates refusing to choose a council in the hope of forcing the central government into reinstating commissioners.[118] In 1925 the rural district councils were wound up and their responsibilities were taken over by the county councils. The old poor law unions were amalgamated or abolished; many workhouses were closed; and county homes were established for the sick and the aged. For those who had hoped for improved conditions, however, the results were often disappointing. According to a harsh verdict, an 'odious, degrading and foreign poor law system' was replaced by an odious, degrading and native system.[119]

The abolition of Dublin Corporation was not widely regretted, and shortly before its disappearance *The Irish Statesman* reported the belief that the corporation's disease 'can be cured only by a drastic surgical operation'.[120] It had been dominated by opponents of the treaty who consistently defied the government. For example, it had tried to secure the release of all political prisoners, a step denounced by Cosgrave as designed 'to keep the unfortunate dupes still on hunger strike. I think it is cruel, inhuman, and unworthy of any citizen of this State'.[121]

Such provocations met with a sharp response, and the corporation was replaced by three government-appointed commissioners. It was claimed that the

Westminster government in its most tyrannical days would not have dared to suppress Dublin Corporation.[122] The commissioners ruled the city for the next six years, to widespread satisfaction; the streets were cleaner and better surfaced, and rates were reduced.[123] When the corporation was restored in 1930 the city boundaries were extended to include the prosperous townships of Rathmines and Pembroke, as well as other districts.

Perhaps in consequence of his years as a member of Dublin Corporation, Cosgrave felt that local government should be conducted independently of party politics. 'It is a matter of business and the question of politics ought not to enter into a well administered Local Government Department or a well administered Co. Council, Borough Council, Board of Guardians, or anything of the sort'.[124] In 1923 Cumann na nGaedheal decided not to contest local elections, and it aimed at returning pro-treaty candidates 'whether our own or nominees of other parties'.[125] Two years later the president declared that local government responsibilities had no connection with party politics. In the past, national issues had been discussed at local level, but now a parliament was available to deal with such matters.[126] This was a noble but unrealistic policy, and it allowed republicans to build up their strength at the expense of Cumann na nGaedheal.

In other respects, too, opportunities to dispense favours were rejected—together with the risk of alienating disappointed candidates. When the government decided to establish a sugar beet factory, for example, it handed over the choice of location to a Belgian expert.[127]

Adherence to such high principles provoked both admiration and dismay. *The Irish Statesman* praised the government for having been 'a miracle of moderation in its application of the gospel of the spoils to the victors', even if some people had been given jobs because of their services during the recent conflict.[128] This moderation was unwelcome to many of Cumann na nGaedheal's followers. The leadership often treated rank and file members with indifference, if not dislike, and it tended to view the party as a propaganda machine at its disposal.[129] Its attitude provoked a natural resentment, and the standing committee complained that

> the Organisation's influence on Government policy and its power to affect patronage has been negligible, if not nil. In parts of the country it is openly recognized that to be connected with Cumann na nGaedheal is, in most cases, a handicap... In general, it is complained that those who won the fight have not done well out of the victory.

From Kerry and Wexford came complaints that contracts and appointments had been given to former enemies.[130] Cosgrave's nomination of prominent unionists to the Senate, a magnanimous gesture aimed at healing old wounds, was a further source of animosity among supporters as well as opponents. At a meeting of the party standing committee in October 1924, one member complained that the government performed good works by stealth, when what was needed was publicity and popular policies. Michael Tierney, a future Cumann na nGaedheal TD and university president, argued that the Civil Service Commission was not a success and that recruitment to the civil service was 'English in substance and tone, and unsuited to this country', but Cosgrave responded that merit, efficiency and suitability were the criteria for appointment. He continued, characteristically, 'We must have value for money'.[131]

Such a programme was too idealistic or ideological, too much at odds with the traditional realities of Irish life, for it to survive without compromises. In particular, at a time of internal party upheaval in 1924, the president appears to have given serious consideration to demands that 'anti-Irish' elements should be removed from the civil service and that government decisions should be implemented 'irrespective of opposition from Permanent Officials'. This would have amounted to a purge. Nothing came of the scheme, and the cabinet did not support it. Cosgrave's anxiety to reunite his party may have triumphed briefly over his commitment to a meritocratic, corruption-free state.[132] But it is quite likely that he was simply playing for time, as he did on other occasions. At a lower level, the president was not above lobbying on behalf of protégés. While his foreign minister Patrick McGilligan was representing the Free State at an imperial conference in London in 1930, Cosgrave wrote to him requesting that he should intervene (in his other role as minister for Industry and Commerce) on behalf of a man who ran a private bus service from Belfast.[133] McGilligan might reasonably have thought that he had more important things to do. Like most people, Cosgrave was anxious to 'look after his own', and he tried to ensure that treaty supporters were given jobs in the early years of the state.[134] But he did so with remarkable restraint. During the civil war it had been essential to appoint only trusted people to certain sensitive offices; for example, he chose his brother Philip (a TD for Dublin North-West, described as an 'unassuming, compassionate and selfless man',[135]) to be governor of Mountjoy Jail. In later years other, more 'normal' criteria were applied.

In general, the first Free State administration tried, with exceptional earnestness, to raise the standards of Irish public life. The pattern did not end with the change of government in 1932, and in later years Seán Lemass continued the defence of meritocracy and the fight against clientelism.[136]

Rationalisation also took other forms; for example, the Railway Act of 1924 amalgamated or absorbed twenty-six separate companies to form the Great Southern Railway Company.[137]

Cosgrave's government has been described as representing Victorian thought categories and values, and as characterised by ruthlessness and clarity of objective; in many respects it 'pursued traditional British policy, but with an authority, a degree of public approbation and a single-mindedness that Irish administrations had lacked almost since the Act of Union'.[138] Such a judgment underestimates the extent to which the new rulers were determined not merely to administer the country more efficiently than their predecessors in Dublin Castle had done, but also to impel Ireland in a different direction.

Making the state more 'Irish'

The 1922 constitution declared that Irish was the national language of the Free State, and it was given equal status with English as an official language. This was a natural development, because the advancement of Irish had been one of the few ideological aims of the revolution. The government felt obliged to atone for its moderation in other matters by adopting a rigid linguistic policy; its members could not afford to be branded as covert West Britons.[139] In 1923 it decided that Irish would become a standard subject in the civil service examination.[140] As minister for Education, Eoin MacNeill ensured that the language would be privileged in schools, at the expense of other subjects. Educational standards were subordinated to nationalist demands. His department's policy of Gaelicising Ireland would be achieved mainly by 'the substitution of Irish for English as the *language* of teaching, recreation and life generally in the Primary and Secondary Schools'. The government must ensure 'that Irish is the superior language socially and economically, in other words that *Irish pays*'.[141] The Irish-language scholar Osborn Bergin described the pattern as follows:

> the people leave the problem to the Government, the Government leaves it to the Department of Education, the Department of Education to the teachers, and the teachers to the school-children. Only the very young are unable to shift the burden to someone else's shoulders, so perhaps they will learn to carry it, and save our faces. After all, infants before the age of reason can do marvels with language, so they may not notice the weight.[142]

The Irish language became a state enterprise, and paradoxically it inspired less interest and effort after independence than it had done before. 'The language revival was initiated by government diktat and failed because the majority was not convinced of its need.'[143]

Cosgrave was well-disposed towards Irish, and he was reported to have studied it after his election for Kilkenny in 1917.[144] Both his sons were given Irish names and they were sent for some months to an Irish-language school in Connemara, at a time when such a step was unusual.[145] He talked about 'the Gaelicisation...of our whole culture'.[146] But like the vast majority of the population he had only a limited command of the language. On the rare occasions when he was asked Dáil questions in Irish one of his colleagues answered on his behalf, and when making speeches in Irish he needed a phonetic guide. For example, his St Patrick's Day address in 1926 included the customary 'top and tail' used by politicians and others over many decades, sandwiching an English-language letter or speech between a few token opening and concluding words in Irish. Speaking to the Irish people at home and abroad he wished them well on the feast day of St Patrick, the apostle of Ireland, and in closing he hoped that God and St Patrick might bless 'the work'. In Irish this ran:

> *Do chine Gaedheal i mbaile is i gcéin, beatha agus sláinte ar theacht don bhFéile Náisiúnta so arís—Féile Phádraig, Aspal na hÉireann...Beannacht Dé agus Phádraig ar an obair.*

It was accompanied by the following guide to pronunciation:

> Dhu kinĕ Gayul ī mailĕ iss i gain baha aggus sláinte err hauckt Dhun vailĕ Nashoontha shu areesh—Failĕ Faudrigg, Aspal ne hÉireann...Bannacht Day ogus faudrig er un ubber.[14]

Most Irish people could do no better, and in the census held a month later only 18.3% of them claimed to be able to speak the language.[148] The real figure was almost certainly lower.

Some people who spoke Irish and flaunted their knowledge were often at a loss for words. De Valera began a speech in the treaty debates by confessing in Irish that his command of the language was insufficient for him to persevere. In 1926 less than 0.4% of Dáil speeches were delivered in Irish, and a decade later the figure was still below 1%.[149] After they came to power even Fianna Fáil ministers were sometimes discomfited by their unfamiliarity with the language that they imposed on the rest of the population.[150] De Valera's 1937 constitution was drafted in English, yet it declared that the Irish version of leg-islation (almost always a translation) must take priority over the English (almost always the original).[151] Cosgrave's position forced him to confront or to conceal a monolingualism that was widely shared.

It may be revealing that he signed minutes of Cumann na nGaedheal meet-ings in Irish until after he lost power, and he switched to English in April and May 1932.[152] His token use of Irish may have been associated with his role as head of government. Similarly, in his extensive correspondence with Bishop Michael Fogarty of Killaloe he invariably signed his name in Irish until two years after he left office; from then onwards, with equal consistency, he used the English form.

He had mixed views on compulsion and he believed that the language revival programme should not impair efficiency.[153] Although his government began the pattern of making Ireland a less culturally pluralist society, some of his colleagues and successors showed considerably greater zeal in enforcing Irish. But the cabinet ignored the demand from the Gaelic League that anyone who derided the language in public should be prosecuted; nor did it agree to the League's request that teachers of Irish should be exempted from taking an oath of allegiance to the state.[154] The Irish language would not be allowed to become an extension or a monopoly of the republican movement.

The policy of Gaelicisation came into conflict with another of Cosgrave's ob-jectives: the integration of southern unionists into the Free State. In contrast to the Northern Irish government's attitude towards its minority, he and his gov-ernment hoped that, over time, ex-unionists would share the same loyalties as the rest of the Free State's population.[155] Here his reasons were both principled and practical. He was instinctively inclined towards reconciliation, and as soon as he achieved power he wanted the support of every possible group and indi-vidual. But such attitudes made it easier for republicans to brand Cumann na nGaedheal as 'West British'.

The government also began the satisfying task of creating a new state symbolism. For example, it decided that the official seal of the state would be a harp, 'but not one containing a female figure'.[156] This was followed by the in-troduction of handsome coins and banknotes and ugly postage stamps. (The new Irish currency was tied to sterling, and it remained so until 1979.) Much attention was given to detail, and in discussing the pig that featured on the half-penny the cabinet requested from the artist designing the coins 'a slight reduction in the fullness of the jowl'.[157] Cosgrave felt that in view of many uses to which money was put, only 'profane matter' should feature on the coinage.

A Catholic priest disagreed and regarded the coins as 'the thin edge of the wedge of Freemasonry sunk into the very life of our Catholicity' in an attempt 'to beget a land of devil-worshippers'.[158]

Another form of national self-expression in the 1920s was the establishment of a national radio service under the Department of Posts and Telegraphs. Radio broadcasting spread slowly, and over the decades it enriched the lives of many Irish people. The service, called 2RN, was launched on 1 January 1926 without a thorough examination of its form and content, but it was intended to have a cultural rather than a political nature.[159] Shortly after the inauguration of the service, Cosgrave wrote a long letter giving his personal impressions of Irish broadcasting. He complained about low standards and he adopted a comparative approach, as in praising German stations for providing the best music and the clearest speakers. He regretted that 'the splendid Beethoven Concert given in Dublin this year' had not been broadcast. In the 'Irish-Ireland' programme he found that 'jigs, reels, hornpipes seem to be always the same, and an anti-British colour has been predominant. It is not clear whether this is super-patriotism or the slave mind'.[160] He despised both these characteristics.

In 1924 the Free State instituted Aonach Tailteann, 'a sort of mixture of a national Olympic Games and a world's fair'.[161] Large crowds gathered in Croke Park and Phoenix Park to watch games, athletics and—most popular of all—motor-cycle races. The games were repeated in 1928, when the motor-cycle race was reported to have attracted 100,000 spectators, and on a much smaller scale in 1932.[162] They were then abandoned.

Other areas proved to be more problematical. It was clear from the beginning that the tone of the new state would be Catholic and that the wishes or demands of the Church leadership would be given every consideration. This development began under Collins, when he agreed to Archbishop Byrne's request for an advance copy of the draft constitution,[163] and the change was much to Cosgrave's taste. The cabinet planned to hand over the site of the General Post Office to the archbishop for the construction of a new cathedral, but legal constraints prevented it from doing so.[164]

Byrne and other members of the hierarchy brought pressure to bear on the government in particular arenas, and ministers felt obliged to act cautiously if they were to avoid embarrassment. In particular, the Church's views were sought and respected in areas such as divorce. Cosgrave wrote to Byrne:

> I have to acknowledge with many thanks the receipt of the memorandum on Catholic Teaching on Marriage.

I hope to be able to show it to some members of the Committee in time for the Meeting.

I do not anticipate any difficulty whatever in the matter of a correct interpretation & action by Catholic members of Oireachtas. The crux of the whole business is how the committee can best decide to put the matter before the two houses.[165]

He asked for the archbishop's opinion whether private divorce bills should be permitted, as had been the case under British rule, and the reply was predictable. Byrne declared that the Church claimed sole jurisdiction in regard to matrimony, and it viewed marriage only as a sacrament. It could not sanction divorce even for non-Catholics; all baptised persons were under its jurisdiction. Any Irish citizens who wanted divorce could emigrate to a state where it was available, and the country would lose nothing by their departure.[166] Later Cosgrave wrote to another bishop 'I must confess that in the beginning I was a child so far as my information and knowledge of the subject was concerned…It was from His Grace [Byrne] that I learned that His Holiness had jurisdiction over all baptised persons'.[167] In the words of an authority on the subject, 'the Church was the mentor and Cosgrave the willing pupil'.[168] Cosgrave subsequently introduced legislation to ensure that divorce would not be tolerated in the Free State, on the ground that 'the whole fabric of our social organisation is based upon the sanctity of the marriage bond'.[169] Elsewhere, governments went further. In Austria, where the concordat with the Vatican was written into the constitution, matrimonial questions were regulated by canon law and not civil law.[170]

The question of film censorship was raised in the Dáil in September 1920. (Five years earlier Cosgrave had proposed that Dublin Corporation should agree to meet the Dublin Vigilance Committee on the subject of objectionable films. He had already presided over one of the committee's meetings.)[171] The draft of a film censorship bill was approved even before the end of the civil war.[172] This measure followed a pattern that was widespread in other countries and it was aimed at works that were seen as 'subversive of public morality'. In the Free State it was necessary to introduce legislation because until then each local authority had been responsible for censorship in its own area, resulting in wide discrepancies.[173] Action was deferred on a proposal to ban films that were offensive to the people of friendly nations. (Examples given were *Beau Geste*, *Mare Nostrum* and *Mademoiselle from Armentières*).[174] Later in the decade new legislation created a harsh and often philistine censorship of books.[175]

The Church also played a central role in Irish education. Standards were low, and in 1924–5 over 490,000 pupils attended national schools while fewer than 23,000 were enrolled for secondary schools.[176] Science and foreign languages were neglected. But reforms were introduced, such as ensuring compulsory attendance in schools and streamlining the vocational educational system.[177] Cosgrave's government, like its successors, was determined to limit state expenditure, and it benefitted financially from the Catholic Church's involvement in running primary and secondary schools—an involvement that was accompanied by a substantial degree of clerical control. This pattern was inherited from the British.[178] In similar fashion, both sides profited from the Church's management of many hospitals. The government saved money by sharing power in regard to education and hospital management. The results of this cooperation were normally popular and beneficial. Only many decades later did it become common knowledge that a minority of Church members had abused their positions in running institutions such as industrial schools and Magdalene laundries. To an extent, the state 'farmed out' some of its responsibilities in health and education.

'AMONG THE NATIONS OF THE EARTH'

Like many Irish nationalists, Cosgrave tended not to devote much attention to the outside world; his interests were focused on Ireland. He informed the Dáil that he had never gone to Continental Europe except on business, or when ordered to do so for his health, or to attend religious ceremonies. He had never left Ireland for holidays, and he never intended to do so.[179] In 1922 George Gavan Duffy, the outgoing minister for Foreign Affairs, quoted Cosgrave's remark at a recent cabinet meeting that Ireland's foreign relations, other than commercial, would be a matter of no importance.[180] The president normally left such matters to his ministers, although his few interventions in the development of foreign policy were significant. Among them was his determination that the Free State should apply for membership of the League of Nations, and that the Anglo-Irish Treaty should be registered with the League as an international agreement.[181] Ireland was admitted to the League as one of the British Commonwealth dominions, despite objections by some republican protesters, and Cosgrave led the large Irish delegation that went to Geneva for the admittance ceremony in September 1923.[182]

Inevitably, his main foreign concerns lay with the United Kingdom, primarily in terms of implementing both the treaty and the recommendations of the boundary commission (a body that would revise the frontier between North and South), but also as a conduit for relations with other governments. Ireland became the first dominion to establish diplomatic links with countries outside the Commonwealth, and Irish representatives were sent to the United States, France, Germany and the Vatican. These diplomats were expected to attack 'the idea that we are a sort of bastard English nation with no distinctive ancestry or civilisation of our own'.[183] The Free State issued its own passports. In the 1920s it played an influential role in international affairs.[184]

Cosgrave made brief appearances at both the 1923 and 1926 imperial conferences, but he left the hard work at these gatherings to colleagues—to Desmond FitzGerald and Eoin MacNeill who were delegates to the conference in the first instance, and to FitzGerald and Kevin O'Higgins, in his role of vice-president, in the second. Sensibly, the government decided not to accept a British offer of hospitality;[185] its independence must not be compromised. The president had no interest in attending receptions in London and he wrote tetchily 'if people have any doubts regarding our leisure time the sooner they are disabused the better…I have no patience with their semi social events'. He did not wish to become absorbed in such festivities; after all, he added, 'we have our own'.[186] He would represent the new Irish state in a responsible and dignified fashion, but would do no more than he felt useful or necessary. For example, he inquired of the Earl of Granard whether it would be appropriate for him to wear his papal decoration when going to Buckingham Palace.[187] But in the group photograph of the dominion prime ministers gathered around George V during the 1926 conference the others sat or stood formally while Cosgrave leaned casually and irreverently against the back of a chair. The king might not have been amused.

The outcome of this conference, at which O'Higgins played a leading role, was to enhance the dominions' independence; in Cosgrave's words, all were 'free to develop on [their] own national lines without restraint or hindrance'.[188] The treaty was simultaneously implemented and vindicated. Towards the end of his life O'Higgins constructed improbable plans for the formal establishment of a Griffithite dual monarchy, but there is no reason to think that the president shared such views. In 1924 FitzGerald, then minister for External Affairs, circulated his colleagues asking their opinions as to whether the Free State should approach the British before presenting the treaty for registration with the League of Nations. Cosgrave replied that he favoured a direct approach, without any British involvement.[189] His government was determined not to play the role envisaged for it by Lionel Curtis, the Colonial Office's adviser on Ireland: that it should 'be content to run like good dogs after the British coach'.[190]

MUTINY

The Irish government had cause for pride in the area of foreign affairs, but most of its problems, achievements and failures lay at home. In 1924 and 1925 Cosgrave's administration had to cope with two major crises: the army mutiny and the boundary commission.

The army had swollen massively during the civil war, and one of the government's most pressing tasks was to reduce its size by two-thirds, from a total of 58,300 to 19,300 (although it was intended that the armed forces should be capable of rapid expansion in times of emergency). Linked to this was the need to weed out men who might have been suitable for a guerrilla campaign against the British but were ill-equipped for life in a regular peace-time force.

Some cabinet members were suspicious of the army in general, and in particular of General Richard Mulcahy, the minister for Defence. Subsequently it was claimed that the reason for the army crisis in 1924 was disharmony within the cabinet.[191] Joe McGrath, the minister for Industry and Commerce, schemed with officers against Mulcahy, and O'Higgins later complained that the government 'didn't know what the Army was doing, and when they did happen to know things about it that it was regarded as a kind of impertinence';[192] he claimed that the general went to cabinet meetings not as a colleague but as a delegate.[193] Factions within the army distrusted each other. Some Collins loyalists, who had already begun causing trouble during their commander's lifetime, formed the IRA Organization (IRAO) to advance their interests and to counter the lingering influence of the IRB. In particular they resented what they saw as IRB domination of the army council, a group consisting of the minister for Defence and the three most senior officers.

In April 1923 the cabinet established a council of defence to increase its control over the military.[194] Cosgrave was a member of this body. Two months later, IRAO members wrote to him and he placated them; he was anxious to ensure that they would not cause any embarrassment before the impending general election. He and Mulcahy met a group of disgruntled officers and listened to complaints that the army was rotten and that Mulcahy was disloyal to Collins's outlook. Cosgrave was emollient, saying that such matters should be discussed in a friendly manner, but Mulcahy left the room in protest. At a subsequent meeting McGrath acted as spokesman for the dissident officers.[195] One of the topics discussed with them was the revival of the IRB, and a year later both Cosgrave and O'Higgins claimed that they had not favoured the brotherhood's continued existence.[196] This would have been consistent with their suspicion of secret societies. The government was pressurised into undermining decisions taken by the army council, and Mulcahy resented his colleagues' interference in military affairs. He failed to inform them that the IRB was still active. Cosgrave was wary of any army reorganisation that would strengthen headquarters at the expense of the units.[197]

In March 1924 two of Collins's former lieutenants, Liam Tobin and Charles Dalton, sent an ultimatum to the president. McGrath delivered it in person. Complaining that the government was not trying to secure a republic they demanded that demobilisation should be suspended and that the army council should be dismissed; 'we can no longer be party to the treachery that threatens to destroy the aspirations of the Nation'. They sought a reply within four days.[198] Some officers seized arms and ammunition before deserting their posts. The government's initial response was firm, and it ordered that the dissidents should be arrested. McGrath promptly resigned from the cabinet and soldiers were sent to his house in search of leading mutineers. Eoin O'Duffy, the police commissioner, was appointed general officer commanding the defence forces; this was effectively a repudiation of the existing army command and therefore a concession to the mutineers. However the cabinet rejected O'Duffy's suggestion that it should meet him once a week.[199]

Cosgrave described the rebel officers' action as 'a challenge to the democratic foundations of the State, to the very basis of Parliamentary representation and of responsible Government' and he declared—with dubious accuracy—that the government had never discussed questions of politics with army officers. McGrath referred to muddling, mishandling and incompetence within the (unnamed but identifiable) Department of Defence.[200] He threatened to address the Dáil on the matter, preferably on the following day, but the cabinet was anxious to prevent such a move; his revelations about divisions within the army and the government would cause serious political damage.

Cumann na nGaedheal TDs held a lengthy meeting that lasted six or seven hours, in the course of which McGrath defended the mutineers. Some other deputies also viewed them sympathetically. According to McGrath, it was decided that if the defiant officers undertook 'to undo, so far as they can, the mischief created by their action…the incident will be regarded as closed'; there would be no victimisation. Other ministers denied that any such bargain had been struck.[201] The government agreed to hold an inquiry into the administration of the army and to consult McGrath on how the inquiry would be conducted.[202] This amounted to another partial capitulation by the government; the mutineers had already achieved some of their aims. They would soon achieve more.

Opportunism

After Cosgrave informed the Dáil of the decision to hold an inquiry, the rebel spokesmen sent him a second letter recognising that 'the Army just as the Police must be subject to the absolute control of the Civil authority'. They claimed that they would have secured their objectives if, as a result of their action, 'the Army situation is righted'.[203] O'Higgins declared that 'in the handling of very delicate situations, there must needs be opportunism', and that the incident was a 'minor calamity'. In a speech that was described as good-humoured, even jocose, Cosgrave too played down the earlier threat in light of the mutineers' new message.[204]

Johnson accused him of accepting the ultimatum and of failing to assert the authority of democratic government. He described the government as acting as if it were responsible to a party meeting rather than to the Dáil.[205] This was a fair comment; Cosgrave and his cabinet had backed down in face of internal party dissent and now treated the mutiny with far less seriousness than before. They wanted to secure a compromise that would end the crisis, so they abandoned their previous severity and made light of the initial challenge to their authority. On 14 March the government decided to allow the mutineers the opportunity to surrender and return weapons, ammunition and other property, in return for which they would be released on parole. O'Duffy was appointed inspector general of the defence forces—removing any uncertainty as to whether he had authority over the army council.[206]

Mulcahy and the army command were dissatisfied with this indulgence towards the IRAO, and also with the powers given to O'Duffy in military affairs. When Gearóid O'Sullivan, the adjutant general, learned that the mutineers were to hold a meeting in Devlin's public house on Parnell Street in Dublin, he concluded, not unreasonably, that they were still plotting against the government. He ignored the cabinet's recent decision that the mutineers should be treated leniently and he ordered that the building should be raided. Two lorries filled with troops arrived at the pub, where they found about forty men in conclave. Shots were fired, and an armoured car trained its machine gun on the building. McGrath rushed to the scene and contacted Cosgrave by telephone.[207] His role was supposedly that of mediator, but in practice he offered the mutineers his support; nonetheless, several of them were arrested. As a concession towards him, he was allowed to buy drinks for the prisoners.[208] One feature of the night's events was that Charles Byrne, Cosgrave's *aide-de-camp*, was among those arrested.[209] Even though O'Duffy was in Monaghan he was aware of the arrests, and it has been suggested that he may have chosen to stay away from Dublin on that night, or that he may even have orchestrated events in order to discredit the army council.[210]

The raid on Devlin's pub brought to an end any serious threat to the state from the IRAO, but it also undermined the government's attempt to achieve a compromise solution. The cabinet's response took many people by surprise. Its main concern was not that its authority had been challenged and that a mutiny had been overcome, but that the army's raid clashed with the government's revised policy of forgiveness. It took no further action against the mutineers, and those arrested in Parnell Street were released on parole. Instead, it punished the army commanders who had crushed the mutiny behind the backs of most members of the cabinet. Mulcahy and the army council were sacked or forced to resign.

Several ministers had been unhappy about the army, in particular about its 'factionalism', and they felt that because of its association with the IRB the army leadership would not be able to deal effectively with the mutineers. They exploited the crisis to dispose of a cabinet colleague and of officers whom they distrusted. Long before the crisis had erupted O'Higgins seems to have waged a vendetta against Mulcahy, and this personal dislike reinforced his general suspicion of the military.

For the closing stages of the crisis Cosgrave was ill, and he missed seven consecutive cabinet meetings that were held in a period of five days, from 18 to 22 March. All of these were chaired by O'Higgins. This provoked speculation that the president's illness might have been diplomatic, and that he might not have wished to confront the problem. It encouraged implausible theories—such as that Cosgrave, operating through McGrath, arranged for the ultimatum as a means of getting rid of O'Higgins (whom he disliked because of his masterful way; he also regarded Mulcahy as 'a pain in the neck').[211] Cosgrave had already chaired seven cabinet meetings dealing with the mutiny between 7 and 15

March, and important decisions (the initial firm response, O'Duffy's appointment to the army, subsequent leniency and the establishment of the committee of inquiry) were taken under his leadership. He retired to his bed only when the crisis seemed to be over; on 14 March *The Cork Examiner* had felt able to conclude 'all's well that ends well'.[212] He was unable to preside at his party's St Patrick's Day dinner, an event that he would probably have wished to attend.[213] No-one could have foreseen that the crisis would erupt once more with the raid on Devlin's pub.

The president's health problems were almost certainly genuine. He had been seriously ill for a month in early 1922; he would be absent again for another two months at the end of 1924, during which he recuperated in Nice; and in 1927 his doctor advised him to take a month away from work.[214] His punctilious conduct of business was interrupted by occasional bad health.

Despite his illness Cosgrave arranged an urgent meeting with Mulcahy and O'Duffy on 17 March.[215] On the following day the cabinet, now chaired by O'Higgins, approved instructions to the army that were based on a letter from Cosgrave to McGrath.[216] The Parnell Street raid took place that evening. It is highly probable that, in the absence of Cosgrave's calm and consensual influence, the ministers, chaired by O'Higgins, were harsher in their treatment of the military than would otherwise have been the case. In his memoir written a few years later, Seán Ó Murthuile, one of the dismissed generals, recalled that Cosgrave appreciated the army's difficulties to a greater extent than any of his civilian colleagues.[217] But O'Higgins seized and held the initiative.

Nevertheless, most of the important decisions taken during Cosgrave's absence were subject to his agreement; in particular, the generals would be dismissed only if he approved. He did. The cabinet recommended to him that Mulcahy should be asked to resign and that O'Duffy should be placed in complete control of the army. He endorsed these decisions when MacNeill and Blythe called to visit him.[218] His colleagues decided that the president should take over the Ministry of Defence, (once again, subject to his agreement), and that during his illness O'Higgins would act on his behalf. This plan was submitted to him, and with his approval, and also that of O'Higgins and MacNeill, a statement on the matter was amended before it was issued to the press. The reference to O'Higgins was removed;[219] it would seem that Cosgrave was determined to avoid creating an impression that O'Higgins had supplanted him. On 21 March he read in the newspapers about his vice-president's statement concerning the dismissal of the chief of staff, and he asked for details and reasons. O'Higgins replied, justifying the government's actions and explaining that the cabinet felt obliged to act swiftly.[220] Later, Cosgrave wrote to his colleagues expressing the wish that final major decisions should not be taken until he had been consulted, and this was then agreed.[221]

Only once was there a partial indication that the president's views did not prevail. He suggested an extension of time for the surrender of the mutineers and of stolen material; like other ministers, he was clearly anxious to placate the IRAO. The cabinet minutes record that this view was 'mentioned', that no extension could be given, but that there would be no discrimination against people who surrendered late if there were reasonable excuses for the delay.[222] Cosgrave was informed regularly of what happened, and he approved his colleagues' actions; there is little or no reason to believe that his illness was feigned. Having been absent from seven cabinet meetings he returned to take the chair on 24 March. He remained minister for Defence for the next eight months, and O'Duffy was soon relieved of his military responsibilities (Peadar MacMahon became army chief-of-staff in March 1924, overlapping with O'Duffy, who formally resigned his army role in February 1925).

McGrath believed that the government had not kept its word to him in his role as the mutineers' representative, and together with eight other deputies he deserted Cumann na nGaedheal. He retired from public life, to become a vastly wealthy businessman. The president did his best to heal the split in the party, but negotiations with the dissident TDs failed—after, it was claimed, 'six months of subterranean intrigues and obscure manoeuvres'.[223] When they resigned from the Dáil at the end of the year the government won seven of the nine contests in the ensuing 'mini-general election'. Sinn Féin gained the other two seats and increased its vote substantially.

A committee of inquiry examined aspects of the mutiny, although its terms of reference precluded investigation of the raid on Devlin's pub and its aftermath, and although the dismissed generals attended its meetings the mutineers refused to do so. Its report censured Mulcahy and both factions in the army, the IRB and the IRAO. Not surprisingly, in the ensuing Dáil debate O'Higgins played the leading role on the government side. As he put it, he took his place in the dock since he had, in a sense, prime responsibility for the dismissal of the army council.[224] He must have felt gratified at claiming credit for what he portrayed as a triumph of democracy. Mulcahy accused Cosgrave of remaining silent, first when the three army heads were swept away, then when his colleagues implied serious charges in the Dáil, and finally after he had been presented with the report of the Army Inquiry. The president replied that he had not the time, inclination or intention to read the evidence given before the inquiry.[225] More might have been expected.

In their handling of the army mutiny the civilians in the cabinet were described as having 'temporized, vacillated, dissimulated, and reneged as only politicians can'.[226] They also behaved unwisely in appearing to repudiate both the army and the IRB—bodies which had played a central role in establishing the democratic state that Cosgrave and his colleagues defended so vigorously. One consequence of the crisis was the departure of both Mulcahy and McGrath, two strong figures who were associated with the War of Independence and who were on the 'Collins' wing of Cumann na nGaedheal. This tilted Cosgrave's government away from Collins's legacy and towards its moderate or 'Redmondite' faction.[227] After the resignations Cosgrave and FitzGerald were the only surviving ministers who had fought in Easter Week. Mulcahy returned to the government three years later, in June 1927, but the crisis increased O'Higgins's influence. He has been described as having been a threat to 'the rather timid Cosgrave…ever eager to fill his leader's ill-fitting presidential shoes'.[228] But for the remaining three years of his life O'Higgins remained in second place, and apart from a brief interval in 1933–4 Cosgrave led his party for another two decades.

The mutiny and its aftermath caused or provoked change in the Irish leadership. It also had more far-reaching consequences. Despite the fact that the Dáil and the general public were often kept in the dark about the crisis and how it was handled, the mutiny actually consolidated democratic, civilian rule. This may have seemed an improbable outcome, given that the men who put down the mutiny were treated severely while those who actually threatened the state were handled in a remarkably indulgent manner; their only punishment was resignation from the army, which would probably have happened in any case. *The Irish Times* drew attention to the apparent conflict between the government's ends and its means, and it pronounced sternly that 'Mutiny has been condoned, and resignation has been the fate of those responsible persons who refused to condone it'.[229] The civilian triumph was secured by the suppression of the mutineers. It was confirmed, ironically, by the unfairly harsh treatment meted out to and accepted by Mulcahy and the senior army officers, who thereby disproved at least some of the allegations made against them. 'The real significance of 1924 was the mutiny that never was'.[230] Military commanders had justifiable grievances, but there was no *coup d'état*.

Following his resignation, McGrath's place in the cabinet was not given to Hogan, at that point an outstandingly able 'extern' minister, but to the new minister for Industry and Commerce, McGilligan, who was a more neutral figure. Cosgrave subsequently appointed as minister for Defence the relatively unknown Peter Hughes, who had no military or administrative experience. This was entirely his decision and the cabinet had not considered it before party members were informed. Mulcahy regarded the appointment as 'a minor tragedy'; it was deeply unpopular among elements in the party who supported the mutineers, and seventeen TDs signed a letter of protest.[231] It was seen as an attempt to downgrade the army's importance and it began 'a policy of calculated neglect of military affairs'.[232] When faced with opposition to his choice the president was unyielding. He was reported as replying that even if the appointment was not politically suitable, 'it is not in my view as essential to pay attention to that as it is to the efficient administration and military efficiency of the Ministry'.[233] At the end of 1924 the French consul speculated that Cosgrave's resignation was imminent, but Mulcahy had noted in late November that the president's attitude was 'not that of a man who was going to get out'.[234] Only a few days earlier the former Cork deputy Liam de Róiste reported the view that the government and the party would split if Cosgrave were to resign.[235] Both Cumann na nGaedheal and the government were weakened by the army crisis, but the president remained in charge.

THE BOUNDARY

The mutiny was a legacy of the civil war. It overlapped with 'unfinished business' from the treaty that preoccupied Cosgrave's government for its first three years. Article 12 of the agreement provided for a boundary commission that would make changes to the border between the two parts of Ireland. In the treaty negotiations the British had rejected the idea of holding plebiscites to re-draw the border; such measures might be appropriate to Continental Europe, where some frontiers were decided by the votes of the relevant populations, but they would not be tolerated within the United Kingdom. They would give the wrong result.

The article was intended to deal with the fact that from a nationalist standpoint Northern Ireland was a gerrymandered entity, whose border was created arbitrarily to satisfy the interests or demands of one community at the expense of the other; one-third of its population wished to belong to the Free State. It had been drawn up carelessly (or at least, vaguely), in contrast to the attention devoted to similar clauses in the recent European post-First World War treaties. In the context of the boundary commission, Thomas Jones, a British government adviser on Irish affairs and a central figure in the 1921 negotiations, observed that the treaty 'was not drafted as an Act of Parliament would be drafted'.[236] In particular, although Article 12 was designed to tackle the problem posed by the large, discontented minority in Northern Ireland, it allowed in theory for a transfer of territory in *both* directions. In 1921 the Irish delegates who negotiated the treaty, as well as the cabinet in Dublin, either failed to notice this fact or failed to perceive its importance. Nor did they try to include safeguards to ensure that 'the wishes of the inhabitants' could not easily be over-ruled by the subordinate 'economic and geographic conditions'. The Irish negotiators were encouraged to believe that substantial transfers of territory would ensue,[237] but this was not reflected in the wording of the treaty. In the Dáil debates on the agreement, Cosgrave had expressed the conviction that it provided

> an opportunity of capturing the Northern Unionists…and with a generous invitation to cultivate and recognise our national identity, and to help us in putting this country in its proper place, I believe that we would effect a united country in a way that was never done before. They are great citizens of this nation even though they differ from us…no one here [the Dáil] has suggested any better way of dealing with them than that laid down here.[238]

Originally, in January 1922, Collins and Northern Ireland's prime minister James Craig decided to ignore the article relating to the boundary commission and to 'agree on behalf of their respective Governments' how the border should be re-drawn.[239] This was an 'astonishingly vague' proposal,[240] and it could be seen as a lack of faith in the settlement that Collins had signed so recently. Nothing came of the plan, and instead he hoped for rapid results from the boundary commission. He wanted it to begin work in July 1922, but the outbreak of civil war wrecked any such hopes; when the Dublin government was unable to control its existing territory it could not realistically hope to acquire any more.

Linked with the boundary question was the provision in the Government of Ireland Act of 1920 (which had created the political entity of Northern Ireland) for the establishment of a 'Council of Ireland'. This body would consist of members from both Irish parliaments, and it would administer services such as railways and fisheries, 'with a view to the eventual establishment of a parliament for the whole of Ireland'.[241] In March 1922 Cosgrave took a hard line on this question and he wrote that all joint meetings of ministers should be held in Dublin; there could not be equality between the two governments; and the number of Belfast ministers should not exceed those from Dublin. Fionán Lynch, then minister for Education, wrote of the Northern government 'there are many ways in wh. we can hamper them without making it appear our actual policy'.[242]

But at the end of that year, as an indication of goodwill, Cosgrave offered to suspend the council for five years—provoking a British official to remark that if Collins were still alive such a gesture would never have been made without securing a substantial concession from the Ulster unionists.[243] Two years later Johnson queried the matter in the Dáil and claimed that the Free State government had no right to vary the provisions of the treaty in so far as they related to the Council of Ireland.[244] Cosgrave expressed privately his bewilderment at why such a favourable position had been abandoned; 'in agreeing to this have we not handed over to the British an authority which might have been the subject of a bargain which could have been more advantageous'. Conveniently, he chose to assign responsibility for suspending the Council of Ireland to all those who were members of the Dáil at that time.[245]

British politicians and governments were increasingly committed to protecting the interests of Ulster unionists, even though the frontiers of Northern Ireland were impossible to defend by the normal democratic standards of the age. From the time of Bonar Law's brief premiership in 1922–3, Britain's aim was to preserve the *status quo* in Ireland. Cosgrave was warned that British public opinion and the press supported Craig—who was playing his cards well.[246] The boundary became frozen over time, Craig's special police force, known as the B Specials, intimidated nationalists; the county councils of Fermanagh and Tyrone, which nationalists controlled, were suspended; PR was abolished at local government level; constituencies were gerrymandered; and the frontier was reinforced by customs posts established by the Free State. In January 1923, in his role as minister for Finance, Cosgrave had proposed this last measure—which Craig must have enjoyed describing as partitionist.[247]

The Irish and British governments made it clear that force would not be used to compel Northern Ireland to relinquish territory, while Craig was equally explicit that he would fight to maintain the area the unionists had obtained in 1920; 'what we have, we hold'. Cosgrave contrasted the 40–45,000 strong B Special police force in the North with the less than 7,000 civic guards in the Free State.[248]

The governor-general, Tim Healy, urged the Irish cabinet to adopt a stiff and unbending attitude; 'Look at Craig. He is like a piece of iron. He never yields'.[249] The Cumann na nGaedheal ministers did not follow Belfast's example, but their position was considerably weaker than Craig's. The wishes of the population in Northern Ireland counted for little or nothing in comparison with the political balance of power in Westminster, which now favoured the unionists. The transfer of extensive areas to the Free State would provoke more opposition in Britain than would minor adjustments to the border.[250]

Cosgrave told Lionel Curtis, with whom he enjoyed good relations and who was often sympathetic to the Free State, that his government had ended its press campaign on the question of the boundary. This action had disquieted many of his followers—particularly in the army.[251] On the other hand, he remarked ruefully that the Northern government was unbending; 'the pinpricks were all on one side and the forbearance all on the other'.[252] He protested bitterly against a 'campaign of hate against the Free State…a very deliberate and very malignant conspiracy' to create ill-feeling between Britain and Ireland.[253]

Like Collins, he preferred to settle the question privately—a policy that co-existed with public demands that Article 12 should be implemented. By the time that he was able to begin this process, the Free State's position was at best unpromising. Initially, however, there had been greater optimism. In October 1922 Cosgrave's government had established a North-East Boundary Bureau headed by Kevin O'Shiel, a Tyrone lawyer who had served as a judge in the Dáil courts and had been an adviser to Collins. This body prepared extensive documentation, and in June 1923 O'Shiel suggested as a minimum claim, beyond which the Free State could not retreat, the transfer to the Free State of all Northern Ireland except Antrim, the extreme eastern portion of Tyrone bordering on Lough Neagh, the eastern half of Derry, North Armagh and North Down.[254]

In a similar vein, Cosgrave concluded a memorandum on the boundary question on a hopeful, even aggressive note. Discrimination against Northern Catholics should come to an end, constituency gerrymandering should be undone and PR should be retained for ten years. The customs barrier should be maintained, and the boundary should be rectified so as to make it a more suitable line:

> we get a fairer deal for our people in the North. We cut away entirely from England. We have full control in the major part of the country and North-East is left without its reserves and may possibly look more to us than across.[255]

He sought information on the condition of Northern nationalists, 'specific in character and capable of substantial evidence'.[256] Later, in 1925, he provided money to assist the nationalists in the Northern Irish general election; satisfactory results would strengthen the case for an extensive transfer of territory to the Free State.[257]

But a gloomy forecast from another source proved to be remarkably accurate. The commission would not seriously weaken Craig's position, and it might recommend an exchange of territories by which Northern Ireland received the Protestant areas of Donegal in exchange for 'a few hungry townlands in the mountains of Tyrone'. The Free State might be better off with the existing border, and nationalists would be far safer if they could get effective guarantees of their rights and liberties in Northern Ireland.[258]

Cosgrave requested the British government to initiate the process of establishing the commission, and he nominated Eoin MacNeill as the Free State representative. This was an unfortunate decision. As a politician MacNeill might have seemed unsuited to a legal or judicial body; as a cabinet minister he would necessarily be 'part-time'; and his approach to his new task was fatalistic. Referring to his age (he was born thirteen years before Cosgrave, and was by far the oldest member of the cabinet) he quoted from *Richard II*, 'the ripest fruit first falls'.[259] He saw himself as a sacrificial victim. O'Higgins and O'Shiel were both uneasy at MacNeill's appointment, and O'Shiel had already proposed MacNeill's brother James, who was then the Irish high commissioner in London.[260] He would probably have been a much better choice.

The British continued to procrastinate, and by the time a conference took place in London in February 1924 the short-lived first Labour government under Ramsay MacDonald had taken office. Despite Irish hopes, it was no more favourably disposed towards the Free State than its Conservative predecessor had been. It proposed a delay of a year in establishing the boundary commission, during which the Council of Ireland could be activated. But MacDonald's administration realised that Cosgrave was keeping strictly to his commitments, and Thomas Jones feared that if the British were to violate the treaty 'a motion will be put through the Dail abolishing the Governor-General and the Oath, thus virtually setting up a Republic'. Shortly afterwards he wrote of the concern that growing opposition to the Irish government might rally round the failure to implement Article 12.[261]

Cosgrave rejected the British proposals, which he saw as inferior to the terms of the 1920 Government of Ireland Act.[262] He wrote, in vain, advocating a census to determine the wishes of the inhabitants of the disputed border areas.[263] This was even less likely to be conceded now than during the treaty negotiations three years earlier. Craig proved adamant, and the attempts to resolve the question by conference broke down. He invited Cosgrave to discuss the matter, provided that the Free State gave up its right to a boundary commission under the treaty, and naturally such an idea was rejected.[264] MacDonald then began to implement Article 12 and Craig refused to nominate a commissioner, with the result that both the Dublin and London parliaments passed legislation enabling the British to appoint a Northern representative.

O'Higgins warned Cosgrave that any possible ambiguities in the treaty should be cleared up before the commission met; otherwise they would be left to the decision of the British-appointed chairman. Hugh Kennedy, the attorney-general, disagreed, and he felt that the Free State could not now admit to an ambiguity it had hitherto denied.[265] This seemed reasonable. At a meeting in August 1924 with the British colonial secretary, J.H. Thomas, Cosgrave argued against any further delay in establishing the boundary commission and he gave a serious warning: an Irish government might come to power that would denounce the treaty.[266] Matters transpired as O'Higgins had warned.

The chairman appointed by the British government was a South African judge, Richard Feetham, a man who had strong imperial beliefs and connections, who had been nominated by Lionel Curtis and who was influenced by him. (After Feetham was appointed Curtis sent him a telegram: 'England expects'.[267] England would not be disappointed.) When the two men met, Cosgrave told Feetham that the Free State had never admitted the possibility of losing any of its territory; the commission's function was to ascertain the wishes of the people within Northern Ireland and determine the boundary accordingly.[268] Feetham had other ideas. His approach was narrowly legalistic, and he was described as refusing 'to look outside the four corners of the written instrument'.[269] Despite this legalism he felt able to ignore one awkward fact: throughout the treaty the unity of Ireland was acknowledged in principle.[270]

His overriding concern was with the continuing viability of Northern Ireland, and not with the large, discontented minority that provided the reason for the commission's existence. No wholesale revision of the map was to be contemplated, and the political circumstances in 1921 that had led to the establishment of a boundary commission were deemed irrelevant to the conditions of 1924–5. He believed that Northern Ireland 'must still be recognisable as the same provincial entity' that had come into existence in 1920.[271]

According to one authority, 'in effect, Feetham claimed that the Commission had been handed a blank cheque, allowing it to do pretty much as it pleased'.[272] He did precisely what Cosgrave had feared: 'Nationalists in Tyrone, Fermanagh, Derry, Armagh are only to be used as filling-in stuff to enable those against Irish unity to maintain a Parliament'.[273] This was a far cry from the naïve expectations of Griffith and Collins during the treaty negotiations that the frontier would be re-drawn to their satisfaction. But the Free State government was a victim as much of its own self-deception as of British duplicity.[274]

As early as its preliminary tour in December 1924 the commission devoted all its attention to border areas rather than to the heartland of Fermanagh and Tyrone; nationalists foresaw, correctly, that only minor adjustments to the frontier could be expected. MacNeill acquiesced weakly. He was an honourable and guileless man who had many other issues on his mind; he seemed 'to have combined integrity with incompetence'.[275] He kept rigidly to the principle of confidentiality and he did not inform his cabinet colleagues of developments as the commission carried out its work. His northern counterpart was more flexible. Craig and his ministers assured their followers that they would be satisfied with the commission's report, while (with good reason) Cosgrave and the Dublin government gave no comparable expression of confidence.[276] They did, however, make plans for implementing the administration of transferred territories.[277]

The settlement

On 7 November 1925 the *Morning Post*, a Conservative newspaper, published what it claimed to be the commission's decision, and the text was illustrated by maps. The report was broadly accurate. Modest amounts of territory were to be transferred in both directions, and while the Free State would gain slightly in terms of area and population, richer land would be awarded to Northern Ireland. According to one complaint, the Free State would receive mountainous countryside, uneconomic holdings, 'the best grouse-shooting in Ireland and very little else'.[278] In particular, the nationalist town of Newry would remain in Northern Ireland. The partisan nature of the award of territory is indicated by the fact that 'Protestants transferred to Northern Ireland were to bring half as many Catholics with them, whereas the Catholics going the other way would bring only one-tenth of their number of Protestants'.[279]

Cosgrave, O'Higgins and Blythe met Cumann na nGaedheal members and a delegation from East Donegal. The president informed the Dáil that the cabinet believed the commission had no authority to transfer territory from the Free State to Northern Ireland. The treaty had established an all-Ireland Free State from which Northern Ireland might secede. Until the commission reported, the Dublin government's powers over Northern Ireland were suspended, but they would come 'into instant operation in any area assigned to the Free State by the Commission. There is no corresponding arrangement whereby the powers of the Government of Northern Ireland are in a state of suspension over any Free State territory'. He argued that the *Morning Post* forecast fulfilled none of the conditions laid down in the treaty, and he complained that

> a most scandalous campaign of intimidation and misrepresenta-
> tion has been waged. A most indecent and flagrant violation of
> judicial procedure has been indulged in…Important personages
> in public life, both in Great Britain and in the Six Counties,
> assisted in the endeavour to influence the Court.[280]

This was for public consumption; in private Cosgrave wanted to bury the commission's report.[281] The prospect of losing southern territory to the North, and the fear of political instability that would result from such a loss, 'weighed more heavily than the failure of the Boundary Commission to meet the Nationalist demand for self-determination'.[282]

MacNeill spoke with Cosgrave, and shortly afterwards he resigned from the commission and from the cabinet; he was succeeded as minister for Education by another History professor in UCD, John Marcus O'Sullivan. Later, he described Feetham's attitude as follows: the combination of the Government of Ireland Act of 1920 and the time that had elapsed since Ireland was divided 'had created a *status quo* which should only be departed from when every element and every factor would compel us to depart from it'. No award could be made that would significantly weaken or undermine Northern Ireland; the Government of Ireland Act was to condition the implementation of the treaty, and not *vice-versa*. He admitted that a better strategist would not have allowed himself to be outmanoeuvred as he had been.[283] MacNeill had remained a member of the commission knowing that Feetham's views were close to those of Craig, and that he would be out-voted by two to one.

The Labour leader Thomas Johnson criticised the government's handling of the matter, claiming that it had placed the Free State in a humiliating position. The independent deputy Bryan Cooper suggested that the polished steel of MacNeill's mind was no match for the cudgel play of his fellow-commissioners.[284]

Cosgrave met the British prime minister, Stanley Baldwin, and some of his cabinet colleagues in London on 26 November. He was reported as having talked for forty minutes before Baldwin and others had their say. He claimed that the intention of Article 12 of the treaty had not been carried out, and he made it clear that he did not want the commission to issue its report. If the new frontier were to be accepted it would be better if the article had never existed. The Irish would prefer if any suggestions for a resolution of the border were to be made by the British. Baldwin pointed out that the Free State would have expected the commission's report to be implemented if it had been favourable, and Cosgrave agreed that this was true. He also suggested that two or three of his ministers might confer with members of the British cabinet.[285] He deplored MacNeill's conduct, yet he must have been aware that in appointing to the commission someone so unsuitable to the task his own judgment was at fault.

He also met Craig, who offered only minimal concessions—such as releasing a few prisoners who had already served almost half their sentences—and who subsequently made it clear to British ministers that Northern Ireland would not sacrifice territory to save Cosgrave's face.[286] He and Craig agreed that they both preferred 'the old line'.[287] Many years later, Wilfred Spender, the head of the Northern Irish civil service, claimed that Cosgrave broke down and burst into tears during his meeting with Craig, but this lacks all plausibility.[288]

The president rejoined his cabinet colleagues, who were unanimous in rejecting the proposals made by the British. Their meeting, which had three other minor items on the agenda, lasted 4¼ hours.[289] As Cosgrave had already suggested to Baldwin, an Irish delegation went to London shortly afterwards, and O'Higgins met Baldwin and Craig. He sought an improvement in the conditions of nationalists in Northern Ireland, referred to a feeling that 'we have been tricked again', and warned that the Irish government might fall if the border were re-drawn according to the boundary commission report.[290] In what Jones described as a brilliant and eloquent statement of the Free State case, O'Higgins sought 'a substantial improvement in the position of the Nationalists in Ulster, an emancipation of the minority'. But his concerns for the Northern nationalists lay partly in the likely impact on the Free State of doing nothing to improve their position; without such an improvement, they would 'raise an outcry which would find an echo in every nationalist breast in the twenty six counties'.[291] He also proposed to Craig that the Free State might be relieved of its obligations to pay a share of the British Empire's debt, as laid down by Article 5 of the treaty.[292]

Craig wished to help the Free State government avoid embarrassment, but he remained determined that any concessions would be made by British taxpayers rather than by Ulster unionists. He saw the Council of Ireland as a potential threat and he suggested that its powers should be transferred to the northern government.[293]

Cosgrave returned to London on 1 December, and he, O'Higgins and John O'Byrne, the attorney-general, resumed negotiations with Baldwin and his ministers. They stressed the fragility of their position, and they were able to present themselves as the only barrier between Britain and the 'wild Irish'.[294] They sought concessions in return for their acceptance of the 1920 border. The president warned that he had received 'something in the nature of an Ultimatum' from his backbench TDs and that there was opposition within his party to any agreement modifying Article 12.[295] He declared that, speaking as an Irishman rather than as a minister, he disliked an arrangement involving a transfer of territory whereby the position of the Catholic minority in the North would be still further weakened.[296] He admitted that he had been forced to abandon his claims against the Belfast government, 'because he saw that it was impossible to obtain their acceptance…He was satisfied that Sir James Craig could not at the present time "deliver the goods"'.[297]

The Irish team was unable to win any significant improvement in the conditions of northern nationalists, so it turned to its second preference. It concentrated on securing benefits for the Free State, and Cosgrave played a leading role in the quest for financial concessions. Using a memorandum written the previous day by the secretary of the department of Finance, Joseph Brennan, he gave an outline of Irish financial and economic problems.[298]

Winston Churchill, now Chancellor of the Exchequer, speculated that Ireland's share of imperial debt might amount to annual payments of £8.25 million for the next 60 years. Cosgrave suggested a lower figure of under £6 million, but he asked how the Irish government could pay even this sum. He raised another possible British concession: that the oath to the king should be made optional. This idea was probably no more than a gambit. It would allow the 48 republican deputies to enter the Dáil, it would weaken the Free State's stability, and it would 'make the republicans a political entity which they were not at present'.[299] Neither side pursued it, and the discussion remained concentrated on financial matters. O'Higgins argued that the British should 'forego phantom millions of money that they could never hope to obtain'.[300] Cosgrave pointed out that no-one had ever expected the Free State would have to pay higher taxes and receive fewer advantages than when it was still part of the

United Kingdom; 'if the Treaty had never been signed, Ireland would have been a liability and not an asset to England'.[301]

Churchill persuaded the British cabinet to abandon Article 5 in return for the Free State's commitment to pay compensation for malicious damages committed in Ireland since January 1919. This was estimated to be in the region of £5 million. The Irish would also make further but moderate transfers. Brennan was critical of what he saw as Cosgrave's readiness to concede superfluous and unwarranted payments,[302] but Michael MacWhite, the Irish representative in Geneva, referred to 'the hell of a fight' that was needed to escape from obligations under Article 5.[303] The Free State would relinquish to the Belfast government the Council of Ireland's powers relating to Northern Ireland, and the position of republican prisoners in Northern Ireland would be reviewed.

At their final meeting, on 3 December, Cosgrave said to Craig 'one of us no doubt will hear from the other?'[304] He hoped, in vain, that while Craig could announce he had given nothing away, 'it was clearly understood between them that every effort would be made to promote goodwill between North and South'.[305] Craig was subsequently invited to Dublin but he never made the journey. Cosgrave wrote to him that many people in the Free State, including the professions and the business classes, saw the agreement reached in the aftermath of the boundary commission report as 'the best contribution so far made by its signatories and their Governments'.[306] Whatever might have been the views of the professional and business classes south of the border, northern nationalists felt betrayed.[307]

Baldwin was amused when after their meeting in Chequers, his official country house, one of the Irish leaders said to him 'We had better travel separately, Prime Minister. To be seen arriving in London together would not be good for either of us'.[308] It is unlikely that Craig was the Irish leader in question.

In the ensuing Dáil debate, Cosgrave claimed that the government had done all it could to ensure a satisfactory report by the commission, but when it seemed that the result would be unfavourable it had acted to remedy the situation. Publication of the decision would have been a national calamity. He referred to the spirit of co-operation and friendship that had characterised the recent negotiations ('in itself a form of union') and claimed that this would

> justify our decision to put this barren question of the Boundary behind us once and for all, and turn our faces towards new methods and new developments. This is surely a course more in harmony with the intentions of the Treaty than the perpetuation

> of a fruitless wrangle as to where a boundary between Irishmen is
> to be drawn.

He claimed that the only real security for minorities was the goodwill and neighbourly feeling of the people among whom they live. 'In abandoning the Council of Ireland, the Free State will lose nothing. It will gain goodwill.' He argued that the agreement removed with one sweep the main outstanding sources of dispute between Ireland and Britain. 'It stabilises our financial position. It secures that we are deprived of none of our citizens'.[309] Four years after the treaty a 'southern' identity had been consolidated. Hogan went further; he saw the result as 'eminently satisfactory' for the Free State and claimed that the agreement improved the original treaty.[310]

Others disagreed. Dáil deputies complained that northern nationalists were being thrown to the wolves and that the government was living in a fool's paradise. The settlement was dismissed as a great victory for innocence and babyish trust. Johnson lamented the abandonment of the Council of Ireland and claimed that the agreement betrayed the intentions of the Irish negotiators who had signed the treaty.[311] Cosgrave's earlier complaints that Craig would not yield an inch, and that northern nationalists suffered from discrimination, were now thrown against him. The government made no defence against the claim that it had not attempted to secure concessions in the matter of the oath—and thereby to secure unity in the Free State. Perhaps Cosgrave had forgotten, or had chosen to forget, his brief reference to the possibility of making the oath optional and not obligatory. Some Cumann na nGaedheal deputies left the party in protest—the second such exodus in less than two years, following the example given by earlier defectors in the aftermath of the army mutiny.

The settlement had the advantage that Cosgrave's government continued to rule a homogenous population, without significant minorities—unlike most of the new European political entities (and Northern Ireland in particular). It was reduced to hoping that Ulster unionists would eventually change their minds, and to repeating the arguments that the president had outlined some time earlier: ultimate unity might come eventually

> if we have good government down here, but good government is
> a lot to ask from a relatively poor country & from a people so
> long divorced from any respect for order.[312]

Time might bring about unification, as it had done in Australia, Canada and South Africa.[313] At different stages in his career Cosgrave made it clear that he would sacrifice the prospect of a 26-county republic in favour of a united Ireland with fewer powers.[314] But he abandoned any fantasies of an early reunification.

Many Irish nationalists who deplored partition felt able to cherish their grievance while at the same time finding the independent state a more comfortable place without the presence of a million Ulster unionists.

There was nothing new or surprising in the government's concentration on the Free State and its interests. Redmond had accepted partition in 1914, and in practice so did the Easter rebels two years later; they planned to launch an insurrection only in the three southern provinces, and to leave Ulster in peace. Their proclamation claimed 'the allegiance of every Irishman and Irishwoman', but they knew that any attempt to involve the north in their rebellion would have resulted in sectarian violence of the sort they were most anxious to avoid. Even for them, as also for their successors in the war of 1919–21, Ulster was 'different'.[315] During the treaty negotiations de Valera subordinated national unity to southern sovereignty. Cosgrave and his ministers followed what was then a well-established tradition.

NEW OPPONENTS

The agreement confirming the border made surprisingly little impact on an electorate whose concerns were confined almost entirely to the Free State, and it removed many potential difficulties. It was nonetheless a humiliation. The treaty had failed to provide the gains that had been widely expected, and Cumann na nGaedheal was accused of endorsing partition. De Valera knew that if his party had been in the Dáil it might have combined with other groups to defeat the measure and bring down the government; Sinn Féin's abstentionist policy was becoming ever more self-destructive. Austin Stack wrote to him saying that, despite the oath, on balance he was inclined to enter the 'so-called Dáil' if the 47 Sinn Féin votes could ensure the rejection of the agreement.[316]

Slowly, de Valera began easing his way out of the grip of obscurantist diehards whose policies led to a dead-end. He moved from authoritarianism to ambiguity, and then to democracy.[317] In 1926 he founded a new party, Fianna Fáil, which showed signs of being more flexible on the question of abstention and which began to pose a more serious threat to Cumann na nGaedheal. But de Valera still insisted on the removal of the oath of fidelity to the king, and Cosgrave refused to budge on the question. Each side was fearful of making a concession that would seem to compromise the stand it had taken in 1922.[318]

The government won fifteen of the twenty-one seats in by-elections held during the lifetime of the fourth Dáil (nine of them caused by resignations after the army mutiny), but its unimpressive performance in the two final contests should have caused alarm. Like other members of his party, and like other heads of government in later decades, Cosgrave was suspicious of PR. He even told Craig that he would 'like it out of the way'.[319] In particular he suggested that it was inappropriate to hold by-elections under PR, because the results disturbed the representation that had been established at general elections. This was a disconcerting stance for someone so committed to democracy, and it may have reflected an incumbent's exasperation with the need for frequent by-election campaigns. As an alternative he urged co-option of a member belonging to the outgoing TD's party. There was strong opposition to this idea, however, and it was abandoned.[320]

Morale among government supporters was low. In early 1927 Cosgrave was warned that in Longford Cumann na nGaedheal and the Farmers' party were very slack in terms of political activity, while the republican party 'holds meetings all over the County, and seems to be full of money'. He agreed that 'Anti-Treaty people are the most industrious'.[321] Apart from lingering disappointment at the result of the boundary commission, further problems lay ahead. The adverse balance of trade had worsened during the previous three years, with a particularly sharp fall in exports of cattle and alcoholic products.[322] Cosgrave had reason to be worried about his party's prospects at the next general election.

Nonetheless, the government persisted in antagonising large sections of Irish public opinion, and even as the election drew near it continued, unwisely, to appeal to voters' heads and not to their hearts. This was in contrast to its opportune enactment of Hogan's Land Bill immediately before the 1923 election. In 1927 the budget was not framed to win over voters.[323] Already in 1924 O'Higgins had introduced a moderate Intoxicating Liquor Bill, describing it as 'as healthy a tonic as one could devise for the nation at present' (but Healy commented privately that it would not add to the government's popularity).[324] His act disallowed judicial discretion, with the consequence that local TDs could not be tempted to corrupt district justices if they were forced to be incorruptible.[325]

With unworldly timing O'Higgins introduced a second such bill in February 1927, only months before the election was due to be held. This measure would reduce the number of public houses and also their opening times. In particular, pubs would be obliged to close for at least one hour (the 'holy hour') in the middle of the day. There was scope for reform; the Free State had one public house per 230 people, while in Scotland the corresponding figure was one per 695. As an example of one abuse among many, in the village of Blacklion in Co. Cavan eight of the twenty houses were licensed premises.[326] But the bill provoked widespread opposition and resentment, particularly among members of Cumann na nGaedheal. *The Irish Statesman* remarked that there was 'something exhilarating about the resolute indifference of Ministers to the interests which they antagonize even while a general election is in sight. Their attitude is one of resolute moral courage'.[327] A month later, Bryan Cooper joked about O'Higgins that 'if he woke up some morning and found that he was popular he would examine his conscience'.[328] His remark could be applied to the government as a whole; it took support for granted and it seemed to disparage the arts of persuasion.

The Clonakilty Licensed Vintners association wrote to Cosgrave protesting vigorously against the planned legislation,

> whereby our property is proposed to be confiscated and our legal rights grievously infringed. We wish to point out that our association is composed of very prominent members of the Cuman na Gaedhal and these members will to utmost of their ability oppose every effort of the Government to impose this confiscatory legislation on the people. That we instruct our local T.Ds. to oppose this bill in the most resolute manner and that we shall watch their voting in the Dail with a view to the power that we control in coming Elections.[329]

The licensed vintners of Clonakilty would have had no respect for Burke's theory of representation, and other lobbyists shared their determination to treat the government and their local deputies as agents or servants. Cosgrave felt obliged to meet a deputation from licensed vintners in his own constituency.[330] To the dismay of the Church of Ireland Temperance Society, the cabinet yielded to pressure and modified the bill;[331] there were limits beyond which it would not adhere rigidly to principle. Nonetheless there was a significant drop in the retail value of alcohol consumed in the Free State—from £20.2 million in 1925 to £12.7 million in 1932.[332]

The government had done much of which it could be proud. A Cumann na nGaedheal election advertisement claimed that the agricultural grant had been doubled and that the Free State had built the largest and most up-to-date sugar factory in Europe.[333] At the party's 1927 ard-fheis, Cosgrave outlined the government's aims and record. Prominent among them were 'the restoration of order and the breaking of a reign of terror'. These goals had been achieved, and 'the conditions of 1922–1923 seem to us now like a bad dream'. Parliamentary and executive institutions were organised. As well as the doubling of the agricultural grant, land was redistributed; tariffs were introduced; work had begun on the Shannon hydro-electric scheme; income tax was cut by half in five years; the duties on tea, cocoa and coffee were abolished; and the duty on sugar was reduced by almost two-thirds, rendering 'the poor man's breakfast table almost entirely tax free'. A unified educational structure replaced 'a scattered heap of systems'. Education, external and financial policies had been designed to inculcate self-reliance.[334] Cosgrave pointed out that in four years the Dáil had passed 183 public and 9 private acts. Thomas Johnson even suggested that 50 years in the future people writing histories would look back at the period and say 'what a great time it was to have lived in'.[335]

Despite economic problems, a growing trade imbalance and dissatisfaction within Cumann na nGaedheal, ministers could take comfort from the republicans' continuing abstention from the Dáil. Mulcahy expected the party to secure a clear majority in the 1927 election but feared that the PR system might limit its gains. *The Irish Times* estimated that with a substantial poll the government might actually increase its representation.[336] (In the event, the proportion of the electorate that voted rose from 59% to 66%.[337]) In his reading of the situation ahead of the election, the French consul Alfred Blanche believed that the government deserved to be swept away, but he forecast that instead it would lose only a few seats and otherwise maintain its present position.[338] Many other observers felt that Cosgrave and his government could face the election with some confidence.

DÁIL EIREANN.

TIGH LAIGHEAN,
BAILE ATHA CLIATH.
10adh Meadhon Fhoghmhair, 1923.

Chun ...... *Liam T Mac Cosgair* ......

Teachta do toghadh do Dháilcheanntar...... *Chontae* ......
Cheathaḋlach - Cill Choinnigh ......

Cuireadh t'ainm chugham mar dhuine de sna baill do toghadh
do Dháilcheanntar...... *Chontae* ......
Cheathaḋlach - Cill Choinnigh ......
chun fónamh sa Dáil do gairmeadh le Furógra dar dháta an 9adh
lá de Lughnasa, 1923; chun teacht le chéile i mBaile Atha Cliath
ar 3 p.m. ar an 19adh lá de Mheadhon Fhoghmhair, 1923.

Do réir Bhuan-Ordú Uimh. 1 de Bhuan-Orduithe Dháil Eireann,
tá orm a chur in úil duit nach foláir duit bheith i láthair im' oifig
i dTigh Laighean, Sráid Chill Dara, Baile Atha Cliath, Dé
Luain an 17adh, no Dé Máirt an 18adh Meadhon Fhoghmhair,
idir 11 a.m. agus 4 p.m., no Dé Céadaoin an 19adh Meadhon
Fhoghmhair idir 11 a.m. agus 2 p.m., chun forálacha Airtiogail 17
den Bhunreacht a chólíona.

LEINSTER HOUSE,
DUBLIN,
10th September, 1923.

To ...... *Liam Thomas Cosgrave* ......
Deputy elected for the...... *County* ......Constituency of
Carlow - Kilkenny

Your name has been returned to me as that of one of the
members elected for the...... *County* ......
Constituency of...... *Carlow - Kilkenny*...to serve in the
Dáil which has been summoned by Proclamation dated the 9th
August, 1923, to meet in Dublin, at 3 p.m., on the 19th September,
1923.

Pursuant to Standing Order No. 1 of the Standing Orders
of Dáil Eireann, I have to notify you that your attendance is
required at my office at Leinster House, Kildare Street, Dublin,
on Monday the 17th, or Tuesday the 18th September, between the
hours of 11 a.m. and 4 p.m., or on Wednesday the 19th September,
between the hours of 11 a.m. and 2 p.m., for the purpose of
complying with the provisions of Article 17 of the Constitution.

Colm O Murchadha

Cléireach na Dála.

Confirmation of Cosgrave's election for the constituency of Carlow-
Kilkenny in the August 1923 general election.

'The more we are together the merrier we'll be', anti-treaty cartoon by Grace Gifford Plunkett, showing Cosgrave drinking champagne with King George V and (?) Stanley Baldwin.

"THE MORE WE ARE TO-GET THE MERRIEF

'LL BE"

DO YOU REALISE THAT 'THE IRISH FREE STATE GOVERNMENT' IN FOURTEEN MONTHS HAVE MURDERED EXECUTED, TORTURED AND IMPRISONED MORE IRISHMEN THAN THE BRITISH DID IN ALL THE YEARS OF THEIR TERROR ?

IT IS SAID by Free State Ministers that we want to bring the English back.   THIS IS A LIE.

BUT if the BRITISH GOVERNMENT is going on fighting us and destroying us as she has been doing since June 28th, 1922, we prefer that she should USE ENGLISH TROOPS, and not our own misguided creatures.

THE FREE STATE MINISTERS are nothing but aggrandised R.I.C. back again amongst us.

Vote Against Everyone of Them.

VOTE AGAINST EVERYONE WHO SUPPORTS THEM.

By your return to your REPUBLICAN ALLEGIANCE You can RE-ESTABLISH UNITY assuring us PEACE and provide the basis upon which we may together build a prosperous and happy national life.

WE SHALL ALL SHARE IN WHAT SHALL BE THE FINAL VICTORY OVER ENGLAND.

What prospect for such happening is there while you have a Government which does all the British Government orders ?

COME BACK TO US: VOTE FOR THE REPUBLIC AND THE REPUBLICAN CANDIDATES.

Vote for National Peace & Prosperity

Patsy Pathrick on Physiognomy

Recorded by SEAN ETCHINGHAM, T.D.

"WHO was the lad was in here to-day?" asked Terry.

"A Physiognomist," replied Patsy. He tould me he's workin' for several newspapers. He'd a lot o' thim picture papers showin' suicides, an' murderers

n' prize bulls an' Shetland ponies side by side with divorced women, an' girls ith a taste in this that an' th'other. He uld me he'd sum up the votin' at the ext election be a study o' the physiognomy o' the ould register. He talked iv ristotle an' all that wonderful genius had ritten on the countenance, an' o' aveter the Swiss pastor. Laveter could ll most everything o' the mind an' anners iv a man be a study o' the physognomy. The nose he tould me was the ing. He spoke o' De Valera, an'——"

"What did he say?" interrupted Terry.

"I know what he'd say to *your* nose,"

apped Patsy. "He needn't be a physognomist to say ye were inquisitive. He edn't be a new Colonial to swear it. He id De Valera's nose showed him to be a man who would distinguish himself in ovements requirin' mental power an' gression. It was a nose that showed ct an' a penetratin' quick cast o' brain. denoted honesty, truth and sincerity. wasn't a nose for a political party leader, was the nose for a National leader. ken with the whole face it denoted a big an—a great man an' a dangerous man the enemies iv his country. Arthur

Griffith's physiognomy, he said, showed self-assertion, an' an autocratic nature. All the newspaper men in England were told to concentrate on Griffith's jaw. They did. It got poor Arthur. They wrote 'bout his massive cast steel jaw, an' when they noticed he took to 'settin' it in front o' shop windows an' public lookin' glasses—"

"They wrote the same about Beckett's jaw," said Terry.

"They did," went on Patsy, "an' Carpentier caught him a crack on it, an' it proved to be glass. One o' the lads in the Dail tould me that poor Griffith kept showin' his jaw to the Deputies. He put it out like the leaf iv a table, an' they all grinned at the propaganda iv' the newspaper citizens iv the Empire. 'Heads up, an' jaws set,' is the way to enter the Empire. Laveter says a well-accentuated jawbone shows courage—good platform

courage. I don't doubt it. I asked him about Mick Collins——"

"Is Mick a great man?" asked Terry.

"He's head o' the Provisional Government," yelled Patsy. "Mick's physiognomy, the lad tould me, showed impulse; he'd be energetic, impatient, an' imitative. He has considerable force an' determination, an' would undertake the managin' department iv he could. He'd organise in every detail, an' like a good county surveyor know as much 'bout the bye roads as the main thoroughfares. Only be this can ye control all the traffic. I was askin' him 'bout some o' the other lads. He says Kevin O'Higgins shows vanity, affectation, an' pretension. Willie Cosgrave shows wit. The best sign o' this is for one eyebrow to be set higher than th' other. He has the taperin' jawbone in combination with the broad forehead. Like Griffith he'd be an unscrupulous politician. I don't mind that, for every mother's child in Ireland knows the ins an' outs o' the politics o' the Dublin Corporation. Ye needn't be a physiognomist to know that."

"I asked the fellow iv he knew any o' the Republicans, an' he said he didn't, 'cept Mellowes. 'I'm really a Free State physiognomist,' says he, 'the Free State is a sentimental title,' says he, 'but it will get a lot o' recruits.' 'That Little

General,' says he, 'ill never make a Colonial. He's an iron face, and doesn't want to cultivate a jaw. Ye'd never get him with a sentimental substance. He'd tell ye 'twas an earthly hell yer Free State, an' he'd call it the Fettered State. An' By the Dog he'd be right,' says he. 'I'd call the face o' Mellowes a merciless face, merciless to an enemy,' says he. I asked him 'bout the women."

"What did he say?" interrupted Terry.

"I've tould ye 'bout yer nose," snapped Patsy. "I spoke to him 'bout the women, an' Be Lloyd George's Dog iv he didn't start talkin' o' Darrel Figgis an' the necessity o' havin' the face shaved to practice physiognomy. He said Darrel was a debater. When I asked him what sort iv a constitution he'd draft the most he could say was that it 'd be a Figgis Constitution, an' that it 'd be fairly 'ithin the four corners o' the articles iv agreement. 'Bout the women, he said he hadn't attended any o' the meetin's o' the new women—the Colonial Cailini as yet, but that he heard they were all out 'agen equality o' franchise."

"Ye could read women's faces," said Terry.

"An' women's necks as well," continued Patsy. "No doubt iv it. Now an' then ye might be led astray by complexion, but ye could play the physiognomist in

Grafton Street any evenin'. To tell ye the truth I never b'lieved much in it. I've seen a useless Johnny with the pointed chin an' a jaw 'most as far out as Arthur Griffith's. I've seen paint an' powder on Grafton Street 'three o'clocks,' an' they'd all the well-marked features o' nose, eyes, mouth, forehead, ears, an' chin, an' yet they hadn't a mind above the butterfly."

"What do ye think o' physiognomy?" asked Terry.

"It's a pastime," said Patsy, "like signin' Articles iv Agreement in the quiet seclusion o' Hans Place."

Irish Fun, May 1922, p. 4, caricatures and pen-picture descriptions of de Valera, Griffith, Collins, Cosgrave and Darrell Figgis.

Opposite: Sinn Féin handbill for the 1923 election.

Cartoon from *The Leader*, September 1923, showing the composition of the Dáil following the general election. Blythe, O'Higgins and Walsh sit on a ministerial bench; Cosgrave flies overhead; Johnson peers out through the fence while Larkin and William O'Brien watch from outside; in the background, de Valera stands beyond the fence.

Resolution of the Archbishops and Bishops of Ireland adopted at their Maynooth meeting 9th October, 1923.

"Hitherto, in obedience to the divine
"law, no divorce with right to re-marry
"has ever been granted in this country.
"The Bishops of Ireland have to say that
"it would be altogether unworthy of an
"Irish legislative body to sanction the
"concession of such divorce, no matter who
"the petitioners may be."

(Signed) X MICHAEL CARD. LOGUE.

'The old-age pensioner's treatment': political cartoon about the 10% cut in the old age pension in 1924.

Opposite: Resolution adopted by the Irish Catholic hierarchy in 1923 on the subject of divorce.

Following pages: 'The president outlines his policies': cartoon about the Free State government's trade protection policy, 14 May 1927.

Phonetic transcription of the text of the opening and closing sentences of Cosgrave's 1926 St Patrick's Day address.

Opposite: Cosgrave and his wife Louisa photographed on board ship 1924.

BROADCAST MESSAGE.

OPENING SENTENCE.

Dhu kinĕ Gayul ĭ mailĕ iss i

gain baha aggus sláinte err hauckt Dhun vailĕ

Nashoontha shu areesh – Failĕ Faudrigg, Aspal

na hÉireann.

Closing Sentence

Bannacht Day ogus faudrig

er un ubber

Cosgrave and his wife Louisa and their sons Liam and Míceál in the garden of their home in Templeogue.

Denomination.	Design.	Decision.
		the Minister for Lands & Agriculture might select the type of animal to serve as a model
Sixpence	Wolfhound	It was decided that the Committee should be requested to ask Mr. Metcalfe to submit a design based on the wolfhound breed - the model submitted not being true to type.
Threepence	Hare	Mr. Metcalfe's design was accepted.
Penny	Hen	Mr. Metcalfe's design was accepted.
Halfpenny	Pig	It was decided that the Committee be requested to ask Mr. Metcalfe to make a slight reduction in the fullness of the jowl of his design of the pig.
Farthing	Woodcock	Mr. Metcalfe's design was accepted.

OBVERSE DESIGN.

Mr. Metcalfe's design of the Harp was accepted

as the obverse for all the denominations in question.

Cabinet minute, 2 May 1927, agreeing designs for Irish Free State coinage; (inset) mould of the original design of the reverse of the halfpenny, and the coin as cast in 1928, amended in line with the minute.

Opposite: Letter from Liam Tobin and Charles Dalton on behalf of the IRAO to Cosgrave, 6 March 1924, demanding a meeting to discuss the removal of the Army Council and the suspension of demobilisation.

The Meeting adjourned at 6.45 p.m.

TO:
President Liam Cosgrave.

Sir,

On behalf of the I.R.A. Organisation we have been
instructed to present the following Ultimatum to the
Government of Saorstat Eireann.

Briefly our position is this:-

The I.R.A. only accepted the Treaty as a means of
achieving its Objects, namely, to secure and maintain a
Republican form of Government in this country.

After many months of discussion with your Government
it is our considered opinion that your Government has not
those objects in view and that their policy is not reconcilable
with the Irish People's acceptance of the Treaty.

Furthermore, our interpretation of the Treaty was that
expressed by the late Commander-in-Chief, General Michael
Collins, when he stated "I have taken an oath of allegiance
to the Irish Republic and that oath I will keep Treaty or no
Treaty". We claim Michael Collins as our leader and again
remind you that even after the Treaty was signed that drastic
action was taken against enemies of the unity and complete
independence of our country. Both in oath and honour bound,
it is our duty to continue his policy and therefore present
this Ultimatum to which we require a reply by 12 noon, 10th
March 1924.

We demand a conference with representatives of your
Government to discuss our interpretation of the Treaty on
the following conditions:-

(a) The removal of the Army Council.

(b) The immediate suspension of Army demobilization
and re-organisation.

In the event of your Government rejecting these proposals
we will take such action that will make clear to the Irish
People that we are not renegades or traitors to the ideals that
induced them to accept the Treaty.

Our Organisation fully realises the seriousness of the
action that we may be compelled to take, but we can no longer
be party to the treachery that threatens to destroy the
aspirations of the Nation.

LIAM TOBIN, Major-General.	President of the Executative Council.
C. F. DALTON, Col.	Secretary to Executative Council.

(over)

Reference No.

TELEPHONE 5166.

Letter to Cosgrave, 20 March 1924,
outlining the decision of the cabinet
on replacing the leadership within
the army and action to be carried
out against mutineers.

OIFIG AN UACHTARÁIN
(The President's Office).

SRÁID MHUIRBHTHEAN UACH.
(Upper Merrion Street),

BAILE ÁTHA CLIATH
(Dublin).

President

The following matters were decided at this morning's meeting of the Executive Council:

(1) The attitude towards men implicated in the Mutiny as set out in the memorandum of the Minister of Defence dated 18th March (which is based upon President's letter to Mr. McGrath) was confirmed with an extension of date mentioned in paragraph (1) to 6 p.m. on Saturday 22nd inst. Until that date all arrests, raids, searches and other aggressive action against the officers concerned will cease. Parole of officers under arrest will not be accepted until after the 22nd inst.

(2) The following temporary appointments made on recommendation of General O'Duffy

    Chief of Staff — Major General Joseph Sweeney

    Adj. General — Col Hugo MacNeill

    Q.M.G. — Col Felix Cronin

(3) The Committee of Enquiry to proceed with its investigations at once

(4) General O'Duffy is to submit at once to the Executive Council a complete list of the officers who resigned. The resignations will be accepted in every case.

20/3/24.

MEETING OF THE EXECUTIVE COUNCIL

WEDNESDAY 19TH MARCH, 1924.   9.30 pm to 9.50 pm

ATTENDANCE.

The following members were present:-

1. Vice President & Home Affairs....Mr. O'Higgins.
2. Finance........................Mr. Blythe.
3. External Affairs................Mr. Fitzgerald.

Members absent:- (see Note at foot)

1. President.......................Mr. Cosgrave.(ill)
2. Industry & Commerce.............Mr. McGrath.
       (resignation accepted 19th instant)
3. Defence........................General Mulcahy.
             (resigned 19th instant)
4. Education......................Prof. McNeill.

Others present:-

1. The Attorney General............Mr. Kennedy.
             ----
1. Secretary to Council............Mr. O'Hegarty.
2. Asst. Sec. do.................Mr. McDunphy.
             ----

1. MINISTRY OF DEFENCE. –Duties undertaken by President.

In connection with the situation caused by resignation

of the Minister for Defence it was decided that the following

statement should be issued to the Press, subject to the approval

of the President:-

> "The President has decided, subject to the approval
> "of DAIL EIREANN, to take up the duties of the
> "Ministry of Defence.   During the illness of the
> "President, the Vice President will act for him
> "in that Ministry".

The Meeting adjourned at 9.50 p.m.

This statement was subsequently submitted to the President

in his home, and with his approval, and the approval of the Vice

President and the Minister for Education, the statement was

amended to the following form and so issued to the Press:-

> "The President has decided, subject to the approval
> "of DAIL EIREANN, to undertake the duties of the
> "Ministry of Defence".

Cabinet minute, 19 March 1924, indicating that a statement to be issued to the press regarding Cosgrave taking up the duties of Minister of Defence was amended at his request, removing the reference to O'Higgins acting for him in his absence.

C. Ó.h. Uigín.

Cosgrave, British prime minister Ramsay MacDonald and Northern
Ireland premier Sir James Craig, at Chequers, May 1924, for
discussions on the border.

Opposite: 'The Long View', cartoon featured in *Punch*, 14 May
1924, John Bull speaking to Cosgrave on the boundary issue.

THE LONG VIEW.

John Bull (*to the President of the Irish Free State*). "I DON'T SAY THIS IS THE BEST FENCE I'VE EVER SAT ON; BUT, IF YOU HOPE ONE DAY TO DISPENSE WITH IT ALTOGETHER, I SHOULDN'T RAISE TOO MUCH TROUBLE ABOUT IT NOW."

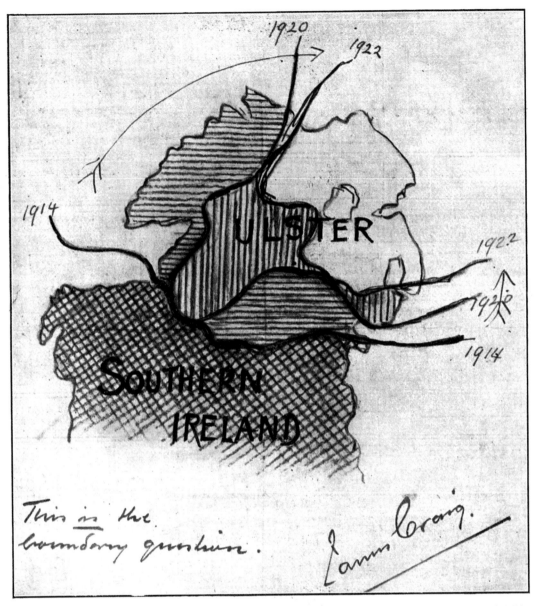

EPITOMISING THE BORDER DISPUTE : A ROUGH MAP, SIGNED BY SIR JAMES CRAIG FOR MR. L. RAVEN HILL, OUR SPECIAL ARTIST IN ULSTER.

'Epitomising the border dispute', map sketched and signed by James Craig and reproduced in *Illustrated London News*, 1 April 1922, indicating the changes to the border of Ulster between 1914 and 1920, when Northern Ireland came into being, and the additional territory being claimed by the Irish Free State in 1922.

Opposite: Minute of provisional government meeting, 21 March 1922 (initialled by Michael Collins), referring to Collins's discussions with Craig in relation to the Council of Ireland, and indicating Cosgrave's agreement (as minister for Local Government), with reservations, with Collins's suggestions.

(1586.) Wt.3—.10,000.3-22.A.T.&Co.,Ltd. PB. 850   Urgent.   Ref. No. Z. 1568

1922

Rialtas Sealadach na hÉireann

Name

Subject   COUNCIL OF IRELAND

2/3/1922

I am anxious that each member of the Provisional Government should see the attached extract from a letter written by Sir James Craig to Mr. Churchill. In my opinion it is important to point out:-

(1) That there is no question of the Council of Ireland arising under the Treaty. This must be made clear, even if we have the desire to deal for certain purposes with the Belfast Parliament. I may say when Sir James Craig and I reached the agreement mentioned, it was suggested that for common purposes certain ministers or a combination of ministers, or the entire Cabinets could meet so as to come to decisions to tide us over the transitional period, or any transitional period.

(2) It would be well to bear in mind that the meeting of Ministers Ministers for Labour, Ministers for Agriculture) while having good results was not on any basis of understanding, and certainly not on any terms of equality as between the Governments. Our powers are of course complete, whereas the powers of the Belfast Parliament are very incomplete.

(3) Generally, I am of opinion that we should keep the Belfast Parliament well within its powers and not give them any assistance except in the most restricted way. I recommend this course now owing to the general condition in Belfast. If they were moving towards the unity of Ireland we could afford to be very much more helpful.

MoC

TO:
Minister for Home Affairs. (in Duggan)
(1) I agree.
(2) Of course there can be no question of equality.
(3) I agree. The suggested meeting of Cabinets might be useful when Belfast functions according to act.
SP. 21/3/22

TO:
Minister for Local Govt. (in Burgess)
(1) I agree, subject to the number of the Belfast contingent not exceeding ours at a joint meeting of the Cabinets, which should be held in Dublin only.
(2) applications for these meetings will generally come from Belfast + from the nature of the case there is not and cannot be equality.
(3) I agree.
EC McN 22/9/22

TO:
Minister for Agriculture. (in Hogan)
see note attached
PH 22/3/22

TO:
Minister for Economic Affairs. (in Higgins)
I concur in all three. but there is provision in article 13 of Treaty re Council of Ireland. It would be utterly unworkable having no real power to administer.
C.Ó.Y. 24/3/22

TO:
P.M.G. (in Walsh)

TO:
Minister for Education. (in Hayes)
I agree to all three. With regard to 3) there are many ways in wh. we can hamper them without making it appear our actual policy.

TO:
Minister for Labour. (in McGrath)
I agree to all three. JMcG
2? MAR 1922

King George V and premiers of the dominions attending the 1926 Imperial Conference. Back row: Walter Stanley Munroe (Newfoundland); Joseph Gordon Coates (New Zealand); Stanley Bruce (Australia); James Hertzog (South Africa); Cosgrave. Front row: Stanley Baldwin (UK), King George V and William Mackenzie King (Canada).

Opposite: Anti-Free State election poster in the aftermath of the civil war.

ONE PROMISE
THAT HOGAN WILL KEEP—

"You did not think that we would execute Irishmen. We did,—
and we will bloody well execute again!"

—Mr. HOGAN (Free State Minister for Agriculture)
speaking at Crossmolina, Mayo, 10/11/24.

—IF YOU VOTE FOR THE
FREE STATE

Cosgrave and others on the steps of the Royal Irish Academy,
Dawson Street, August 1924, for the visit of Prince Riza Mirza
Khan. Cosgrave was elected a member of the Academy in 1927.
(Front row also includes O'Duffy, O'Higgins, FitzGerald and Hugh
Kennedy; W.B. Yeats, a member of the senate, is in the third row.)

Cosgrave posing while a model is sculpted for a bust by American artist G.F. Waters, 1925.

Cosgrave and his sister Joan, with Hugh and Clare Kennedy at the Wolfe Tone anniversary.

'the Government,
like Tennyson's brook,
goes on for ever'.

- CONFRONTING FIANNA FÁIL, 1927–32 -

Opening image: '*The Plunge*', cartoon
published in the *Daily Mail*, 27 August
1927, Cosgrave jumping into a general
election and pulling de Valera in with him.

IN THE election campaign of May–June 1927 the government outlined its plans for the future, flaunted its achievements and ridiculed its opponents. It emphasised its road improvement programme and the Shannon hydro-electric scheme—the project to develop an electricity-generating station on the lower reaches of the River Shannon at Ardnacrusha, Co. Clare, on which work had begun in 1925. Cosgrave claimed that Cumann na nGaedheal had chosen honesty over popularity, and with excessive optimism he assured an audience that the days of political patronage and jobbery were over.[1] He denounced de Valera, criticising his record at the time of the treaty negotiations and during the civil war. He blamed his rival for both the £15 million spent on the army during the civil war and the £7 million paid in compensation for damage done to property during the conflict. He attacked Fianna Fáil's continued abstention from the Dáil, comparing it to a football team that stood on the sideline, and he displayed his characteristic treatment of hecklers by describing one of them as 'a gentleman with auburn hair who seems to have all the responsibility of the world on his shoulders'.[2] For three evenings in a row his campaigning ended at midnight, and he claimed to have addressed 27 meetings in one week in the run-up to polling day.[3] Half-way through the campaign he could speak only in a whisper, although his voice soon recovered.[4]

Despite Cosgrave's robust electioneering it was remarked that he was almost alone in giving a reasoned defence of the government's principles and policies; many of its spokesmen, including ministers, indulged freely in personal attacks on their opponents.[5]

In some respects Cumann na nGaedheal's campaign was undisciplined or inefficient. For example, O'Higgins complained that in Roscommon prospective candidates who were not selected at the party convention subsequently ran as independents; while in South Mayo five candidates competed for five seats, when only three of them might be expected to win.[6] (The reality turned out to be even worse: two were elected.) It was claimed that many Cumann na nGaedheal candidates seemed to think it was their leaders' business to carry them to victory on their backs.[7]

There was speculation that de Valera might modify or even abandon the policy of abstention, and one repeated message in the party's pre-election advertisements was that 'Fianna Fáil is going in', but in the end it remained true to its convictions and its members refused to take the oath or their seats.

The result of the election on 9 June was a severe disappointment to the government. It lost 16 seats, securing only 47 to Fianna Fáil's 44, while other parties and independents achieved an impressive total of 62. Cumann na nGaedheal won only 27.4% of the first preference vote, a drop of 11.5%. In a striking change from the patterns of 1922 and 1923, the party gained fewer first preference votes and fewer seats than the combined anti-treaty forces of Fianna Fáil and Sinn Féin. Smaller groups performed far better than expected, and *The Irish Statesman* complained that the country had elected a Dáil containing representatives of 'the shreds and tatters of every futile party'.[8] But the government had lost more heavily to Labour and to the new National League, headed by John Redmond's son William, than to Fianna Fáil.

De Valera and his deputies tried to enter the Dáil on 23 June without signing the oath (described by the clerk as 'a little formality'), but they were rebuffed. Their absence simplified the election of a new administration. With misplaced confidence Cosgrave had declared that he would not form a government with a mere fifty seats, but in the event the only solution was for him and his ministers to 'acquiesce in having office thrust upon them'.[9] He was once again elected president of the Executive Council, by 68 votes to 22. He had already declared that he would not accept the presidency in the capacity of

> a super-policeman to maintain law and order while allowing the country to drift along economically, nationally and internationally…We have no intention of imperiling our good relations with Great Britain to secure a dishonest saving of faces, or to acquiesce in a national deception.[10]

He brought Richard Mulcahy back into the cabinet, although not in his former controversial position as minister for Defence. That post went to Desmond FitzGerald and Mulcahy took over Local Government. (Decades later he claimed that, initially, Cosgrave had not wanted to reinstate him, but he had made it clear that if he were not appointed to a ministry he would no longer support the government.[11] He remained popular with many party members.) His return to the cabinet was seen as providing a counterweight to the influence of Kevin O'Higgins, but on the other hand the vice-president now held the Justice and External Affairs portfolios.

Everything changed on 10 July. As O'Higgins walked alone to Sunday mass in Booterstown he was assassinated by three members of the IRA. The shock was immense; only weeks earlier *The Irish Times* had expressed a widespread view that 'the sinister shadow of the gunman has vanished'.[12] Now, the symbol of law and order in the new state had been brutally murdered and the terror of the civil war seemed to have been revived. When Cosgrave was late returning to his house from mass that morning, because of a punctured car tyre, his wife became terrified that he too had been shot.

The following day Thomas Johnson met the president. He was aware that two ministers (FitzGerald and John Marcus O'Sullivan) were ill; he believed that three others (Cosgrave himself, Patrick McGilligan and Patrick Hogan) were worn out, and he concluded that without O'Higgins the government was weak. Cosgrave was later described as having looked pale and incredibly frail on the day of O'Higgins's funeral.[13] In these circumstances Johnson suggested that, if it were necessary, Labour would be ready to join an all-party coalition. Naturally such a coalition would consist only of parties that were already in the Dáil, so Fianna Fáil was automatically excluded. His overture was ignored; in his words, it was 'spurned and flouted'.[14]

CRISIS AND SURVIVAL

Instead of cooperating with the opposition, the government planned a drastic series of responses to O'Higgins's murder, thereby implementing Cosgrave's promise that the assassin's bullet would not succeed in terrorising the country.[15] The cabinet decided to introduce a Public Safety Bill and other measures. The most significant of these was an Electoral Amendment Bill, which laid down that all candidates for election to the Dáil would be obliged to swear that if elected they would take the oath of fidelity to the king. Fianna Fáil would therefore be compelled either to observe the terms of the treaty—and to function as a normal political party on conditions determined by the government—or be excluded from national politics. De Valera would have to abandon one of his party's core policies or relinquish his painstaking efforts to work his way back to effective political activity. He would be forced to choose between being consistent and being constitutional.[16] (Such a move by the government had been suggested in the past. For example, in 1924 the Irish-American judge Daniel Cohalan had proposed that 'vacant' Dáil seats might be filled by holding new elections. Cosgrave had turned down this idea because of its impact on Northern Ireland, where nationalists abstained from parliament. 'If we declare those seats vacant in our area, the North East follows suit, and one of the main objections to the North-East goes'.[17])

At a subsequent meeting with Labour leaders following O'Higgins's assassination, the president claimed that ministers were not physically capable of conducting a strenuous election campaign to fill the seats left empty by the Fianna Fáil abstentionists. He, Blythe and McGilligan argued that if the police and the army did not act decisively against republican militants some of the government's supporters would get out of hand, and it would be impossible to prevent their unauthorised attacks. After this encounter Johnson concluded that ministers 'were determined to make a demonstration of their power and intention to meet violence with violence'.[18] Opposition leaders rejected the cabinet's efforts to secure cross-party support for its package of measures.

The obvious appeal of the government's policy was accompanied by the danger that republicans might then feel pressurised to return to the methods of the civil war.[19] It was a gamble. On the other hand, Cosgrave could have insisted on humiliating de Valera by making it even more difficult for him to take the oath, but he refrained from doing so. From his point of view the ideal solution would have been a split in Fianna Fáil, with the consequence that some of its members would enter the Dáil (as one, Patrick Belton, had already done) while the extremist section would be marginalised. Alternatively, the united party would take the oath and would automatically replace Labour as the leading opposition party, thereby threatening the government's position. In such a case, ministers hoped, the public would repudiate Fianna Fáil because it had abandoned a policy it had cherished for the past five years—a policy that was associated with its members' actions before and during the civil war. Each side feared making a concession that would seem to compromise its earlier stance, so from Cosgrave's point of view it was crucial that de Valera should be made to swallow his words when taking the oath.

To the surprise of many observers de Valera gave way, although in practice he had little choice; he had spent the past five years denouncing the oath, but he had also spent four of those years trying to demarcate himself from the IRA and to regain power by political means. He decided that the oath was 'merely an empty political formula', and on 11 August he and his followers entered the Dáil at last. Cosgrave's feelings must have been mixed, even though he described the end of Fianna Fáil's abstention from parliamentary politics as the best thing that had happened during the past five years.[20] His natural satisfaction that the Free State would now become a normal, functioning democracy was accompanied by the danger that a change in public opinion might bring to power a leader and a party he despised.

In combination with Labour and Redmond's National League, de Valera would have sufficient votes to overcome the informal alliance of Cumann na nGaedheal, the farmers and the independents. Calculations were made, and there was a general expectation that the government was doomed to defeat on a motion of no confidence, probably by one vote. The three opposition parties agreed that following such a result, Labour and the National League should form a government and that it should be supported from the back-benches by Fianna Fáil. This would be a marriage of opposites, and the prospect of Labour's dependence on Fianna Fáil provoked the image of 'a very gentle lamb leading to the pastures a pack of wolves, silent but hungrily licking their chops'.[21] Cumann na nGaedheal was described as being reconciled to bowing out, and it was claimed subsequently that Cosgrave had urged army officers to show loyalty to the expected new administration.[22] *The Irish Times* even published the names of Johnson's likely 'cabinet'. This was the result of an extraordinary scoop by which its deputy editor, Bertie Smyllie, fortified by a bottle of whiskey, assembled the information from torn-up scraps of paper that Labour leaders had thrown into a waste-basket after a meeting in the Powerscourt Arms Hotel in Enniskerry, Co. Wicklow.[23]

In the event, one of Redmond's deputies voted with the government on the confidence motion on 16 August, and another—the famous Alderman John Jinks of Sligo—simply vanished. He had sat behind his leader throughout the debate, but then failed to vote in the division lobbies. Rumours circulated that he had been plied with drink, or that he had been kidnapped by practical jokers. Subsequently, Jinks explained that he had made clear his opposition to the National League's policies and, having heard the arguments in the debate, he left the Dáil and went back to his hotel. Not long before he had been listed as a 'doubtful' voter.[24] The result was a tie, and the government was saved by the casting vote of the *ceann comhairle* or speaker, Cosgrave's close friend Michael Hayes.

The president was described as looking bewildered by what had happened, but he seized his opportunity and promptly adjourned the Dáil until October. Seán T. O'Kelly, who until then had spoken only in Irish, was so flabbergasted by the turn of events that he lapsed into English.[25] When the government won two by-elections soon afterwards, one occasioned by the assassination of O'Higgins and the second by the death on 15 July of Countess Markievicz, Cosgrave acted decisively. On the advice of the attorney-general, John A. Costello, he dissolved the Dáil on 25 August, less than two months after it had assembled, and he called new elections for 15 September. There were reports that some members of his cabinet had not been informed about the dissolution.[26] De Valera denounced this move as sharp practice, although it was an expedient that he would adopt with remarkable success on three later occasions.

J.J. Walsh, the minister for Posts and Telegraphs and chairman of Cumann na nGaedheal, was a committed protectionist and was therefore at odds with central aspects of the government's policy. During the campaign for the September election he followed Jinks's example and he too disappeared. He had always been a troublesome colleague. For example, at the first meeting of the third Dáil in September 1922 Johnson had referred to 'the disadvantages of Mr. Walsh's temperament', and Walsh's fellow-ministers came to share this view. (A year after Johnson made his comment, Mulcahy wrote to Cosgrave complaining about the postmaster general.[27]) To the government's great embarrassment he left the country without warning as the election campaign began. He was later encountered in Paris on his way to take a holiday in Luzern. He then sent a telegram resigning from the party and denouncing the policies of his former colleagues. The resignation of the party chairman weakened the government's argument that it represented stability and continuity.[28] To lessen the risk of losing Walsh's seat, Cosgrave decided to take his place and run for election in Cork Borough, as well as in his old constituency of Carlow-Kilkenny. (Contesting a number of constituencies was common at the time, but a candidate could represent only one and so would have to choose if elected to two or more; vacancies would be filled through by-elections) He was accustomed to taking on extra burdens. At this time he—briefly—combined the presidency with the ministries of Justice, External Affairs and Defence.[29]

A second election campaign so soon imposed a heavy financial burden on all parties, but particularly on the smaller groups and the independents. Only 265 people ran for election in September, as opposed to 377 in June; the number of 'third party' candidates, outside the ranks of Cumann na nGaedheal and Fianna Fáil, dropped by more than half, from 193 to 88.[30] They were squeezed, and the two large groups benefitted at their expense. In June the main parties had won only 53% of the vote; in September their share rose to 72%.[31]

After the traumatic events of the summer the campaign was fought more bitterly than had been the case three months earlier. The background to the September election—a violent attack on the state in the form of the assassination of a government minister—favoured Cosgrave and his party. Cumann na nGaedheal was able to afford extensive advertising, which sometimes occupied half of a newspaper page, and it employed the advertising agency O'Kennedy-Brindley to assist with its campaign material. A celebratory booklet published after the election began 'Nothing more remarkable in political propaganda has ever been attempted in Great Britain or Ireland than the huge press advertising campaign of the Government Party', which, it boasted, had been carried through without a hitch.[32] As before, the government's publicity was balanced between recording its achievements, making promises for the future and warning the electorate against the dangers posed by Fianna Fáil. It claimed that during the past five years de Valera's actions had cost the country approximately £10 million a year—money that could have paid for 40,000 workers' houses and made possible an increase rather than a decrease in the old age pension.[33] Fianna Fáil's acceptance of the oath of fidelity encouraged government speakers to distinguish between 'facts' and 'formulas', while Labour's Johnson was vulnerable to Ernest Blythe's taunt that he had an 'insane desire to be a Minister at any price'.[34] Cosgrave campaigned zealously. He was described as having travelled over 2,000 miles and having addressed over 100 meetings within a fortnight. As had been the case in June, some crowds waited until after midnight to hear him.[35] In Claremorris, Co. Mayo, tar barrels burned in the streets and young men held aloft blazing sods of turf impaled on pitchforks.[36] Cosgrave stressed the government's economic management of the country's affairs—for example, he pointed out that a decade earlier the annual cost of the judiciary for all Ireland had been £58,000; now, in the Free State, it had been reduced to £25,000.[37] He dismissed de Valera as a slacker, a shirker and a man afraid to tackle a job and work hard.[38]

In the second election of 1927 Cumann na nGaedheal performed better than Fianna Fáil, winning 62 seats to its opponent's 57; its vote increased by 11% as opposed to Fianna Fáil's 9%. With the support of independents Cosgrave was able to continue in office for another 4½ years. He topped the poll in both his constituencies, and he chose to move from Kilkenny to Cork Borough, where he remained for the rest of his career. (Seán MacEntee was therefore unjust in describing the president as a bird of passage in the constituencies that he represented.[39])

Cosgrave remarked that Cumann na nGaedheal had won exactly the number of seats he had predicted. However, he had not expected that the smaller parties would have lost so heavily—and therefore he had not anticipated that Fianna Fáil would have performed so well; he consistently miscalculated the republicans' appeal to the electorate. He wrote that after five years in office various measures, reforms and laws passed to deal with crime, 'all made enemies—I do not know if any of them made friends'.[40] In the September election Cumann na nGaedheal had much in its favour and, as Cosgrave claimed, Fianna Fáil could not face the electorate with confidence. In these circumstances the narrowness of the gap between the two parties should have caused the government serious concern about a future election fought in less promising conditions.[41]

De Valera's opponents ridiculed him for needing five years to realise that the oath was no more than an empty formula, but 35% of Irish voters seemed not to care. Instead of punishing him for his inconsistency they rewarded him for having changed his mind. In contrast, both Labour and Redmond's National League fared poorly, and the voters had little patience with their recent opportunistic and unsuccessful manoeuvres. Johnson lost his seat.

Before the Dáil met Cosgrave negotiated with Michael Heffernan, the leader of the Farmers' Party, and an alliance was formed. When the new Dáil met on 11 October he was re-elected president with a majority of six votes; he appointed Heffernan as a parliamentary secretary or junior minister in the Department of Posts and Telegraphs, and the farmers supported the government throughout the sixth Dáil.

Fianna Fáil was dismissed as 'raw from the political backwoods',[42] but the party adapted to parliamentary politics, sometimes painfully, and it became accustomed to Dáil procedures. It developed a 'welfarist' programme and appealed to those with social and economic as well as political grievances; it was able to project the interests and reproduce the self-image of the petty-bourgeoisie.[43] But it was reluctant to abandon its links with the IRA and the rhetoric of struggle. For example, in 1928 Seán Lemass claimed in the Dáil that the main purpose of the civic guards was 'to suppress any attempt on the part of the young men of Ireland to organise themselves to achieve what many of the Ministers on the front Bench opposite were fighting to achieve a few short years ago'.[44] By implication, or extension, the Free State government had taken over the role of the British. The following year, de Valera repeated the message: 'you are regarded here as…the agents of British authority in this country'.[45]

CONSOLIDATION AND INNOVATION

Perhaps excessively influenced by de Valera's misjudgments in 1921–2, Cosgrave continued to under-estimate his opponent. In 1927 he wished that de Valera 'were as strong as he is unfortunately weak'.[46] Some years later he revealed the personal animosity between the two men, describing his rival as 'a type of arrested mental development', and as

> this man who wants to have himself regarded as a pacificator, as
> a great man, with great ideals who, when he uses one sentence
> follows it with another which makes it impossible for anybody to
> understand what he means; this man who, pretending to show

respect for me, dislikes me more and has greater hatred for me than any other man in this country has for another.[47]

When Cosgrave sent a St Patrick's Day message for transmission to the United States the International Broadcasting Corporation censored passages such as 'Mr. de Valera's insane campaign of destruction in 1922 and 1923'.[48] (De Valera too seemed to think in personal terms, and in listing the parties' strength after the September 1927 election he began 'Fianna Fáil 57 Cosgrave 61'.[49] He also discouraged social contacts between his TDs and members of Cumann na nGaedheal.[50])

The president's relations with other Fianna Fáil politicians such as O'Kelly and MacEntee were predictably poor, but he described Lemass appreciatively as a businessman (a term he used about himself), and in discussing a housing bill he distinguished between de Valera's two principal lieutenants: 'Deputy Lemass was, I think, the first who came to the kernel of it. Deputy O'Kelly carefully avoided it.'[51] In 1932 he said that he would prefer to see a practical politician like Lemass as president than an 'impractical dreamer' like de Valera.[52]

Cosgrave continued to flourish in parliamentary debates, and he remained personally popular, but his government came under increasing pressure from Fianna Fáil as the opposition grew steadily in confidence. The new party was populist and well-organised, and it spread rapidly; by 1928 it had over a thousand branches throughout the country.[53] Cumann na nGaedheal, by contrast, became increasingly an elitist, 'establishment' party, and it felt able to consider forming 'a high-class Politico-Social club…[that] would form the nucleus of a Party Institution which would represent the best elements of the Community'.[54] Ministers were accused of having joined the establishment and were mocked for dressing in formal clothes on formal occasions. They appeared to be comfortable when they wore top hats.

The last Cumann na nGaedheal administration was characterised by an absence of the crises that had marked the years 1922–7. No-one resigned from the cabinet. But as the government was forced on the defensive it engaged in some dubious manoeuvres. In 1925 Cosgrave had written that although the Dáil and Senate were sovereign assemblies and could do what was wrong, the constitution provided the necessary safeguards to deal with such wrongs.[55] Three years later in 1928, however, his government seemed to take a different view. Fianna Fáil planned to abolish the oath to the king by using the 'initiative' clause in the constitution—which provided for a referendum to be held on a particular question if 75,000 voters signed a petition to that effect. When

Fianna Fáil amassed 96,000 signatures the government responded forcefully, and controversially, by removing the referendum and initiative clauses from the constitution.[56] One reaction to this move was that the republicans wished to destroy the Free State constitution, and they watched with satisfaction as the government itself began the work of demolition.[57] It subsequently renewed for another eight years the period during which the constitution could be amended by ordinary legislation—a short-sighted action that would benefit de Valera in the 1930s. By such measures it eliminated most of the devices that had been introduced in 1922 to curb party government.[58] It was not prepared to allow what it saw as legal anomalies to obstruct the business of the state and provide unnecessary opportunities to its enemies. Nevertheless, the Free State slowly became a more 'normal' and peaceful society, and in 1929 Cosgrave could declare that Ireland was a crimeless country and its population one of the most law-abiding in the world.[59]

The cabinet continued its efforts to impose efficiency and modernity on a people that it often saw as reluctant or hostile. For example, it began an overhaul of local government. It was no longer satisfied with dismissing county councils and corporations and replacing them with state-appointed commissioners, as had happened between 1923 and 1927. In later years a new system was introduced that increased the power of Dublin administrators over local politicians—who were often recalcitrant and irresponsible. Following American models, professional city and county managers were appointed. In some cases the results were remarkable. Most notably, Philip Monahan, the 'lord protector' of Cork, won the citizens' deep respect during his 35 years as commissioner and city manager.[60]

Throughout the 1920s Cosgrave's government continued its efforts to undo the damage caused by the violence of the years 1916–23, and in particular of the civil war; the task that was begun in the Free State's early years continued until the end of the decade. Rebuilding railway lines and bridges was a priority. In Dublin, the General Post Office, the Custom House and the Four Courts complex, including the Public Records Office—which the republicans had destroyed in an act of exceptional vandalism—were all restored.[61] In 1928 the government established the Manuscripts Commission, and two years later it provided a grant to help create the Irish Folklore Institute. Cosgrave was reported to have had a personal interest in the state of the nation's archives.[62]

Over a period of several years he involved himself in the efforts to provide the capital with a Municipal Art Gallery, thereby enhancing the city's claim to benefit from Hugh Lane's disputed will. In 1929 he handed over the magnificent Charlemont House on Parnell Square, which had been built in 1765, as a gift from the government to the city of Dublin. It opened as a gallery four years later, and the debt of honour to Lane had been repaid.

The Free State was also able to benefit from the services of Edwin Lutyens, who would have designed the gallery crossing the River Liffey if Lane's own ideas for a gallery had materialised. Lutyens planned one of the most striking monuments erected in Ireland during the first decades of independence. This was another matter in which Cosgrave had a direct and detailed involvement. For years there had been controversy over the plans to erect a memorial in Dublin to the Irishmen who had been killed in the First World War. A large sum of money, over £40,000, was raised for this purpose, but the government was conscious of the dramatic change in attitudes towards the war in the years that had followed the Easter Rising. It was reluctant to allow such a monument be raised in a prominent position, and it turned down proposals for sites in locations such as Merrion Square and Phoenix Park. The issue remained unresolved for years. Eventually, Cosgrave became irritated by requests and complaints and he took the matter in hand. After outlining possible means of using the funds he consulted the cabinet (some of whose members needed to be prodded), he approached the Office of Public Works, he discussed the matter with its principal architect T.J. Byrne (an old friend), and he secured agreement that a memorial would be built on a site (in Islandbridge, to the south-west of the city) that was at the time used for allotments.[63] In this location the memorial would benefit from a certain degree of invisibility.[64] The government made a lavish contribution of £50,000, which contrasted with its refusal to build a worthy cenotaph to Griffith, Collins and O'Higgins,[65] and Lutyens produced an imaginative design. Cosgrave continued to be involved in the planning of the project, and he held meetings with the architect and others.

Perhaps with the possibility of a change of government in mind he was 'most anxious' that work on the site should begin before the end of 1931,[66] and preparations duly commenced on 30 December, only ten weeks before he left office. The workforce consisted of ex-servicemen drawn equally from the Irish and British armies, and the memorial was completed in 1939.[67] Even though the state contribution was based on the presumption that the park would be a public amenity, and even though one critic complained that the memorial would be situated in 'a distant backwater which will be used as a playground for the children of Inchicore',[68] the park was neglected for decades. Until 1988 it was opened to the public for only one day a year.

The greatest triumph of Cosgrave's final term of office, however, was the completion of the Shannon hydro-electrical project. In the 1920s the Free State had the lowest electricity consumption in Western Europe, apart from Portugal. An ambitious scheme to harness the waters of the Shannon was the brainchild of an Irish engineer, T.A. McLaughlin. In the course of 1923 he and several ministers discussed his ideas to dam the river and build a power station at Ardnacrusha, a few miles from Limerick City. He approached Cosgrave in December that year, and his later recollection was that the president 'had a great deal of other things on his mind…he was not very interested'. Cosgrave himself told the Dáil that at this first meeting he turned down, on his own responsibility, the proposal for developing the Shannon.[69] But a month later, at a second meeting that was also attended by Minister for Industry and Commerce Joe McGrath, Finance Minister Ernest Blythe and Attorney-General Hugh Kennedy, it was decided to undertake a technical and commercial assessment of the scheme. The German firm Siemens-Schuckert was encouraged to make proposals, and the government appointed a committee of international experts that approved in their broad outline the plans as submitted. The project was one of the largest in the world at the time, and it was of great psychological importance for the Free State, stimulating public self-confidence when it was badly needed.[70] Allowing for the difference in scale, the Shannon scheme may bear comparison with the Tennessee Valley Authority established by the US Congress in the mid-1930s to revitalise a region that had been badly affected by the Great Depression. The mere fact that the contract for the Shannon scheme went to a German and not a British company was an affirmation of national independence. One observer remarked that it was a quick decision,

> but it was a decision. Not in a hundred years would that swift decision have been taken by Dublin Castle, nor could it have been carried through the British Parliament. The only thing that the British Parliament ever did quickly about Ireland was to pass a Coercion Act.[71]

The government drove a hard bargain and kept to it.[72] As the work progressed it was obliged to intervene to a greater extent than originally anticipated; private enterprise was unwilling to become involved because the profits would be insufficient. Although it was a radical measure for a conservative administration it involved no ideological change—rather an adaptation to circumstances.[73] Within the cabinet the new minister for Industry and Commerce, Patrick

McGilligan, was the dominant force behind the development, but after a hesitant start Cosgrave gave it his consistent support, and his detailed knowledge of the proposals emerged at numerous points.[74] The construction work was accompanied by labour disputes, and McGrath, who had been forgiven for his desertion of the government in 1924 during the army mutiny, was given the role of combating the trade unions. The president formally inaugurated the scheme at a grand ceremony in July 1929 in front of the cabinet, 50 deputies and senators and other dignataries. He pressed an electric switch, opening the sluice gates to the new canal that would divert water to the power station, and over the next few months the waterway was flooded. In the years between 1930 and 1937 electricity sales in the Free State increased five-fold.[75] The scheme was central to the new state's infrastructure.

The government intervened in other areas where private capital was unable or unwilling to participate. For example, in 1927—on an issue closely related to the development of the hydro-electric scheme—it established the Electricity Supply Board. This was a corporate body to control and develop the country's electricity network. In the same year it passed legislation to set up the Agricultural Credit Corporation, a bank to finance agriculture. These provided models for the 'semi-state bodies' that characterised Irish life for many years to come. But in general Cosgrave believed in private rather than state enterprise, and he welcomed the impact of the Irish Hospitals Sweepstakes, a lottery established in 1930 to finance hospitals and medical services as the state was unable to meet the expenses involved. 'The hospitals are very fortunate—twelve months ago bankrupt, today rich beyond their dreams'.[76] In fact much of the money went to enrich the organisers of the Sweepstakes, such as Joe McGrath, beyond most people's dreams.

Despite various reforms and improvements, much of the population lived and died in miserable conditions. For a majority of Irish citizens, the 1920s was a decade of static or declining real income and diminished employment opportunities.[77] The infant mortality rate in Dublin was almost twice that of London and more than double that of New York, while 66,000 people lived in dwellings with four or more people to a room.[78]

Housing remained an urgent problem, despite Cosgrave's long-standing concern with the question. In 1928 he told the Dáil that during the previous six years the government had provided about 14,000 houses, at a cost to the state of about £1.8 million, although he conceded that most people 'will tell us that three or four times that number is required'. Later, he announced that

60,000 houses were needed, affecting perhaps 400,000 people, but that the burden on taxpayers must be taken into account and it was not a good time to borrow money. It was 'the merest nonsense' to claim that money could solve the problem.[79] As in earlier years, he saw himself as a prisoner of economic circumstances, and he felt unable to translate his goodwill into positive action on the scale that he and others would have wished. Like almost all European leaders of the time, he did not think in 'Keynesian' terms. But, in the 1920s, nor did Keynes. During that decade the emphasis in Ireland was placed on good middle-class housing, and the government provided grants for civil service employees to build large homes.[80] Determined to avoid constructing new slums, and 'seduced by dreams of garden suburbs', Cosgrave's administration opted for suburbanisation, rather than inner-city development of the sort that he had championed in the 1910s. This became the dominant approach to housing in Dublin and led to it becoming a low-rise, low-density city.[81] A housing bill in 1931 prepared the way for later, more ambitious construction programmes that characterised the Fianna Fáil government in the 1930s.[82] But in general Cumann na nGaedheal governments took few measures to improve the position of the poor.[83]

Emigration, which had dried up during the First World War, resumed with the return of peace, and a pattern was re-established that endured for many decades. Between 1924 and 1927 over 100,000 people, most of them young, emigrated to North America or Australia.[84] This inability to provide jobs for people at home was mortifying for nationalists who had blamed emigration on the failings of British rule.

The government might have had only limited success in tackling social and economic problems—problems that, it never tired of emphasising, had been compounded by the republican campaign of destruction during the civil war. But in areas such as 'Gaelicising' the state and making it conform more closely to Catholic ideals, projects already begun during its first term, it was able to implement changes that were largely to its satisfaction—and to the satisfaction of the powerful lobbies that advocated them. As befitted a co-founder of the Gaelic League, Eoin MacNeill was an enthusiastic language revivalist. His successor as minister for Education, John Marcus O'Sullivan, was less passionately committed to using and enforcing the Irish language, but the campaign continued nonetheless. It was led by the minister for Finance, Ernest Blythe, who declared that he cared more deeply about Irish than about any other political question.[85] This ensured that the language revival was funded more generously than many other government measures. He wanted thousands of books printed in Irish, and in fixing their price and arranging for their sale there should be no attempt 'to put the scheme on a commercial basis'.[86] Elsewhere he was more stringent.

An Irish Language Commission was established in 1926, and the government continued to subsidise the Gaeltacht in a moderate fashion. Although Cosgrave acknowledged the worth of a commission on the Gaeltacht, he caused disquiet by hinting that the cost of some schemes it recommended might be prohibitive. Subsequently, official zeal in initiating projects was never matched by consistency and vigour in their application.[87] Yet according to *The Leader*, which was an advocate of the cause, even the government's enemies admitted that its efforts in standing by the Irish language were beyond reproach; later the journal pronounced that the Cumann na nGaedheal record on the language question was 'a hundred per cent'.[88] Over generations Irish became associated with the state rather than with the people, who ignored their leaders' exhortations and persisted obdurately in speaking English.

ROME RULE

Another element of continuity between Cosgrave's earlier and final administrations was the close links between church and state, although his last years in power were also marked by tensions and disagreements. Almost all the hierarchy continued to support the government and its party. In September 1927 Cosgrave wrote to Archbishop Byrne acknowledging his large subscription to the general election fund, the size of which had surprised him. A year later he thanked Bishop Fogarty of Killaloe for his 'princely contribution'.[89] He remained on excellent terms with many within the clergy, he and Fogarty visited each other's houses frequently and they rode together, and while on holidays in Connemara he remarked that he had been invited to stay with both the papal nuncio and the bishop of Cloyne, 'so that I'm like a pensioner of the Church'.[90]

Cosgrave was able to use his clerical contacts to good effect in his support of the Legion of Mary, an association of people who served the church on a voluntary basis, which had been founded in Dublin by Frank Duff in 1921. Byrne was hostile towards this body, but despite their friendship Cosgrave had no qualms in undermining the archbishop's efforts to marginalise the Legion. In 1931 he arranged an appointment for Duff with the newly arrived nuncio, Paschal Robinson, who encouraged him and ensured that he was able to meet the pope.[91] When Cosgrave lost office a year later Duff wrote to him that

You have placed me under immeasurable obligations to you which can never be repaid. In all difficulties and at all important moments of the things I had in hand, I turned to you, and you were never found wanting…The services you have rendered to the Legion of Mary are incalculable.[92]

Despite his success in defending Duff against the archbishop, the president had reason to view the influence of the Church in Irish politics with wariness and apprehension. The government felt obliged to intervene when disputes concerning some priests' payment of income tax escalated to the point where one of them was prosecuted. Cosgrave negotiated with Byrne and it was agreed that all priests would return a figure that would leave them below the income tax threshold.[93] In July 1928 he warned the chief justice, Hugh Kennedy, about a planned article containing a reference to his attendance at a Masonic garden party in Clonskeagh, while also offering reassurance that he had managed to avert its publication.[94] Some time later, Senator James Douglas, a Quaker, wrote to Cosgrave in distress, protesting that an attempt was being made to prevent him from holding any office in the Free State on the ground that his stand on divorce was antagonistic to the Catholic Church and its members—a claim he dismissed as slanderous.[95]

Elsewhere, Cosgrave and his colleagues had to tread carefully to avoid the wrath of Catholic zealots. There were demands for censorship of publications, to complement the earlier censorship of films. (This was not a specifically Irish pattern, and numerous other states had already imposed censorship of what was regarded as obscene and indecent material, or of works advocating contraception and abortion.[96]) In Cork some priests denounced the 'pagan' government from the pulpits.[97] Vigilante squads, sometimes armed, destroyed British newspapers and burned or otherwise removed public library copies of books by 'immoral' writers such as Byron, Turgenev, Conan Doyle, Shaw, Yeats and Synge. A devotional work on a book on Jesus Christ by a Dominican priest Fr Didion was purged, probably because the author's name was confused with that of Renan.[98]

In 1926 the government established a Committee on Evil Literature (consisting of two clergymen, two professors and a national teacher) to advise on whether censorship should be extended. It came under pressure from various groups—from newspapers; from bodies such as the Irish Vigilance Association, the Catholic Truth Society of Ireland and the County Mayo Board of Health; from Fianna Fáil; and from many of its own supporters.

Eventually it succumbed and in 1928 James Fitzgerald-Kenney, the minister for Justice, introduced a censorship bill. Its initial form was shoddy and careless, allowing extensive powers to pressure groups and lobbies. The measure was opposed by many Protestants and by the intelligentsia, a group that carried little or no weight in Irish public life.[99] The bill was changed in various respects (92 amendments were proposed in the Dáil and 42 in the Senate).[100] But the Catholic Truth Society believed that the 'Christian and Catholic attitude is expressed in the Bill, and that it should not be whittled down'.[101] In the numerous debates on the matter Cosgrave made only one brief intervention, relating to the expenditure involved.[102] Like several of his colleagues, he did not seem to relish the fight. The party newspaper claimed, in vain, that the government had 'just as much a duty to protect its citizens against the ignorant fanatic as against the propagandists of vice'.[103] The final version, banning publications that advocated contraception or that were deemed to be 'indecent or obscene', was less drastic than had been intended originally, but the thoroughness with which it was implemented made independent Ireland an object of international ridicule for the next 40 years.

In enforcing certain Catholic beliefs and opinions Cosgrave and his government reflected accurately the wishes of the great bulk of Irish public opinion. Their decision to introduce legislation that they clearly did not want 'was a tribute to the organization, skill and sheer bloody-mindedness of the moral reformers'.[104] The ultra-Catholic lobby was to be feared.

Shortly after the censorship bill was enacted, the secretary of the Catholic Truth Society wrote to the minister for Justice asking that *Roper's Row*, a novel by Warwick Deeping, should be referred to the censorship board. Fitzgerald-Kenney refused. He believed that a book should not be banned because one page out of 400 contained rhetorical questions about contraception. The society's secretary went over his head, appealed directly to Cosgrave, and threatened to 'publish the correspondence with comments, unless you may be able to induce a change of heart and a change of attitude in the Department'. Against civil service advice the president gave way, and he suggested that the book should be referred to the censorship board, as requested. He explained that he wanted to prevent an attack on the act within a few weeks of its passing (although he suspected that it would be undermined by the actions of people such as the complainant) and he foresaw the possibility of an amending bill being advocated.[105] This did not prove necessary, and those who demanded censorship were soon satisfied with the implementation of the act. As an early indication of its enthusiasm, the censorship board joined *The Times* book club, borrowed books, banned them, and returned them.[106] In the 1930s the board banned 1,200 books and 140 periodicals.[107] The system endured until 1967.

THE LIBRARIAN AND THE ARTIST

By far the most significant conflict between the government and elements of the Catholic Church was the case of the Mayo librarian. A section of the clergy distrusted libraries because they were conduits to the dangerous outside world.[108] There was outrage when Letitia Dunbar Harrison, a Protestant who had been educated in Trinity College, was appointed as the county librarian in July 1930. She had charge of more than 13,000 books and served almost 10,500 readers scattered over 150 centres.[109] The initial pretext for objecting to her appointment was her inability to speak Irish, but the reasons were sectarian.

The dean of Tuam complained that a century after Catholic Emancipation a Protestant ascendancy was being created in Mayo.[110] When the county council refused to appoint Dunbar Harrison, the government dissolved it for failing to carry out its statutory duty. This move was described by the Catholic newspaper *The Standard* as 'a course worthy of Moscow', and by a Cumann na nGaedheal supporter as 'toleration run riot'.[111] A Dáil deputy compared it to the actions of Nero and the Spanish Inquisition.[112] Journals such as *The Catholic Bulletin* and *The Catholic Mind* joined in the onslaught on the librarian and on the system that had permitted her appointment. Branch libraries closed in protest, and in his Lenten pastoral Archbishop Gilmartin of Tuam found it 'gratifying to see how the representatives of our Catholic people are unwilling to subsidise libraries not under Catholic control'.[113] In the words of a later commentator, books were spoken of as if they were dangerous drugs.[114] Fianna Fáil exploited the situation, and de Valera protested against centralisation of power in Dublin. (He soon changed his mind.) Cosgrave informed the Dáil that Dunbar Harrison was the best-qualified applicant for the post, that the selection board was comprised of appropriately experienced members and that they were all Catholics.[115] This did nothing to appease the opposition. His attitude was that 'we Catholics ought not to fear Protestants', but that it seemed as if Mayo was fearsome. He added that if Catholics must be appointed to certain positions, the advertisements should be worded accordingly.[116] This was not permitted under the Local Authorities Act.

The government received welcome support from various quarters, but it was appalled by the prospect of a Church–state quarrel. (When in power de

Valera, too, went to great lengths to avoid public disputes with the Church.[117]) Cosgrave tried to resolve the problem in a discreet manner, and he sent an emissary, Joseph Glynn, to Tuam to meet the vicar general and the archbishop. Glynn claimed that if the Catholic bishops made the new claim that a librarianship was a sensitive post, similar to that of a teacher, the president would take up the matter sympathetically with his colleagues. He also stressed the difficulties that would be involved. For example, he quoted Cosgrave's concern with the rights of minorities and the details of implementation; 'it would not be fair to tax non-catholics for the maintenance of the library if a non-catholic could not receive an appointment'. But he made it clear that 'if the bigger question were settled' it would be possible to promote Dunbar Harrison out of Mayo to a post in Dublin.[118] The Church expanded the range of its discontents, and Archbishop Harty of Cashel warned that he would denounce the government if Protestant doctors were appointed to dispensaries in his diocese. A Catholic doctor trained in Trinity College would be equally objectionable.[119]

Cosgrave too showed firmness; if the bishops claimed that librarians should be placed in the same category as teachers he would accept the decision but he would not implement it. (Desmond FitzGerald went further and said that in such an event he would resign.[120]) It is remarkable that, despite his concern with retaining the Catholic vote, the president held out for so long and against such odds.[121]

Gilmartin wanted the government to intimate its willingness and anxiety to reach an understanding with the bishops in all questions where there might be a clash between Catholic Church discipline and the laws of the state or articles of the constitution.[122] He made further demands, and Cosgrave drafted a reply in which he stressed that there were limits to the government's power to satisfy the Church if it were to fulfil its duties conscientiously. 'We cannot impose religious tests—and that, I fear, is what is proposed for our adoption in this case'. He could not envisage a solution along the lines proposed by the archbishop.[123] But in practice he felt obliged to give way. Responding to a suggestion by Gilmartin, Cosgrave and the Education minister John Marcus O'Sullivan replied that the government could not promise in writing to remove Dunbar Harrison, and nothing could be done immediately, but in effect they confirmed Glynn's earlier point: if it were possible to do so, at a suitable time the government would see whether a position outside Mayo could be found for her.[124]

In the Dáil de Valera argued that the people of Mayo were justified in insisting on a Catholic librarian, and he claimed that dispensary doctors should be of the same faith as the majority population.[125] (Here too he changed his mind after coming to power.) Cosgrave was robust in defending the procedures that had been adopted, but he did not take the opportunity of arguing that it might be the government's duty to ensure fair play for Protestants.[126]

Shortly before the 1932 general election a suitable position *was* found for Dunbar Harrison. The cabinet decided that it would be in the public interest to transfer her from Mayo, and she was appointed as librarian in the Department of Defence—much to her delight.[127] She did not stay there long. One happy feature of her turbulent year in Mayo was that she fell in love with a Methodist minister who was based in Castlebar, and when she married him she was obliged to resign from the public service.[128] In political terms the result was not clear-cut. Fianna Fáil increased its number of seats in Mayo from four to five in the 1932 election, but it did so at the expense of Labour. Although the fall in Cumann na nGaedheal's first preference vote in Mayo exceeded the national average, its total of four seats was unchanged.

An unfortunate and improbable by-product of the prevalent 'culture of censorship' at the time was the treatment of the artist Harry Clarke. The government planned to make a presentation to the International Labour Office (ILO) in Geneva, and it commissioned Clarke to design a stained glass window. He chose as a theme his interpretation of excerpts from the work of fifteen modern Irish writers, but his completion of the project was delayed by the impact of tuberculosis—that soon killed him, at the age of 41.

The government was unhappy at the idea of the state being represented abroad by passages from literary works that were banned at home. Perhaps this is understandable in light of the onslaughts that it had to face from the Catholic lobby. Cosgrave was an admirer of Clarke's stained glass, and some years earlier he had been generous in his praise when opening an exhibition of the artist's work.[129] Nonetheless, he drafted a letter to Clarke directing that the panel illustrating Liam O'Flaherty's novel *Mr. Gilhooley* should not be included in the window being crafted for the ILO—adding that this would be in Clarke's own interest as well as in that of others. He found himself 'in deep water' when it came to proposing an alternative, and he wrote that he would like the benefit of Clarke's judgment. (Gordon Campbell, the secretary of the Department of Industry and Commerce, re-drafted the letter and it was his version that was actually sent.[130]) Clarke was surprised and worried by this message, and he protested that it would be impossible to meet Cosgrave's conditions; but he stressed that he had alternatives to offer, and he invited the president to inspect the glass in his studio.[131]

Campbell accompanied his minister, Patrick McGilligan, to the studio where they examined the window, and subsequently the government's opposition deepened even further; Joyce and Seamus O'Sullivan now joined O'Flaherty as 'unsuitable' writers. It was felt that 'the inclusion of scenes from certain authors as representative of Irish literature would give grave offence to many of our people'.[132] Not merely did the government fear embarrassment, but there was also concern that any controversy might damage the future business of Clarke's firm (most of whose commissions came from religious sources).[133] This was a valid point. The panels were transported to the ante-room of the council chamber in Government Buildings for inspection by the cabinet, and Cosgrave's friend Bishop Fogarty was among those who admired them. While objecting to the figures of 'the satyr and the girl', he nonetheless regarded the window as the finest modern stained glass he had seen anywhere in Europe, 'of beautiful colouring, and a richness equal or almost equal to the very old glass of early medieval times'.[134] It remained outside the cabinet room for over two years, until after the change of government, and while there it was damaged.

The cheque in payment for the work arrived three weeks after Clarke's death.[135] Cosgrave was sent a mocking article about the window that had been published in *The Catholic Bulletin*; he replied that he did not intend to read such 'rubbish', but he expressed concern about what was being done in response to a letter from Clarke's widow. Subsequently he met her and he accepted her offer of buying back the window for the same price (£450) that the government had paid for it.[136] It is now in the Wolfsonian Museum in Florida.

SUCCESSES ABROAD

Cosgrave's deep religious faith was widely known and respected. Far more people shared Liam de Róiste's admiration of him, 'a really virtuous, pious man', than shared the disparagement of a Danish resident in Ireland who referred to him as 'Holy Willie'.[137] But even if sometimes on the defensive, he was prepared to challenge the Church establishment when he felt it appropriate to do so. In particular, the government was determined to establish formal diplomatic relations with the Vatican. This was an aspect of the pattern of consolidating the Free State's separate identity, and it would also have the attraction of weakening the impact of the Irish College in Rome, whose rector was a committed opponent of the treaty.[138] Such a move was opposed by the Catholic hierarchy; the bishops dreaded the appointment of a nuncio who would bring to an end their near-monopoly of clerical contacts with the Vatican. They lost, and diplomatic relations were established in 1930.

Cosgrave also was deeply involved in another 'Catholic' triumph, and it was under his government that most of the preparations were made for the Eucharistic Congress that was held in Dublin in June 1932. But by then de Valera was in power, and he was able to take the credit for his predecessor's efforts.

The Vatican connection represented only one facet of Irish foreign policy. For years the Free State made little impact in the League of Nations,[139] but towards the end of the 1920s it became more assertive. It was elected to a 'dominion' seat on the council of the League in 1930. Far more important was its success in expanding the opportunities provided by the treaty and helping to end Britain's dominant position in the Commonwealth. The pattern established in the early years of independence was maintained during Cosgrave's final administration. In public the government stressed that the treaty was sacrosanct but in private it tried to secure minor concessions from the British.[140] Under Patrick McGilligan (who for years served both as minister for External Affairs and for Industry and Commerce—a strange combination) Ireland played a prominent role in the Imperial Conferences of 1929 and 1930. These climaxed in the Statute of Westminster, which laid down that the British parliament could no longer legislate for any of the dominions, and that they could repeal or amend any act of the London parliament that affected them. In McGilligan's words, an imperial system that took centuries to elaborate had been brought to an end within four years.[141] Cosgrave, however, believed firmly that the statute was subordinate to the Anglo-Irish Treaty, and that it simply expressed the constitutional position achieved by and through the treaty.[142]

Churchill, who was by now effectively an opposition back-bencher even though the Conservative party dominated the British government, argued that the Irish Free State should be excluded from any provision that might allow it to evade or repudiate the terms of the treaty. But Cosgrave helped disarm opposition to the statute by sending a letter to the prime minister (MacDonald, once again), in which he stressed that the treaty could be altered only by consent, that the Irish government viewed it with 'solemnity', and that any amendment of the statute would be wholly unacceptable. This letter was read out in the House of Commons.[143]

The statute was enacted only weeks before Fianna Fáil came to power, and it facilitated de Valera's onslaught on the treaty. But there is no reason to think that if Cosgrave had won the 1932 election he would have changed his mind and adopted a similar approach; his government's policy was always to exploit the treaty rather than to dismantle it. He believed that the Commonwealth was as far removed from the British Empire of his boyhood as people in the 1930s were from the Battle of Waterloo.[144]

He and his government were accused of having forgotten the 'stepping-stone' argument used in the treaty debates, and of having ignored Griffith's incantation that 'this is no more a final treaty than this is the final Irish generation'.[145] But after coming to power de Valera admitted that

> the Twenty-six Counties here, as a result of the 1926 and 1930 conferences, had practically got into the position—with the sole exception that instead of being a Republic it was a monarchy— that I was aiming at in 1921 for the whole of Ireland…I am prepared to confess that there have been advances made that I did not believe would be made at the time.[146]

As in 1923 and 1926, Cosgrave left the detailed negotiations at the 1929 and 1930 Imperial Conferences to his minister for External Affairs. He sent McGilligan an appropriately generous letter of appreciation in which he wrote that 'it was to a considerable extent more my duty than your responsibility to undertake these negotiations and to achieve the results'.[147] He made occasional visits to mainland Europe, but his most dramatic foreign venture was a visit to the United States and Canada in February 1928. For the first time, an Irish nationalist leader crossed the Atlantic not in search of funds that he might use to weaken or end British rule in Ireland, but as the head of an independent government.

Before the journey he confessed to being nervous, to feeling like an amateur player about to make his first appearance on the professional stage.[148] But despite being marred by mishaps, the visit was a triumph. His ship was delayed by bad weather, the journey from Southampton to New York lasted nine days rather than seven, and in consequence his tour was curtailed. In Canada, the train engine jumped the track and ploughed through several rail cars on a siding. Cosgrave was unhurt, and according to contemporary accounts he comforted the injured and dying railway personnel.[149]

He visited New York, Chicago, Philadelphia and Ottawa; he met President Coolidge, Prime Minister Mackenzie King and numerous politicians and businessmen; and he received much attention from the American and Canadian press. Some of this was unfamiliar; 'he has become a "star" actor—for cinema camera men follow him from sunrise to sunset'.[150] De Valera was also in the

United States at that time, trying to raise funds, and it was reported that they overlapped in the same hotel.[151] The visit also attracted widespread attention in Ireland. One commentator praised the president's performance, and in particular how 'he spoke of an Ireland full of hope for the future'.[152] He was welcomed back to Ireland with cavalry, planes and fireworks.[153] Some months later the American secretary of state, Frank Kellogg, paid a short visit to Dublin.

PROBLEMS AT HOME

Foreign successes, however gratifying they were at the time, and however significant they would be in the long term, were overshadowed by the impact on Ireland of the Great Depression. The reverberations of the Wall Street crash in October 1929 reached Ireland in the course of the following year, undermined the government's policy of free trade and forced it to retreat from the policy summed up by Hogan: 'I would rather have one preference from England economically than all your tariffs'.[154] In a world in which most countries adopted economic protection, the Irish government felt obliged to do likewise—thereby opening itself to the taunt that it was now, belatedly, following policies that Fianna Fáil had advocated for several years. The value of exports fell by nearly a quarter in 1930–1; the volume of exports that had been achieved in 1929 was not approached again until 1948—and then in a depreciated currency.[155] Unemployment rose, and Cosgrave's final two years in power were dominated by economic and political problems.

In March 1930 Cumann na nGaedheal was defeated in the Dáil by two votes on a Fianna Fáil motion that would have added £300,000 to the cost of old age pensions. Twenty-two deputies were absent for the vote, and the result was blamed on the government's neglect of the group of independent TDs; according to *The Irish Times*, 'consistent contempt of its wishes and interests has imbued it with a spirit of apathy…They cannot reconcile the Government's frugal attitude to old age pensions with its orgy of expenditure on the compulsory propagation of the Irish language'.[156] The cabinet decided to resign and challenged its opponents to provide an alternative administration.

The two main opposition parties refused to support one another, and although Labour was deeply critical of Cumann na nGaedheal's policies it did not forgive de Valera's recent declarations in which he indicated his continuing ambivalence towards the Dáil. The result was that both he and T.J. O'Connell of Labour were supported only by their own deputies, while enough independents rallied behind Cosgrave to ensure that he was re-elected president by fifteen votes. He promptly re-appointed his cabinet. However it was unwise to have allowed such a crisis to erupt through the absence of government deputies, and it reminded the public of the old age pension question that had provoked so much resentment only six years earlier. *The Manchester Guardian* might respect Cosgrave's 'austere determination to set a limit to the charitable impulses of the Dail', but Fianna Fáil was able to contrast this reluctance to pay for pensions with the government's (treaty-imposed) readiness to disburse substantial sums to 'ex-British Judges, Officials, and Police'.[157]

The Irish Statesman referred admiringly to Cosgrave's courage and dexterity as he refused to whittle down his policy in an effort 'to buy off groups which held his fate in the hollow of their hand. Not the least of his triumphs was that as he managed it the thing seemed quite easy to do'.[158] But his position grew weaker as the depression worsened and as prices for agricultural products collapsed. Cumann na nGaedheal won all four by-elections held in 1927–9 (although in one case only narrowly), while it lost two out of three held in 1930–1. At the end of 1930 the president was able to point out that although agriculture was passing through a phase of acute depression, Irish citizens had an appreciable margin for savings, the social services were relatively good and the national debt comparatively low. Ireland's credit rating was among the strongest in the world.[159] The Free State's experience of the crisis was less catastrophic than that of numerous other countries, but the 1932 election would prove that many voters were unimpressed by such comparisons.

Between April and August 1930 Cosgrave was ill and he spent months away from his desk; he missed seventeen out of eighteen successive cabinet meetings, but after his return he was absent for only one more during the rest of his term of office.[160] For relaxation, whether healthy or recuperating, he rode and played golf, he travelled around Ireland, took holidays in Connemara, Rosslare and elsewhere, although (following the pattern of the times) he did not venture abroad except on business or pilgrimage.

His Northern counterpart James Craig was able to indulge in frequent cruises, but Cosgrave had enough problems to keep him at home. The number of days lost to strikes increased dramatically between 1928 and 1931.[161] The turn of the decade saw the IRA resume its campaign of violence—and, as was almost always the case between 1922 and 1939, its actions took place in or were directed against the independent Irish state rather than in or against Britain or Northern Ireland.[162] In many respects these IRA activities were a continuation of the civil war rather than an attempt to renew the conflicts of 1916–21. Policemen and warders were attacked; witnesses, jurors and others were intimidated and even murdered; and railway lines were torn up. Shots were fired at the soldiers guarding Cosgrave's house as they returned from duty.[163] Eoin O'Duffy, the police commissioner, warned that the IRA was on the verge of open insurrection.[164]

From the point of view of the Catholic and conservative establishment, an alarming feature of this violence was the emergence of new socialist-republican groups, in particular Saor Éire, and there were exaggerated fears of a Communist threat to Ireland. McGilligan had little faith in the existing Dáil, where Cumann na nGaedheal was weakened by its coalition partner, and he speculated that the government might seek a mandate to rule for a year by decree, with 'absolute control' and without needing parliamentary approval for its measures.[165] (This would have followed the contemporary pattern of Brüning's government in Germany between 1930 and 1932.) Moderate Labour leaders shared the government's belief in the 'Red peril', and two TDs broke with the party to side with the government on the question.[166]

As in 1922 the president solicited the help of the Catholic hierarchy, and once more it rallied round. After holding a secret meeting with Cardinal MacRory in August 1931 Cosgrave sent a seventeen-page memorandum to him and the other bishops, in which he warned of a Communist-inspired conspiracy that aimed at 'the abolition of government as we understand it, the confiscation of property, the destruction of the existing order, and the creation of a state of anarchy'. The conspirators were described as appealing 'to the poverty of the poor, to the cupidity of the dishonest, to the envy of the unsuccessful…Rents, debts, etc. are exploitations of the poor in the interest of the rich'. The government sought episcopal support for the legislation it planned to introduce.[167] The bishops obliged, and their pastoral denouncing revolution and Communism read almost like a paraphrase of some of the documentation provided by Cosgrave.[168] At least in part, the government's actions can be seen as a response to Fianna Fáil's increasingly close relationship with the Catholic Church (and after de Valera came to power he surpassed Cumann na nGaedheal in moral zeal).[169]

When Cosgrave introduced a repressive Public Safety Bill in the Dáil in October 1931 he stressed the need for establishing military tribunals. He warned that the IRA's attack on the courts had been completely successful, and that the ordinary law-abiding citizen had been placed at the mercy of the least scrupulous element of the community. Saor Éire was 'simply an organisation for setting up in this country a State on the lines of the Russian Soviet Republic'.[170] The new legislation established military tribunals that could impose the death penalty. Despite the public emphasis on Communism, the government's main target was the IRA and its tactics were opportunistic; unable to trump Fianna Fáil's green card it resorted to a red scare.[171] The act was criticised widely, but—as during the civil war, and again after O'Higgins's assassination in 1927—drastic measures succeeded, if only temporarily, in crushing republican acts of violence.

DEFEAT

The 1932 general election was held in surprisingly calm and peaceful circumstances; the main exception was the murder of a Cumann na nGaedheal TD, Patrick Reynolds, in Co. Leitrim, but this was the action of a disgruntled former supporter rather than of political opponents. Yet as in the past, the IRA campaign achieved one of its main objectives: it succeeded in branding the government as intolerant and authoritarian. This image was reinforced by the foolish prosecution of Frank Gallagher, the editor of *The Irish Press*, de Valera's new daily paper, on the grounds of seditious libel. The trial, which took place during the election campaign, enabled Fianna Fáil to portray Cosgrave's administration as waging a campaign against the freedom of the press, and also to distract attention from its own continuing close links with the IRA. By the 1930s the public was no longer prepared to accept measures that were more appropriate to the early days of the state and the civil war.[172]

This blunder was one of several during Cumann na nGaedheal's last year in office. In 1930 Cosgrave wrote that the government might have paid more attention to 'political' stunts. Ministers were unable to travel around the country and they were often out of touch with the people.[173] Yet they antagonised voters by introducing an emergency budget; income tax was increased, the tax on petrol was raised and the salaries of teachers and the police were reduced. On polling day Cumann na nGaedheal was punished by groups it had alienated, most notably when the owners of small buses placed their vehicles at the disposal of Fianna Fáil in protest against the recent tax.[174] It has been argued that Cosgrave and his colleagues regarded the state finances as being 'too serious a business to be the subject of party political considerations. This was an era of relative innocence'.[175] Yet, as a Cumann na nGaedheal supporter wrote later, 'if the Government really desired a renewal of confidence at the polls its actions immediately before the election bordered on lunacy'.[176] Having earlier stressed the importance of its majority support, it now made a virtue of its unpopularity.[177] An administration that regarded the opposition as dangerous and unfit to hold power should have done more to avoid defeat.

In Ireland as elsewhere politicians were often at the mercy of civil servants and bankers. When Britain left the gold standard in 1931, Sidney Webb, who had been in government until only five weeks earlier, complained that 'nobody told us we could do this'.[178] In a similar fashion, the Irish cabinet depended on experts such as J.J. McElligott, the secretary of the Department of Finance, who warned that securing a balanced budget was a test universally applied to measure a government's ability.[179] All Irish economists opposed 'any minor divergences from the canons of free trade and neoclassical economics'.[180]

Mere longevity acted against the administration; and two years before the election *The Irish Statesman* had commented that in both parts of Ireland 'generations seem to pass; events recede almost into myth and history, but the Government, like Tennyson's brook, goes on for ever'.[181] There was a widespread feeling that a change was overdue. Three years before the 1932 dissolution of the Dáil *The Leader* referred to de Valera as 'possibly, if not probably, the President of the next Government'. In 1930 Cosgrave had accepted that there would be a change in the administration of the country sooner or later, and declared that according to all the political rules he and his colleagues 'should have been turned out years ago'.[182] Fianna Fáil seemed increasingly like a government in waiting, and it stalked Cumann na nGaedheal.[183]

In summer 1931 Cosgrave reported that he and his colleagues had resisted pressure for a general election.[184] Difficulties increased, and less than two months later the Department of Finance prepared a gloomy memorandum lamenting that the harvest was poor, trade was stagnant and tax yields would be low; drastic economies in expenditure would be needed.[185] McGilligan worried about the prospect of declining revenue, falling prices, growing demands for services, increasing unemployment and the absence of emigrants' remittances. He believed that 'it would be sheer madness to think of trying to operate repressively throughout a miserable and poverty-stricken twelve-month' and wondered if an election might be feasible in February 1932.[186] But in November Blythe told a party meeting of the cabinet's decision that until economic and other difficulties had been dealt with a general election would be undesirable.[187]

In the event, the election *was* called for February, as McGilligan had hoped and earlier than the president had anticipated. (It could have been postponed until October, and Cosgrave might have been wise to stick to his original plan.) The timing was conditioned partly by the Imperial Economic Conference that was scheduled for the following July, if not sooner. Cosgrave was aware that Britain, Australia and New Zealand had all held elections in the recent past, and that if the Irish government did not possess a recent popular mandate its position at the conference would be weakened. The Free State might not get 'the best bargain' if other dominions felt that another party could soon be in office. He felt that any decisions reached would not be binding on a Fianna Fáil government. Apart from his concerns about the economic conference, he believed that 'when financial issues of the first importance may arise at any moment, it is advisable to get a new Parliament without delay'. No-one saw any immediate likelihood of improved conditions. He had already told several bishops that he intended calling the election after the Eucharistic Congress in June, and accordingly he intended contacting the archbishop of Dublin to inform him of the change of plan.[188] His tone did not augur well for the government's chances. Nor did the fact that the opposition put forward more candidates than Cumann na nGaedheal.

The campaign was fought in dismal weather, and in Roscommon town Cosgrave was observed by a seven year-old schoolboy who decades later remembered

> a thin face blue with cold, gesturing hands red with cold, hair rising in the cold like a cockatoo's and a deep collar turned right up about the ears against the wind.[189]

In his speeches Cosgrave argued that Ireland was fortunate in comparison with wealthier countries, but it could not hope to plough a lonely furrow; that the treaty could not be altered without the consent of both sides; and that Fianna Fáil would 'let loose once more upon the people the instigators of disorder and crime'.[190] He stressed economic circumstances, and in a Carlow factory he informed his audience that the world's battles were being fought in the workshops and fields.[191] As he had done so often in the past, he emphasised the citizens' duties: they should take the responsibility of shouldering their own share of the government of the state.[192] Cumann na nGaedheal looked back on its achievements while in office and boasted with some justification that it had not changed its policy to win votes. De Valera was the obvious target in the party's claim that it had never put forward five contradictory policies at the same time.[193] As in the past, it made the basic mistake of drawing attention to its opponent.

Cosgrave forecast that a victory for Fianna Fáil would result in internal disturbances; it would facilitate an armed conspiracy that was spreading Communism under a thin guise of patriotism and that had been solemnly condemned by the hierarchy.[194] But the government proposed no plans for the future. The IRA reduced the scale of its activities, although only temporarily, thereby reducing the impact of the government's warnings.[195] Cumann na nGaedheal ran the only two female candidates in the election.

Fianna Fáil played down its demand for a republic, and it concentrated on issues such as the removal of the oath, partition, the Irish language and the retention of the land annuities. It portrayed itself as being more Catholic than the government, which many of its speakers associated with unionists and Freemasons.

Cumann na nGaedheal won 57 seats to Fianna Fáil's 72, and the party's share of the vote fell by 3.4%—even though it had swallowed up the National League, some farmers and some independents.[196] This was even worse than Cosgrave had expected. He had thought that the government would lose eleven seats and gain two or three, but in the event it gained none.[197] The result should not have surprised anyone; in Britain, Germany, the United States and elsewhere, democratic governments were swept away by the Great Depression. But in Ireland the consequences were enduring, and Fianna Fáil would remain the largest party in the state for an uninterrupted period of 79 years.

Rumours circulated that elements hostile to de Valera planned to prevent his assumption of power, but with one exception there is no evidence of such a conspiracy and there is good reason to doubt it. The exception was O'Duffy, the commissioner of the civic guards, who took soundings among army officers to see if there would be sufficient support to stage a *coup* if de Valera were to be elected.[198] The chief of staff made it clear that the army would support a democratically elected government, however objectionable it might be, and he removed suspect officers from positions where they might have been able to cause trouble. Mulcahy later claimed that when Major-General Hugo McNeill had suggested a *coup d'état* against the new government he told the man not to be an ass.[199]

Cosgrave heard reports, made enquiries and was reassured quite accurately that everything was under control.[200] He admitted that some threats had probably been made, with the result that the Fianna Fáil leadership became alarmed, and he warned O'Duffy against taking action.[201] It is significant that O'Duffy was the only figure to be dismissed from a state office when the new government consolidated its position by calling and winning an election in 1933. De Valera had ample opportunity to investigate the matter once he was in power. If he had been able to uncover any evidence of a wider conspiracy it would have been in his interest to publicise it and immediately remove those responsible from positions of influence. He did neither.[202]

It may be a sign of Cosgrave's suspicion of the incoming administration that in the interval between the election and the first meeting of the new Dáil he offered the post of secretary of the Department of Industry and Commerce to John Leydon, one of the ablest of the country's civil servants. Sensibly, Leydon decided to wait and allow the incoming minister to make the appointment. In this respect Cosgrave's fears were unfounded; Seán Lemass, who became the new minister at the department, appointed Leydon to the post, and the two men formed a successful team for many years to come.[203]

When the newly elected Dáil met on 9 March 1932 de Valera was elected president by 81 votes to 68. (It is said that before the vote Cosgrave calmly played pontoon with John Marcus O'Sullivan.[204]) It was ironic, if not tragic, that in one respect this was the culmination of what Cosgrave had fought to attain throughout the previous decade: the people's will had triumphed, and a peaceful, democratic change of government had taken place. Soon afterwards, in opposition, he claimed that the presence of Fianna Fáil deputies in the Dáil was proof and satisfaction that the persuasive methods adopted by his government were not without their fruit.[205] But the fruit was bitter to the taste. He was the victim of one of his greatest achievements.

After the election, but before the transfer of power, Cosgrave concluded philosophically

> if it is over—we might have done better—but God's will be done.
> I hope the country will not suffer in any way, but personally I feel
> glad to be out of politics.[206]

He would never return to power, but he would remain in politics for another twelve years.

Following pages:
'Rally round President Cosgrave', 1927 Cumann na nGaedheal election poster.
'Prosperity in the Free State', anti-Cumann na nGaedheal election handbill, 1927.
'Friendly warning', political cartoon showing Kevin O'Higgins 'raking up the past', published in the *Herald*, 28 May 1927. O'Higgins was assassinated by members of the IRA on 10 July 1927.

RALLY ROUND PRESIDENT COSGRAVE

THE MAN WHO NEVER WEN BACK ON HIS WORD AND CAN BE TRUSTED TO SEE YOU SAFELY THROUGH

VOTE GOVERNMENT

Published by Cumann Na nGaedheal, 5 Parnell Square, Dublin.   Printed by the Temple Press, Temple Bar, D

"PROSPERITY" IN THE FREE STATE.

"The Free State is the most prosperous country in Europe" said Mr. Cosgrave twelve months ago in Paris.

"The last five years had been a period of extraordinary advancement" said Mr. Desmond Fitzgerald four months ago in Dunlaoghaire.

The following extracts from the Official Free State Estimates for 1926-27 show where this "prosperity" and "advancement" has been:—

President's Department

Mr. Cosgrave's Salary	£2,500
Parliamentary Secretary to the Executive Council	£1,200
Parliamentary Secretary	£1,000
Secretary	£1,200
Assistant Secretary	£794
Aide-de-Camp to President	£562
Higher Executive Officer	£371
*Bonus	£1,142
Travelling Expenses	£500
Incidental Expenses, including uniforms for President's Chauffeurs	£150
Allowance to Mr Cosgrave for use of his private car	£500

The above salaries do not include the bonuses.

Department of Agriculture.

Minister H.gan's salary	£1,700
Allowance for Private Sec.	£150
Secretary	£1,200
Allowance for Private Sec	£100
Assistant Secretary	£1,000
Agricultural Director	£950
Principal Clerks (two)	£1,544
Account	£673
Staff Officers (three)	£1,865

The above salaries do not include the bonuses.

Total cost in salaries, wages and allowance not including bonus £110,074.

Land Commission.

Commissioners (two	£2,837
Assistant Commissioner	£1,200
Private Secretaries to Commissioners	£300
Secretary	£1,130
Second Secretary	£900
Assistant Secretary	£672
Examiner of Title	£1,000
Examiners of Title (two)	£1,734
Examiners of Title (two)	£1,600
Examiners of Title (temporary)	£3,360

The above salaries do not include the bonuses.

Total cost of Department in salaries and allowance £258,175.

Department of Fisheries.

Minister Fionan Lynch's Salary	£1,700
Allowance for Private Sec.	£100
Secretary	£830
Staff Officer	£564
Higher Executive Officers	£876
Junior Executive Officer	£1,786
Clerical Officers	£2,263
Chief Inspector of Fisheries	£675
Inspectors of Fisheries	£1,2
Superintendents	£1,314
Local Fisheries Officers	£1,674
Bonus	£6,645

The above salaries do not include the bonuses.

Total cost of Department in salaries and allowances £21,826.

* Cost of Governor General's Establishment £27,133.

The foregoing are only a few items from the Official Estimates of the Free State Government. They serve, however, to show why the cost of governing 26 Counties is about £30,000,000 a year, and explain why the people are crushed beneath an intolerable load of taxation.

Is it any wonder there are Unemployment, Starvation and Emigration in the country when the people's money is thus squandered on a British Governor General, on an ornamental and useless Senate, and on an army of highly paid Ministers and Officials?

Cosgrave and Michael Hayes leading O'Higgins's funeral procession past Government Buildings, July 1927. Also in the photograph are Diarmuid O'Hegarty, Eamonn Duggan, Patrick McGilligan, J.J. Walsh and Fionán Lynch.

Opposite: Cumann na nGaedheal election poster for September 1927 election, denouncing Fianna Fáil for taking the oath of allegiance and entering the Dáil in August, having refused to do so since 1922.

They took the Oath
to save their party
—they would not take it in 1922 to save the country from Civil War

THE Oath to-day is the same as it was in 1922—an oath to obey the will of the majority of the people. Not a syllable has been altered. Mr. De Valera and his friends would not take it then. They preferred to plunge their country into the horrors of civil war. If they had taken it then there need have been no "wading through blood."

Why did they not take it in 1922? Because, in the words of their leaders, "the people did not matter; they were mere sheep, to be driven."

Why have they taken it now? Ever since they took it they have been busy contradicting one another in an attempt to hide their real motives. Now they pretend to put the nation's peace above party advantage.

The latest "explanation" is that they took the oath they say they will not keep in order to safeguard "innocent" gunmen from the Public Safety Act.

If to defeat the Public Safety Act was their object, why did they not think it necessary to "humiliate" themselves until after this Act had become law and they were too late to defeat it?

it was the Electoral Amendment Bill that brought them in—it put an end to their plans to destroy the State from outside the Dail.

They would not enter the Dail in 1922 because their gunmen were then in power outside. They have gone in now because their gunmen have been driven to cover, and they want to use the Dail to put them in power again.

The Fianna Formula for "National Peace" is to "invite all men who stand for Irish Independence to enter the Army."

THE PUBLIC KNOW WHAT THAT MEANT IN 1922.

Mr. McEntee lets the cat out of the bag . . . .

"Whatever justification Mr. Cosgrave's Government had for the Public Safety Bill . . . . there was none for the Electoral Amendment Bill . . . . After that (the Electoral Amendment Bill), Fianna Fail was not going to allow personal pride to prevent them from taking the oath."

—Sean McEntee at Malahide on August 14

_and discloses another "Empty Formula"!

Give your Vote to
Cumann na nGaedheal

The Party that has given you National Peace in spite of the Empty Formulists

Copy Cable sent at 8 p.m. 15.III.1927 to

The International Broadcasting Corporation,
165 Broadway,
NEW YORK CITY,

        Following is Statement asked for in wire of 14th STOP

(1)   Mr. De Valera's insane campaign of destruction in
1922-23 by which he endeavoured to wreck the Treaty between
Ireland and Great Britain cost the State no less than 75
million dollars in Army expenditure and twenty-eight million
dollars in compensation for direct destruction of life and
property of which twenty-three million dollars have already
been paid. For nearly two years the normal life of the
country was practically at a standstill, while Mr. De Valer's
dupes in the name of freedom strained every nerve to deprive
their country of life and liberty. Their honesty of purpose
may be judged from the fact that banks were a special
object of their attack and from these robbed hundreds of
thousand of dollars. Rails were torn up, roads broken and
bridged destroyed, telephone and telegraph wires cut and
stolen and communication by every means repeatedly
interrupted;   the total cost to the State in direct expenditure, taking no account of consequential losses to farmers
and business men over one hundred and three million dollars.

(2)   It might have been thought that an infant State of
little over 3,000,000 people commencing life under such
                                        circumstances

Kevin O'Higgins, Michael Hayes, Cosgrave, Hugh Kennedy, Desmond FitzGerald and Ernest Blythe, all wearing top hats and tails.

Opposite: Part of Cosgrave's 1927 St Patrick's Day message for broadcast in the United States, which is highly critical of de Valera and republican activity during the civil war. This part of the speech was censored by the International Broadcasting Corporation.

LUNCHEON

tendered by

Hon. William Hale Thompson
Mayor of Chicago

in honor of

Liam T. Cosgrave
President of the Irish Free State

Saturday, January the twenty-first
nineteen hundred and twenty-eight

Main Dining Room
The Drake Hotel
Chicago

With every good wish
Wm Hale Thompson
Mayor

Cosgrave with the mayor of Chicago, William Hale Thompson, 22 January 1928, during his trip to the United States and Canada.

Opposite: Invitation, signed by Mayor Thompson, to lunch held in honour of Cosgrave during his visit to Chicago in January 1928.

Cosgrave speaking to the press during his visit to the United States,
28 January 1928.

Opposite: Cosgrave opening the rebuilt General Post Office,
1929, with a silver key that was presented to him as a memento of
the occasion.

Following pages:
'Night's candles are burnt out', painting by Seán Keating (1929)
of the completed dam for the hydro-electric station at
Ardnacrusha.

'Visit the Shannon Works! See this mighty project in the making',
ESB poster promoting visits to the 'Shannon Scheme' at
Ardnacrusha during its construction.

'The campaign against Evil Literature has started', political
cartoon relating to the culture of censorship of the time.

Visit the Shannon Works!

See this Mighty Project in the making

Arrangements have been made with the Great Southern Railway to issue <u>Return Tickets at Single Fares</u> from all stations on its system to Limerick on week-days, available for return within three days including day of issue, from now on until the 29th of September inclusive.

Conducted Tours daily from the I. O. C. premises
Sarsfield Street, Limerick :—
1st Tour leaves at 10.30 a.m., returning 1.30 p.m.
2nd   „   „   2.30 p.m.,   „   6.30 p.m.
BUS FARE 4/- (Children Half-price)
Guide's services free.

Those not wishing to avail of these Conducted Tours should apply direct for a permit, giving date of proposed visit.
Conducted Tours on SUNDAYS for large excursion parties ONLY—

Apply to The ELECTRICITY SUPPLY BOARD

GUIDE BUREAU, STRAND BARRACKS, LIMERICK

O'LOUGHLIN
PRINTER
FLEET STREET
DUBLIN

THE CAMPAIGN AGAINST
EVIL LITERATURE HAS
STARTED

24th Sept 30

Dear Mr Clark

I have been considering
the subjects introduced in the Staun
Seun ??? since I had the pleasure
of seeing it on Monday last.

I have come to the conclusion
that O'Flahertys ??? works should
not be included — ??? that connection
has not excluded your own interests
as well as those of others.

In making any suggestion
as to an alternative I find myself in
deep water & would like to have the
benefit of your judgment.

Sincerely yours
??? ??? ???

Inside the window panel: "...come towards him dancing, moving ...folds of the veil, so that they ...folded slowly, as she danced. ...in Gilhooley. by LiamOFlaherty."

"I know the great gift we will give to the Gael will be a memory to pity and sigh over; and I shall be the priestess of tears. Deirdre. by George Russell."

Panel 6 of the Harry Clarke window commissioned for the ILO building in Geneva, depicting the scene from Liam O'Flaherty's novel 'Mr Gilhooley' about which Cosgrave had expressed reservations, and George Russell's 'Deirdre'.

Opposite: Draft letter from Cosgrave to Harry Clarke, 24 September 1930, regarding the content of panels for the stained glass window, commissioned by the government for the International Labour Office building at the League of Nations, Geneva.

Following pages:
Draft letter from Cosgrave to Archbishop Gilmartin of Tuam, 11 March 1931, pointing out it was not possible for the government to discriminate on religious grounds in making appointments to public posts.

'Government by the rich and for the rich', Fianna Fáil poster for 1932 general election, criticising Ernest Blythe.

'We want no "Reds" here', Cumann na nGaedheal poster 1932, warning of the dangers of Communism.

Anti-Fianna Fáil poster for the 1932 general election.

My Lord Archbishop,

      Your letter of the 4th instant is but further evidence of Your Grace's continued interest and goodwill. ~~On this~~ and ~~occasion~~ I can but repeat the sincere gratitude to which I have ~~had~~ had already to give expression.

      I should particularly like to thank Your Grace for the trouble you have taken in ascertaining the views of various persons of influence in Mayo. In this connection it may not be out of place to mention that when I spoke of a restoration of the good relations happily existing between the Ecclesiastical Authorities and the Government, I had in mind the Executive entrusted with the administration of the Law, rather than ~~any~~ a particular group member belonging to a definite political party, who, for the moment, happen to bear the responsibility.

      I fear, however, that those whom ~~Your Grace~~ consulted *you were so kind as to consult* ~~have not had present to their minds~~ *will a view to arriving at a solution of the present difficulties do not really grasp in the matter of the Govt.* the effective limits of the Government's powers ~~if it~~ conscientiously ~~performs~~ *to fulfil* its duties.

      As I explained to Your Grace at our interview *in the* to *applied in favour of or* discriminate against any citizen - ~~or to exercise a preference for~~ a citizen - *on the ground of religion* on account of religious belief, would be to ~~conflict with~~ *repudiate* some of the fundamental principles on which this State is founded. *We cannot impose religious test.*

      That the librarianship question as a whole can be solved as an educational position is open to considerable doubt. The Hierarchy has not as a whole made such claim, and obviously general legislation for the country - not particular legislation for a particular part - would be to recognise the Law, and the Minister had no option but to take effective steps for its enforcement.

      It is with deep regret, therefore, that I am unable to see a solution along the lines indicated in Your Grace's letter.

GOVERNMENT
BY THE RICH
AND
FOR THE RICH

VOTE
FOR FIANNA FÁIL

WE WANT NO
'REDS' HERE!
KEEP THEIR
COLOUR OFF
YOUR FLAG!
VOTE FOR
CUMANN
NA n GAEDHEAL

NO GOODS TAKEN
FROM WINDOW !

Supplies from
Goods Stores
only !

Published by Cumann na nGaedheal, 5 Parnell Square, Dublin, and Printed by Browne and Nolan, Ltd., Printers, 41 and 42 Nassau Street, Dublin.

Our New Half-Sovereign?

Worth its Face Value !

'not be always at the beck and call
of mob movements'.

Opening image: 'Our new half-sovereign',
anti-de Valera election poster, 1932.

THE British had hoped that Cumann na nGaedheal would win the 1932 election, and after the change of government in Dublin they waited impatiently for its return to power. There should be 'no disloyalty to Mr. Cosgrave'.[1] They were anxious to avoid taking steps that might weaken him and consolidate de Valera's position. Cosgrave played a balancing act. On the one hand he sent emissaries to London with the message that Britain should not capitulate in its dispute with the new Irish administration.[2] Some members of Fianna Fáil accused the opposition of aiding the enemy. Seán Lemass claimed that Cumann na nGaedheal was intriguing behind the government's back to secure a new agreement and to provide the British with

> the last penny which Mr. Cosgrave's tax-gathering machine would be able to squeeze out of the Irish farmers if he was returned to power…There is a definition of treason in any standard dictionary, and I invite Mr. Cosgrave and his colleagues to look it up.[3]

But even while he was still president he had urged London not to adopt an aggressive attitude in the event of de Valera taking office.[4] Later, he expressed doubts about Desmond FitzGerald's claim that Britain had a right to refuse to lift tariffs against Irish imports; 'there may be a case for the British contention, it's not for us to make it'.[5] He would not damage Ireland's national interests.

For ten years he and his government had argued that the treaty provided the state with sufficient freedom. During the recent election campaign he declared that he did not know what more the Free State could ask than the decision of the Imperial Conference of 1926: all the dominions were co-equal with Britain.[6] But de Valera knew what more he could ask—or what he could take. In the course of the next six years he tore up the treaty that Cumann na nGaedheal had maintained so conscientiously and he succeeded in removing the few remaining limitations to Irish sovereignty. He appealed to traditional anti-British sentiment, and where Cosgrave had chosen co-operation he preferred confrontation. Although his measures provoked retaliation, he did all this with relative impunity. Despite the warnings of disasters to come, the independent Irish state enhanced rather than damaged its international reputation. Defenders of the 1921 settlement were soon left with nothing to defend; even their valued role as champions of democracy would be undermined by their own miscalculations.

Fianna Fáil settled comfortably into office and quietly appropriated many of its predecessor's achievements. Cosgrave noted how 'it appears that de Valera dominates the others in all things'.[7] Some years earlier O'Higgins had written that 'the "Chief" is gone, for better or worse, in Irish politics'.[8] He was wrong; the chief was back. There would be no more public quarrels or ministerial resignations, as there had been in the early 1920s. The new government showed drive and determination, and Cumann na nGaedheal soon became marginalised. As early as November 1932 Cosgrave's old friend the earl of Granard was reported to have described him as a spent force.[9] But it was noted that when he mingled with the public he was more popular than his party or his former cabinet colleagues.[10]

In April 1932 de Valera took the first steps to abolish the oath to the king. Ten weeks later the 'Economic War' began, when the Irish government defaulted on the land annuities—the repayment of loans made to Irish farmers by British governments under the land acts. These amounted to £3 million a year. (The two agreements concerning payments that had been concluded between the previous administration and the British were not approved by the Dáil.) The money was collected as before, but it remained in Dublin and was placed in a suspense account pending arbitration. The British responded by imposing duties on Irish livestock, thereby recouping much of the money that they would have received through the annuities, and in turn, the Irish taxed British coal. Even though the conflict eased with the 'coal-cattle pacts' of 1935–7 (whereby each side raised its quota for those key exports), it came to an end only in April 1938.

For many farmers the consequences of the dispute were grim. The value of Irish exports crashed and the price of cattle fell by more than half, leading to widespread hardship among middling and large farmers—who, conveniently for the new administration, were largely supporters of Cumann na nGaedheal. Others benefitted from the fall in the price of beef, and *The Sunday Times*'s correspondent noted that cheap meat was associated by the masses with a Fianna Fáil government.[11]

De Valera combined these radical measures with cautious and conservative policies elsewhere. Long before, in 1927, William Redmond described Cosgrave and his government as having been converted from poachers to gamekeepers, and he saw no reason why de Valera and his colleagues should not do the same.[12] They did. Now that Fianna Fáil ministers were in power they began to accept the legitimacy of the state, and later they would prove themselves stern in its defence. But traces of their earlier ambivalence remained, and in a revealing remark while sparring with Cosgrave in the Dáil, Seán MacEntee referred to the government as 'an institution which owes its origin to you'.[13]

In the course of the 1930s Fianna Fáil moved to the centre of the Irish political spectrum and by the end of the decade it had become unambiguously democratic. It was both populist and entrepreneurial. It provided stable, efficient administration, and it emphasised the symbolic rather than the violent side of militant republicanism.[14] De Valera displayed a skill that he had lacked in 1921–3, and many former opponents were won over by his combination of aggression and moderation. Soon Yeats was able to remark 'I am a Cosgrave man…but I believe that de Valera is dead right in his dispute with Great Britain', and he compared the new president to Swift as representing a nation's 'turbulent self-assertion'.[15]

FIANNA FÁIL TRIUMPHANT

De Valera was anxious to escape from his dependence on Labour support in the Dáil, and in January 1933 he called a snap election. Although Cumann na nGaedheal was caught off guard it was able to learn from its past mistakes; in particular the party dropped the purely negative approach that had made so little impact a year earlier, and it informed voters of what it would do if it regained power. Cosgrave's personality was emphasised, in contrast to earlier and later campaigns, and he was portrayed as a man of honour, principle and consistency.[16] He promised that he would end the Economic War in three days, and FitzGerald even claimed that if Cosgrave returned to office he would cross to London that very night and negotiate a settlement.[17] This was a popular commitment in many quarters, and in Waterford 60 dock labourers, who had suffered from unemployment because of the conflict, contributed towards Cumann na nGaedheal funds.[18]

Cosgrave also declared that he would introduce a two-year moratorium on the payment of annuities, and that they would subsequently be resumed at half the existing rate. This represented a change from the policy he had followed while in power. He attacked what he described as the government's strategy of 'perpetual and aimless war with our neighbours, bankruptcy for our farmers, and the imposition of extravagant taxation in the pursuit of unthinking and ill-considered economic schemes'.[19] De Valera stressed the need for strong government, and he repeated his commitment to abolishing the oath, retaining the annuities and protecting Irish industries. But during the campaign he was warned privately that his manifesto contained no reference to partition; it was therefore most important that he should emphasise this grievance in his remaining speeches.[20] He provided comical relief when he dashed by mistake into a Cumann na nGaedheal convention in Limerick town hall before being directed to his own party headquarters.[21]

Cumann na nGaedheal resumed the innovative pattern that it had shown in September 1927, when it had successfully employed an advertising company to assist in running its election campaign, and Cosgrave was the first Irish party leader to feature in a 'talkie' film. This circulated the country in a large van (with the politically appropriate registration plate ZZ 1916), equipped with a projector and screen, and free open-air showings were provided.[22] Election leaflets were scattered from a plane.[23] Once again Cosgrave was unlucky with the weather in Roscommon, where one of his speeches was delivered in a blinding snowstorm, while at the other extreme he addressed a crowd estimated at 40,000 in College Green in Dublin.[24] He gave good advice to constituency executives, trying to ensure that the party would not lose seats by splitting its vote between too many candidates, but in some areas his recommendations were ignored—to the party's detriment.[25]

Large crowds welcomed him on his tours, and in his final address he declared that all the signs pointed towards a record victory.[26] He wrote afterwards 'we never had better meetings or more enthusiasm'.[27] But some of the patterns were ominous. In an editorial supporting Cumann na nGaedheal *The Irish Times* conceded that de Valera was backed by 'the raw, young people on the new register…almost to a boy and girl'.[28]

The poll, of over 81%, was the highest ever recorded in an Irish election. De Valera secured the free hand he had sought, gaining a further five seats and winning an overall Dáil majority—of one. By contrast, Cumann na nGaedheal lost nine seats and almost 5% of the first preference votes it had obtained a year earlier. In Cork Borough, Cosgrave received more votes than any candidate in the country except de Valera, O'Kelly and MacEntee. Other former ministers were less popular: Ernest Blythe was defeated in Monaghan; Patrick Hogan had a narrow escape in Galway; and in Kerry John Marcus O'Sullivan and Fionán Lynch were elected on the last count.[29]

Before and after the dissolution of the Dáil Cosgrave had held discussions with Frank MacDermot, the leader of the National Farmers' and Ratepayers' League (soon to become the Centre Party), but they failed to agree on the formation of a new political grouping.[30] Some of Cumann na nGaedheal's support drifted to the Centre, which won 9% of the vote; MacDermot's party had many policies similar to those of Cumann na nGaedheal, but it also had the attraction of novelty. The Centre won 30% as many first preference votes as were gained by Cumann na nGaedheal, which lost five seats in constituencies where Centre Party candidates polled well. (MacDermot claimed that Centre candidates swelled the opposition vote to a higher total than it would otherwise have reached.[31])

After the election the British lost hope in an early Cosgrave restoration and reconciled themselves to living with de Valera for the foreseeable future. A year later, Cosgrave advised London that it could not expect de Valera's government to collapse and it should come to a settlement with him.[32]

The Blueshirt parenthesis

The 1933 election was the most violent in the history of independent Ireland; among many other incidents, some of Cosgrave's supporters were attacked in Co. Kerry and 50 people were injured in a confrontation in Dublin.[33] This followed a pattern that had developed throughout the previous year: a return to civil war politics. One of the first actions of the Fianna Fáil government in 1932 had been to release political prisoners, and now that the tables were turned many IRA men seized the opportunity to take revenge on their once-dominant opponents. Within weeks of the transfer of power Cosgrave and McGilligan were howled down at a public meeting by IRA members shouting the slogan 'no free speech for traitors'. Such activities soon became widespread.

The Fianna Fáil government turned a blind eye to the extremism displayed by some of its own supporters, and at times it even seemed to endorse violent paramilitary organisations. Shortly after coming to power de Valera visited Skibbereen, Co. Cork, and the civic guard formed a guard of honour on one side of the street while the local IRA lined up on the other. De Valera ignored the police, but he took the salute from the IRA and inspected its detachment before entering the town.[34] When Blueshirts and the IRA mobilised at the same place the guards were consistent in ordering only the Blueshirts to redirect or discontinue their parades and rallies.[35] Opponents of the government lost confidence in the state.

Within weeks of de Valera's re-election General Eoin O'Duffy was dismissed as commissioner of the guards. The government's critics viewed him as a martyr, and its action provoked strong criticism from Cosgrave and other opposition leaders. (They ignored the fact that when they were in power they had viewed his insubordination with growing unease and had decided to dismiss him if they won the election.[36]) They feared, wrongly if understandably, that his removal might mark the beginning of a purge of public officials, but de Valera stood firm against such pressure from his party members in a way similar to that in which Cosgrave had resisted *his* followers during the early years of the state.[37] The new president was happy to exploit the talents of many former opponents.

O'Duffy took over the leadership of the Army Comrades Association (later called the National Guard), an organisation that had been founded in the previous year to protect Cumann na nGaedheal speakers and meetings from attack. This body soon adopted fascistic symbols, such as the blue shirt uniform and the Roman salute. Only a small minority, most notably Blythe and O'Duffy, sympathised with the authoritarian patterns spreading across Continental Europe. It was perhaps significant that Blythe preferred to spell 'comrades' with a 'k', giving the association what he regarded as the striking initials AKA.[38] The overwhelming majority of the association's members saw themselves as decent and upstanding members of society who were under threat from a republican mob that endangered free speech.[39] The 'Blueshirts' adopted much of the paraphernalia of the anti-democratic Right, but few of them were actually fascists; they were

> simply traditional conservatives, decked out in fashionable but ideologically ill-fitting continental garb…The shirt and the salute marked the summit of their ideological achievement.[40]

They added colour to the drabness of life in the 1930s.[41]

O'Duffy announced that he would lead a parade of 20,000 of his followers to the memorial commemorating Griffith, Collins and O'Higgins that stood outside Leinster House. Such gatherings had been held annually in the time of the previous government, but now the circumstances were completely different. Some observers wondered whether the parade might be the prelude to an attempt to seize power, modelled on Mussolini's 'march on Rome' eleven years earlier. Was he planning a coup? He said not, probably truthfully, but the government was understandably worried.

The government's initial response was to order the confiscation (allegedly for 'stock-taking') of weapons that were held legally by Blueshirts and members of Cumann na nGaedheal—but weapons in the hands of republicans were not confiscated. Soon afterwards the National Guard was suppressed, while the IRA remained undisturbed.[42] Cosgrave accused Fianna Fáil of providing political sensations to divert attention from the economic condition of the state, and he demanded that the government should act impartially.[43] It then banned O'Duffy's parade, using emergency legislation that had been introduced under the previous administration in 1931, and that was suspended but not repealed after Fianna Fáil had come to power. Thereby it regained the initiative, and O'Duffy backed down. As a result of this defeat he became prepared to compromise with politicians, a group he had hitherto viewed with distaste or even contempt.

From June 1933 renewed meetings were held to merge Cumann na nGaedheal and the Centre Party. Subsequently these talks widened to involve the Blueshirts. Cosgrave showed no sign of enthusiasm at their inclusion and it seems that any reservations he might have had were shared by some of his front-bench colleagues—in particular by Patrick Hogan.[44] But having lost two general elections in rapid succession, the former ministers were in a weak position when dealing with men who conveyed an impression of energy and aggression. Some party members approached O'Duffy and invited him to accept the leadership of the new party.[45]

When Cosgrave announced the merger to a Cumann na nGaedheal convention in September 1933, he outlined the need for unity against Fianna Fáil, described the negotiations with the Centre (but not the Blueshirts) and claimed that 'a full appreciation of the services and public work of General O'Duffy was present in the minds of the members of the Centre Party'. He made no such claim for the Cumann na nGaedheal representatives at the meetings. The result of the discussions was that O'Duffy would become president of the newly formed Fine Gael party. Cosgrave never mentioned the Blueshirts in his speech, and (at least by implication) as far as he was concerned O'Duffy was chosen as leader in a purely personal capacity.[46] Cosgrave, Frank MacDermot and James Dillon of the Centre Party would become vice-presidents, and others were added later. The party's programme was thoroughly democratic and it showed little trace of Blueshirt influence; this was the price demanded by the constitutional parties for accepting O'Duffy's leadership.[47] Among Fine Gael's aims was resistance to 'the claims of any self-declared army or dictatorship, to exercise political authority, or to interfere with individual liberty for Communistic or other ends'.[48]

Cosgrave was prepared to sacrifice his leadership of the strongest element in the new alliance; he saw the prospect of achieving unity against de Valera as being more important than maintaining his own position in the party. Many of his followers welcomed the change. When O'Duffy arrived at the Cumann na nGaedheal meeting to decide on forming a new party all the delegates sprang to their feet and cheered for several minutes.[49] Much as supporters of the treaty had revered Collins and tolerated the IRB in 1922, now they accepted 'a leader disdainful of parliamentary democracy'.[50]

Twenty years later MacDermot claimed that he would have far preferred Cosgrave as leader of the new party to O'Duffy, but that because some of his colleagues disagreed with him the merger could not have been achieved unless he gave way. The Centre would have welcomed Patrick Hogan as leader, but he was unwilling to play the part. MacDermot recalled that it was Cosgrave who had first suggested O'Duffy's name.[51] However this seems at odds with Cosgrave's notable lack of enthusiasm in his speech announcing the formation of the party in September 1933. For Centre politicians, the choice of O'Duffy as leader lessened the risk of their being subsumed into Cumann na nGaedheal.[52]

The general was not a member of the Dáil, and Cosgrave was able to continue without interruption as the leader of the parliamentary opposition. Each of the three components of the new party, including the Blueshirts, appointed six members of the executive, and Cosgrave had to exclude some of his former cabinet colleagues. Only ten of the twenty-four members of the Fine Gael executive were Dáil deputies.[53] Hogan was unhappy with these developments and his withdrawal to the backbenches—and often from the Dáil itself—was a serious loss to the party. But there were several other reasons for this action: he was defeatist and resentful after Fianna Fáil came to power and implemented policies he deplored; he became a husband and father; and he concentrated on his legal practice in Co. Galway.[54]

The new party's policy stressed its commitment to democracy, its opposition to Communism, its determination to abolish PR and its plan to establish industrial and agricultural corporations—a manifestation of the belief, then popular in some quarters, that class conflict should be replaced by cooperation between trade and professional organisations. No attention was paid to many of the views that O'Duffy had expressed in the course of the previous year. But the merger gave a badly needed veneer of legitimacy and respectability to the Blueshirts, and they in turn provided the political opposition with a populism and dynamism that it had lacked.

The National Guard was banned, as was its successor the Young Ireland Association, and the Fine Gael headquarters was raided by police. In a scene reminiscent of de Valera's capture in Ennis ten years earlier, O'Duffy was arrested while making a public speech in Westport, Co. Mayo, but his detention was soon deemed illegal and he was released at the demand of the high court.[55] Numerous meetings addressed by Cosgrave, O'Duffy and others were attacked, and stones and bottles were hurled at speakers and their cars. In Leitrim a visit by the two leaders was marked by shots, a baton charge, the felling of trees and the blocking of roads by stones. The platform on which they were due to speak was doused with petrol and set on fire.[56] In separate incidents four Blueshirts died of their injuries after having been beaten or shot. In contrast to skirmishes involving uniformed political armies in Continental Europe, the Blueshirts were more often the victims than the perpetrators of thuggish behaviour.[57]

Much of the violence in 1933–4 was a consequence of the Economic War. Calves were slaughtered because there was no market for them, there was widespread hardship and many farmers refused to pay annuities to the government. In some cases their cattle and other belongings were seized, sales of their belongings were disrupted and battles took place. Like most prominent figures in Fine Gael, Cosgrave was dismayed when party members resorted to lawlessness. He claimed that when governments conspired against the liberties of the people some of them were driven to oppose the law—but he condemned such conduct nonetheless, and he argued that 'it is possible for men and women to combine peacefully for the protection of their rights'.[58]

Many of the meetings he addressed were accompanied by Blueshirts, who formed a guard of honour and saluted with arms extended. Such behaviour was at odds with every aspect of his past and future career and there is no reason to think that he welcomed it; he may have 'recoiled from these developments with horror'.[59]

Cosgrave stayed carefully aloof from the paramilitary aspects of the movement. In contrast to some of his colleagues he never wavered in his adherence to democracy, and an Italian Fascist complained of him that he was 'completely permeated by democratic principles'.[60] Prominent members of Cumann na nGaedheal such as Mulcahy, Blythe and FitzGerald admired the Blueshirts' forcefulness, and on occasion some of them wore the blue uniform—at times even in the Dáil, to Cosgrave's embarrassment.[61] He could hardly discipline them for following the example set by the party leader, but he did not join them. He retained his customary attire of white shirt, wing-collar and bowler hat; no-one could have looked less like Hitler or Mussolini.

He was always reserved in his statements concerning the Blueshirts. Although they provided bodyguards at party meetings he hardly ever mentioned them after they had become formally linked with Fine Gael. When he did, it was to criticise the government for banning them.[62] He described the blue shirt as inoffensive and he referred to 'St Patrick's blue'.[63] He praised

O'Duffy in public (he could hardly have done otherwise) and described him as an Irish leader with an Irish name (a blatant allusion to de Valera). In one speech he declared that the party could not mark its appreciation of O'Duffy's long and faithful service to the country in a better manner than by asking him to take over the leadership of the movement. 'He was worthy of the office'.[64] He attacked the government's treatment of the general, its claim that the courts hampered the executive and its failure to protect its political opponents from attack. He reiterated his party's opposition to the use of arms. It had 'stood for majority rule all along since 1922'.[65]

On occasion he deferred to the new 'corporatist' strand in his party. In replying to a paper on the Corporative Society by James Hogan (a UCC professor of History and a brother of the former minister for Agriculture), he rejected the idea that every effort to realise Catholic social principles in action should be condemned as dictatorship. He believed that the plan of reorganising society along vocational lines, in accordance with authoritative Christian principles, should be common ground on which all Irish Catholics could agree. The opinions of Protestants were not mentioned. He hoped that economic and social questions might be removed from political disputes, and he rejected the 'bogies' of social division and class war, but he also wished to give workers' organisations a new status and a new dignity.[66]

He continued to be busy in the Dáil and on public platforms. For the most part his speeches were concerned with issues such as the government's faults, increased taxation, the danger of Communism, annuities, the decline in cattle exports caused by the dispute with Britain and the hardship that resulted from that conflict. He opposed the government's plans to abolish the Senate.[67]

In all the excitement generated by the Blueshirts, Cosgrave was relegated to the margins; the Labour leader William Norton remarked that O'Duffy was awarded streamer headlines and leaded type in the newspapers, while his predecessor was confined to two or three lines.[68] Even James Dillon was reported to have described him as a 'spent force'.[69] But despite this demotion the former leader remained personally popular, and on a tour of Donegal O'Duffy commented bitterly on the lack of support for the Blueshirts, while it was noted that Cosgrave aroused warm feelings.[70] This may be the reason why the general 'disappeared' during the leaders' tour of the county and returned unobtrusively to Dublin.[71]

In a break with what had been Cumann na nGaedheal's traditional policy, O'Duffy decided to contest the local elections in June 1934, and his position as president of Fine Gael was weakened by the party's failure to stage a breakthrough at this level. He expected an overwhelming victory but by the standards he had set the results were disappointing; Fianna Fáil won 728 seats, Fine Gael 596, Labour 185 and other candidates 371.[72] Cosgrave conceded that 'we have not yet completed electoral machinery up to full efficiency point'.[73]

O'Duffy was normally obliged to modify his extremist tendencies and, with exceptions, the Fascist strand in the movement was muffled and marginalised; the Blueshirts were increasingly overshadowed by their politically minded partners. But the general's radicalism re-emerged from time to time. Some of his statements became even wilder than before; he encouraged Blueshirts to prevent the seizure of cattle, and he even threatened war against Northern Ireland.[74] In September 1934, nearly two years after the Nazis had come to power, he praised Hitler's achievements in Germany.[75] The Belfast *Irish News* claimed that Cosgrave was critical of him, while James Hogan denounced his 'destructive and hysterical leadership' and resigned from the party's national executive.[76]

Cosgrave made it clear that he wanted a showdown; he did not share Dillon's view that there should be a 'patch up'. In what for him was a stinging indictment he claimed that the de Valera government's political policy was safer than O'Duffy's. The new leader differed fundamentally from his colleagues on matters of party management and national reunification. Cosgrave saw him as unreliable and inconsistent, and he believed that to rehabilitate him in the public mind would be an almost insuperable task.[77] The other members of the party leadership were determined to remain within the law and they could not tolerate his erratic opinions and behaviour. O'Duffy had to go.

The general was presented with an ultimatum, tactfully described as 'points of agreement', according to which all party officers were 'to deliver only carefully prepared and concise speeches from manuscripts in future. Interviews to Press to be given only after consultation and in writing'. Not surprisingly, O'Duffy rejected these terms and he resigned.[78] The role of the members and the party traditionalists in rejecting his excesses showed that their dominant political allegiance was to the liberal democracy that had emerged following the years of the Irish revolution.[79] Fine Gael was lucky that a two-months-long newspaper strike in Dublin concealed its upheavals from many of the electorate.

RETURN OF THE VETERAN

The party that had rushed to embrace O'Duffy now rediscovered Cosgrave's virtues; it reverted to a reliable and trusted figure who did not provide excitement but who inspired confidence. (In a similar manner, in August 1922 the provisional government had welcomed him as a chairman whose style con-

trasted with Collins's dynamic but dangerous impetuosity.) When a party convention formally elected Cosgrave president of Fine Gael in March 1935 he
noticed that no-one present inquired why O'Duffy had left.[80] His return to the
leadership provoked mixed feelings; he was attacked in some quarters, and
Michael Tierney saw his reinstatement as removing any chance of beating de
Valera in the near future.[81] James Hogan, a persistent critic, wrote that 'to Mr.
Cosgrave's omissions, ineptitudes and utter want of vision and initiative I at-
tribute most of Fine Gael's misfortunes. He was so sure O'Duffy was a great
man that he sat still and let him run amok for a whole year'.[82] Yet Cosgrave did
more than anyone else to ensure that his party's links with the Blueshirts
amounted to no more than an embarrassing parenthesis rather than an ominous
new beginning.

The historian Nicholas Mansergh was not surprised when, after O'Duffy's
sudden departure in September 1934, Cosgrave took over as acting party
leader; the former Cumann na nGaedheal ministers had treated him with
great deference during his temporary eclipse. A month later Cosgrave wrote
to him referring to 'a mild political sensation of which you may have heard',
and Mansergh saw this as an example of his characteristic quality: a quiet,
sub-acid humour.[83]

The reinstated leader faced a problematic inheritance. In some quarters the
new party would find it difficult to regain Cumann na nGaedheal's hard-earned
reputation for solidity and for indifference to the whims of the electorate. Its
links with the Blueshirts had made it a fashion victim, 'momentarily modish,
perhaps, but soon faintly ridiculous'.[84] Cosgrave was impervious to fashion.
But the Blueshirts had been expensive, and Dillon warned that the party owed
£8,000—£3,000 of which was due immediately—and that 'our creditors are
pressing'.[85] (Some months earlier Cosgrave had pointed out that over 80% of
the party's subscriptions came from Dublin city and county.)[86] Internal disputes continued and the inconvenient paramilitary allies were slow to disappear.
As late as February 1936 a large body of Blueshirts welcomed Cosgrave to
Fermoy.[87] The following October a meeting of the Fine Gael standing committee chaired by Cosgrave decided that the actions of Ned Cronin, O'Duffy's
successor as director general of the Blueshirts, were 'subversive to the interests
of the Organisation' and his membership of the party was terminated.[88] The
force was disbanded.

Corporatism also proved hard to shake off. Even after Cosgrave had resumed
the leadership, one of the party's fourteen objectives was the development of a

corporate system based on the principles enunciated by the papacy.[89] The model might be Roman, but at least it was provided by the Rome of Pius XI rather than of Mussolini. This was as far as he went in his concessions to the views that were briefly in vogue among party members, and he soon retreated from them, never to return. The corporate state was allowed to fade away quietly, and in the following year even Fine Gael's publicity organ *United Ireland* admitted that the policy was no longer popular.[90]

While his opponents were distracted by these internal feuds, de Valera continued to implement his long-term programme. Stage by stage he dismantled the treaty. The oath of fidelity to the king (by now called 'oath of allegiance' even by many of those who accepted or defended it) was removed, then the Senate, then the governor-general, and finally the constitution was abolished. All these moves helped to marginalise the extremists in the IRA and lure back into the political system many others who were hostile to the Free State.[91] He legitimised the polity he had done so much to delegitimise ten years earlier.[92]

De Valera showed that he was able to do what Cosgrave and others said he could not do, and he left them with no convincing arguments against him. The roles of a decade earlier were now reversed. Until 1927 he had ignored the Irish state, arguing that it was impossible for him and his followers to take the oath. He was forced to break his promises and submit to terms imposed by his enemies, but he was able to wriggle his way off the horn on which he had impaled himself.

In a similar manner, Cosgrave's assertions that the treaty was sacrosanct, and his forecasts that disaster would follow any attempt to contravene it, were all disproved after 1932. It was difficult to answer the question de Valera posed to his opponents who had argued that the treaty gave Ireland the 'freedom to achieve freedom': were those 'who acted on that policy now going to say that there is to be a barrier and a perpetual barrier to advancement?'[93] Fine Gael was unable to develop an alternative policy, while de Valera's actions confirmed that the treaty *did* grant Ireland the freedom to achieve freedom—as Collins had claimed in 1921–2. He was indifferent to taunts that he had thereby vindicated his enemy and had proved himself wrong. For Cosgrave, it was galling to see the opponent whom he despised undoing much of his work, ruling with competence and authority and establishing himself as the unchallenged Irish leader.

De Valera allowed the IRA free rein as long as it attacked supporters of Cumann na nGaedheal/Fine Gael; in 1934 the military tribunal convicted nearly four times as many Blueshirts as members of the IRA.[94] But when its atrocities provoked widespread disgust and the organisation began to threaten his own position, he changed tack and banned it. Fianna Fáil benefitted from the widening breach with the IRA, and de Valera won support from moderates who had earlier regarded him with suspicion.

The government also undertook an ambitious social programme. A decade earlier Blythe had been complimented because one of his budgets 'holds the scales of justice even between rich and poor'.[95] Fianna Fáil was able to appeal to those who felt that the scales should not be even and that they should be tilted in favour of the weak and vulnerable. It continued and expanded the housing programme that the Cosgrave administration had begun at the end of its term of office. Of almost 91,000 houses built between 1923 and 1938, more than 65,000 were constructed after 1932.[96] Unemployment benefits and old age pensions were also increased—and so were taxes. The serious damage done to agriculture during the Economic War was matched by a rise in industrial employment, partly as a consequence of wide-ranging tariffs. Fianna Fáil also sought economic self-sufficiency, although with only limited results.

Government ministers were kept busy running their departments, but after losing office Cosgrave found that he had time on his hands. He began breeding shorthorn cattle, with considerable success. In his correspondence he reported rumours concerning de Valera's likely actions, the prospects of ending the Economic War on relatively favourable conditions and the likelihood of an early general election. He went on pilgrimage to Rome in March 1934 and found 'a great air of business about Italy'. A year later his doctors ordered him to go to the Continent and, accompanied by two priests, he visited France and Spain. He was impressed by Barcelona, which he thought resembled a miniature London.[97] His and his party's financial worries lessened in 1938, when he received an allowance of £800 per year as leader of the largest opposition party.[98]

PARTY PROBLEMS

A decade earlier it had been suggested that Cosgrave would have benefitted from a few years in opposition.[99] But having been in power for so long he found it difficult and frustrating to adjust to the role of a leader who had no prospect of an early return to office. He remained active politically; for example, in a period of three weeks in October 1935 he was scheduled to address meetings on different days in Navan, Carlow, Ennis and Hospital.[100] The party was dissatisfied, however, and the following year it was suggested that he might travel more widely around the country.[101] Fine Gael drifted; some deputies were lazy; and in 1935 the director general of the party complained that it was impossible to have any work done at headquarters or in the constituencies while members of the standing committee were apathetic in attending meetings.[102] It was decided that each TD would meet Cosgrave and discuss his intentions and location.[103] Little or nothing happened, and in October 1936 he wrote to deputies deploring internal differences and difficulties, and complaining that they deflected attention from major problems.[104] Economies became necessary; that summer the party newspaper *United Ireland* had ceased publication. Cosgrave and Dillon shared an office in the party headquarters.[105] One meeting was held without raising 'any possibly awkward questions about whether a quorum was present'. Some deputies thought that the weather (in mid-November) was too cold to attract crowds at outdoor rallies. The minutes recorded bleakly 'It was ordered that the party re-assemble at 9.45 p.m. It did not.'[106]

Fine Gael remained an unhappy family. Cosgrave reported general agreement that there must be harmony within the party's own ranks; 'if we cannot bring about cordiality, candour and confidence between ourselves we cannot expect the public to support us'.[107] The well-disposed *Irish Times* agreed, and it referred to Fine Gael's sorry spectacle of indecision and internal disagreement, its policy of persistent attack.[108] *The Leader* lamented that the opposition was not a satisfactory fighting force. It saw the national political struggle as one between Cosgrave and de Valera, while it dismissed other politicians as 'also rans'; Cosgrave was the outstanding opposition figure, but he was calm and 'not a play-actor or firebrand'.[109]

A correspondent wrote to him that although people were losing confidence in Fianna Fáil there was no sign of them turning to Fine Gael: 'our policy or utterances are too cautious or too negative…caution may paralyse a party in opposition and rob it of the power to launch an offensive.'[110] *The Irish Times* regretted that Fine Gael had toyed with futile expedients, none of which could be expected to make a real impression on the people. It had been speaking with many voices.[111] But one powerful voice was silenced. Although Patrick Hogan had kept aloof from party affairs since the events of 1933–4 he remained a formidable political figure, and his death in a car crash in July 1936 was a grievous blow to his party. Cosgrave lamented that 'our best man is gone'.[112]

At the end of that year Richard Mulcahy drafted an extraordinary letter to Cosgrave, running to nineteen numbered headings, in which he launched an attack on his leader's style of management. He demanded that Cosgrave should inform his associates of his opinions on important matters; it was futile to leave them guessing. He contrasted this to his own efforts to give the party the impression that somewhere in its ranks there was 'authority, guidance and grip'. He accepted that in the early days of opposition there might have been something to be said for Cosgrave's reticence, even though it had permitted the intrusion of O'Duffy, MacDermot and Cronin into the party's leadership. He went so far as to suggest that Cosgrave's policy might be to allow Fianna Fáil win the next election, but if that were not the case the opposition needed leadership 'of a non-reticent, non-enigmatical kind'. As party leader, Cosgrave should be dynamic and forward-looking. Mulcahy ended by stating that he would discuss the matter after Christmas.[113]

It is uncertain if the letter was ever sent, or if the discussion ever took place, but the fact that such views were put on paper indicates a malaise at the highest ranks of the party and dissatisfaction with its leader. Seven years and three further election defeats elapsed before Cosgrave handed over the reins to Mulcahy. Both men might have been forgiven for showing impatience with their party colleagues, who must often have seemed passive and slothful.

Cosgrave continued to argue that he could settle the Economic War. He complained that de Valera's policies had allowed Britain to regulate Irish trade, and he argued that a government's first duty should be to regain economic independence.[114] He queried and harried ministers on issues such as the electoral register, details of expenditure and the Central Bank Bill. He warned that 'if you depreciate people's incomes, decrease their capital investments, and absorb their savings, you cannot expect from these people that sense of citizenship which formerly existed here in this country'.[115] He remained sceptical about Fianna Fáil's industrialisation policy; 'as one person goes into a factory another leaves the land either to the Irish cities or England'.[116] He defended the election of some TDs by university graduates, principally because of the medical profession's record in improving public health, and he retained his distaste for populism. He argued in favour of representation in the Dáil 'that will not be always at the beck and call of mob movements and that will not have to depend for its existence on always doing something that is popular'.[117]

As in the past, he was a sharp and sometimes abusive debater. He informed one deputy that he had increased in weight since he came into the Dáil, if not in intellectual capacity; he asked another was he looking for a certificate to qualify him for a mental home; and he told Lemass 'if you mean what you have said, it is humbug'.[118] He accused MacEntee of wallowing in vulgarity, and—although a short man—he drew attention to others, such as O'Kelly, who were even smaller.[119] On one occasion MacEntee complained that Cosgrave was being most disorderly, and Lemass described him as a master in the art of interruption.[120] In general, however, he spoke at a higher level than many of his supporters or opponents.

His opponents' position seemed unthreatened. De Valera not only continued to dominate Irish national politics, but he also became a prominent international figure who was active in the League of Nations. By contrast, Cosgrave was more narrowly focused on Ireland, and he was relatively uninformed about European affairs. In early 1937 he expressed doubts about the feeling in Britain that Germany would move east and that war was almost certain.[121] He viewed the world from a Catholic standpoint. Only days before the Munich agreement of September 1938 he reported that the Czechoslovak leaders Masaryk and Beneš held high office in the Masonic Order. Nazi persecution in Austria was on a vastly greater scale than anything Ireland had experienced under the Black and Tans, but 'they say this persecution of "Jews" is mere propaganda, that it includes and is directed towards Catholics'.[122] His reference to Jews should not be misunderstood, and there is no evidence whatever that he shared a still-prevalent anti-Semitism.

In some instances Fine Gael's attitude towards foreign disputes was inconsistent and muddled; 'the coherence and sense of purpose which had marked the pro-Treaty party's conduct of external affairs while in office had collapsed in opposition'.[123] It was divided in its response to Mussolini's invasion of Abyssinia in 1935, and initially Cosgrave was among those who criticised the government's support of League of Nations sanctions against Italy. He complained that de Valera had failed to extract concessions from the British (in the context of the Economic War) as a return for supporting sanctions.[124] He argued that British economic measures against the Free State impaired its ability to join in the League's activities.

This stance was unpopular and Fine Gael subsequently changed its mind—but too late to prevent MacDermot's resignation from the party. He rejected the idea that the Free State had a bargaining position and that 'we were free to choose between honouring our engagements and dishonouring them'. Fine Gael should have supported the government when it was in the right.[125] (MacDermot had in fact long planned to leave, and a year earlier he decided to postpone this step because he did not want to hit the party when it was down.[126]) De Valera's old enemy P.S. O'Hegarty wrote that the president 'is in the right for the first time in his political career'.[127]

The Spanish Civil War also proved contentious. Cosgrave favoured Franco's Nationalists, believed that the Irish representative should be withdrawn from Madrid and distinguished between 'patriots' and the 'Red Government'; the conflict in Spain was 'a war for the victory or defeat of Communism and all it stands for'.[128] Increasingly Fine Gael emphasised the religious aspect of the struggle. *The Irish Times* deplored a 'patently vote-catching attitude towards the problems of Abyssinia and Spain'.[129]

Such efforts at vote-catching had only limited results, and after five years in opposition the party was still in an unhealthy condition. By 1937 it was clear that a general election must take place in the near future, and although the government was unpopular Fine Gael was badly placed to make the most of its opportunities. The party's director of elections complained that in six constituencies nothing whatever had been done to prepare for the election.[130] MacDermot claimed that in Roscommon Fine Gael's organisation could hardly be said to exist.[131] It had no obvious partners, and the unhappy experience of the merger with the Centre and the Blueshirts must have made Cosgrave and his colleagues wary of any new alliance. In opposition the party had drifted further to the right, influenced by the collaboration between Fianna Fáil and Labour in 1932–3, and thereby it abandoned the middle ground to its enemy. Fine Gael was Cumann na nGaedheal writ small.[132]

The electoral act of 1935 benefitted Fianna Fáil by reducing the size of many constituencies and ensuring that in subsequent elections it would gain considerably more seats than its proportionate share of the votes.[133] Cosgrave later criticised what he described, with notable moderation, as a 'clever rearrangement of constituencies—I use no harsher word'.[134] (At the time, his objections had centred on the treatment of counties Cork and Donegal.[135]) Even though *The Irish Times* hoped wistfully that Fine Gael might snatch an unexpected victory, from the beginning of 1937 it was generally taken for granted that Fianna Fáil would be able to form the next government.[136] McGilligan was quoted as saying that there was no possibility of Cosgrave's party returning to power in the near future.[137]

TWO ELECTIONS

Early in 1937 de Valera introduced a draft new constitution. The old one was ragged and threadbare, and its authority had been undermined in 1928 when the Cumann na nGaedheal government doubled from eight to sixteen years the period during which it could be amended by ordinary legislation. By 1936, 48 of its 83 articles had been amended.[138] De Valera wanted a fresh start, a 're-foundation' that would wipe from the record his opponents' successful government of the state throughout its first decade. The name 'Irish Free State' would disappear and be replaced by 'Éire' or 'Ireland', while the title of the office that Cosgrave had occupied, 'president of the executive council', was succeeded by that of 'taoiseach'. While retaining most of the strengths of its predecessor, the new constitution would have the advantage of being 'home-grown' and of escaping any association with the treaty that de Valera hated so much. Thereby it reconciled many republicans to the independent Irish state.

Cosgrave sensibly ignored a letter from a former government colleague urging him to resist 'the Suffragette agitation arising out of the Constitution…their poisoned fangs were everywhere in evidence'.[139] But he attacked the draft as being entirely the work of one man; as being a party measure (he complained that on no issue had a free vote been allowed); as exalting the authority of the prime minister at the expense of his cabinet colleagues (ministers ought to possess security and a measure of independence); as giving the state president unjustifiably wide powers; and as endangering equality between the sexes. He thought it absurd that the Irish text of the new constitution would predominate in the case of disputes in courts of law, even though it was a translation of the original English version. The people would be given neither the time nor the opportunity to exercise a wise judgment on the document.[140] He dismissed its treatment of partition as 'make-believe'.[141] But the Fine Gael party did not support MacDermot's proposal that the constitution should recognise Ireland's membership of the Commonwealth and George VI as king of Ireland.[142] It appreciated that irreversible changes had taken place since 1932.

De Valera called an election for 1 July 1937, the same day as the referendum on the constitution. The campaign was tame and uneventful, in contrast to the excitement of four years earlier. An observer at one of Cosgrave's election meetings noted that while he dealt effectively with interruptions he also meandered, and that when he raised good points it was only to play with them and then to move on to side issues.[143] But on other occasions he was sharp and forceful. A heckler asked him did he stand for an all-Ireland republic and he 'rapped out the answer: "I do not"'. The commentator added

> There is not much nonsense about Cosgrave. Of course, he did not mean that for ever and for ever he was against an all-Ireland Republic…Cosgrave meant that here and now he does not stand for an all-Ireland Republic. Neither does de Valera.[144]

In his speaking tours he emphasised high taxation, the increased cost of basic items of food, the irrelevance of the new constitution and how the Fianna Fáil government had divided the country. He claimed that when he left office the national debt was £32 million, and five years later it stood at £61 million.[145]

Fine Gael performed relatively well. It retained the same number of seats, although the Dáil's membership had been reduced, but it failed to pick up any of the eight lost by Fianna Fáil. Its share of the vote rose by 4.4%—the only increase in the seven elections held between those of September 1927 and 1951—although it fell by 5% from the combined Cumann na nGaedheal/ Centre vote in 1933. But Labour was the main beneficiary of Fianna Fáil's un-popularity, and its proportion of the vote rose from 5.7% to 10.3%.[146] Mulcahy was defeated in Dublin North-East and FitzGerald in Kilkenny, although Mulcahy returned to the Dáil in the following year. Cosgrave's constituency lost one of its members, and for the first time he was unable to secure the election of a party colleague. The constitution was endorsed by a narrow majority, and Fianna Fáil remained in power. As a sign of changing times the new British prime minister, Neville Chamberlain, was on balance satisfied with the result.[147] De Valera now represented stability and respectability; he was the man with whom the British could do business.

After the election Cosgrave argued that Fianna Fáil had fought with three great advantages: it had re-drawn the constituencies to its own benefit; it had secured support from groups that gained from government expenditure raised by increased taxation; and its financial resources far surpassed those of Fine Gael—which was now left with a debt of £5,000.[148] Cosgrave wrote to FitzGerald in early 1938 that the party's 'staff is small, the work of this [Senate] Election is falling to a small number…the task of securing support has had to be undertaken individually'.[149]

In the context of a possible coalition with Fianna Fáil he was scornful of the cabinet's expertise and he felt that it did not have 'a single competent or even able administrative financier or economist'—although he did view the party's elec-toral support with an appropriate respect.[150] By now he had good reason to do so.

Cosgrave was sounded out unofficially as to whether he might run for the new office of national president. He refused, on the grounds that popular elec-tion was a bad system and that in principle the party was opposed to an elected head of state.[151] Perhaps the abuse of presidential power in Germany between 1930 and 1933 provided a warning of the dangers that such a pattern could entail. The elderly and apolitical Douglas Hyde was chosen as a consensual candidate.

In April 1938 de Valera secured an advantageous settlement of the Economic War. Annuities were cancelled, in return for a lump sum payment of £10 million; favourable terms were obtained for Irish exports to Britain; and the treaty ports were handed over to Irish control, thereby making it possible for Ireland to remain neutral in a future war. Having learned from his mistake in 1921, de Valera conducted the negotiations in London himself. Even though he was dismayed by Hitler's acts of aggression he benefitted from Chamberlain's policy of appeasement. Faced with threats from Germany, and also, if more distantly, from Italy and Japan, the British government wanted at least to tidy up the minor irritation on its western flank. As a result it made concessions to Ireland that would have been unthinkable a few years earlier; if the Irish 'won' the war it was for political reasons.[152] (In similar fashion, shortly afterwards Britain placated the Arabs in Palestine in order to reinforce its position in the Middle East.[153])

In a less than plausible speech Cosgrave informed the government that he did not begrudge it any advantage it might derive from the settlement. He argued that such an agreement could have been secured at any stage during the past five or six years, and he claimed that the government had simply implemented Fine Gael policy. Fianna Fáil denied his claim that he could have obtained the ports years earlier but had chosen not to do so for financial reasons.[154] People paid more attention to de Valera's achievement in ending the Economic War than to the fact that he had started it.

De Valera seized on the first opportunity to call a general election; this arose in June 1938 when he was defeated in a minor vote on the question of arbitration in civil service disputes. Cosgrave suspected that some Fianna Fáil deputies had been ordered to be absent from the Dáil for the vote and thereby provide a pretext for an election.[155] In the campaign he fought doggedly, criticising the government for extravagance and for the high cost of living. He claimed that its industrial policy had been of little benefit to the country, and he even accused it of wanting 'something like Hitlerism'.[156] Some of his causes were far from populist; for example, he promised that if it were returned to power Fine Gael would restore the recently abolished university seats in the Dáil.[157] But with the ending of the Economic War one of his main weapons had been whisked from his hands.

Cosgrave complained that the opposition had been caught at a disadvantage, but initially he still expected the government to lose votes—and probably also seats; he felt that it was difficult to see how it could improve its position. Soon reality set in, and he lamented that his party 'will not do nearly as well as the last time'.[158] It did not. The Dáil had 138 members and Fine Gael ran only 76 candidates (compared with 95 a year earlier), showing how little faith it had in being able to form a government on its own. It lost three of those seats it already held. With almost 52% of the vote, Fianna Fáil gained eight seats, mainly at the expense of Labour. For the first time since 1922 Cosgrave failed to top the poll, and soon afterwards he dismissed the rumour that he intended resigning as leader of the party. (The previous year it had been suggested that he might be glad to escape from the turmoil of politics.)[159]

In light of de Valera's diplomatic triumph only two months earlier Fine Gael's performance was respectable, but the party remained sluggish. In 1936 its standing committee met sixteen times; in 1937, seven; in 1938, eight and in 1939, five. Some staff members were sacked and others were forced to accept reductions in their salaries.[160] It seemed doomed to permanent opposition.

NEUTRALITY

With the outbreak of war in September 1939 Cosgrave overcame his reservations and he supported the Emergency Powers Bill, which effectively licensed the government to rule by decree. The normal parliamentary legislative functions were suspended.[161] The Dáil voted unanimously in favour of Irish neutrality; any other course would have divided the country and would probably have led to violence. He wrote that apart from the merits of the war 'which, in the circumstances, held a secondary place', neutrality was the only method of preserving any measure of national unity. He was concerned about the possible erosion of citizens' rights and liberties, but had he been in office he would have done the same as de Valera. He argued that Irish neutrality proved the genuine independence of Commonwealth states.[162]

However he was not always consistent. In July 1940, shortly after the fall of France, he sent a remarkable letter to de Valera. He wrote that

> We share the Government's view that a hostile invasion by Britain
> is not contemplated…The position therefore is a probable hostile
> attack from one side, and an offer of assistance from the other…If
> owing to our lack of defensive power a substantial German force
> lands in this country the destruction that must inevitably follow
> from the efforts of the other belligerent to expel them is appalling
> to contemplate…if the Government in changing circumstances

feel it necessary to depart from the policy of neutrality in which they have had our support up to the present my colleagues and I would be prepared to give them our fullest support in such a change of policy.

The taoiseach turned down the idea of co-ordinating defence plans with Britain on the grounds that 'if we invite military assistance from one side, immediate attack by the other side, with all its consequences, will be almost inevitable'. Cosgrave then reiterated his view that 'changing circumstances may conceivably make it in the best interests of the country to take that step before actual invasion'.[163] In practice de Valera implemented the spirit of these proposals, but neutral Ireland's collaboration with the Allies was carried out in secret. The last thing he wanted from Fine Gael was support that might have to be acknowledged in public.

Cosgrave continued to underpin the government's policy, even though the idea of a wartime coalition was rejected. An all-party defence conference was established but it achieved little and he chose not to be a member—just as he had earlier decided not to take his place on the Council of State established by the new constitution. He and his colleagues were frustrated at being given little information.[164] His refusal to meet de Valera also created problems. For example, when the taoiseach sought a discussion with some members of Fine Gael a preliminary conference took place in Cosgrave's house; Mulcahy and Dillon then spoke with de Valera and O'Kelly; and finally they reported back to a meeting at which Cosgrave was present.[165] (Subsequently a reference was made to his 'almost fantastic hatred' of the government.[166])

In December 1939, when the IRA seized most of the Irish army's stock of ammunition, he taunted Fianna Fáil that 'you are now seeing the fruits of what you sowed yourself'; he viewed the IRA as the spiritual successors of de Valera and others who took arms against the state in the civil war.[167] However while he claimed to have no belief in internment, he would not object if the government were convinced that it was the only means of securing the safety of the state.[168] This was a logical extension of his conduct during the civil war. In similar fashion, de Valera now behaved as Cosgrave had done when he was in power; hundreds of IRA members were interned, six of them were executed and three others were allowed die on hunger strike.

Cosgrave's support of neutrality was a sensible and statesmanlike approach, even though it could be seen as an abandonment of the Commonwealth connection that he and his party had defended for so long. It also removed a further difference between them and Fianna Fáil. He felt obliged to refrain from criticising the government's foreign policy; anything suggesting a deep cleavage of opinion might encourage 'adventures' against Irish territory. He argued that independent Ireland should devote all its energies to avoid the danger of reconquest by Britain or occupation by and subordination to Germany. With British assistance it might be possible to resist a German attack, but the Germans could not help repel a British invasion—which, resulting in hostilities, would completely disorganise the country's economic life.[169] He and his colleagues also gave their enthusiastic support to the defence forces, and he addressed meetings urging men to enlist.

De Valera made virtually no reciprocal gestures, and in political terms the opposition's patriotic support of the government's measures did Cosgrave and his party little good. In 1941 he lamented that the public saw Fine Gael as 'a political wet nurse to "the boys in office"', and more than two years later a reason he gave for another electoral defeat was the widespread feeling that the country had 'an ideal opposition exercising a wise restraint'.[170] In November 1940 the novelist Elizabeth Bowen reported from Dublin to the Dominions Office that 'Mr. Cosgrave seems (these days) to be negligible', and some weeks later another visitor to Dublin described him as living 'deep in the wilderness of opposition'.[171]

However marginalised he may have been, he continued to advocate his deeply held beliefs on government and citizenship. In January 1940 he told the Dáil that the state

> will never progress, either spiritually, morally, economically, culturally, or in any other way unless we lay down for ourselves proper orders and proper regulations, for the conduct of public policy, for correct appreciation of the citizen's rights and duties, his responsibility and his obligations as well as his rights.[172]

Two years later he returned to the theme and he demanded 'as a guiding principle and a guiding rule in this country that there must be law and order, that there must be one fountain of control in this country and that we will tolerate no other'.[173] It was characteristic of him that he wrote to Fogarty praising the bishop's pastoral on truth and honesty.[174]

As opposition leader he was zealous in monitoring the government's activities, seeking to protect citizens' liberties and querying the implementation of censorship—which was often imposed in a bigoted and partisan manner. He complained that even the pope was censored and that Irish radio provided fewer details of the latest papal encyclical than the BBC had done. Irish people were not allowed to express their views on the invasions of Poland and Finland.[175] He also resisted successfully the government's proposal that the maximum lifetime of a Dáil should be extended from five to six years.[176]

Fine Gael remained demoralised and ineffective, and Dillon antagonised all sides by his outspoken remarks. In early 1940 he made a speech on the war that was at odds with party policy, but Cosgrave viewed it as an expression of a personal opinion that did not necessitate any response.[177] In July 1941 Dillon went further, appealing in favour of Ireland joining the allies. Cosgrave confessed that he had had no idea such a statement would be made, and he retained his belief that it was desirable and necessary to present a national front. He argued that

> The duty and responsibility of every person in public life is not neutrality; it is not taking part in this conflict; it lies in ensuring the security and stability and integrity of this country. If that is better served by a policy of neutrality, then it is our duty to accept and adopt that policy.[178]

The vast majority of Irish people believed that the national interests were 'best served by a policy of neutrality'. Another TD could not imagine 'how a political party can exist and have amongst its leaders such a wide divergence of opinion as has been expressed by Deputy Dillon and Deputy Cosgrave'.[179] It was not the sort of conduct that would have been tolerated from one of de Valera's lieutenants, but Cosgrave pardoned his colleague once more on the ground that people should be allowed to speak their minds and learn from experience.[180] Nevertheless, when Dillon returned to the theme yet again in the following year, Cosgrave felt obliged to accept his resignation—although the parting was amicable on both sides.[181]

His unruly colleague rejoined Fine Gael a decade later and became its leader from 1959 to 1965. But in 1942 Cosgrave feared that if such views were to be implemented the country would be placed in a vulnerable position, while the British and Americans would be no better off than before. He told the visiting Labour MP Aneurin Bevan that the state would not join the war even in return for an all-Ireland parliament.[182]

Cosgrave's speeches on the country's foreign policy were described as being stronger and clearer than those of any of his front-bench colleagues.[183] But, perhaps irked by Dillon's remarks, his defence of neutrality included a passage that seemed to be at odds with his long-term democratic commitments.

> Democracy may have as many sins to its credit and may be as faulty a form of government as autocracy.
>
> From what one either sees or reads of the course of history with regard to democracy, there is just as much to its discredit as there can be said to be to its credit. That it has worked well in one country or two there is no doubt whatever. That it is perhaps the most despicable form of Government in regard to one of the Continental countries there is no doubt either.[184]

On foreign policy he was an uncertain guide, but such sentiments were far removed from his theory and practice in Irish affairs. Despite all his electoral disappointments he never wavered in his determination that his own people should have the right to choose their governments in a democratic manner.

The Dáil met rarely (on only 66 days in 1942) and the diminution of party conflict during the war gave Cosgrave more time for non-political activities. He remained closely involved in Church affairs and he welcomed the appointment as archbishop of Dublin in November 1940 of John Charles McQuaid, a man whom he admired and who had visited the Cosgrave family every Christmas Eve for years.[185] (He continued to do so after his elevation.) His sons began their professional careers, Míceál in Goffs bloodstock auctioneers and Liam as a barrister. He read histories such as Hammond's *Gladstone and the Irish Nation*.[186] Like the rest of the country he and his family suffered from shortages of food and fuel, but his enjoyment in riding and hunting was undiminished. He followed the war closely, although he had few sources of accurate information. In his correspondence he reported rumours that the Germans had attempted an invasion of Britain in November 1940, that Ireland would be invaded, and that the Labour politician Stafford Cripps might succeed Churchill as prime minister. He admired Roosevelt's 'masterly genius' in managing American public opinion.[187]

COUP DE GRÂCE

As the war dragged on and as party politics remained subdued, Cosgrave intervened less frequently in debates and, to an even greater extent than in the past, he allowed his colleagues play the leading roles. Fine Gael became ever more torpid. In happier times the party's TDs met weekly, but only four meetings were held in 1941 and three in 1942.[188] He lamented that Fine Gael had great difficulty in persuading its followers to contest local elections, and that many of them chose to run as independents.[189] In March 1943, with yet another general election imminent, it was reported that although a policy committee had been established the previous May it had not met.[190] The reality was even worse; the committee had been formed much earlier, in June 1941. And it was perhaps revealing that although he had chaired the meeting that set up this committee, he was not a member. The party standing committee did not meet for another six months.

Cosgrave made it clear that his aim was to form a national coalition after the election, following the pattern of other European countries. He admitted, however, that this would in reality be impossible, 'if for no other reason than the existence of the head of the Government at the present moment'.[191] Many people shared the view that the divisions between the two main parties were by now largely artificial. James Hogan believed that seeking a national government was a blunder, because it drew attention to the fact that Fianna Fáil and Fine Gael were no longer divided by any major policy differences.[192]

De Valera rejected any involvement in a coalition—although, as was pointed out, he had been prepared to support one in the very different circumstances of August 1927.[193] (Cosgrave had then argued in the opposite sense.) Labour made no commitment on the subject. In his election speeches Cosgrave criticised the excessive use of emergency orders and the rise in the cost of living. He promised to restore agricultural prosperity.[194] In power, Fine Gael would provide £2.5 million to establish a scheme of family allowances.[195] The 1943 campaign witnessed a large number of independent candidates, the highest in any election between 1927 and 1977.[196] Fine Gael was described as forecasting that it would win 50 seats, and Fianna Fáil 56.[197]

The result was a heavy blow to Cosgrave and his party. There was widespread dissatisfaction with wartime conditions, and there had been speculation that Fine Gael would improve its position. De Valera's government lost its gains of five years earlier, its total of deputies fell from 77 to 67, and its overall majority disappeared; it was now in a minority of four. But Fine Gael fared even worse, its number of seats dropped from 45 to 32, and its first preference vote from 429,000 to 307,000.[198] Even more clearly than had been the case ten years earlier, the beneficiaries of an anti-government mood were Labour and independents; they, and not the main opposition party, were the choice of those who wanted to punish the government. Twenty-two candidates from outside the three main parties were elected. Richard Mulcahy, John A. Costello and

John Marcus O'Sullivan were among the losses for Fine Gael (although the first two would regain their seats a year later). But Cosgrave remained popular, and in Cork he headed the poll once again. Among the few comforts for the party was the election of his son Liam for Co. Dublin, and he was one of only three new Fine Gael deputies. He would remain in the Dáil without interruption until 1981. Within a matter of months he became one of the most prominent speakers on the opposition benches.

The reasons Cosgrave gave for the poor result included the fear of war, misgivings regarding de Valera's conduct if he were to be defeated and claims that only the government could hope to secure a Dáil majority.[199] He wrote phlegmatically that the outcome was disappointing for everybody; 'it was an interesting time'.[200] But his disappointment must have been greater than that of any other leader. By now, with the solitary exception of the 1937 result, his party's share of the vote had declined steadily in the five general elections since September 1927.

Fine Gael was widely written off, its recovery being described as almost impossible, its position irretrievable.[201] Perhaps symbolically, the party sold its headquarters on Merrion Square and moved to smaller premises on Hume Street.[202] In effect, this latest defeat marked the end of Cosgrave's leadership. He was ill, suffering from colds and influenza.[203] But he remained active in the new, eleventh Dáil, discussing topics such as wheat cultivation, army pensions and neutrality.[204] In the last debate of 1943, before the Christmas adjournment, he interrogated Lemass about aspects of the Children's Allowances Bill.[205] He did not re-enter the Dáil chamber for another twenty years.

Following pages:
Letter from Cosgrave to Diarmuid O'Hegarty, secretary of the Department of the President, 8 March 1932, expressing his appreciation for the work of the staff of the department during his time as president.

'Now on Tour: Thomas's Troupe of Imperial Artistes', poster advertising the 21 January 1933 issue of *An Phoblacht*, satirising Cosgrave and government ministers.

'Now is your chance!', Cumann na nGaedheal election poster for 1933, encouraging women voters to 'Bring back Cosgrave'.

'The farmer cannot pay', Cumann na nGaedheal advertisement, *Irish Independent*, 17 January 1933.

Eoin O'Duffy at a Blueshirt rally, *c.* 1935; to his left is Lord Mayor Alfie Byrne; Cosgrave is behind O'Duffy.

8th March, 1932.

My dear Mr O'Higaf.

On leaving Office I desire to express my high
appreciation of the manner in which the exceedingly heavy
responsibilities and arduous duties of this Department have
been discharged during the past difficult years.   The test
which was placed on the Public Service as a whole and on
the loyalty and ability of each Public Servant individually
was probably the heaviest and the most severe in the history
of public administration in this country,   In addition to
the many difficulties ordinarily associated with a change
in Government and policy new Departments had to be set
working from the foundation and much reconstruction had
to be accomplished by the Departments of State.   The
highest praise is due to the manner in which the leaders
and the staffs of your Department successfully grappled
with those difficulties and with work which had increased
both in volume and complexity.

It is a pleasure to me to place on record that a
high sense of public duty has been displayed individually
and collectively throughout the Service during a period of
exceptional stress and strain.   Ministers join with me
in sincere appreciation of the admirable work which has
been accomplished.

Very Sincerely Yours

Liam E. MacCosgair

D. O'Hegarty, Esq.,

Price **2** Pence

AN PHOBLACHT.
THE REPUBLIC.

Price **2** Pence

New Series, Vol. VII., No. 50.   SATURDAY, 21st JANUARY, 193

NOW ON TOUR:

THOMAS' TROUPE
OF IMPERIAL ARTISTES

Cream de-ficit Vanishing

"I USE IT REGULARLY, HENCE MY LOVELY UNRIVALLED CHEEK"

SAYS MISS R. NESTA BLITHE ONCE FAMOUS LEADING LADY IN "PIRATES OF FINANCE"

Ashes of Ruses Powder

"ABSOLUTELY THE ONLY THING TO SAVE MY FACE —" SAYS DAME MARCIA O'SULLIVAN OF ABERDEEN HALL.

NEGOTIATION CREAM

"INVALUABLE FOR REMOVING THOSE SUPERFLUOUS AIRS. I OFTEN USE IT ON MY TWO KNEES —" SAYS MDE. CORKSCREW, STAR OF INNUMERABLE ROYAL COMMAND PERFORMANCES AT THE EMPIRE THEATRE

J. BULL'S 'Balmy SHAM POOH!

"FRIDAY NIGHT IS ALWAYS MY Balmy NIGHT —" SAYS PRETTY PATTY HOGAN STAR TURN OF THE IMPERIAL FOLLIES.

Georgian OATHMEAL SOAP

"PRESERVES THAT IMPERIAL COMPLEX(ION)" SAYS MADAME FIZZ-KENNI THE WELL-KNOWN BOOTY SPECIALIST.

Rouge de Rogue LIPSERVICE

"BOTH ON AND OFF THE STAGE I FIND IT AN EXCELLENT FAKE UP—" SAYS CHARMING MEG GULLAGAIN NOW PLAYING IN 'BITTERSWEET'

LAST APPEARANCE
POSITIVELY!

NOW IS YOUR CHANCE!

FIANNA FAIL promised the WOMEN of Ireland to find Work for their Husbands and Sons. Since FIANNA FAIL came into power the

NUMBER OF UNEMPLOYED

HAS RISEN BY OVER

73,000

FIANNA FAIL has added to the Household Expenses by a Multitude of Taxes.

WOMEN
OF THE FREE STATE

Put out the Government that has caused so much unemployment, worry and want, and REDUCED THE STANDARD OF LIVING in every home.

BRING BACK COSGRAVE—HE WILL BRING BACK GOOD TIMES

Published by Cumann na nGaedheal, Printed at The Metropolitan Printing Works, Talbot Street, Dublin.

THE FARMER

Three times in ONE YEAR!

Fianna Fail admit that there is only one profitable market for the Farmer's exports.

They have recklessly ruined that market.

They have deprived the Farmer of the £9,000,000 he used to get for his exports.

They confess that there is no alternative market.

They have destroyed the Farmer's capacity to earn.

They have taxed everything he uses from tea and tobacco to buckets and manures.

They made him provide Bounties for exporters and relief for the British consumer.

THEY WERE DETERMINED TO MAKE THE FARMER PAY ALL HIS ANNUITY

At Ennis on April 10th Mr. de Valera said :—

"I must repeat once more that the Government will cont'nue to collect the Annuities and that the farmer must continue to pay them. . . The money belongs to the State."

In Dail Eireann on August 5th, Mr. de Valera said :

"There can be no remission of these (Land Annuities) payments at the present time."

Send Your Subscriptions to the

COSGRA VICTORY FUND

Address:

Mr. W. T. COSG

3 Merrion Sq

Dublin

★ **VOTE**

YOU CANNOT RICHER BY MAK

FOR THE

COSGR

K.A.A.

CANNOT PAY

Who made them change?
COSGRAVE!

In Dail Eireann on November 16th, Mr. Cosgrave moved a resolution that—
"The collection of Annuities should be suspended during the period of the Economic War."
Fianna Fail and Labour defeated this motion and voted to continue the policy of Lost Markets, Taxes and Writs.

COSGRAVE'S POLICY IS:

1. To STOP the Economic War.
2. To recover for the Farmer his export market.
3. To restore his earning capacity.
4. To reduce his Taxes.
5. To give him TWO YEARS WITHOUT ANY ANNUITIES and allow him to get back his losses of the last 10 months.
6. To reduce his Annuities, after that by HALF.

AKE THE TOWNS
THE FARMER POORER

VE
CANDIDATES!

COSGRAVE
WILL REDUCE TAXATION

M^cENTEE HAS IMPOSED
£6,000,000 EXTRA TAXATION
DURING THE PAST TEN MONTHS

The Country CANNOT Stand Another McENTEE Budget

COSGRAVE
KEEPS HIS WORD

VOTE	BELTON, PATRICK
1, 2, 3, 4, 5	BYRNE, JOHN JOSEPH
IN THE ORDER	COLLINS-O'DRISCOLL, Mrs.
OF YOUR CHOICE	MULCAHY, RICHARD
	RICE, VINCENT

FOR THE
CUMANN NA nGAEDHEAL CANDIDATES

Printed by the JUVERNA PRESS, LTD., 12 Upper Liffey Street, Dublin, and Published by Patrick F. O'Reilly, Solicitor, 66 Dame Street, Dublin, Election Agent for the Candidates.

Min Mulcahy and Richard Mulcahy, Alfie Byrne and Cosgrave on the steps of the Pro-Cathedral following mass to mark the installation of Douglas Hyde as the first president of Ireland, 25 June 1938.

Opposite: 'Cosgrave will reduce taxation', 1933 election poster in support of Cosgrave.

Fine Gael

UNITED IRELAND

✦

3 MERRION SQUARE
DUBLIN

3.

Here I should tell you that at that meeting pretty
strong language was used by several people on the subject of
the offensive resolution which had been passed at the League
of Youth Congress, and there had been the most disgusting
scene between O'Duffy and Professor Hogan in the course of
which O'Duffy abused Hogan like a fishwife.

When we reached the room where we were to meet I immediately
put the question of O'Duffy's speeches ~~to the~~ issue by stating
that I had seen the General in his room, and by repeating what
I had said to him. The General very obviously avoided this
discussion and brought forward the general question of the
land annuities and our attitude to Northern Ireland. A very
long discussion ensued and it became abundantly clear that
O'Duffy had given no consideration to either question, but had
made up his mind that it would be a popular thing to do
something 'dramatic" in respect of either or both of them, and
that therefore his proposal for a "No Rent" manifesto and for
the appointment of a Commissioner of the Blueshirts for
Northern Ireland would be popular and should be adopted without
reference to the consequences that might follow from either
decision. The end of the discussion was that he professed to
accept our view and to suggest that his proposals were little
more than gestures made with a view to precipitating some
definite action by the National Executive of Fine Gael. We
then reverted to the question of the ~~undiscriminating~~ nature
of his speeches and of the safeguards that would be necessary
to provide against their recurrence, and we parted most
amicably under the impression that all was well, having agreed
to meet on the following Wednesday at 8.30 with a view to
making final arrangements for the meeting at the Mansion House
preparatory to having them confirmed by the Standing Committee
which was to meet on Thursday.

However, Burke received a letter from the General on the
Tuesday morning announcing his resignation from the Fine Gael
Organisation. We submitted this to the Standing Committee on
Thursday morning and decided to summon the National Executive
and the Central Council of the League of Youth by wire for

DÁIL ÉIREANN

TIGH LAIGHEAN
(Leinster House)

BAILE ÁTHA CLIATH
(Dublin)

— 4—

A duty to serve has fallen upon us all, and we are asking young men and old to risk their all in the defence of the country. The future of " politics " or of political parties is of no importance at this hour, when sacrifices are being demanded from our soldiers and our people and destruction threatens the existence of our State and people.

I am strongly of opinion that discussions should immediately be entered into with a view to estimating the imminence and extent of the danger, and deciding the steps, of whatever nature, that must be taken to defend the country against it.

W. T. Cosgrave

Final page of letter from Cosgrave to the then taoiseach, Eamon de Valera, 9 July 1940, suggesting that in the light of danger of invasion by Germany, Fine Gael would be prepared, if necessary, to support the abandonment of the policy of neutrality.

Opposite: Page of letter from James Dillon to Frank MacDermot, September 1934, noting O'Duffy's resignation from the Fine Gael organisation.

AWARD CERTIFICATE.

Any further Communications on this subject should be addressed to— 👉 and the above number quoted.

An Roinn Cosanta,

Brainse Airgeadais,

Colaiste Caoimhin,

Glasnaoidhea...

Baile Atha Cli...

................*15 Eanair*..........1954.

I am directed to inform you that in accordance with the terms of the Militar... Service Pensions Act, 1934, the Minister for Defence has granted you a pension o...

£..51...5s...0d.... (Fifty-one pounds and five shillings....) per annum

The pension is payable as from the....7th December, 1949...

In accordance with the provisions of the Military Service Pensions (Amendment) Ac...

1953, the pension is increased to £.76. 17s. 6d.................. (Seventy-six pound...

seventeen shillings and.........) per annum as from the 1st January, 1953.
sixpence.

The pension payable in respect of the period ended 31st December, 1952, i... subject to deduction under Section 20 (1) of the Act in respect of receipts by you fro... Public Monies and it is your duty to inform the Minister at once if you were in receip... of Public Monies as defined by Section 20 (1) of the Act in respect of that period.

....

a/s Rúnaí.

*To... Liam T. MacCosgair, Uas.,

................Beechpark, Templeogue,

................Co. Dublin.

Section 20 (1) of the Mil. Ser. Pensions Act, 1934, defines Public Moneys as—"Any remuneratio... pension, or allowance payable out of public moneys, whether provided by the Oireachtas or out of th... Central Fund or by means of the poor rate or any other rate imposed by a local authority.

Extract from Mil. Ser. Pensions Act, 1934, Section 19 (1) & (2)— " If any person with a view... obtaining either for himself or any other person a grant or payment of a pension under this Act, make... signs or uses any declaration, application or other written statement knowing the same to be false, suc... person shall be guilty of an offence under this section, and shall be liable, on summary conviction there... to a fine not exceeding twenty-five pounds, or to imprisonment for a period not exceeding six months, or... the discretion of the Court to both such fine and imprisonment.

If any person so convicted as aforesaid is in receipt of a pension obtained by reason of such fal... declaration, application, or other written statement he shall forfeit such pension as from the date of su... conviction."

N.B.—This Certificate is no security whatever for debt. It should be carefully preserved, as it will be... the greatest assistance to you when completing the Pension Warrants, which will be sent to you.

*In the event of the death of the person to whom this Form is addressed, the person who notifies th... death to the local Registrar of Deaths should deliver this Form and any other Pension papers held b... deceased, to him, and will receive from him the sum of one shilling for so doing.

SP.19 2000 5-53 2/501...

Cosgrave with his son Liam, daughter-in-law Vera and grandchildren
Liam T., Mary and Ciarán, at home in Beechpark, May 1965.

Opposite: Cosgrave's military service certificate for 1916, valid under the
Military Service Pensions Act (1934) and the Amendment Act (1953),
issued on 5 December 1953.

'That noble unrequited gentleman'

- THE ELDER STATESMAN, 1944–65 -

Opening image: Drawing of
Cosgrave by Frank Leah.

IN January 1944 Cosgrave retired from the leadership of his party and from public life. Towards the end of the previous year he had told Bishop Fogarty of his intentions, and by late October rumours had begun to circulate in Dublin. He soon informed his senior colleagues.[1] *The Leader* commented that there was no public expectation of his retirement, yet it caused no surprise.[2] According to one account his colleagues regarded him more as a friend and a counsellor than as a leader.[3] This in itself would have been sufficient reason to resign.

He departed at a low point in his party's fortunes, when he was virtually the only survivor in the Dáil of the government that he had led a dozen years earlier. Almost all his principal colleagues were gone: Blythe and Hayes lost their seats in 1933, Hogan died in 1936, and FitzGerald was defeated in 1937. Now he was deprived of the support of Mulcahy, Costello and O'Sullivan. The only members of his cabinet still in the Dáil were McGilligan, Fionán Lynch and James Fitzgerald-Kenney (and within months McGilligan would be the sole survivor of this trio). Apart from that of September 1927, every election result had proved disappointing.

Cosgrave explained that he took his decision to retire on the grounds of ill-health, and another reason he gave was that younger men should not be hampered by older men clinging on.[4] But after twelve years in opposition, with Fianna Fáil apparently entrenched in power, with some of his cherished achievements dismantled, with many of his expectations and warnings disproved by de Valera's triumphs, and with his party apparently in terminal decline, the prospect of yet further frustration and disappointment must have provided an incentive to bow out. At the request of his constituency executive he retained his seat, if only because there was no suitable candidate to contest a by-election, but he did not attend any further meetings of the Dáil and he made clear his intention to stand down at the next general election. He would not draw his deputy's salary of £480 per annum, and it was later claimed that he never took up his pension.[5] His semi-detached position proved to be short-lived, however, as the Dáil was dissolved less than four months later.

His announcement provoked numerous expressions of concern for his health and good wishes for his retirement. It was typical of him that every reply was different, and he took up points made in all his correspondents' letters. Among the many messages he received was one from John Maffey, the British representative in Dublin, who assured him that he had 'the rare gift of healing & that can remove mountains, & indeed it shifted quite a number'.[6] O'Sullivan wrote to him explaining away their electoral misfortunes: 'You never subordinated statesmanship to mean political expediency. You preferred defeat, fighting for decency in public life, to victory won by cheap and unworthy methods.'[7] His former private secretary acknowledged the help, kindness, generosity and comradeship he had received.[8] In turn Cosgrave paid tribute to his colleagues, remarking to FitzGerald that 'it was my privilege and it is now my consolation to have been associated with men of blameless lives, of outstanding ability, a selflessness without precedent. They gave me the praise & they took the blame'.[9] (One recurring and perhaps revealing theme in his replies to letters was his references to his colleagues' 'blameless lives'.)

He was self-critical, and he regretted that his government had concentrated on its immediate work while neglecting to take the public into its confidence, 'not realising that it is those who advertise who must sell'.[10] He appreciated that he and his colleagues had failed in the sphere that they considered the least important, but which was actually the most important, and whose true significance they had not recognised: the retention of popular support.[11] Some time earlier he had declared that the revolutionary generation had not brought about a significant improvement in the country's living standards; the two main parties 'were able to make a revolution, but so far as building up the country and making it a place for Irish men and women to live in is concerned, examining these two decades, we would venture to express the hope that the next two decades will be far better'.[12]

But he also had reason to be proud of his record, and he took satisfaction in having brought together representatives of different nationalist traditions— although not, of course, the radical republicans who had opposed the treaty. This was illustrated by the fact that the sons of John Redmond and John Dillon had joined his party (even if James Dillon had departed temporarily).[13]

When he said farewell to his political colleagues it was observed that he looked cheerful, 'a man who had cast off care for the holidays, and is now out to enjoy himself'. This vitality was contrasted to his unhealthy appearance in recent years.[14] His farewell address to his party was described as lacking any sign of defeatism, and 'there was no mistaking that it was Cosgrave's Ard-Fheis'.[15]

Even though Mulcahy was briefly without a Dáil seat he was chosen as the party's leader, and he occupied this post until 1959. (It was his colleague John A. Costello, however, who headed two Fine Gael-led governments between 1948 and 1957.) But the new management proved no more successful than the old—despite Mulcahy's heroic work as, year after year, he travelled around the country every weekend on his autocycle.[16] In the general election of May 1944 the party fought under difficult circumstances and experienced another severe defeat, losing a further two seats while Fianna Fáil gained nine. In Cork Cosgrave was succeeded by an independent—a man who, a year earlier, had been his unsuccessful running-mate and who now quadrupled his vote. Jumping ship had proved to be a good career move. In early 1946 it was remarked that, notwithstanding all Mulcahy's efforts, Fine Gael's decline had continued uninterruptedly, and that when Cosgrave retired the bottom seemed to fall out of the party.[17]

LIFE AFTER POLITICS

Long before this, in early summer 1944, he had been interviewed in his home by a Dutch journalist. The writer described the house, with its grand piano, its small study and its portraits of Parnell, Count John McCormack and (surprisingly) the former German president, Field-Marshal von Hindenburg. Blackbirds and thrushes sang in the hedged-in garden, and in the surrounding fields shorthorn cows waded 'knee-deep in the luscious buttercups'. Cosgrave remarked that retirement was not as easy as it seemed, and that he had to detach himself gradually from public life. In reality, however, the change appears to have been made with considerable speed and with little or no regret. The interviewer's account of their meeting conveys an impression of serenity.[18]

Cosgrave cut his links with party politics; for the rest of his life he made no political speeches, and he stayed away from almost all Fine Gael activities. He made an exception for those that had a historical connection, such as commemorations of the treaty. From 1952 onwards he received a pension for his services in the years after 1913.[19]

His example of a 'clean break' and of a conscious detachment from political affairs became the normal pattern for retired Irish heads of government. He maintained his refusal to attend meetings of the Council of State. A year after he stood down from politics he made it clear to his former colleagues that he would not consider running for the office of president; as had been the case in 1937, he refused to be a candidate in a contested election. At the end of 1945 he reported that he took no interest in political matters because it would be unfair on Mulcahy to make any comments.[20] But in private he was kept informed about current events by his son Liam, who rose steadily through the Fine Gael ranks. In turn, he passed on news and gossip to Fogarty in Ennis.

His memory lingered on despite his inactivity, and seven years into his retirement it was claimed that, particularly in rural constituencies, the electoral choice was still between 'Dev' and 'Cosgrave'.[21] (Long after Cosgrave had left political life Michael Hayes continued to preface letters to him with the greeting 'Dear Boss'. Oliver St John Gogarty, ever-teasing, used to address him as 'Dear Ard-Rí' or 'Dear High King'.) Fine Gael party members continued to mention him frequently and respectfully in their speeches, but as time went on 'Cosgrave' referred increasingly to the son and not to the father. Even though Fine Gael's decline continued, at least in terms of votes, the particular circumstances of 1948 enabled it to return to power as the leading partner in a coalition. This was a source of much delight to Cosgrave, and after the change of government it was noted that he had been a keen follower of the events of the previous few weeks.[22] He made no comment, however, when Costello proclaimed a republic soon afterwards.

Occasionally he spoke at public events, such as a meeting of the Bloodstock Breeders and Horse Owners Association and the inauguration of a fund for a memorial to the founder of the Christian Brothers. (He described the latter as 'Ireland's votive offering to Christianity, its contribution to civilisation, its thanksgiving to Providence for preservation from infidelity'.)[23] Like most Irish politicians he was assiduous in attending funerals, but he continued the practice when it no longer offered him any electoral advantage. In the early 1960s he participated in a BBC programme on Gogarty.[24] He and his friends collaborated in a long-term and frustrating effort to control the content of Padraic Colum's biography of Griffith and to reduce the number of errors.[25] But he resented the nuisance of having to answer requests for his own memoirs; he had none, and he did not intend to write any.[26]

Despite Cosgrave's deep commitment to majority rule, in one of his rare speeches he criticised what he saw as the modern fallacy whereby—in the context of Communism—statesmen exalted democracy to the sphere of a religion.[27] Only once during his last two decades did he become embroiled in controversy. In December 1953 he chaired a debate on partition in the Literary and Historical Society in UCD. His remarks were moderate, except perhaps for his claim that the only authority exercised by Rome on independent Ireland was an insistence that its people should keep the Ten Commandments. But James McSparron, an Ulster Unionist MP who also spoke on the same occasion, accused him of having attacked the constitutional position of Northern Ireland and went on to demand that he should also criticise de Valera's violations of the treaty. This led to one of the numerous debates characteristic of the letters columns of *The Irish Times*.[28] Others joined happily in the fray but Cosgrave resumed his silence.

In private and from a distance he could be forthright in his views. When a group of bankers criticised a speech by Costello he dismissed them as 'a nervous lot, old-fashioned, conservative, introspective', and he believed it would be better for the government to undertake works that would increase employment and production than to invest in England or elsewhere.[29]

He attended functions in venues such as the National Museum and the French embassy, but he went to the theatre or cinema only on very rare occasions. Ernest Blythe claimed that Cosgrave had no interest in the Abbey Theatre and that he had boasted of never having attended any of its performances. Myles na Gopaleen's reaction was 'that was a stern sort of vow but I hope Mr. Cosgrave has been wise enough to keep it still'.[30] At home he continued to read works of history and economics, and he corresponded about recent writings on subjects such as Edward Carson or the Earl of Derby's visit to Dublin in 1921.[31] He acknowledged receipt of books on India and Don John of Austria, and he was impressed by an article in the *Ecclesiastical Record*.[32] His favourite novelist was Canon Sheehan (a common taste at the time), but most fiction held little appeal for him. He ignored some critical or hostile historical writings, and years after their publication he remarked that he had not read Pakenham's *Peace by Ordeal* or Macardle's *Irish Republic*.[33] As he had done in the past, he read *The Irish Independent* every day.

He enjoyed listening to the radio.[34] He bred and sold award-winning dairy cattle. He walked regularly and he drove a car until he was in his seventies. He rode twice a week in season with the Ward Hunt, claiming that for someone in good health there was no better exercise.[35] He often attended race meetings although he seldom put money on a horse, and his interest in bloodstock continued to the end of his life. In old age he would sit in the sun on a bench by the paddock in the Phoenix Park, his umbrella between his knees and his hands crossed on its handle, watching the horses come out. A story goes that one day he shared the bench with the poet Patrick Kavanagh, and they sat together for some time. Eventually Kavanagh broke the silence and said

> Forgive me for intruding, Mr. Cosgrave…I know all about intrusion. People are constantly intruding on me, in pubs and everywhere else, and I know how evil it is. But I would just like to tell you that I have admired you all my life. You're a gentleman.

To his surprise and delight Cosgrave turned and answered

> Ah, Mr. Kavanagh, I know your work of course and I admire it
> very much. It's no intrusion at all, I assure you. It gives me great
> pleasure to meet you.

They shook hands and relapsed into silence.[36] Kavanagh's respect was displayed in public as well as in private, and shortly before Cosgrave's death the poet wrote of him as 'that noble unrequited gentleman'.[37]

In 1946 the Fianna Fáil government appointed him to the Racing Board, where one of his colleagues was Judge Wylie. Throughout the ten years during which he served as the board's president he assisted the industry in various ways, such as assigning funds to improve racecourses. He resigned when Gerard Sweetman, the Fine Gael minister for Finance, imposed a levy on Racing Board revenue, but he resumed his membership a year later at the request of James Ryan, the new Fianna Fáil minister.[38] In such matters he was apolitical.

Religion remained central to Cosgrave's life. In old age he served mass in the Franciscan Church in Merchant's Quay and subsequently for the Passionists in Mount Argus.[39] He mentioned having had 'a grand day' with the Holy Ghost fathers.[40] He wrote in friendly fashion to Gogarty, advising that his advancing age warranted doing something about the state of his soul.[41] He visited Rome again and met the pope. In the 1960s he belonged to a Legion of Mary group that gathered in Blackrock. When he learned in 1963 that a hostel belonging to the Legion was to be closed down by the Dublin Health Authority he approached his old opponent Seán MacEntee, who was then minister for Health, and the decision was reversed.[42] He died as a member of the Third Order of St Francis.[43]

His wife Louisa was concerned principally with the family and the house, although she also engaged in charitable work and was a governor of the Royal Hospital for Incurables.[44] After a short illness, she died in June 1959 at the age of 76. Cosgrave's son Liam and his family then moved in to Beechpark and kept him company for the last six years of his life. He was an indulgent grandfather.

Newspapers rarely reported his activities, apart from mentioning his continuing attendance at funerals, requiem masses, race meetings and other such events. An Irish journalist wrote he had 'done his job, he retired quietly to the outskirts of Dublin, and nobody thought much about him after that'.[45] From time to time references, both positive and negative, were made to aspects of his time in office. In his last two decades the public seemed to forget the disappointments of his years in opposition and he was increasingly associated with the foundation of the state and his exercise of power. But in *The Irish Times* Myles na Gopaleen turned him into an almost mythical or legendary figure in his crowded pantheon. In one column he announced that Cosgrave and Alfie Byrne used to wear bowler hats, 'but that's because they're *Dublin* men'; presumably this was not an offence, as it would be for others who lived beyond the Pale. In an article on the Rolls Royce car he pronounced that 'Willie Cosgrave, Joe McGrath, Powerscourt and myself are the only men entitled to call themselves Masters of the Rolls; and every man-jack of them a success in his own rite'.[46] He claimed that Cosgrave's abolition of Dublin Corporation eliminated 'a swarm of wasters, tipplers, touchers and gobhawks who had been quartered on public funds'.[47]

Brendan Behan also entertained friends with his performance of 'Mr. Cosgrave's visit to Mountjoy'. In this sketch the then president went to inspect the conditions of hunger-striking prisoners and was accosted by Maud Gonne MacBride, who resented the fact that she had not been arrested together with her companions. She abused him as 'Imperialist! Lackey! West Briton! Liar!' and demanded 'Arrest me! Arrest me!' He replied 'Madame. Imperialist I may be. Lackey I may be. Liar I may even be. But I am not a collector of curiosities'.[48]

In December 1961 Cosgrave's portrait by Seán O'Sullivan was hung in Leinster House, and in June 1963, after an interval of nearly two decades, he returned to the Dáil to listen to the address by President John F. Kennedy. First he and then Seán T. O'Kelly made their way to sit among the diplomats in the distinguished visitors' gallery, and deputies from all parties gave them standing ovations. The two men, initially close colleagues in Dublin Corporation and subsequently long-term opponents, embraced briefly.[49] Towards the end of his life Cosgrave broke a pattern that had endured for forty years, and at a social event in the papal nunciature in Dublin he and de Valera engaged in polite conversation.

In 1963 Seán Lemass, who was now taoiseach, wrote to him concerning the publication of documents relating to the treaty negotiations. In his reply Cosgrave noted that 'almost daily one is brought up against some frightful "historical" issues derived, no doubt, from "historians"', but he ended by expressing his satisfaction that Lemass was 'in vigorous good health. God be with you'. The taoiseach reassured him that only 'bona-fide' historians would be given access to documents.[50] In many ways they were kindred spirits, and they respected each other's characters and achievements.[51] A few months later Cosgrave was approached by Lord Beaverbrook, who might not have qualified as a 'bona-fide' historian but who expressed an interest in buying the papers of O'Higgins, Collins, Redmond, Dillon and Healy.[52] Beaverbrook operated on a grand scale.

It was a source of great satisfaction and pride that his son Liam was elected first as leader of Fine Gael in April 1965, and then as president of the party in October that year, only a month before Cosgrave's death.

He had always been frail and his health continued to cause concern, but the end came with merciful speed. On 15 November he served mass as usual. He had a heart attack that evening as he sat talking with his family by the fireside, he was taken to bed, and he died less than a day later, on the evening of 16 November. His death was unexpected; Frank Duff heard the news in Rome, and subsequently he received a letter from Cosgrave indicating that he was in excellent health.[53]

Surviving friends and former colleagues were generous in their assessments of his career, but de Valera was more reserved in his reaction. In a formal statement the president simply regretted Cosgrave's death and also the fact that political differences had marred their earlier close friendship, but the brief official statement paid no tribute to his old enemy's achievements.[54] This was in contrast to the magnanimity displayed by Lemass, who in his Dáil tribute praised

> the privations and the sacrifices which he endured so that national freedom might be ours, the capacity he displayed in presiding over the administration while responsibility was his, the grace with which he handed over responsibility when the people so willed, the dignity with which he carried out his duties as Leader of the Opposition and later as a private member of this House, the generosity of spirit with which he lent his hand to the defence of the State in a time of national danger.[55]

Cosgrave was buried in a simple grave in Goldenbridge Cemetery in Dublin. The state funeral took place in steady rain, and an army guard of honour saluted his remains as the procession passed the former South Dublin Union, where he had fought alongside Eamonn Ceannt and Cathal Brugha nearly 50 years before. There was no elaborate ceremony and no oration. The state buried one of its founding fathers with an appropriate dignity. Many priests attended, but it was ironic that at the funeral of a man who was so closely identified with the Catholic Church, and who was on excellent terms with so many bishops, no representative of the Irish hierarchy was present. All its members were in Rome for the closing stages of the Second Vatican Council.

In 1955 Desmond Williams wrote a long, discerning and positive assessment of Cosgrave's career in *The Irish Times*. The former president was described as being able to claim outstanding credit for a society that was both conservative and 'liberal' in its constitution; he understood the mixed nature of the Irish people; he sought reconciliation; he was skilled in handling his cabinet; he picked a distinguished team of senior civil servants; he was calm where some of his ministerial colleagues were dogmatic and passionate; and of him it could truly be said '*de re publica bene meruit*'.[56] But this profile was exceptional and— largely through lack of evidence—historians did not begin to investigate the period of the Irish revolution and the Free State until after Cosgrave's death; during his lifetime only a handful of serious scholarly works examined the record of his government.[57] In 1964–5 a beginning was made, when a radio series brought together a group of historians and others who lectured on the events of the years between 1922 and 1937.[58]

Cosgrave's reputation has grown slowly with the years, but his image and his legacy remained unfocused. In 2010 an incident took place that illustrates the extent to which he had been neglected by posterity. In the course of her research on the artist Seán Keating the art historian Éimear O'Connor happened upon a roll of old paintings, in the middle of which was revealed his long-lost portrait of Cosgrave. It had been commissioned in 1923 and was exhibited once that year, after which Keating removed it from its stretcher, stored it away, and never showed it again. There is no evidence to suggest why the painting remained with him; perhaps the sitter was not happy with the work, or it may be that there was no money to pay for it. Its rediscovery might seem symbolic of the re-emergence to public consciousness of a figure who had for long been neglected.[59]

When the former president retired from public life the satirical journal *Dublin Opinion*, which was normally sympathetic to Fianna Fáil, featured a cartoon in which 'Ireland' introduced him to an elderly robed figure with the words 'Mr. Cosgrave, this is History. I've a kind of feeling he's going to do you rather well.'[60] As is so often the case, History was not in a hurry, but in the long run this forecast has been vindicated. When evidence began to accumulate from the mid-1960s onwards scholars could engage in research on the history of the revolutionary period and the Irish Free State. Its first administration has been subjected to scrutiny, and the results have been mainly positive. One historian concluded that although Cosgrave's vision was limited, his instincts were con-servative and he had failed in the context of historical expectations, his government's achievement was nonetheless historic. 'It was due in large measure to him that things did not fall apart, that the centre did hold'.[61]

Cosgrave was one of very many people in the ranks of the Irish Volunteers, the IRA, the Dáil government, the Sinn Féin party and (indirectly) the home rule party whose combined efforts created the independent Irish state. He was the most significant of those who consolidated it. His determination, even ferocity, in fighting and winning the civil war—in marked contrast to his normal mildness—has commanded widespread respect, even if the executions carried out by the army under his administration have remained controversial. For some people they have remained unforgiven. In many areas he and his colleagues were successful in building on the treaty, although they did not implement Collins's belief that it was no more than a stepping-stone. They were authoritarian in defending the people's right to choose their government.

Late in life he confessed that his cabinet included one half-statesman (O'Higgins) but no politicians; it has also been suggested that he was the only politician in a government of talented individuals.[62] He is honoured in Fine Gael as one of the founders and the long-term leader of the pro-treaty party—even though (like most of his ministers) he gave it only intermittent attention and viewed it without apparent warmth. Naturally there has been criticism, which in retrospect he shared, that his concern with administration was matched by neglect of the party and of public opinion.

Cosgrave's long years in opposition must be considered a failure, although he mitigated the consequences of his party's flirtation with the Blueshirts. Despite his self-effacement at this time he—more than any of his colleagues—helped to prevent Fine Gael from slipping towards extremism, and he ensured that in all significant respects it became and remained a continuation of Cumann na nGaedheal.

Unsurprisingly, his social and economic values were those of the 1920s rather than of the late twentieth or early twenty-first century. His governments were too cautious in tackling the problems of the poor, although his prudence in handling the state's finances would gain a new respect many decades later.

His passionate commitment to majority rule, his ability to reconcile elements such as Redmondites and southern unionists to the independent Irish state (although not others, including some who recognised the state only when they could control it), and his instinctive willingness to respect the popular verdict when it turned against him in 1932, have been almost universally esteemed. W.T. Cosgrave occupies a prominent and honourable place in the Irish democratic tradition.

Letter from Cosgrave to 'Albert', 12 October 1962, expressing the hope that no-one would write a biography of him.

Beechpark,

Templeogue

Co. Dublin.

12th October 62

Dear Albert.

Autograph as requested enclosed.

No one to my knowledge has written a "life" of me & it is to be hoped no one shall.

Taylor's life of Collins is well done. Collins was the greatest Irishman of our generation and indeed of many other generations.

[illegible]

[illegible]

[illegible] Cosgrave

Telephone:
Dublin 95253

BEECHPARK,
TEMPLEOGUE,
CO. DUBLIN

9th Feby 44

My dear Desmond.

For months past I have been putting off writing to you. Now it has come to pass.

We have had a long and I hope fruitful association which calls for an acknowledgement on my part which this letter must fall far short of expressing.

I thank you for your friendship - for the honour of having been a colleague in an eventful period. for all the labours you performed in such a distinguished manner with such beneficial results for the State - and the Government of which you were a member.

I thank you for your patience which I so often tried by [conduct?] [fashioned?] after Job.

Letter from Cosgrave to Desmond FitzGerald, 9 February 1944,
following his retirement from the leadership of Fine Gael,
acknowledging that during his time as president he was fortunate to
have colleagues of 'blameless lives, outstanding ability, a selflessness
without precedent', who gave him the praise while 'they took the blame'.

A courageous man needs no tribute – but I must pay this tribute to yours – a more courageous man I never met. And your moral courage was even greater.

We have had many differences during those years. Well I knew you well enough to appreciate that on a question of principle – you could not give way. On any other differences – it was merely there to be composed.

This break with public life is painful. It was my privilege and it is now my consolation when been associated with men of blameless lives – of outstanding ability – a selflessness without precedent. They gave me the praise & they took the blame.

I thank you finally for that last speech. May God grant you Mr Fitzgerald – & yours His choicest blessings. With affection admiration & gratitude Believe me

very sincerely

William T. Cosgrave

My dear J.D.

I was particularly pleased to get your letter, which went back farther than any other. Any recollection of that incident with Rev. Br. Lanigan was but the haziest, even as to who said that about the Lord Mayoralty. Perhaps the sequel may interest you. It was my wish to escape the office and after the 1920 Municipal Election when the Sinn Fein majority was big, some people were insistent on my nomination. Now Ald. Kelly to my mind was the obvious selection. No one who had not been a "participant" in 1916 was acceptable to certain people. Ald. Kelly was arrested a short time before the day of the Election, had been transported to Wormwood Scrubbs and while there was duly elected Lord Mayor.

It was not only an honour but a privilege to have as associates such men of rare distinction as I had during my period in public life. They were unselfish, industrious, competent, and constructive and they had the highest sense of public duty.

Sean Milroy has been engaged for some months getting material for a life of Griffith. Your reference to Rooney is probably the second I have seen in amny years. Milroy's early chapters dealing some belated credit to that very remarkable man. You say truly that the present generation is painfully unfamiliar with these 40 years. We have been examining the list of people still living who were closely associated with Griffith who is not yet 22 years dead; the number is not only relatively but actually small.

These two Collins and Griffith were very different. Griffith had the misfortune to make poor selections of men for his work - in public matters. Collins had a gift of getting the best available. Griffith w rked hard. Collins still harder. Griffith had on occasion fixed principles to which Collins gracefully deferred and vice versa. A story appeared in the Sunday Independent concerning Collins and myself, the point of which was missed. On the day appointed for the elected members to sit in the "Parliament of South Ireland" I went into the room where Griffith and Collins met first just prior to the hour fixed. Tension was obvious. A.G. "Mr. Collins won't allow this meeting today because the British refuse to release some prisoners". "What do you say?" Cosgrave "The Brish prior to this meeting are dealing with a political party. After this meeting they deal with a Government." Collins "Call the meeting". He needed no persuasion. No man saw a point clearer, certainly no man saw it quicker. His death ranks as a tragedy along with Brian Bory.

There were exhilerations during that period, extending over many years. Public Office is however lonely all that unnecessary deference arousing impatience.

We might have failed in ending the former administration here and that would have been nad. We could not afford to fail in constructing another that would have been disastrous. Success in the reconstruction was largely due to the loyal co-operation of the three services - Army and Garda, regulating - the Civil Service in the field of construction. And on each man in his own sphere depended the future as well as the present. For your own special labours in that work I thank you cordially and sincerely.

You may observe that the only order in this letter is that it follows to some extent the points in your owwn and you will exercise your indulgence towards it.

God be with you and prosper you and yours and all your work.

Very sincerely yours,

WM.T.C.

Typescript of a letter from Cosgrave to Joseph Rush, 9 February 1944, responding to a letter marking his retirement, in which Rush had reminisced about a school teacher referring to Cosgrave as 'the future Lord Mayor of Dublin'. Cosgrave also recalls an interaction with Griffith and Collins and the work of building the state.

Letter from Cosgrave to the then taoiseach, Seán Lemass, January 1963,
regarding publication of documents relating to the treaty negotiations,
and expressing Cosgrave's distrust of historians.

Pairc na mBeathog,

Tigh Molog

Co. Baile Atha Cliath.

A Thaoisigh a chara,

My recollection is that the Secretary to the
Government wrote to me in the early 30's on a proposal
then under consideration to publish these documents.
My reply at the time was that I was opposed to the
publication, citing that it was unlikely we would be
favoured by the documents (if any) passing between
British Ministers on the negotiations.

When first charged with responsibility in
Government in 1922 it was reported to me that there
were no documents in the Archives dealing with these
matters, and in consequence my list of these letters
was made available by me for the State Archives. It is
now over forty (40) years since I read these papers –
a rather long interval to expect clear remembrance.

Mr. Packenham called on me about the time the
question of publication arose in the 30's. Unless my
recollection is much at fault he told me he was writing
about the period. It was rumoured at the time that he
had been afforded an opportunity of reading these
documents. No one had a right to grant anyone such a
facility. My recollection about the interview is that
I told him (Mr. Packenham) it was rather strange writing
on these matters having had access but to one side. He
published a book which I had not time then or since to
read.

On the final paragraph of your letter – I have
nothing further to add to what I wrote already. I agree –
should you decide to grant permission to historians – with
the safeguards set out in (a) and (b) save that "any
historian" is too wide a description. Almost daily one is
brought up against some frightful "historical" issues
derived, no doubt, from "historians".

Quite well, thanks, and I am glad to observe from
the papers that you are in vigorous good health.

God be with you.

Sincerely,

(Signed) W.T. COSGRAVE.

IRELAND : " Mr. Cosgrave, this is History. I've a kind of feeling he's going to do you rather well."

'Mr Cosgrave: This is history', cartoon published in *Dublin Opinion*,
February 1944, p. 216.

Opposite: Photograph of Cosgrave riding with the Ward Hunt, in the 1930s.

'As one president to another', political cartoon, published in the *Chicago Tribune*, January 1928, showing Cosgrave meeting President Calvin Coolidge during his trip to the United States. Original drawing by John McCutcheon, presented to Cosgrave by the artist.

Opposite: Photograph of Cosgrave, at home, May 1965.

AS ONE PRESIDENT TO ANOTHER.

Endnotes

ABBREVIATIONS

BMH	Bureau of Military History
BNA	British National Archives, London
CCCA	Cork City and County Archives
DDA	Dublin Diocesan Archives
DIB	*Dictionary of Irish Biography*
DIFP	*Documents on Irish Foreign Policy*
KDA	Killaloe Diocesan Archives, Ennis
NAI	National Archives of Ireland
NLI	National Library of Ireland
TCD	Trinity College Dublin
UCDA	University College Dublin Archives
WS	Witness statement

Opening image: 'The sympathetic listener', political cartoon, published in the *Herald*, 19 March 1931, depicting Uncle Sam listening to Cosgrave's St Patrick's Day message.

1. THE PRESIDENT

[1] NAI, Department of the Taoiseach (DT), S 4522, W.T. Cosgrave to Fr M.A. McGrath, 22 December 1922.

[2] *Irish Times*, 7 December 1922, 7; *Freeman's Journal*, 7 December 1922, 5.

[3] NLI, P 7398, French Ministry of Foreign Affairs, *Europe, 1918-1929, Irlande*, vol. 3, 110, Alfred Blanche to Raymond Poincaré, 9 December 1922.

[4] Nicholas Mansergh, diary, 22 September 1935, in Diana Mansergh (ed.), Nicholas Mansergh, *Nationalism and independence: selected Irish papers* (Cork, 1997), 120–1.

[5] *Senate debates*, vol. 10, 811 (4 July 1928); available at: debates.oireachtas.ie.

[6] John M. Regan, *The Irish counter-revolution 1921–1936: treatyite politics and settlement in independent Ireland* (Dublin, 1999), 130.

[7] Bill Kissane, *The politics of the Irish Civil War* (Oxford, 2005), 125.

[8] W.T. Cosgrave, 'Comments', *Studies*, 22 (88) (December 1933), 553.

[9] Diarmaid Ferriter, *The transformation of Ireland, 1900–2000* (London, 2004), 304.

[10] NAI, DT, S 5983/20(13), Cosgrave, speech to Cork Industrial Development Association, 5 September 1928.

[11] Robert Skidelsky, *John Maynard Keynes: the economist as saviour 1920–1937* (London, 1992), 479.

[12] *Dáil debates 1921–1922, Debate on the treaty*, 359 (9 January 1922).

[13] *Dáil debates*, vol. 14, 1206 (26 February 1926); available at: debates.oireachtas.ie.

[14] UCDA, John A. Costello MSS, P190/313(2), Speech, Fine Gael ard-fheis, 20 February 1940.

[15] Hackett, diary, 8 March 1932, in Lis Pihl (ed.), *Signe Toksvig's Irish diaries, 1926–1937* (Dublin, 1994), 413, n. 16. Hackett was equally harsh in his comments on de Valera.

[16] Frank Callanan, *T.M. Healy* (Cork, 1996), 616; Edward MacLysaght, *Changing times: Ireland since 1898* (Gerrards Cross, 1978), 129.

[17] Paul Canning, *British policy towards Ireland, 1921–1941* (Oxford, 1985), 90.

[18] Mackenzie King, diary, 30, 31 January 1928, quoted in Francis M. Carroll, 'Official visits: President Cosgrave comes to Ottawa', *Canadian Journal of Irish Studies* 36 (2) (Fall 2010), 185. Long after Cosgrave left office his photograph remained in King's study, see John Hearne to Joseph Walshe, 22 November 1940, in Michael Kennedy *et al.* (eds), *Documents on Irish Foreign Policy* (*DIFP*): vol. VI (Dublin, 2008), 397.

[19] Winston Churchill, *The world crisis: the aftermath* (London, 1929), 349.

[20] V.S. Pritchett, *Dublin: a portrait* (London, 1967), 5–6.

[21] *Irish Times*, 9 September 1922, 9.

[22] *Irish Statesman*, 7 January 1928, 416.

[23] Cosgrave MSS, Cosgrave to Michael Hayes, 3 February 1944. The Cosgrave papers have not been archived or catalogued as this book goes to press, so precise source references cannot be provided.

[24] Callanan, *T.M. Healy*, 610.

[25] CCCA, U271/A/46 and 52, Liam de Róiste, diary, 25 October 1922, 14 February 1925.

[26] DDA, Byrne MSS, 466, Office of the president of the executive council, Cosgrave to Archbishop Byrne, 12 February 1925.

[27] Cosgrave MSS, Earl of Granard to Cosgrave, 16 November 1925, Cosgrave to Granard, 24 November 1925.

[28] BMH, WS 1054, 5, Eilis Aughney, witness statement.

[29] Oliver St John Gogarty, *As I was going down Sackville Street* (London, 1937), 15.

[30] NAI, D/T, S 5983/40, Speech, 15 January 1930.

[31] NAI, D/T, S 5983/13, Speech to Trinity College Historical Society, 26 October 1927.

[32] Cosgrave MSS, W.T. Cosgrave, interview with Edward J. Lawler, *Boston Sunday Post*, 5 February 1928; also Cosgrave MSS, Cosgrave to John Marcus O'Sullivan, 2 February 1944.

[33] UCDA, Hugh Kennedy MSS, P4/826(12–13), New York Supreme Court proceedings, 8 June 1923.

[34] KDA, Fogarty MSS, 33, 93–40/i, Cosgrave to Bishop Michael Fogarty, 22 February 1940; UCDA, Kennedy MSS, P4/1211(1), Cosgrave to Hugh Kennedy, 29 June 1926.

[35] See, for example, Michael Tierney, *Eoin MacNeill: scholar and man of action* (Oxford, 1980), 359; UCDA, Kennedy MSS, P4/419, Cosgrave to Kennedy, 30 September 1924.

[36] St John Ervine, *Craigavon, Ulsterman* (London, 1949), 480; NLI, Johnson MSS, 17,162, Johnson, memorandum, July 1927.

[37] UCDA, MacEoin MSS, P151/905, Cosgrave to Seán MacEoin, 13 March 1928.

[38] Anthony J. Jordan, *W.T. Cosgrave, 1880–1965: founder of modern Ireland* (Dublin, 2006); Stephen Collins, *The Cosgrave legacy* (Dublin, 1996).

[39] On de Valera's concern with his historical image, see Diarmaid Ferriter, *Judging Dev* (Dublin, 2007), 10–11; Patrick Murray, 'Obsessive historian: Eamon de Valera and the policing of his reputation', *Proceedings of the Royal Irish Academy* 101C (2) (2001), 37–65.

2. BECOMING A POLITICIAN

[1] Michael Hayes, *Sunday Independent*, 21 November 1965, 9.

[2] *Thom's official directory* (Dublin, 1878), 1411; (Dublin, 1886), 1426.

[3] Moira Lysaght, 'Memoir', 84 (unpublished; in the possession of Charles Lysaght).

[4] Cosgrave MSS, Cosgrave to Stephen Gwynn, 22 January 1944.

[5] *Weekly Irish Times*, 12 October 1929, 9.

[6] *Dáil debates*, vol. 44, 1740 (15 November 1932).

[7] Much of the information in these paragraphs is derived from Cosgrave MSS, Liam Cosgrave, 'Recollections of the Life of W.T. Cosgrave' (2004), 1–3; and from NAI, 1194/15, Liam Cosgrave to Stephen Rynne, 24 May 1978.

[8] Lysaght, 'Memoir', 84.

[9] Kees van Hoek, *People and places* (Tralee, 1944), 33; Cosgrave MSS, Cosgrave, 'Recollections', 7–8.

[10] DDA, O'Brien Institute admission register, 1888–1972.

[11] John Patrick Walsh, A comparative analysis of the reading books of the Commissioners of National Education and of the Christian Brothers, 1831-1900; unpublished MA dissertation, UCD, 1982, 339, 358, 367.

[12] Cosgrave MSS, Cosgrave to Agnes Martin, 29 January 1944.

[13] Jim Cantwell, pers. comm. 'Research notes on the O'Brien Institute'.

[14] Cosgrave MSS, Joseph D. Rush to Cosgrave, 6 February 1944.

[15] DDA, O'Brien Institute admission register, 1888–1972.

[16] UCDA, Hayes MSS, P53/217(5), Hayes to Sean Milroy, 1 May 1943.

[17] Cosgrave MSS, *Boston Sunday Post*, 15 January 1928.

[18] *Dáil debates*, vol. 87, 826 (2 June 1942).

[19] *Thom's official directory* (Dublin, 1909), 1592; (Dublin, 1921), 1630.

[20] *Freeman's Journal*, 24 September 1909, 4.

[21] Lysaght, 'Memoir', 85.

[22] Elizabeth Malcolm, 'The rise of the pub: a study in the disciplining of popular culture'. in James S. Donnelly, Jr. and Kerby A. Miller (eds), *Irish popular culture 1650–1850* (Dublin, 1998), 50–77: 51.

[23] Thomas Burke, cited in Kevin C. Kearns, *Dublin pub life and lore: an oral history* (Dublin, 1996), 29.

[24] *Dáil debates*, vol. 9, 237 (24 October 1924).

[25] Sheila Carden, *The Alderman: Alderman Tom Kelly (1868–1942) and Dublin Corporation* (Dublin, 2007), 21; Mary E. Daly, *Dublin: the deposed capital: a social and economic history 1860–1914* (Cork, 1984), 205.

[26] *Irish Daily Independent*, 12 March 1900, 6; Eunan O'Halpin, 'Cosgrave, William Thomas', in James McGuire and James Quinn (eds), *Dictionary of Irish Biography* (*DIB*) (Cambridge, 2009), vol. 2, 880–1; available online at: dib.cambridge.org.

[27] *United Irishman*, 9 December 1905, 1.

[28] *Sinn Féin*, 9 March 1907, 1; 14 December 1907, 1; 28 December 1907, 1.

[29] *Irish Independent*, 10 March 1908, 6.

[30] *Sinn Féin*, 27 March 1909, 4.

[31] *Freeman's Journal*, 5 January 1909, 4.

[32] *Freeman's Journal*, 6 January 1909, 4.

[33] Seán Lemass, *Dáil debates,* vol. 33, 1042 (27 February 1930).

[34] *Sinn Féin*, 28 August 1909, 3.

[35] *Sinn Féin*, 28 December 1907, 2; 9 January 1909, 2.

[36] Licensed Vintners Association, minutes, vol. 16, 19 January 1909.

[37] *Irish Independent*, 25 January 1909, 6.

[38] *Irish Independent*, 14 June 1909, 5; 22 June 1909, 5.

[39] Dublin Corporation reports, 1912, No. 4.

[40] *Irish Independent*, 8 March 1909, 7.

[41] *Sinn Féin*, 12 June 1909, 4; 19 June 1909, 4; 26 June 1909, 4.

[42] *Freeman's Journal*, 19 August 1908, 4; 18 August 1910, 10.

[43] *Irish Independent*, 13 May 1910, 9; *Sinn Féin*, 4 June 1910, 4.

[44] Jacinta Prunty, *Dublin slums, 1800–1925* (Dublin, 1998), 157–8.

[45] *Sinn Féin*, 19 November 1910, cited in Tom Kelly, *The streets of Dublin 1910–1911* (Dublin, 2013; Sheila Carden (ed.)), 35.

[46] Prunty, *Dublin slums*, 219; Joseph V. O'Brien, *'Dear, dirty Dublin': a city in distress 1899–1916* (Berkeley, 1982), 28, 134.

[47] *Report of the departmental committee appointed by the Local Government Board for Ireland to inquire into the housing conditions of the working class in the City of Dublin* (London, 1914), 3–4.

[48] *Irish Independent*, 22 March 1910, 7.

[49] Municipal Council minutes, 15 April 1912, 274; León Ó Broin (ed.), *William E. Wylie and the Irish Revolution 1916–1921* (Dublin, 1989), 27.

[50] Carden, *Alderman*, 136–7.

[51] Municipal Council minutes, 3 April 1911, 245–6.

[52] Municipal Council minutes, 18 July 1911, 384; *Irish Independent*, 19 July 1911, 5.

[53] Municipal Council minutes, 15 March 1915, 128–31.

[54] *Sinn Féin*, 12 February 1910, 5.

[55] Municipal Council minutes, 11 November 1907, 480–1; 12 July 1909, 366.

[56] *Irish Worker*, 23 September 1911, 2; 30 September 1911, 2.

[57] *Irish Independent*, 19 January 1912, 6.

[58] O'Brien, *'Dear, dirty Dublin'*, 55.

[59] Municipal Council minutes, 19 March 1913, 187–9; 23 June 1913, 355–6.

[60] Municipal Council minutes, 22 August 1913, 436–7; 8 September 1913, 458-9; *Irish Independent*, 9 September 1913, 5.

[61] Municipal Council minutes, 19 September 1913, 462–5.

[62] R.F. Foster, *W.B. Yeats: a life. I. Apprentice mage* (Oxford, 1997), 497.

[63] Yeats to Gregory, 11 May 1916, Allan Wade (ed.), *The letters of W.B. Yeats* (New York, 1953), 612.

[64] See below, 254–5.

[65] Municipal Council minutes 1 September 1913, 440; Pádraig Yeates, *Lockout: Dublin 1913* (Dublin, 2000), 92.

[66] Municipal Council minutes, 7 February 1916, 111.

[67] *Sinn Féin*, 12 October 1912, 5.

[68] *Sinn Féin*, 8 October 1910, 1.

[69] *Leader*, 10 January 1914, 539.

3. FIGHTING FOR INDEPENDENCE

[1] David Fitzpatrick, 'Militarism in Ireland, 1900–1922', in Thomas Bartlett and Keith Jeffery (eds), *A military history of Ireland* (Cambridge, 1996), 379–406: 384.

[2] *Irish Independent*, 30 April 1914, 6.

[3] *Freeman's Journal*, 26 November 1913, 9.

[4] BMH, WS 268, 1, Cosgrave, witness statement; *Dáil debates*, vol. 7, 3148 (26 June 1924).

[5] BMH, WS 268, 1–2, Cosgrave, witness statement.

[6] BMH, WS 203, 4, Edward O'Neill, witness statement; BMH, WS 1624, 1, Patrick Loughran, witness statement.

[7] BMH, WS 268, 3–6, Cosgrave, witness statement.

[8] BMH, WS 175, 11, John Styles, witness statement.

[9] BMH, WS 1624, 1, Patrick Loughran, witness statement.

[10] BMH, WS 1511, 4, Gerald Doyle, witness statement.

[11] Lysaght, 'Memoir', 85–6.

[12] *Irish Independent*, 16 March 1916, 4.

[13] Lysaght, 'Memoir', 92.

[14] BMH, WS 268, 6, Cosgrave, witness statement.

[15] Charles Townshend, *Easter 1916: the Irish rebellion* (London, 2005), 173.

[16] A Volunteer, 'South Dublin Union area', *Capuchin Annual*, 1966, 202, 209.

[17] BMH, WS 305, 1, Patrick Smyth, witness statement.

[18] BMH, WS 304, 16, James Coughlan, witness statement.

[19] BMH, WS 268, 6(b), Cosgrave, witness statement; Max Caulfield, *The Easter rebellion* (London, 1964), 78–9.

[20] BMH, WS 297, 2, 4, Annie Mannion, witness statement.

[21] BMH, WS 186, 9, Thomas Doyle, witness statement.

[22] Major Francis Fletcher Vane, cited in Paul O'Brien, *Uncommon valour: 1916 and the battle for the South Dublin Union* (Dublin, 2010), 76.

[23] A Volunteer, 'South Dublin Union area', 208.

[24] BMH, WS 305, 2, Patrick Smyth, witness statement.

[25] Brugha to Thomas Ashe, 26 March 1917, cited in Seán Ó Lúing, *I die in a good cause: a study of Thomas Ashe, idealist and revolutionary* (Tralee, 1970), 112.

[26] Cosgrave MSS, *Boston Sunday Post*, 15 January 1928.

[27] Seamus Cullen, 'Bridget Nixon 1855–1934', *Dublin Historical Record* 66 (spring/autumn 2013), 68.

[28] BMH, WS 203, 5, Edward O'Neill, witness statement.

[29] Lysaght, 'Memoir', 90.

[30] Thomas J. Morrissey SJ, *William O'Brien 1881–1968: socialist republican, Dáil deputy, editor, and trade union leader* (Dublin, 2007), 106.

[31] Adrian Hardiman, '"Shot in cold blood": military law and Irish perceptions in the suppression of the 1916 rebellion', in Gabriel Doherty and Dermot Keogh (eds), *1916: the long revolution* (Cork, 2007), 225–49: 236, 245.

[32] BMH, WS 268, 15, Cosgrave, witness statement.

[33] On Wylie, see Myles Dungan, *Conspiracy: Irish political trials* (Dublin, 2009), 282, 291.

[34] Cosgrave MSS, Form for assembly and proceedings of field general court martial on active service.

[35] BMH, WS 268, 4, 6, Cosgrave, witness statement.

[36] NLI, MS 44,674, Cosgrave, 'Account of treatment of prisoners'; Ó Broin, *W. E. Wylie,* 28–29.

[37] Cosgrave MSS, Form for assembly and proceedings of field general court martial.

[38] Robert D. Marshall, 'Lieutenant W.E. Wylie K.C.: the soldiering lawyer of 1916', in Felix M. Larkin and N.M. Dawson (eds), *Lawyers, the law and history: Irish Legal History Society discourses and other papers 2005–2011* (Dublin, 2013), 120–47: 132.

[39] UCDA, de Valera MSS, P150/524, De Valera, memorandum, 3 July 1969.

[40] BMH, WS 268, 18–19, Cosgrave, witness statement.

[41] BMH, WS 268, 20, Cosgrave, witness statement.

[42] J.J. Walsh, *Recollections of a rebel* (Tralee, 1944), 42–3.

[43] BMH, WS 1511, 43–6, Gerald Doyle, witness statement.

[44] BMH, WS 865, 7, Jack Plunkett, witness statement.

[45] BMH, WS 244, 16–17, John McGallogly, witness statement.

[46] UCDA, de Valera MSS, P150/529, Joe McGuinness to Count Plunkett, Easter Sunday 1917.

[47] UCDA, MacNeill MSS, LA1/G/158, Reply to questionnaire for ex-prisoners; LA1/G/150, MacNeill to Margaret McNeill, 26 March 1917.

[48] Municipal Council minutes, 8 January 1917, 11.

[49] Thomas J. Morrissey SJ, *Laurence O'Neill (1864–1943), lord mayor of Dublin (1917–1924), patriot and man of peace* (Dublin, 2013), 67.

[50] British National Archives, London (BNA), CO.904/103, County Inspector's report, Kilkenny, 1 August 1917.

[51] Jim Maher, *Kilkenny People*, 26 May 1995, 13.

[52] *Freeman's Journal*, 7 August 1917, 3.

[53] *Irish Independent*, 9 August 1917, 3.

[54] *Irish Independent*, 27 September 1917, 3.

[55] *Freeman's Journal*, 13 August 1917, 3.

[56] Charles Townshend, *The republic: the fight for Ireland's independence, 1918–1923* (London, 2013), 120.

[57] BMH, WS 653, Mrs. T.M. Sullivan, witness statement; NLI, O'Brien MSS, 8556(15), Healy to William O'Brien, 15 September 1917.

[58] BMH, WS 268, Cosgrave, witness statement, note 3; Cosgrave MSS, Liam Cosgrave, 'Recollections', 13, 21.

[59] Callanan, *T.M. Healy*, 529.

[60] NLI, MS 24,357(2), Cosgrave to Kathleen O'Doherty, 10 July 1917; Cosgrave to Irish National Aid and Volunteers Dependants Fund, 9 December 1917; NLI, MS 23,468, minutes, National Aid Association, 11 December 1917; Caoimhe Nic Dháibhéid, 'The Irish National Aid Association and the radicalization of public opinion in Ireland, 1916–1918', *Historical Journal* 55 (3) (2012), 705–29: 720.

[61] BMH, WS 1280, 57, Eamon Broy, witness statement.

[62] Lysaght, 'Memoir', 90.

[63] *Irish Independent*, 9 October 1917, 3.

[64] Municipal Council minutes, 17 December 1917, 510–1.

[65] 'Hell in Dublin and the Corporation', *New Ireland*, 17 November 1917, 28–9; 'Hell in Dublin', *New Ireland*, 15 December 1917, 89.

[66] BNA, CO.904/23/5 (21), Sinn Féin convention report.

[67] UCDA, de Valera MSS, P150/575(26), Sinn Féin convention report, 25 October 1917.

[68] Lawrence William White, 'MacDonagh, Joseph', *DIB*, vol. 5, 918.

[69] *Irish Independent*, 11 June 1918, 1.

[70] Morrissey, *William O'Brien*, 160.

[71] *Irish Independent*, 26 June 1918, 2; William Murphy, *Political imprisonment and the Irish, 1912–1921* (Oxford, 2014), 120.

[72] NLI, O'Neill MSS, 35,294(4), Joseph MacDonagh to Laurence O'Neill, 18 December 1918; Aodh Quinlivan, *Philip Monahan: a man apart. The life and times of Ireland's first local authority manager* (Dublin, 2006), 23.

[73] BNA, HO.144/1582/335439, Correspondence and notes, 17 May–10 June 1918.

[74] NLI, O'Neill MSS, 35,294(3), Cosgrave to Laurence O'Neill, 19 November 1918.

[75] Cosgrave MSS, Cosgrave to Henry Dixon, 1 January 1919.

[76] NLI, O'Neill MSS, 35,294(3), Cosgrave to O'Neill, 19 July 1918; NLI, Byrne MSS, 33,735, Cosgrave to T.J. Byrne, 22 January 1919.

[77] NLI, Stack MSS, 17,090, Collins to Austin Stack, 7 March 1919.

[78] NLI, MS 23,468, Minutes, National Aid Association, 22 March 1919.

[79] Liam Cosgrave, 'Recollections', 6–7.

[80] Cosgrave MSS, Memorandum.

[81] Frank Flanagan, *Reminiscences of 'the pope' Flanagan* (Dublin, 2010), 13, 17.

[82] Eamonn MacThomáis, *Me jewel and darlin' Dublin* (fourth edition, Dublin, 1983), 42.

[83] *Freeman's Journal*, 15 January 1923, 5.

[84] *Dáil debates*, vol. 33, 1148 (27 February 1930).

[85] Arthur Mitchell, *Revolutionary government in Ireland: Dáil Éireann 1919–22* (Dublin, 1995), 158.

[86] BMH, WS 414, 4, Eveleen Lawless, witness statement.

[87] *Dáil debates, 1919–1921*, 270 (11 March 1921).

[88] NAI, DE 1/2, Cabinet minutes, 17 July 1920.

[89] *Evening Telegraph*, 19 January 1920, 1; Pádraig Yeates, *A city in turmoil: Dublin 1919–21* (Dublin, 2012), 79.

[90] Municipal Council minutes, 23 January 1912, 64; 23 January 1914, 14.

[91] Cosgrave MSS, Cosgrave to Joseph D. Rush, 9 February 1944; Carden, *Alderman*, 166–7.

[92] William O'Brien, *Forth the banners go. Reminiscences of William O'Brien* (Dublin, 1969), 170.

[93] NAI, Dáil Éireann (DE) 1/2(41), Cabinet minutes, 20 February 1920.

[94] *Irish Bulletin*, 26 March 1920.

[95] *Freeman's Journal*, 26 March 1920, 5.

[96] *Irish Independent*, 30 March 1920, 6; *Freeman's Journal*, 30 March 1920, 5.

[97] BNA, HO.144/1582/335439, Cosgrave, request for parole, 13 April 1920; *Freeman's Journal*, 19 April 1920, 3; Cosgrave MSS, Cosgrave to Padraic Colum, 18 October 1922; BMH, WS 268, Note 1, Cosgrave, witness statement; Morrissey, *Laurence O'Neill*, 119.

[98] *Irish Independent*, 30 June 1920, 6.

[99] *Freeman's Journal*, 13 August 1920, 6.

[100] *Dáil debates, 1919–1921*, 185 (29 June 1920); 218–23 (17 September 1920).

[101] UCDA, de Valera MSS, P150/1376, O'Higgins to O'Hegarty, 5 January 1921.

[102] Cosgrave MSS, T.J. McArdle to Cosgrave, 14 June 1937.

[103] BMH, WS 501, 42, T.J. McArdle, witness statement.

[104] NAI, Dáil Éireann Local Government (DELG), 7/22, O'Higgins to secretary, Donegal County Council, 7 February 1921.

[105] Mitchell, *Revolutionary government*, 56.

[106] Cosgrave MSS, Cosgrave, 'Statement on relations between Michael Collins, Cathal Brugha and Austin Stack', n.d..

[107] *Dáil debates, 1921–1922 (private sessions)*, 36 (22 August 1921).

[108] BMH, WS 449, 6, Cosgrave, witness statement.

[109] *Dáil debates, 1919–1921*, 253 (25 January 1921).

[110] NAI, DE 1/2, Cabinet minutes, 19 December 1919.

[111] Tom Garvin, *1922: the birth of Irish democracy* (Dublin, 1996), 66.

[112] Cosgrave MSS, Cosgrave to Thomas Crosbie, 28 January 1944.

[113] *Dáil debates, August 1921–June 1922*, 375 (10 May 1922).

[114] NAI, DELG 27/31, J. Bennett to Department of Local Government, 27 November 1921.

[115] Mel Cousins, *The birth of social welfare in Ireland, 1922–52* (Dublin, 2003), 27.

[116] NAI, DELG, 16/9, Cosgrave to clerk of the union, Manorhamilton, 6 September 1921.

[117] *Dáil debates, 1919–1921*, 271 (11 March 1921); circular 30 September 1920, cited in BMH, WS 501, 105, T.J. McArdle, witness statement; *Dáil debates, August 1921–June 1922*, 35 (17 August 1921).

[118] NAI, DE 2/84, Cosgrave to Stack, 3 May 1921.

[119] NAI, DELG, 30/11, Cosgrave to secretary, Westmeath County Council, 28 September 1921.

[120] UCDA, de Valera MSS, P150/575(14–5), Sinn Féin Convention Report, 25 October 1917.

[121] *Dáil debates, 1921–1922 (private sessions)*, 37 (22 August 1921).

[122] NAI, DE 1/3(160), Cabinet minutes, 24 November 1921.

[123] Martin Maguire, *The civil service and the revolution in Ireland, 1912–38* (Manchester, 2008), 98–9.

[124] *Dáil debates 1921–1922 (private sessions)*, 36 (22 August 1921).

[125] Cosgrave MSS, *Boston Sunday Post*, 22 January 1928; BMH, WS 268, Note 1, Cosgrave, witness statement; Mary E. Daly, *The buffer state: the historical roots of the Department of the Environment* (Dublin, 1997), 60–1.

[126] Municipal Council minutes, 3 May 1920, 287, Cosgrave to governor, Bank of Ireland, 29 April 1921.

[127] Yeates, *A city in turmoil*, 150.

[128] *Dáil debates, 1921–1922 (private sessions)*, 35 (22 August 1921).

[129] NAI, DELG 11/23, Cosgrave to O'Higgins, 11 August 1921; Cosgrave to secretary, Galway County Council, 11 August 1921.

[130] NAI, DELG 5/18, O'Higgins to Cosgrave, 26 September 1921.

[131] NAI, DELG 16/9, O'Higgins to Cosgrave, 7 October 1921; Cosgrave and O'Higgins, 'Memo on condition of rate collection in County Leitrim to show the need for extraordinary methods in this county', 10 October 1921.

[132] NAI, DE 1/2(125), Cabinet minutes, 6 July 1920.

[133] NAI, DE 2/44, Report in re building dispute, 16 October 1920; O'Hegarty, minute, 23 October 1921.

[134] NAI, DE/1/1(50), DE/1/2(4, 7, 17), Cabinet minutes, 19 September, 3 October, 10 October, 31 October 1919.

[135] *Freeman's Journal*, 28 October 1920, 5.

[136] *Dáil debates, 1919–1921*, 151-2 (20 August 1919).

[137] NAI, DE 2/396, Diarmuid O'Hegarty to de Valera, 24 February 1921. The original proposal is missing from the file but its content can be deduced from the response.

[138] *Irish Independent*, 13 September 1919, 5.

[139] BMH, WS 939, 123, Ernest Blythe, witness statement.

[140] Cosgrave MSS, Cosgrave to Fr E.J. Doherty, Glencree, 23 January 1944; Fr James McDonnell-Moran, *Sunday Press*, 21 November 1965, 4.

[141] NAI, DE 1/3, Cabinet minutes, 27 November 1921.

[142] For example, NAI, DELG 3/6, Kevin O'Higgins (?) to Thomas Bolger, 8 December 1920.

[143] UCDA, de Valera MSS, P150/1376, De Valera to Cosgrave, 19 January 1921.

[144] *Dáil debates*, vol. 40, 305, 316, 373–4 (15, 16 October 1931).

[145] O'Halpin, 'Cosgrave', *DIB*, vol. 2, 882.

[146] BMH, WS 680, 21, Nicholas O'Dwyer, witness statement.

[147] Mark Sturgis, diary, 22 December 1920, in Michael Hopkinson (ed.), *The last days of Dublin Castle: the Mark Sturgis diaries* (Dublin, 1999), 98.

[148] Simone Téry, *Irish Statesman*, 22 September 1928, 48; BMH, WS 939, 123, Blythe, witness statement.

[149] BMH, WS 501, 39–40, T.J. McArdle, witness statement.

[150] *Freeman's Journal*, 29 November 1920, 7; *Irish Independent*, 16 November 1920, 5; 6 January 1921, 6.

[151] *Irish Independent*, 18 May 1921, 6.

[152] Sturgis, diary, 7 May 1921, in *Last days of Dublin Castle*, 174.

[153] CCCA, U271/A/35, Liam de Róiste, diary, 25 January 1921.

[154] CCCA, U271/A/37, Liam de Róiste, diary, 22 May 1921.

[155] Terence de Vere White, *Kevin O'Higgins* (London, 1948), 47.

[156] *Dáil debates, 1919–1921*, 255 (25 January 1921).

[157] UCDA, de Valera MSS, P150/1376, O'Higgins to Diarmuid O'Hegarty, 5 January 1921.

[158] *Dáil Debates, 1919–1921*, 269 (11 March 1921).

[159] UCDA, O'Higgins MSS, P197/5(2), O'Higgins to Brigid Cole, n.d. (1920–1).

[160] O'Higgins to Cole, n.d. (1921?), UCDA, O'Higgins MSS, P197/49(2).

[161] Daly, *Buffer state*, 67.

[162] UCDA, O'Higgins MSS, P197/14(5), O'Higgins to Cole, n.d. (1920–1).

[163] UCDA, de Valera MSS, P150/1376, de Valera to Cosgrave, 17 January, 4 April 1921, to O'Higgins, 28 April 1921.

[164] BNA, CO.904/23, Collins to de Valera, 17 February 1921, de Valera to Collins, 18 June 1921, Epitome of letters captured.

[165] UCDA, de Valera MSS, P150/1377, Collins to de Valera, 15 October 1921.

[166] Peter Hart, *Mick: the real Michael Collins* (London, 2005*)*, 257–8.

[167] NAI, DE 2/7, appendix (d), Collins, statement of receipts and expenditure, 23 January 1921; UCDA, de Valera MSS, P150/1377, Collins to de Valera, 10 February 1921.

[168] See Ronan Fanning, *Fatal path: British government and Irish revolution* (London, 2013), 249–60.

[169] BMH, WS 767, 85–9, Patrick Moylett, witness statement. Moylett states 'Mr Cosgrave, his four men (whose names I do not know), and myself…', 86.

[170] UCDA, Mulcahy MSS, P7A/209(150), Seán Ó Murthuile, memoir.

[171] J. Anthony Gaughan, *Austin Stack: portrait of a separatist* (Dublin, 1977), 157.

[172] UCDA, de Valera MSS, P150/1473, Notes, 24 July 1921.

[173] UCDA, Hayes MSS, P53/222(69), P53/324(1), Michael Hayes to Padraic Colum 20 August 1952; Michael Hayes, memorandum, 20 April 1963.

[174] NAI, DE 1/3(118A), Cabinet minutes, 9 September 1921; David Fitzpatrick, *Harry Boland's Irish revolution* (Cork, 2003), 232–3.

[175] *Dáil debates, 1921–1922 (private sessions)*, 95–96 (14 September 1921).

[176] Regan, *Irish counter-revolution*, 15-16.

[177] Michael Laffan, *The partition of Ireland 1911–1925* (Dublin, 1983), 80–1.

[178] Gaughan, *Austin Stack*, 163, 167.

[179] Ruth Barrington, *Health, medicine and politics in Ireland 1900-1970* (Dublin, 1987), 93.

[180] Cosgrave to county councils and boards of guardians, 27 September 1921, cited in BMH, WS 501, 108, T.J. McArdle, witness statement; NAI, DE 1/3(159), Cabinet minutes, 24 November 1921.

[181] NAI, DELG, 11/23, Cosgrave to chief of inspection, 19 September 1921.

[182] *Freeman's Journal*, 10 October 1921; 2, 3 October 1921, 5.

[183] Jason K. Knirck, *Imagining Ireland's independence. The debates over the Anglo-Irish Treaty of 1921* (Lanham, 2006), 77–8, 88.

4. DEFENDING THE TREATY

[1] *Dáil debates, 1921–1922 (private sessions)*, 118 (14 December 1921); NAI, DE 1/3(182), Cabinet minutes, 3 December 1921.

[2] *Dáil debates, 1921–1922 (private sessions)*, 173 (15 December 1921).

[3] NAI, DE 1/3(182), Cabinet minutes, 3 December 1921.

[4] TCD, Childers MSS, 7814, Childers, diary, 4 December 1921.

[5] The Earl of Longford and Thomas P. O'Neill, *Eamon de Valera* (London, 1970), 168; O'Higgins confirmed this disagreement, see *Dáil debates 1921–1922* (private sessions), 173 (15 December 1921).

[6] Michael Laffan, *The resurrection of Ireland: the Sinn Féin party, 1916–1923* (Cambridge, 1999), 359.

[7] Collins, *The Cosgrave Legacy*, 24-5.

[8] TCD, Childers MSS, 7814, Childers, diary, 8 December 1921.

[9] Cosgrave MSS, *Boston Sunday Post*, 22 January 1928.

[10] Morrissey, *Laurence O'Neill*, 205–6.

[11] BMH, WS 465, 11, Mary O'Sullivan, witness statement; Tim Pat Coogan, *De Valera; long fellow, long shadow* (London, 1993), 284.

[12] Cosgrave MSS, *Boston Sunday Post*, 22 January 1928.

[13] *Dáil debates, 1921–1922, debate on the treaty*, 108 (21 December 1921).

[14] Padraig de Búrca and John F. Boyle, *Free State or Republic? Pen pictures of the historic treaty session of Dáil Éireann* (Dublin, 1922), 7, 24, 25.

[15] 'Nichevo' (Bertie Smyllie), *Irish Times*, 21 January 1922, 9.

[16] *Dáil debates, 1921–1922, debate on the treaty*, 102–8, 358 (21 December 1921, 9 January 1922).

[17] *Dáil debates, 1921–1922, debate on the treaty*, 357 (9 January 1922).

[18] *Dáil debates, 1921–1922 (private sessions)*, 277 (6 January 1922).

[19] *Irish Independent*, 3 January 1922, 5.

[20] Maureen Wall, 'Partition: the Ulster question (1916–1926)', in Desmond Williams (ed.), *The Irish struggle 1916–1926* (London, 1966), 79–93: 87; Laffan, *Resurrection of Ireland*, 232.

[21] Cosgrave MSS, Cosgrave to Joseph D. Rush, 9 February 1944.

[22] *Weekly Irish Times*, 21 January 1922, 2; UCDA, Mulcahy MSS, P7/B/29(6), Cosgrave to Collins, 19 August 1922.

[23] Morrissey, *Laurence O'Neill*, 210.

[24] NAI, G1/1. P.G.71, Cabinet minutes, 13 February; P.G.93, 10 March 1922.

[25] UCDA, de Valera MSS, P150/1546, Cosgrave to de Valera, 12 January 1922.

[26] Ulick O'Connor, *Oliver St. John Gogarty* (London, 1964), 186–7.

[27] NAI, G1/1, P.G.5; P.G.12; P.G.20, Cabinet minutes 17, 18 and 20 January 1922.

[28] *Dáil debates, August 1921–June 1922*, 300–1 (27 April 1922).

[29] *Dáil debates, August 1921–June 1922*, 259, 446–7, 454 (26 April, 18 May 1922).

[30] *Irish Times*, 17 June 1922, 7.

[31] DDA, Byrne MSS, 466, Office of the president of the executive council. Cosgrave to Byrne, 22 June 1922.

[32] Finola Kennedy, *Frank Duff: a life story* (London and New York, 2011), 78–9.

[33] *Dáil debates, 1919–1921*, 130 (19 June 1919).

[34] NAI, G1/1, P.G.30, Cabinet minutes, 25 January 1922.

[35] Laurence O'Neill to Thomas Johnson, 30 June 1922, *Irish Labour Party and Trade Union Congress report*, 1922, 32.

[36] *Dáil debates*, vol. 3, 660 (4 May 1923).

[37] Cyril Barrett, 'Visual arts and society, 1921–84', in J. R. Hill (ed.), *A new history of Ireland VII: Ireland 1921–84* (Oxford, 2003), 587–620: 600.

[38] NAI, G1/1, P.G.3, Cabinet minutes, 16 January 1922.

[39] UCDA, Mulcahy MSS, P7a/182, Cosgrave to Richard Mulcahy, 3 January 1924.

[40] *Dáil debates, August 1921–June 1922*, 124, 195, 430 (28 February, 2 March, 17 May 1922).

[41] *Dáil debates, August 1921–June 1922*, 430, 432 (17 May 1922).

[42] *Dáil debates, August 1921–June 1922*, 300 (27 April 1922).

[43] NAI, D/T, S 8139, 8, Cosgrave, interview, 27 February 1923.

[44] *Senate debates*, vol. 1, 2080 (3 August 1923).

[45] NAI, D/T, S 2978, Memorandum, 12 April 1922.

[46] BNA, Cab. 21/249, 22/N/60(7 and 8), Conference on Ireland with Irish ministers, 26, 27 May 1922.

[47] Cosgrave MSS, Liam Cosgrave, 'Recollections', 33.

[48] *Irish Independent*, 1 June 1922, 8.

[49] Michael Hopkinson, *Green against green: the Irish Civil War* (Dublin, 1988), 110–1.

[50] NAI, D/T, S 8139, Cosgrave, memorandum, n.d. (*c.* 31 December 1922).

[51] *Freeman's Journal*, 10 June 1922, 6.

[52] *Irish Independent*, 12 June 1922, 6.

[53] *Weekly Irish Times*, 17 June 1922, 1.

[54] *Irish Times*, 10 June 1922, 2; *Irish Independent*, 10 June 1922, 7.

[55] Bill Kissane, *Explaining Irish democracy* (Dublin, 2002), 151.

[56] Laffan, *Resurrection of Ireland*, 400–9; Michael Gallagher, 'The pact general election of 1922', *Irish Historical Studies*, XXI (84) (September 1979), 413–20.

[57] *Dáil debates*, vol. 1, 771 (26 September 1922); *Irish Times*, 7 December 1922, 5.

[58] Michael Gallagher (ed.), *Irish elections 1922–44: results and analysis* (Limerick, 1993), 3; *Nationalist* (Carlow), 24 June 1922, 8.

[59] John M. Regan, *Myth and the Irish state* (Sallins, 2013), 118–20; Mulcahy, *Dáil debates*, vol. 1, 172–3 (12 September 1922).

[60] Cathal O'Shannon, *Evening Press*, 19 November 1965, 12.

[61] NAI, G1/2, P.G.45, Cabinet minutes, 1 July 1922.

[62] NAI, G1/2, P.G.57, Cabinet minutes, 12 July 1922.

[63] UCDA, Kennedy MSS, P4/588(4), Kennedy to Cosgrave, 3 April 1923.

[64] NAI, G1/2, P.G.45, Cabinet minutes, 1 July 1922.

[65] *DIFP*, vol. I (Dublin, 1998), 488: Collins to Cosgrave, 5 August 1922.

[66] NAI, G1/2, P.G.68; G1/3, P.G.80; P.G.93, Cabinet minutes, 22 July, 3 August, 18 August 1922.

[67] NAI, G1/2, P.G. 58, Cabinet minutes, 12 July 1922; Regan, *Myth and the Irish state*, 12.

[68] UCDA, Mulcahy MSS, P7/B/29(177), Collins to government, 26 July 1922.

[69] NAI, G1/2, P.G. 72, Cabinet minutes, 26 July 1922.

[70] Regan, *Irish counter-revolution*, 80; *Myth and the Irish state*, 14, 68, 83, 134.

[71] UCDA, Kennedy MSS, P4/558(1–3), Kennedy to Cosgrave, 3 April 1923.

[72] NAI, D/T, S 2817, Cosgrave, memorandum, 12 August 1922.

[73] NAI, D/T, S 1393, Gavan Duffy to Collins, 24 July 1922.

[74] NAI, D/T, S 8143, Cosgrave to Mícheál Ó Cuill, 4 August 1922.

[75] NAI, G1/2, P.G.41, P.G.57, P.G.69; G1/3, P.G.86, P.G.93, Cabinet minutes, 29 June, 12 July, 24 July, 9 August, 18 August 1922.

[76] UCDA, Kennedy MSS, P4/241, Michael McDunphy to Hugh Kennedy, 22 August 1922; NLI, Collins MSS, 40,420/12(3), Collins to Cosgrave, 3.30 p.m., 21 August 1922.

[77] NAI, G1/3, P.G. 96, Cabinet minutes, 22 August 1922.

[78] UCDA, FitzGerald MSS, P80/694(1), Minute, n.d. (22 August 1922?) on Patrick Hogan, draft reply to Labour Party.

[79] NAI, G1/3, P.G. 97, Cabinet minutes, 23 August 1922.

[80] NAI, G1/3, P.G. 100, Cabinet minutes, 25 August 1922.

[81] Maryann Gialanella Valiulis, *Portrait of a revolutionary: General Richard Mulcahy and the founding of the Irish Free State* (Dublin, 1992), 172; Tierney, *Eoin MacNeill*, 311–2.

[82] Paul Murray, *The Irish Boundary Commission and its origins 1886-1925* (Dublin, 2011), 124.

[83] NAI, G1/3, P.G. 99, Cabinet minutes, 24 August 1922.

[84] NAI, G1/3, P.G.101, Cabinet minutes, 26 August 1922.

[85] NAI, G2/1, C.1/37, Cabinet minutes, 29 January 1923.

[86] Valiulis, *Portrait of a revolutionary*, 174–5; BMH, WS 939, 179, Blythe, witness statement.

[87] NAI, G1/3, P.G.107, Cabinet minutes, 4 September 1922.

[88] Clare O'Halloran, *Partition and the limits of Irish nationalism* (Dublin, 1987), 141–3; Eamon Phoenix, *Northern nationalism: nationalist politics, partition and the Catholic minority in Northern Ireland, 1890–1940* (Belfast, 1994), 258–9.

[89] TCD, Childers MSS, 7816, Molly Childers, diary, 9 June 1922.

[90] UCDA, Blythe MSS, P24/70, Blythe, memorandum, 9 August 1922. See Daithí Ó Corráin, '"Ireland in his heart north and south": the contribution of Ernest Blythe to the partition question', *Irish Historical Studies*, XXXV (137) (May 2006), 63–4.

[91] NAI, D/T, S 11,209(21), Minutes, 11 October 1922.

[92] *Dáil debates*, vol. 1, 76 (11 September 1922).

[93] *Dáil debates*, vol. 1, 30, 55 (9 September 1922).

[94] NAI, D/T, S 1689A , 'Ministerial & other salaries etc.', memorandum, 23 January 1948; NAI, D/T, S 3557, Hogan, memorandum, 25 January 1924.

[95] *Dáil debates,* vol. 1, 29 (9 September 1922).

[96] The cabinet ministers were O'Higgins (Home Affairs, later Justice); MacNeill (Education); Joe McGrath (Industry and Commerce); Blythe (Local Government, subsequently moved to Finance); Mulcahy (Defence); and Desmond FitzGerald (External Affairs). The three 'non-cabinet' ministers were Patrick Hogan (Agriculture); Fionán Lynch (Fisheries); and J.J. Walsh (Postmaster General).

[97] BNA, CO.739/7, Hugh Martin to Lionel Curtis, 11, 13 September 1922.

[98] CCCA, U271/A/47, Liam de Róiste, diary, 29 November 1922.

[99] UCDA, Hayes MSS, P53/304(230), Interview, Mulcahy and Michael Hayes, n.d..

[100] Regan, *Irish counter-revolution*, 100.

[101] Cosgrave MSS, Cosgrave to Stephen Gwynn, 22 January 1944.

[102] NAI, D/T, S 2925, Cosgrave to Michael McDunphy, n.d (*c*. 2 September 1922).

[103] Frank Henderson to Ernie O'Malley, 26 September 1922, Cormac O'Malley and Anne Dolan (eds), *'No surrender here!' The civil war papers of Ernie O'Malley* (Dublin, 2007), 228.

[104] *Weekly Irish Times*, 14 October 1922, 1.

[105] Patrick Murray, *Oracles of God: the Roman Catholic Church and Irish politics, 1922–37*, (Dublin, 2000), 70–2.

[106] Hopkinson, *Green against green*, 199; *Irish Statesman*, 22 September 1928, 48; *Irish Times*, 16 June 1938, 5.

[107] Terence Dooley, *The decline of the big house in Ireland: a study of Irish landed families, 1860–1960* (Dublin, 2001), 189–90.

[108] *Dáil debates*, vol. 1, 74 (11 September 1922).

[109] NAI, D/T, S 1784, Confidential reports, 26 August and 2 September 1922, captured first by republicans and then by government forces.

[110] Wade, *Letters*, 690: Yeats to Olivia Shakespear, 9 October 1922.

[111] CCCA, U271/A/46, Liam de Róiste, diary, 8 August, 9 September 1922.

[112] NAI, P 7398, *Irlande*, vol. 3, 106, Blanche to Poincaré, 29 November 1922.

[113] O'Malley and Dolan, *'No surrender here!'*, 175: O'Connor to Ernie O'Malley, 12 September 1922.

[114] *Dáil debates*, vol. 1, 807 (27 September 1922).

[115] NAI, D/T, S 8142, Cosgrave, memorandum, n.d. (early December 1922).

[116] NAI, D/T, S 8141, Cosgrave to E.P. Culverwell, 2 October 1922.

[117] *Dáil debates*, vol. 1, 808, 877 (27 September 1922).

[118] *Dáil debates*, vol. 1, 876 (27 September 1922).

[119] *Dáil debates*, vol. 1, 76 (11 September 1922).

[120] *Dáil debates*, vol. 1, 2364 (28 November 1922).

[121] Regan, *Irish counter-revolution*, 113.

[122] Collins, *Cosgrave Legacy*, 38.

[123] *Dáil debates*, vol. 2, 94 (8 December 1922); *Irish Times*, 9 December 1922, 6, editorial.

[124] *Dáil debates*, vol. 2, 49 (8 December 1922).

[125] DDA, Byrne MSS, 466, Office of the president of the executive council, 1922, Draft, Byrne to Cosgrave, 10 December 1922.

[126] Murray, *Oracles of God*, 74, 84–8.

[127] BMH, WS 939, 193, Blythe, witness statement.

[128] NAI, D/T, S 8139(3), Cosgrave, interview, 27 February 1923.

[129] Hopkinson, *Green against green*, 190–1.

[130] Eunan O'Halpin, *Defending Ireland: the Irish state and its enemies since 1922* (Oxford, 1999), 31–3.

[131] BMH, WS 939, 195, Blythe, witness statement.

[132] NAI, D/T, S 3306, Memorandum, 20 January 1923.

[133] UCDA, Mulcahy MSS, P7/B/101(18), Cosgrave to Mulcahy, 25 January 1923.

[134] DDA, Byrne MSS, 466, Office of the president of the executive council, Cosgrave to Byrne, 18 March 1923.

[135] NAI, G1/3, P.G.9(a), P.G.62(a), Cabinet minutes, 19 September, 16 November 1922; BNA, CO.739/7, Lionel Curtis to John Chancellor, 4 October 1922.

[136] DDA, Byrne MSS 466, Office of the president of the executive council, Cosgrave to Byrne, 19 April 1923.

[137] NAI, G2/1, C.1/84, Cabinet minutes, 16 April 1923.

[138] Murray, *Oracles of God*, 185–92.

[139] NAI, G2/1, C.1/85, Cabinet minutes, 17 April 1923.

[140] *Dáil debates*, vol. 2, 94 (8 December 1922); NAI, D/T, S 8139(5), Cosgrave, interview, 27 February 1923. The final point related to a republican attack on the home of Sean McGarry, a pro-treaty TD, which resulted in his young son being burned to death.

[141] *Manchester Guardian Commercial, European reconstruction series. Ireland, section one*, 15 March 1923, 5.

[142] Maryann Gialanella Valiulis, '"The man they could never forgive". The view of the opposition: de Valera and the civil war', in F.J. O'Carroll and John A. Murphy (eds), *De Valera and his times* (Cork, 1983), 92–9.

[143] *Irish Times*, 18 March 1922, 8.

[144] *Freeman's Journal*, 17 August 1922, 5; NAI, D/T, S 8139, Cosgrave, memorandum, n.d. (c. 31 December 1922).

[145] NAI, D/T, S 8139 (8), Cosgrave, interview, 27 February 1923.

[146] Sean Cronin, *The McGarrity Papers* (Tralee, 1972), 125: de Valera to Joe McGarrity, 10 September 1922.

[147] Joan C. Cullen, Patrick J. Hogan TD, minister for Agriculture, 1922–1932. A study of a leading member of the first government of independent Ireland. Unpublished PhD thesis, Dublin City University, 1993, 62.

[148] NLI, O'Kelly MSS, 27,707(353), Seán T. O'Kelly, Memoirs.

[149] NAI, D/T, S 585, Memorandum, 1 February 1924.

[150] M.P. McCabe, *For God and Ireland: the fight for moral superiority in Ireland 1922–1932* (Dublin and Portland, 2013), 150.

[151] *Dáil debates*, vol. 1, 807 (27 September 1922).

[152] NAI, D/T, S 8139(7), Cosgrave, interview, 27 February 1923.

[153] *Dáil debates*, vol. 1, 2363 (28 November 1922).

[154] BNA, CO/164, Prison censor's report, November 1918.

[155] J. Anthony Gaughan (ed.), *Memoirs of Senator James Douglas, concerned citizen* (Dublin, 1998), 87.

[156] *Dáil Debates*, vol. 1, 684, 774 (25, 26 September 1922).

[157] Leo Kohn, *The constitution of the Irish Free State* (London, 1932), 80, 112, 114.

[158] Ronan Keane, 'The voice of the Gael. Chief Justice Kennedy and the emergence of the new Irish court system, 1921–1936', *Irish Jurist* 31 (1996), 205–25: 223.

[159] *Dáil debates*, vol. 1, 774 (26 September 1922).

[160] *Irish Times*, 23 August 1923, 8.

[161] NAI, D/T, S 8139, Cosgrave, memorandum, n.d. (c. 31 December 1922).

[162] UCDA, Kennedy MSS, P4/826(71–2), New York Supreme Court proceedings, 8 June 1923.

[163] *Irish Times*, 14 September 1927, 11.

[164] Kissane, *Politics of the Irish Civil War*, 107.

[165] NAI, D/T, S 1801H , J.H. Thomas to Cosgrave, 16 June 1924.

[166] *Dáil debates*, vol. 34, 398 (2 April 1930); *Leader*, 31 March 1928, 202.

[167] Jason Knirck, *Afterimage of the revolution. Cumann na nGaedheal and Irish politics, 1922–1932* (Madison WI, 2014), 45.

[168] Ronan Fanning, *Independent Ireland* (Dublin, 1983), 42.

[169] Brendan Sexton, *Ireland and the Crown, 1922–1936: the governor-generalship of the Irish Free State* (Dublin, 1989), 76–7.

[170] Keith Middlemas (ed.), Thomas Jones, *Whitehall diary, vol. III: Ireland 1918–1925* (Oxford, 1971), 218: Thomas Jones, diary, 16 November 1922.

[171] Callanan, *T.M. Healy*, 600.

[172] Frank MacDermot, *Irish Times*, 1 June 1957, 7.

[173] *Dáil debates*, vol. 40, 369 (16 October 1931).

[174] NAI, D/T, S 8139(5), Cosgrave, interview, 27 February 1923.

[175] Cosgrave MSS, Cosgrave to Granard, 5 September 1924.

[176] NAI, G2/3, C.2/26, Cabinet minutes, 30 November 1923.

[177] DDA, Byrne MSS 466, Office of the president of the executive council, 1923, Cosgrave to Byrne, 28 October 1923.

[178] Paul Bew, *Ireland: the politics of enmity 1789–2006* (Oxford, 2007), 442.

[179] McCabe, *For God and Ireland*, 187; O'Halpin, *Defending Ireland*, 44.

[180] C.S. Andrews, *Man of no property* (Dublin and Cork, 1982), 68.

[181] Conor Brady, *Guardians of the Peace* (Dublin 1974), 150.

[182] Owen Dudley Edwards, *Éamon de Valera* (Cardiff, 1987), 109.

5. Building the Free State

[1] UCDA, Healy MSS, P 6/A/98, T.M. Healy to Annie Healy, 27 July 1924. See Muiris MacCarthaigh and Maurice Manning, *The houses of the Oireachtas: parliament in Ireland* (Dublin, 2010), 25–7.

[2] Emmet O'Connor, *Syndicalism in Ireland 1917–1923* (Cork, 1988), 159.

[3] Ciara Meehan, *The Cosgrave party: a history of Cumann na nGaedheal, 1923–33* (Dublin, 2010), 6–9; Laffan, *Resurrection of Ireland*, 420–2.

[4] *Leader*, 7 July 1923, 509.

[5] NAI, D/T, S 3306, Robert Kelly to T.M. Healy, 17 September 1923.

[6] Frank Munger, *The legitimacy of opposition: the change of government in Ireland in 1932* (London/Beverly Hills, 1975), 19–20; Regan, *Irish counter-revolution*, 113.

[7] UCDA, Mulcahy MSS, P7a/182, Cosgrave to Mulcahy, 3 January 1924.

[8] UCDA, Mulcahy MSS, P7a/182, Cosgrave to O'Rahilly, 17 August 1923.

[9] KDA, Fogarty MSS 33, 1-23/i, Cosgrave to Fogarty, 12 December 1923.

[10] *Irish Times*, 13 August 1923, 8; 23 August 1923, 8.

[11] *Freeman's Journal*, 20 August 1923, 7.

[12] CCCA, U271/A/49, De Róiste, diary, 11 August 1923.

[13] *Irish Times*, 24 June 1927, 7.

[14] V.S. Pritchett, *Midnight oil* (London, 1971), 119.

[15] Simone Téry, *Irish Statesman*, 22 September 1928, 48; C.H. Bretherton, *The real Ireland* (London, 1925), 168. The first writer was French, the second English.

[16] *Irish Times*, 26 January 1924, 9.

[17] 'Politicus', *Sunday Independent*, 6 October 1929, 8.

[18] *Irish Statesman*, 5 November 1927, 201.

[19] *Irish Statesman*, 5 November 1927, 201.

[20] *Dáil debates*, vol. 33, 1163–4 (27 February 1930).

[21] For example, *Dáil debates*, vol. 20, 1439–41 (3 August 1927); *Senate debates*, vol. 9, 260 (9 August 1927).

[22] John Horgan, *Seán Lemass, the enigmatic patriot* (Dublin, 1997), 59.

[23] *Irish Independent*, 6 June 1927, 8; NAI, Johnson MSS, 17,162, Johnson, memorandum, 19 August 1927.

[24] *Irish Times*, 23 May 1927, 3.

[25] Robert Elgie and John Stapleton, 'The parliamentary activity of the head of government in Ireland (1923–2000) in comparative perspective', *Journal of Legislative Studies* 10 (2/3) (Summer/Autumn 2004), 154–73: 161.

[26] NAI, D/T, S 3678A , Gearoid McGann to Liam Tobin, 20 June 1923; McGann, memorandum, 28 June 1923; Cosgrave MSS, Edward A. Lawler, *Boston Sunday Post*, 15 January 1928.

[27] NAI, D/T, S 5241, Memoranda, n.d. (May 1925).

[28] For example, see UCDA, Mulcahy MSS, P7/B/195, Mulcahy, memorandum, n.d. (January 1924); record of meeting, 25 June 1923.

[29] Sean Etchingham, 'Patsy Pathrick on Physiognomy', *Irish Fun*, May 1922, 4.

[30] Jones, diary, 9 February 1923, *Whitehall diary*, vol. III, 219.

[31] Sean O'Casey, *Inishfallen, fare thee well* (London, 1949), 166.

[32] UCDA, Kennedy MSS, P4/588(1, 5), Cosgrave to Kennedy, 30 April 1924, Kennedy to Cosgrave, 1 May 1924.

[33] Michael Kennedy, *Ireland and the League of Nations 1919–1946: international relations, diplomacy and politics* (Dublin, 1996), 49.

[34] Aengus Nolan, *Joseph Walshe: Irish foreign policy, 1922–1946* (Cork, 2008), 33.

[35] Charles S. Maier, *Recasting bourgeois Europe: stabilization in France, Germany and Italy in the decade after World War I* (Princeton, 1975), 581.

[36] *Irish Statesman*, 1 August 1925, 643.

[37] UCDA, Mulcahy MSS, P7/C/99 (61, 63), Mulcahy, diary, 25 and 26 November 1924.

[38] *Leader*, 8 December 1923, 413.

[39] UCDA, Mulcahy MSS, P7/C/99 (107), Simone Téry, *Irish Statesman*, 13 October 1928, 109; Mulcahy, diary, 18 January 1925.

[40] Ernest Blythe, *Irish Times*, 19 November 1965, 8; see Brian Farrell, *Chairman or chief? The role of taoiseach in Irish government* (Dublin, 1971).

[41] NAI, G2/2, C.1/137, Cabinet minutes, 26 July 1923.

[42] Ronan Fanning, *The Irish Department of Finance 1922–58* (Dublin, 1978), 108, 135.

[43] Fanning, *Irish Department of Finance*, 189; Leon Ó Broin, *No man's man: a biographical memoir of Joseph Brennan—civil servant and first governor of the Central Bank* (Dublin 1982), 129.

[44] Fanning, *Independent Ireland*, 52.

[45] Mary E. Daly, *Industrial development and Irish national identity, 1922–1939* (Syracuse, 1992), 14.

[46] UCDA, Kennedy MSS, P4/1388, Kennedy to Cosgrave, 18 August 1923.

[47] UCDA, Mulcahy MSS, P7D/3(6), Mulcahy, 'Side glance note', 19 August 1963.

[48] UCDA, Mulcahy MSS, P7/B/254, Mulcahy, memorandum, 25 March 1923.

[49] UCDA, Mulcahy MSS, P7/D/3(6), Mulcahy, 'Side glance note', 19 August 1963.

[50] Fanning, *Irish Department of Finance*, 100.

[51] Cormac Ó Gráda, *A rocky road: the Irish economy since the 1920s* (Manchester, 1997), 108.

[52] Ó Gráda, *A rocky road*, 229.

[53] Draft notes of conference, 1 December 1925, *DIFP*, vol. II (Dublin, 2000), 508.

[54] NAI, D/T, S 11,724, Cosgrave to Judge Daniel Cohalan, 11 September 1924.

[55] T.O. Lloyd, *Empire to welfare state: English history 1906–1985* (Oxford, 1986), 120, 152; Noreen Branson, *Britain in the Nineteen Twenties* (London, 1975), 70.

[56] J.J. Lee, *Ireland 1912–1985: politics and society* (Cambridge, 1989), 109.

[57] UCDA, McGilligan MSS, P35a/4, Cosgrave to Fr P. Coffey, 27 October 1922.

[58] KDA, Fogarty MSS 33, 13–29/iii , Cosgrave to Fogarty, 18 May 1929.

[59] CCCA, U271/A/47, Liam de Róiste, diary, 14 November 1922.

[60] K. Theodore Hoppen, *Ireland since 1800. Conflict and conformity* (2nd edn, Harlow, 1999), 191.

[61] George O'Brien, 'The budget', *Studies* 14 (54) (June 1925), 177.

[62] UCDA, Cumann na nGaedheal/Fine Gael MSS, P39/Min/1(441), Cosgrave, standing committee meeting, 10 October 1924.

[63] Cousins, *Birth of social welfare*, 32–3.

[64] Cormac Ó Gráda, '"The greatest blessing of all": the old age pension in Ireland', *Past and Present*, 155 (May 2002), 124–61: 148.

[65] *Dáil debates*, vol. 3, 1112 (18 May 1923).

[66] T.K. Daniel, 'Griffith on his noble head: the determinants of Cumann na nGaedheal economic policy, 1922–32', *Irish Economic and Social History* 3 (1976), 55–65: 59–60.

[67] Dermot McAleese, 'Anglo-Irish economic interdependence: from excessive intimacy to a wider embrace', in P.J. Drudy (ed.), *Ireland and Britain since 1922* (Cambridge, 1986), 87–106: 88.

[68] Lee, *Ireland 1912–1985*, 113.

[69] NAI, D/T, S 3557, Hogan, memorandum, 24 January 1924; Cosgrave, 'Derating of agricultural land', *Studies* 26 (104) (December 1937), 648–54: 648.

[70] Cormac Ó Gráda, *Ireland: a new economic history 1780–1939* (Oxford, 1994), 386.

[71] *Leader*, 5 February 1927, 5.

[72] UCDA, Blythe MSS, P24/617(7), 'Policy of the Cumann na nGaedheal party by President Cosgrave', June 1927.

[73] Maguire, *Civil service and the revolution in Ireland*, 178.

[74] O'Halpin, *Defending Ireland*, 87; Nicholas Mansergh, *The Irish Free State: its government and politics* (London, 1934), 257.

[75] *Saorstát Éireann Irish Free State official handbook* (Dublin, 1932), 89.

[76] Cosgrave MSS, John Marcus O'Sullivan to Cosgrave, 28 January 1944.

[77] *Irish Statesman*, 3 January 1925, 520; *Irish Times*, 11 May 1927, 8, editorial.

[78] *Irish Statesman*, 17 July 1926, 507.

[79] NAI, D/T, S 8139(7), Cosgrave, interview, 27 February 1923.

[80] *Dáil debates*, vol. 41, 585 (27 April 1932).

[81] *Dáil debates*, vol. 1, 1876 (20 October 1922); UCDA, Cumann na nGaedheal/Fine Gael MSS, P39/Min/1(465), Cumann na nGaedheal annual convention, minutes, 29 January 1924.

[82] Tom Garvin, *The evolution of Irish nationalist politics* (Dublin, 1981), 146.

[83] UCDA, McGilligan MSS, P 35a/4, Cosgrave to Fr P. Coffey, 27 October 1922.

[84] *Irish Statesman*, 9 February 1924, 679.

[85] UCDA, Blythe MSS, P24/617(16), Cosgrave, 'Policy of the Cumann na nGaedheal party', June 1927.

[86] Jeffrey Prager, *Building democracy in Ireland: political order and cultural integration in a newly independent nation* (Cambridge, 1986), 202–3.

[87] Margaret O'Callaghan, 'Language, nationality and cultural identity in the Irish Free State, 1922–7: the *Irish Statesman* and the *Catholic Bulletin* reappraised', *Irish Historical Studies* XXIV (94) (November 1984), 226–45: 241.

[88] Garvin, *1922*, 62; Bew, *Ireland: the politics of enmity*, 445–6.

[89] Alvin Jackson, *Ireland 1798–1998* (Oxford, 1999), 285.

[90] Donal O'Sullivan, *The Irish Free State and its senate* (London, 1940), 123.

[91] NAI, D/T, S 3192, Hogan to Cosgrave, 7 April 1924.

[92] Mary E. Daly, *The first department: a history of the Department of Agriculture* (Dublin, 2002), 115.

[93] Terence Dooley, *'The land for the people'. The land question in independent Ireland* (Dublin, 2004), 58.

[94] Terence Dooley, 'Land and politics in independent Ireland, 1923–48: the case for reappraisal', *Irish Historical Studies* XXXIV (134) (November 2004), 175–97: 181–2, 184.

[95] Dooley, *'The land for the people'*, 94.

[96] UCDA, Blythe MSSP24/617(14), Policy of the Cumann na nGaedheal party by President Cosgrave, June 1927.

[97] Liam McNiffe, *A history of the Garda Síochána* (Dublin, 1997), 28.

[98] Mary Kotsonouris, *Retreat from revolution: the Dáil courts 1920–24* (Dublin, 1994), 62, 99.

[99] UCDA, Kennedy MSS, P4/1083(1), Kennedy, draft for Cosgrave, n.d.; P4/1090(1), Cosgrave to judiciary committee, 29 January 1923.

[100] W.N. Osborough, *Studies in Irish legal history* (Dublin, 1999), 279; Raymond Byrne and J. Paul McCutcheon, *The Irish legal system* (4th edn, Dublin, 2003), 56–8.

[101] Kotsonouris, *Retreat from revolution*, 115

[102] Keane, 'Voice of the Gael', 213, 223.

[103] Kotsonouris, *Retreat from revolution*, 114–9, 159.

[104] UCDA, Kennedy MSS, P4/1389, Cosgrave to Kennedy, n.d. (August 1923).

[105] Denis Gwynn, *The Irish Free State, 1922–1927* (London, 1928), 168.

[106] Hugh Geoghegan, 'The three judges of the Supreme Court of the Irish Free State, 1925–36', in Larkin and Dawson, *Lawyers, the law and history*, 29–53:53; Keane, 'Voice of the Gael', 221–2.

[107] *Senate debates*, vol. 2, 677 (6 February 1924).

[108] John McCarthy, *Kevin O'Higgins: builder of the Irish state* (Dublin, 2006), 265–8.

[109] Maguire, *Civil service and the revolution in Ireland*, 194–5.

[110] Maguire, *Civil service and the revolution in Ireland*, 227.

[111] NAI, D/T, S 1932, Ministers and Secretaries Act, 1924.

[112] *Dáil debates*, vol. 5, 917 (16 November 1923); Fanning, *Irish Department of Finance*, 73.

[113] Elaine A. Byrne, *Political corruption in Ireland, 1922–201. A crooked harp?* (Manchester, 2012), 25.

[114] NAI, D/T, S 4315A, Cosgrave to Diarmuid O'Hegarty, n.d. (March 1925).

[115] *Dáil debates, 1919–1921*, 269 (11 March 1921); NAI, G1/3, P.G.52(a), Cabinet minutes, 3 November 1922.

[116] *Dáil debates*, vol. 24, 131–2 (6 June 1928).

[117] Daly, *Buffer state*, 155–8.

[118] Daly, *Buffer state*, 119; F.S.L. Lyons, *Ireland since the famine* (second edition, London, 1973), 484.

[119] Seamas Ó Cinnéide, cited in Lee, *Ireland 1912–1985*, 124.

[120] *Irish Statesman*, 10 May 1924, 261.

[121] *Dáil debates*, vol. 5, 1001 (21 November 1923); Morrissey, *Laurence O'Neill*, 220–1, 228–9.

[122] *Leader*, 31 May 1924, 389.

[123] *Irish Statesman*, 29 August 1925, 777; 26 March 1927, 57; O'Brien, '*Dear, dirty Dublin*', 275.

[124] *Dáil debates, August 1921–June 1922*, 291 (26 April 1922).

[125] UCDA, Cumann na nGaedheal/Fine Gael MSS, P39/Min/1 (141–2), Meeting of standing committee, 13 January 1925.

[126] UCDA, Blythe MSS, P24/616(10), Address, Cumann na nGaedheal convention, 13 May 1925.

[127] Cullen, Patrick J. Hogan, 163.

[128] *Irish Statesman*, 9 February 1924, 679.

[129] Regan, *Irish counter-revolution*, 211.

[130] UCDA, FitzGerald MSS, P80/1101, Statement of view of standing committee, 10 October 1924; UCDA, Cumann na nGaedheal/Fine Gael MSS, P39/Min/1 (334), organisers' report, 13 July 1923.

[131] UCDA, Cumann na nGaedheal/Fine Gael MSS, P39/Min/1 (439–41), Minutes, standing committee, 10 October 1924.

[132] Regan, *Irish counter-revolution*, 214–9.

[133] UCDA, McGilligan MSS, P35d/16, Cosgrave to McGilligan, 23 October 1930.

[134] See, for example, Tom Garvin, *Nationalist revolutionaries in Ireland 1858–1928* (Oxford, 1987), 31.

[135] Pauric A. Dempsey, 'Cosgrave, Philip Bernard Joseph', *DIB*, vol. 2, 880.

[136] Tom Garvin, *Judging Lemass: the measure of the man* (Dublin, 2009), 135–6.

[137] Brian Girvin, *Between two worlds. Politics and economy in independent Ireland* (Dublin, 1989), 27.

[138] Kissane, *Politics of the Irish Civil War*, 37, 151; Oliver MacDonagh, *Ireland: the union and its aftermath* (London, 1977), 106.

[139] Oliver MacDonagh, *States of mind: a study of Anglo-Irish conflict 1780–1980* (London, 1983), 119.

[140] NAI, G2/1, C.1/23, Cabinet minutes, 3 January 1923.

[141] NAI, D/T, S 3717, Ministry of Education, 'The Gaelicizing of Ireland' (memorandum, 1924).

[142] Osborn Bergin, 'The revival of the Irish language. Comment', *Studies* 16 (61) (March 1927), 17–20: 19–20.

[143] Donal P. Corcoran, *Freedom to achieve freedom. The Irish Free State 1922–1932* (Dublin, 2013), 225, 227.

[144] BMH, WS 384, 38, J.J. O'Kelly, witness statement.

[145] *The Star*, 14 June 1930, 87.

[146] *Dáil debates*, vol. 5, 49 (20 September 1923).

[147] NAI, D/T, S 5111/1, President's broadcast message, 17 March 1926.

[148] *Saorstát Éireann, census of population, 1926*, vol. 10, (Dublin, 1934), 129.

[149] *Dáil debates, 1921–1922, debate on the treaty*, 7 (14 December 1921); J.L. McCracken, *Representative government in Ireland: a study of Dáil Éireann, 1919–48* (Oxford, 1958), 134.

[150] For example, Seán MacEntee, *Irish Times*, 16 November 1933, 7; Frank Aiken, cited in Maurice Manning, *James Dillon: a biography* (Dublin, 1999), 108.

[151] *Constitution of Ireland*, Article 26, 6.

[152] UCDA, Cumann na nGaedheal/Fine Gael MSS, P39/Min/3(132–5), Minutes, party meetings, 28 April–19 May 1932.

[153] *Leader*, 28 May 1927, 402.

[154] *Irish Statesman*, 17 April 1926, 144; NAI, G2/5, C.2/265, Cabinet minutes, 19 May 1926.

[155] Ewan Morris, *Our own devices: national symbols and political conflict in twentieth-century Ireland* (Dublin, 2005), 66–7.

[156] NAI, G2/1, C.1/17, Cabinet minutes, 28 December 1922.

[157] NAI, G2/5, C.2/336, Cabinet minutes, 2 May 1927.

[158] KDA, Fogarty MSS 33, 8–28/v, Cosgrave to Fogarty, 12 December 1928; R.F. Foster, *W. B. Yeats: a life II: the arch-poet 1915–1939* (Oxford, 2003), 334.

[159] Richard Pine, *2RN and the origins of Irish radio* (Dublin, 2002), 114, 145.

[160] UCDA, Blythe MSS, P24/467(7), Cosgrave to Blythe, 17 October 1927.

[161] R.F. Foster, *The Irish story. Telling tales and making it up in Ireland* (Harmondsworth, 2001), 103.

[162] Mike Cronin, 'Projecting the nation through sport and culture: Ireland, Aonach Tailteann and the Irish Free State, 1924–32', *Journal of Contemporary History* 38 (3) (July 2003), 395–411: 409.

[163] NAI, G1/2, P.G.33, Cabinet minutes, 12 June 1922.

[164] NAI, G2/1, C.1/26, Cabinet minutes, 9 January 1923.

[165] DDA, Byrne MSS, 466, Department of the president of the executive council, Cosgrave to Byrne, 4 March 1924.

[166] NAI, D/T, S 4127, Eamonn Duggan to Cosgrave, 20 March 1923, describing Byrne's opinions.

[167] NAI, D/T, S 4127, Cosgrave to James Downey, coadjutor bishop of Ossory, 21 September 1925.

[168] Murray, *Oracles of God*, 114.

[169] *Dáil debates*, vol. 10, 158 (11 February 1925).

[170] Anthony Rhodes, *The Vatican in the age of the dictators 1922–45* (London, 1973), 147.

171 Department of Home Affairs, report, 17 September 1920, *Dáil Debates, 1919–21*, 215; Kevin Rockett, *Irish film censorship. A cultural journey from silent cinema to internet pornography* (Dublin, 2004), 46, 384.

172 NAI, G2/2, C.1/98, Cabinet minutes, 4 May 1923.

173 *Senate debates*, vol. 1, 1127–9 (6 June 1923).

174 NAI, D/T, S 5473, Henry O'Friel, secretary, Department of Justice to Diarmuid O'Hegarty, 23 June 1927.

175 See, 260–2.

176 John Coolahan, *Irish education: history and structure* (Dublin, 1981), 47.

177 On vocational education, see Donald Harman Akenson, *A mirror to Kathleen's face: education in independent Ireland 1922–1960* (Montreal, 1975), 33–4.

178 J.H. Whyte, *Church and state in modern Ireland, 1923–1979* (Dublin, 1980), 16–19.

179 *Dáil debates*, vol. 13, 51 (3 November 1925).

180 Gavan Duffy to Cosgrave, 20 June 1922, *DIFP*, vol. I, 467.

181 Kennedy, *Ireland and the League of Nations*, 27–8, 62–3.

182 Donal Lowry, 'The captive dominion: imperial realities behind Irish diplomacy, 1922–49', *Irish Historical Studies* XXXVI (142) (November 2008), 202–26: 208.

183 Joseph Walshe to Daniel Binchy, 25 February 1930, cited in Michael Kennedy, 'Our men in Berlin: some thoughts on Irish diplomats in Germany 1929–39', *Irish Studies in International Affairs* 10 (1999), 53–70: 55.

184 Conor Cruise O'Brien, 'Ireland in international affairs', in Owen Dudley Edwards (ed.), *Conor Cruise O'Brien introduces Ireland* (London, 1969), 104–34: 108–9.

185 NAI, G2/5, C.2/268, Cabinet minutes, 1 June 1926.

186 Cosgrave, minute to FitzGerald, n.d. (mid-April 1924), *DIFP*, vol. II, 282.

187 Cosgrave MSS, Cosgrave to Granard, 29 October 1926.

188 NAI, D/T, S 5983/4, Speech, 2 November 1926.

189 FitzGerald, memorandum, 26 June 1924; Cosgrave, minute, n.d., *DIFP*, vol. II, 311.

190 Canning, *British policy towards Ireland*, 113.

191 UCDA, Mulcahy MSS, P7A/209(254), Seán Ó Murthuile, memoir.

192 UCDA, Mulcahy MSS, P7B/254, Mulcahy, memorandum, 21 March 1923.

193 *Dáil debates*, vol. 7, 3157 (26 June 1924).

194 NAI, G2/1, C.1/85, Cabinet minutes, 17 April 1923.

195 UCDA, Mulcahy MSS, P7/B/195, Records of meetings, 25 June, 4 July 1923.

196 *Dáil debates*, vol. 7, 3124, 3148, 3158-9 (26 June 1924).

197 NAI, G2/3, C.2/27, Cabinet minutes, 4 December 1923.

198 NAI, D/T, S 3678A, Liam Tobin and C.F. Dalton to Cosgrave, 6 March 1924.

199 NAI, G2/3, Cabinet minutes, 11 March 1924.

200 *Dáil debates*, vol. 6, 1896–7 (11 March 1924).

201 UCDA, Mulcahy MSS, P7/B/196, *Manchester Guardian*, 14 March 1924; *Dáil debates*, vol. 6, 2367–8, 2375–7 (26 March 1924); Maryann Gialanella Valiulis, *Almost a rebellion: the Irish army mutiny of 1924* (Cork, 1985), 58–9.

202 NAI, G2/3, C.2/64, Cabinet minutes, 12 March 1924; *Dáil debates*, vol. 6, 1971–6, 1982–3 (12 March 1924).

203 NAI, D/T, S 3678A, Tobin and Dalton to Cosgrave, 12 March 1924.

204 *Dáil debates*, vol. 6, 1984–5, 2000, 2002, 2019–24 (12 March 1924); *Irish Independent*, 13 March 1924, 6.

205 *Dáil debates*, vol. 6, 1988 (12 March 1924).

206 NAI, G2/3, C.2/65, Cabinet minutes, 14 March 1924.

[207] *Irish Times*, 19 March 1924, 5.

[208] Kevin O'Higgins, *Dáil debates*, vol. 6, 2225 (19 March 1924).

[209] UCDA, Mulcahy MSS, P7/B/196, Mulcahy, memorandum, 19 March 1924; NLI, P 7399, *Irlande*, vol. 4, 152, Blanche to Poincaré, 30 March 1924; *Dáil debates*, vol. 6, 2221, O'Higgins (19 March 1924).

[210] Fearghal McGarry, *Eoin O'Duffy: a self-made hero* (Oxford, 2005), 135–6.

[211] NAI, D/T, S 3678E, Maurice Moynihan, memorandum citing views of Michael J. Costello expressed ten days earlier, 22 December 1948.

[212] UCDA, Mulcahy MSS, P7/B/196, Press extract.

[213] NLI, P 7399, *Irlande*, vol. 4, 152, Blanche to Poincaré, 30 March 1924.

[214] Cosgrave MSS, Cosgrave to Granard, 13 December 1927.

[215] UCDA, Mulcahy MSS, P7/B/196, Cosgrave to Mulcahy, 17 March 1924.

[216] NAI, G2/3, C. 2/67, Cabinet minutes, 18 March 1924.

[217] UCDA, Mulcahy MSS, P7a/209(231), Ó Murthuile, memoir.

[218] NAI, G2/3, C.2/68, Cabinet minutes, 19 March 1924.

[219] NAI, G2/3, C.2/69, Cabinet minutes 19 March 1924.

[220] NAI, D/T, S 3678A, Gearoid McGann to Diarmuid O'Hegarty, 21 March 1924, O'Higgins to Cosgrave, 21 March 1924.

[221] NAI, G2/3, C.2/72, Cabinet minutes, 21 March 1924.

[222] NAI, G2/3, C.2/73, Cabinet minutes, 22 March 1924.

[223] *Irish Statesman*, 17 January 1925, 587; see Thomas Morrissey SJ, *A man called Hughes: the life and times of Seamus Hughes 1881–1943* (Dublin, 1991), 189.

[224] *Dáil debates*, vol. 7, 3155 (26 June 1924).

[225] *Dáil debates*, vol. 7, 3128, 3149 (26 June 1924).

[226] O'Halpin, *Defending Ireland*, 51.

[227] See Patrick Maume, *The long gestation: Irish nationalist life 1891–1918* (Dublin, 1999), 218–9.

[228] Anne Dolan, *Commemorating the Irish Civil War. History and memory, 1923–2000* (Cambridge, 2003), 32.

[229] *Irish Times*, 20 March 1924, 6, editorial.

[230] Lee, *Ireland 1912–1985*, 103.

[231] UCDA, Mulcahy MSS, P7/99(54–6), Mulcahy, diary, 20 November 1924; Marie Coleman, 'Hughes, Peter', *DIB*, vol. 4, 839; Regan, *Irish Counter-Revolution*, 223–4.

[232] Eunan O'Halpin, 'The army and the Dáil—civil/military relations within the independence movement', in Brian Farrell (ed.), *The creation of the Dáil* (Dublin, 1994), 107–21: 119.

[233] UCDA, Mulcahy MSS, P7/C/99(78), Mulcahy, diary, 2 December 1924.

[234] NLI, P 7399, *Irlande*, vol. 5, 38, Blanche to Edouard Herriot, 31 December 1924; UCDA, Mulcahy MSS, P7/C/99(69), Mulcahy, weekly comment, 29 November 1924.

[235] CCCA, U271/A/252, De Róiste, diary, 18 November 1924.

[236] Thomas Jones, diary, 31 July 1924, *Whitehall diary*, vol. III, 234.

[237] Murray, *Boundary commission*, 99–104, 116.

[238] *Dáil debates, 1921–1922, debate on the treaty*, 106–7 (21 December 1921).

[239] NAI, D/T, S 1801A, Memorandum, 21 January 1922.

[240] Michael A. Hopkinson, 'The Craig–Collins pacts of 1922: two attempted reforms of the Northern Ireland government', *Irish Historical Studies* XXVII (106) (November 1990), 145–58: 148.

[241] Government of Ireland Act (1920), Clause 2.1.

[242] NAI, D/T, S 1834A, Minutes, 22 March 1922.

[243] James Masterman-Smith, cited in Kevin Matthews, *Fatal influence: the impact of Ireland on British politics, 1920–1925* (Dublin, 2004), 99.

[244] *Dáil debates*, vol. 7, 2373–9 (13 June 1924).

[245] NAI, D/T, S 1834A, Cosgrave, memorandum, n.d. (mid-June 1924).

[246] UCDA, Blythe MSS, P24/129(12), A.W. Cope to Cosgrave, 13 May 1924.

[247] NAI, G2/1, C.1/30, Cabinet minutes, 16 January 1923; Murray, *Boundary commission*, 150.

[248] NAI, North-Eastern Boundary Bureau (NEBB), 1/8/34, Cosgrave to James McNeill, 1 May 1924.

[249] Kevin O'Shiel, notes, 30 January 1924, *DIFP*, vol. II, 265.

[250] Laffan, *Partition*, 101–2.

[251] Curtis to Jones, 28 June 1923, Jones, *Whitehall diary*, vol. III, 223. On Curtis's relations with Cosgrave, see Fanning, *Irish Department of Finance*, 126–8.

[252] BNA, CO 904/18, N.G. Loughnane to Curtis, 17 April 1923.

[253] Paul McMahon, *British spies and Irish rebels: British intelligence and Ireland, 1916–1945* (London, 2008), 189.

[254] NAI, G2/2, C.1/116, Cabinet minutes, 5 June 1923.

[255] Memorandum, 17 January 1924, *DIFP*, vol. II, 252.

[256] NAI, NEBB 1/8/27, Cosgrave to Boundary Bureau, 8 January 1924.

[257] O'Halloran, *Partition*, 149–50.

[258] UCDA, McGilligan MSS, P35d/106, Louis J. Walsh to McGilligan, 5 November 1923.

[259] Geoffrey J. Hand, 'MacNeill and the boundary commission', in F.X. Martin and F.J. Byrne (eds), *The scholar revolutionary: Eoin MacNeill, 1867–1945 and the making of the new Ireland* (Shannon, 1973), 199–275: 216.

[260] Eda Sagarra, *Kevin O'Shiel: Tyrone nationalist and Irish state-builder* (Sallins, 2013), 220–1; McCarthy, *Kevin O'Higgins*, 189–90; Hand, 'MacNeill and the boundary commission', 210.

[261] Jones, diary, 2 February, 30 March 1924, *Whitehall diary*, vol. III, 226, 228.

[262] NAI, D/T, S 1801E, Cosgrave, 'Notes of the president', 2 February 1924.

[263] NAI, D/T, S 1801H, Cosgrave to MacDonald, 4 June 1924.

[264] Jones, diary, 31 July 1924, *Whitehall diary*, vol. III, 233.

[265] NAI, D/T, S 1801R, O'Higgins to Cosgrave, 7 May 1924; Kennedy to Cosgrave, 9 May 1924.

[266] Resumé, 2 August 1924, *DIFP*, vol. II, 330.

[267] Murray, *Boundary commission*, 199.

[268] Cosgrave, memorandum, 6 July 1924, *DIFP*, vol. II, 315; Cosgrave to Feetham, 10 July 1924, *DIFP*, vol. II, 320.

[269] Memorandum (by Hugh Kennedy?), 19 September 1925, *DIFP*, vol. II, 433.

[270] Nicholas Mansergh, *The unresolved question. The Anglo-Irish settlement and its undoing, 1912–72* (New Haven and London, 1991), 193.

[271] Feetham, memorandum, 11 September 1925, Geoffrey J. Hand (ed.), *Report of the Irish boundary commission 1925* (Shannon, 1969), 49.

[272] Matthews, *Fatal influence*, 220.

[273] NAI, D/T, S 11,724, Cosgrave to Cohalan, 11 September 1924.

[274] Enda Staunton, *The nationalists of Northern Ireland* (Dublin, 2001), 96.

[275] Lee, *Ireland 1912–1985*, 147.

[276] Denis McCullough, *Dáil debates*, vol. 13, 610–1 (19 November 1925).

[277] NAI, G2/4, C.2/223, Cabinet minutes, 2 November 1925.

[278] *Dáil debates*, vol. 13, 619 (19 November 1925).

[279] Hand, 'MacNeill and the boundary commission', 249.

[280] *Dáil debates*, vol. 13, 634–8, (19 November 1925).

[281] Hand, 'MacNeill and the boundary commission', 256.

[282] Murray, *Boundary commission*, 193.

[283] *Dáil debates*, vol. 13, 800–2 (24 November 1925).

[284] *Dáil debates*, vol. 13, 808, 810 (24 November 1925).

[285] Draft notes, 26 November 1925, *DIFP*, vol. II, 475–7; BNA, Cab. 27/295, minutes, Cabinet committee on Irish affairs, 26 November 1925.

[286] BNA, Cab.27/295, 1A(25), Committee on Irish affairs, minutes, 26 November 1925, 3rd minute.

[287] Cosgrave MSS, Cosgrave, memorandum, 26 November 1925.

[288] O'Halloran, *Partition*, 112.

[289] NAI, G2/4, C.2/230, Cabinet minutes, 27 November 1925.

[290] Minutes, 28 November 1925, *DIFP*, vol. II, 481–3.

[291] Jones, diary, 29 November 1925, *Whitehall diary*, vol. III, 240–1; summary of statements, 29 November 1925, *DIFP*, vol. II, 490.

[292] BNA, Cab.27/295, CP 501(25), Minutes, 29 November 1925.

[293] McCarthy, *Kevin O'Higgins*, 216.

[294] McMahon, *British spies and Irish rebels*, 194.

[295] Draft notes, 1 December 1925, *DIFP*, vol. II, 497.

[296] Draft notes, 1 December 1925, *DIFP*, vol. II, 507.

[297] BNA, Cab. 27/295, C.A./H/48, Cabinet committee, 1 December 1925, 3rd minutes; draft notes, 2 December 1925, *DIFP*, vol. II, 513.

[298] Brennan, memorandum, 30 November 1925, *DIFP*, vol. II, 491–6; draft notes, 1 December 1925, *DIFP*, vol. II, 497, 501.

[299] Draft notes, 1 December 1925, *DIFP*, vol. II, 500–3.

[300] Draft notes, 2 December 1925, *DIFP*, vol. II, 518.

[301] BNA, Cab. 27/295, C.A./H/48, 5th minutes 2 December 1925.

[302] Ó Broin, *No man's man*, 134.

[303] Michael Kennedy, *Division and consensus: the politics of cross-border relations in Ireland, 1925–1969* (Dublin, 2000), 14.

[304] Draft notes, 3 December 1925, *DIFP*, vol. II, 528.

[305] Draft notes, 2 December 1925, *DIFP*, vol. II, 522.

[306] Ervine, *Craigavon*, 507.

[307] Phoenix, *Northern nationalism*, 332–4.

[308] Keith Middlemas and John Barnes, *Baldwin: a biography* (London, 1969), 364.

[309] *Dáil debates*, vol. 13, 1301, 1303, 1306–7, 1313 (7 December 1925).

[310] *Dáil debates*, vol. 13, 1322, 1387 (7 December 1925).

[311] *Dáil debates*, vol. 13, 1319, 1321, 1436, 1479–84 (7 and 8 December 1925).

[312] UCDA, Kennedy MSS, P4/419, Cosgrave to Kennedy, 30 September 1924.

[313] *Dáil debates*, vol. 61, 1390 (22 April 1936).

[314] For example, *Dáil debates, debate on the treaty*, 107 (21 December 1921); *Dáil debates*, vol. 41, 584 (27 April 1932).

[315] See, for example, Fearghal McGarry, *The Rising. Ireland: Easter 1916* (Oxford, 2010), 219–20; Townshend, *The Republic*, 179–80, 280–2.

[316] UCDA, de Valera MSS, P150/1936, Stack to de Valera, 4 December 1925.

[317] Kissane, *Politics of the Irish Civil War*, 188.

[318] Munger, *Legitimacy of opposition*, 20.

[319] Jones, diary, 1 December 1925, *Whitehall Diary*, vol. III, 244.

320 UCDA, Cumann na nGaedheal/Fine Gael MSS, P39/Min/1(480, 483), Minutes, Cumann na nGaedheal standing committee, 20 November, 11 December 1925.

321 Cosgrave MSS, Granard to Cosgrave, 25 March 1927, Cosgrave to Granard, 26 March 1927.

322 *Irish Times*, 26 May 1927, 6.

323 *Leader*, 30 April 1927, 293.

324 NAI, D/T, S 3703, O'Higgins, 'Intoxicating liquor Bill, prefatory note', 27 March 1924; UCDA, Healy MSS, P6/A/98, Healy to Annie Healy, 27 July 1924.

325 Madeleine Humpheys, 'Jansenists in high places': a study in the relationship between the liquor trade and manufacturing industry and the Cumann na nGaedheal government, 1922–1932, unpublished MA thesis, UCD, 1991, 144.

326 NAI, D/T, S 4251A, *Intoxicating Liquor Commission report August 1925*, 17, and Second Schedule (a), 1.

327 *Irish Statesman*, 12 February 1927, 539.

328 *Dáil debates,* vol. 19, 436 (29 March 1927).

329 NAI, D/T, S 5319, Telegram to Cosgrave, 11 February 1927.

330 NAI, D/T, S 5319, Edward Duggan to Cosgrave's secretary, and accompanying note, 15 February 1927.

331 NAI, D/T, S 5319, Resolution, 3 March 1927.

332 Humphreys, 'Jansenists in high places', table I, 17a.

333 *Leader*, 14 May 1927, 357.

334 UCDA, Blythe MSS, P24/617(1–12), 'Policy of the Cumann na nGaedheal party by President Cosgrave, June, 1927'.

335 *Dáil debates*, vol. 19, 2621, 2623 (20 May 1927).

336 UCDA, Mulcahy MSS, P7b/66, Mulcahy to John J. Sheehan, 28 May 1927; *Irish Times*, 20 May 1927, 6.

337 Gallagher, *Irish election results 1922–44*, 44, 84.

338 NLI, P 7399, *Irlande*, vol. 6, 169, Blanche to Aristide Briand, 8 June 1927.

6. CONFRONTING FIANNA FÁIL

1 *Irish Times*, 3 June 1927, 4.

2 *Irish Times*, 27 May 1927, 5.

3 *Irish Independent*, 27 May 1927, 9; *Irish Times*, 30 May 1927, 4.

4 *Irish Independent*, 30 May 1927, 8.

5 *Irish Times*, 14 June 1927, 6, editorial.

6 NAI, MacDermot MSS, 1065/1/1, O'Higgins to Frank MacDermot, 18 May 1927.

7 *Irish Statesman*, 18 June 1927, 346.

8 *Irish Statesman*, 9 July 1927, 415.

9 *Leader*, 2 July 1927, 509.

10 *Dáil debates*, vol. 20, 14–15 (23 June 1927).

11 UCDA, Mulcahy MSS, P7/D/3(8–9), Mulcahy, conversation with Peadar MacMahon, 19 August 1963.

12 *Irish Times*, 30 May 1927, 6, editorial.

13 *Irish Times*, 13 July 1937, 8.

14 NLI, Johnson MSS, MS 17,162, Johnson, memoranda, July and 19 August 1927.

15 *Irish Independent*, 11 July 1927, 7.

[16] Eunan O'Halpin, 'Politics and the state, 1922-32', in Hill, *A new history of Ireland, VII*, 86–126: 121.

[17] NAI, D/T, S 11,724, Cohalan to Cosgrave 10 January 1924, Cosgrave to Cohalan 18 February 1924.

[18] NLI, Johnson MSS, 17,162, Johnson, memoranda, July and 19 August 1927.

[19] Munger, *Legitimacy of opposition*, 21.

[20] *Irish Times*, 12 August 1927, 7.

[21] *Irish Statesman*, 20 August 1927, 559.

[22] *Irish Independent*, 17 August 1927, 7; Michael Hayes, cited in Meehan, *The Cosgrave party*, 100–1.

[23] *Irish Times*, 15 August 1927, 7; J. Anthony Gaughan, *Thomas Johnson, 1872–1963: first leader of the Labour Party in Dáil Éireann* (Dublin, 1980), 310; Morrissey, *William O'Brien*, 249–50.

[24] *Irish Times*, 18 August 1927, 7; *Irish Independent*, 13 August 1927, 7.

[25] *Irish Times*, 17 August 1927, 7.

[26] David McCullagh, *The reluctant taoiseach: a biography of John A. Costello* (Dublin, 2010), 64–5; Meehan, *Cosgrave party*, 116.

[27] *Dáil debates*, vol. 1, 44–5 (9 September 1922); UCDA, Mulcahy MSS, P7a/179(49), Mulcahy to Cosgrave, 5 July 1923.

[28] Paul A. Kelly, Convincing the voters: the electoral appeal of Cumann na nGaedheal 1923–32. Unpublished MA thesis, UCD, 1981, 72.

[29] NAI, DE 2/6, C.3/12, Cabinet minutes, 29 July 1927.

[30] Gallagher, *Irish elections 1922–44*, 85, 116.

[31] Lee, *Ireland 1912–1985*, 79–80.

[32] Brian O'Kennedy, *Making history. The story of a remarkable campaign* (Dublin, 1927).

[33] *Irish Times*, 2 September 1927, 5.

[34] *Irish Times*, 29 August 1927, 5.

[35] *Irish Times*, 10 September 1927, 6; 12 September 1927, 4; 15 September 1927, 7.

[36] *Irish Independent*, 8 September 1927, 8.

[37] *Irish Times*, 2 September 1927, 8.

[38] *Irish Times*, 7 September 1927, 5.

[39] *Dáil debates*, vol. 31, 527 (5 July 1929).

[40] Cosgrave MSS, Cosgrave to Granard, 22 September, 3 October 1927.

[41] Kelly, Convincing the voters, 75.

[42] *Weekly Irish Times*, 15 October 1927, 8, editorial.

[43] Richard Dunphy, *The making of Fianna Fáil power in Ireland 1923–1948* (Oxford, 1995), 16–17, 66.

[44] *Dáil debates*, vol. 22, 1428 (20 March 1928).

[45] *Dáil debates*, vol. 28, 1404 (14 March 1929).

[46] Cosgrave MSS, Cosgrave to Granard, 3 October 1927.

[47] NAI, D/T, S 2547A, Cosgrave to Diarmuid O'Hegarty, 10 January 1931; *Dáil debates*, vol. 40, 358–9 (16 October 1931).

[48] NAI, D/T, S 5111/3, Speech, 15 March 1927.

[49] UCDA, de Valera MSS, P150/2095, De Valera, note, n.d. (September 1927).

[50] Garvin, *Judging Lemass*, 129.

[51] *Dáil debates*, vol. 33, 1151 (27 February 1930); vol. 26, 822 (24 October 1928).

[52] Manning, *James Dillon*, 51.

[53] Micheál Martin, *Freedom to choose: Cork and party politics in Ireland, 1918–1932* (Cork, 2009), 138.

[54] NLI, James Douglas MSS, 49,581(44), John Costello to James Douglas, 22 February 1928.

55 NAI, D/T, S, 4127, Cosgrave, memorandum, n.d. (February 1925?).

56 Kohn, *The constitution of the Irish Free State*, 242–4.

57 NLI, P 7504, *Irlande*, vol. 7, 90, Blanche to Briand, 8 June 1928.

58 Alan J. Ward, *The Irish constitutional tradition: responsible government and modern Ireland 1782–1992* (Dublin, 1994), 223.

59 *New York Times*, 12 April 1929, cited in Seosamh Ó Longaigh, *Emergency law in independent Ireland* (Dublin, 2006), 90.

60 Quinlivan, *Philip Monahan*, 218–30.

61 John Byrne and Michael Fewer, *Thomas Joseph Byrne, nation builder* (Dublin, 2013), 67–97; on the destruction of the national archives, see UCDA, Kennedy MSS, P4/283/9, Hugh Kennedy, memorandum, n.d. (*c.* 1 July 1922); Ernie O'Malley, *The singing flame* (Dublin, 1978), 100, 104; and David Edwards, 'Salvaging history: Hogan and the Manuscripts Commission', in Donnchadh Ó Corráin (ed.), *James Hogan, revolutionary, historian and political scientist* (Dublin, 2001), 116–32: 117–9.

62 Michael Kennedy and Deirdre McMahon, *Reconstructing Ireland's past. A history of the Irish Manuscripts Commission* (Dublin, 2009), 12.

63 NAI, D/T, S 4156A, Cosgrave 'notes for his personal use', 28 February 1929; Michael McDunphy, memoranda, 18 and 19 November 1929.

64 Keith Jeffery, *Ireland and the Great War* (Cambridge, 2000), 118.

65 Dolan, *Commemorating the Irish Civil War*, 37–8.

66 NAI, D/T, S 4156B, M. MacDonnchadha to J. J. McElligott, 19 December 1931.

67 Jeffery, *Ireland and the Great War*, 121; Nuala C. Johnson, *Ireland, the Great War and the geography of remembrance* (Cambridge, 2003), 108–11.

68 NAI, D/T, S 4156B, *Sunday Times*, 31 August 1930.

69 RTÉ interview, 1967, quoted in Lothar Schoen, 'The Irish Free State and the electricity industry', in Andy Bielenberg (ed.), *The Shannon scheme and the electrification of the Irish Free State* (Dublin, 2002), 28–47: 32, 156, n. 16; *Dáil debates*, vol. 10, 2015–6 (3 April 1925).

70 James Meenan, *The Irish economy since 1922* (Liverpool, 1970), 169.

71 Stephen Gwynn, cited in *Irish Times*, 18 October 1965, 12.

72 Maurice Manning and Moore McDowell, *Electricity supply in Ireland: the history of the ESB* (Dublin, 1985), 51.

73 Schoen, 'Irish Free State', 47.

74 Manning and McDowell, *Electricity supply in Ireland*, 36.

75 Brendan Delany, 'McLaughlin, the genesis of the Shannon scheme and the ESB', in Bielenberg, *Shannon scheme*, 11–27: 19.

76 KDA, Fogarty MSS 33, 34–31/ix, Cosgrave to Fogarty, 19 November 1931; Marie Coleman, *The Irish sweep: a history of the Irish Hospitals Sweepstake 1930–87* (Dublin, 2009), 32, 139.

77 Ó Gráda, *A rocky road*, 228.

78 *Irish Statesman*, 9 June 1928, 267; 28 September 1929, 66.

79 *Dáil debates*, vol. 26, 825 (24 October 1928); vol. 28, 1629, 1632–3 (20 March 1929).

80 Ferriter, *Transformation of Ireland*, 318.

81 Byrne and Fewer, *Thomas Joseph Byrne*, 60; Ruth McManus, *Dublin, 1910–1940: shaping the city and suburbs* (Dublin, 2002), 125.

82 Eamonn Dunne, Revolution or resignation? Radical politics and social change in Dublin, 1922–36. Unpublished MA thesis, UCD, 1985, 16.

83 Cousins, *Birth of social welfare*, 55.

84 Dunphy, *Making of Fianna Fáil power*, 56.

[85] *Dáil debates*, vol. 23, 759 (2 May 1928).

[86] UCDA, Blythe MSS, P24/448(9), Blythe to controller, Stationery Office, 4 December 1931.

[87] Mary O'Grady, Attitudes and policies towards the Gaeltacht, 1922–1932. Unpublished MA thesis, UCD, 1985, 23, 52.

[88] *Leader*, 5 February 1927, 8; 24 December 1932, 523.

[89] DDA, Byrne MSS, 466, Politics general 1924–25, 1927, Cosgrave to Byrne, 16 September 1927; KDA, Fogarty MSS 33, 8–28/v, Cosgrave to Fogarty, 12 December 1928.

[90] KDA, Fogarty MSS 33, 20-30/v, Cosgrave to Fogarty, 9 July 1930.

[91] Kennedy, *Frank Duff*, 114–6,

[92] Cosgrave MSS, Frank Duff to Cosgrave, 8 March 1932.

[93] Dermot Keogh, *The Vatican, the bishops and Irish politics, 1919–39* (Cambridge, 1986), 162–3.

[94] UCDA, Kennedy MSS, P4/1424, Cosgrave to Kennedy, 22 July 1928.

[95] Douglas to Cosgrave, 3 January 1929, in Gaughan (ed.), *Memoirs of Senator James G. Douglas,* 117.

[96] Michael Adams, *Censorship: the Irish experience* (Alabama, 1968), 33–4.

[97] CCCA, U271/A/54, Liam de Róiste, diary, 20 March 1927.

[98] *Irish Statesman*, 22 September 1928, 45; 13 October 1928, 103; 9 March 1929, 4.

[99] Peter Martin, *Censorship in the two Irelands, 1922–1939* (Dublin, 2006), 82–90.

[100] NAI, D/T, S 5381, Censorship of publications bill, committee, 20 February and 25 April 1929.

[101] NAI, D/T, S 5381, Memorandum, 24 November 1928.

[102] *Dáil debates*, vol. 28, 81–2 (20 February 1929).

[103] *The Star*, 26 January 1929, 4, editorial.

[104] Martin, *Censorship in the two Irelands*, 69.

[105] NAI, D/T, S 2325, Henry O'Friel, secretary, Department of Justice, to Frank O'Reilly, 19 October 1929; O'Reilly to Cosgrave, 25 October 1929; Cosgrave to O'Friel, 28 October 1929.

[106] Martin, *Censorship in the two Irelands*, 91.

[107] Adams, *Censorship*, 71.

[108] Pat Walsh, *The curious case of the Mayo librarian* (Cork, 2009), 112.

[109] *The Star*, 25 January 1930, 7.

[110] *Catholic Bulletin*, January 1931, 3.

[111] *Standard*, 13 December 1930, 10, editorial; NAI, D/T, S 2547A, Sean Ruane to Liam Burke, general secretary, Cumann na nGaedheal, 14 December 1930.

[112] Thomas Mullins, *Dáil debates*, vol. 39, 524 (17 June 1931).

[113] NAI, D/T, S 2547A, Lenten pastoral, February 1931.

[114] Jack White, *Minority report: the anatomy of the Southern Irish Protestant* (Dublin, 1975), 100.

[115] *Dáil debates*, vol. 36, 1340–1 (11 December 1930).

[116] NAI, D/T, S 2547A, Cosgrave to Diarmuid O'Hegarty, 10 January 1931.

[117] For example, see Ferriter, *Judging Dev*, 221–2.

[118] NAI, D/T, S 2547A, Glynn, memorandum, n.d. (February 1931).

[119] NAI, D/T, S 2547A, Minutes, 11 and 13 February 1931.

[120] NAI, D/T, S 2457A, Cosgrave and FitzGerald, memoranda, n.d. (February 1931).

[121] Jordan, *W.T. Cosgrave*, 148.

[122] NAI, D/T, S 2574A, Gilmartin to Glynn, 27 February 1931.

[123] NAI, D/T, S 2547B, Cosgrave, draft letter to Gilmartin, 11 March 1931.

[124] NAI, D/T, S 2547B, Unsigned memorandum of meeting, 15 April 1931.

[125] *Dáil debates,* vol. 39, 517–9 (17 June 1931).

[126] *Dáil debates,* vol. 39, 494–501 (17 June 1931); Whyte, *Church and state in modern Ireland*, 46.

[127] NAI, G2/8, C.5/109, Cabinet minutes, 22 December 1931.

[128] Walsh, *Curious case*, 201–2.

[129] *Irish Times*, 4 August 1925, 5.

[130] NAI, D/T, S 4367A, Draft, Cosgrave to Clarke, 24 September 1930; Cosgrave to Clarke, 25 September 1930.

[131] NAI, D/T, S 4367A, Clarke to Cosgrave, 26 September 1930.

[132] NAI, D/T, S 4367A, Cosgrave to Clarke, 30 September 1930.

[133] NAI, D/T, S 4367A, Draft (not sent), Campbell to Lennox Robinson, 30 September 1930.

[134] NAI, D/T, S 4367A, Michael McDunphy to Cosgrave, 15 April 1931, Fogarty to Cosgrave, 15 April 1931.

[135] Nicola Gordon Bowe, *The life and work of Harry Clarke* (Dublin, 1929), 229.

[136] NAI, D/T, S 4367A, Cosgrave, note, 5 March, 28 May 1931.

[137] CCCA, U271/A/52, De Róiste, diary, 14 February 1925; Signe Toksvig, diary, 19 February 1932, *Signe Toksvig's Irish diaries*, 153.

[138] Keogh, *The Vatican*, 135, 137.

[139] Michael MacWhite, memorandum, 14 April 1928, *DIFP*, vol. III (Dublin, 2002), 186.

[140] Knirck, *Afterimage of the revolution*.

[141] *Dáil debates*, vol. 39, 2291 (16 July 1931).

[142] *Irish Times*, 11 December 1933, 8.

[143] Cosgrave to MacDonald, 21 November 1931, John Dulanty to Joseph Walshe, 25 November 1931, *DIFP*, vol. III, 867–8, 874.

[144] *Dáil debates*, vol. 41, 583 (27 April 1932).

[145] *Leader*, 29 January 1944, 9.

[146] *Senate debates*, vol. 15, 938 (2 June 1932), cited in McCullagh, *Reluctant taoiseach*, 99–100.

[147] UCDA, McGilligan MSS, P35d/17, Cosgrave to McGilligan, 25 November 1931.

[148] *Irish Times*, 12 January 1928, 7.

[149] Carroll, 'President Cosgrave comes to Ottawa', 183.

[150] *Weekly Irish Times*, 28 January 1928, 9.

[151] *Irish Times*, 4 February 1928, 7.

[152] *Leader*, 25 February 1928, 92.

[153] *Irish Statesman*, 18 February 1928, 531.

[154] *Dáil debates*, vol. 40, 3058 (17 December 1931).

[155] Lee, *Ireland 1912–1985*, 190; Meenan, *Irish economy*, 94.

[156] *Irish Times*, 29 March 1930, 8, editorial.

[157] *Irish Independent*, 31 March 1930, 11; 29 March 1930, 10.

[158] *Irish Statesman*, 5 April 1930, 88.

[159] *Dáil debates*, vol. 36, 64 (19 November 1930).

[160] Cosgrave MSS, Cosgrave to Granard, 17 September 1930; NAI, G2/8, Cabinet minutes.

[161] Kissane, *Politics of the Irish Civil War*, 171.

[162] Brian Hanley, *The IRA, 1926–1936* (Dublin, 2002), 74, 78–83.

[163] *Irish Times*, 13 November 1930, 7.

[164] McGarry, *Eoin O'Duffy*, 183.

[165] UCDA, McGilligan MSS, P35d/113(1–2), McGilligan to Joseph Walshe, 18 September 1931.

[166] Thomas J. Morrissey SJ, *Edward J. Byrne, 1872–1941: the forgotten archbishop of Dublin* (Dublin, 2010), 190–1; Niamh Puirséil, *The Irish Labour Party 1922–73* (Dublin, 2007), 34–5.

[167] NAI, D/T, S 5864B, Cosgrave to MacRory, 13 August 1931; Cosgrave to Irish bishops, 10, 17 September 1931.

[168] *Irish Independent*, 19 October 1931, 9; Murray, *Oracles of God*, 322.

[169] Murray, *Oracles of God*, 136; David Fitzpatrick, *The two Irelands 1922–1939* (Oxford, 1998), 230.

[170] *Dáil debates*, vol. 40, 41–5 (14 October 1931).

[171] McGarry, *Eoin O'Duffy*, 185; Ronan Fanning, *The four-leaved shamrock: electoral politics and the national imagination in independent Ireland* (Dublin, 1983), 10.

[172] Terence Brown, *Ireland, a social and cultural history 1922–2002* (London, 2004), 130.

[173] KDA, Fogarty MSS 33, 24-30/ix, Cosgrave to Fogarty, 13 December 1930.

[174] *Irish Times*, 17 February 1932, 7.

[175] Dermot Keogh, *Twentieth-century Ireland: revolution and state-building* (revised edition, Dublin, 2005), 60.

[176] O'Sullivan, *Irish Free State and its senate*, 283.

[177] Knirck, *Afterimage of the revolution*, 151.

[178] A.J.P. Taylor, *English History 1914–1945* (Oxford, 1965), 297.

[179] UCDA, McGilligan MSS, P35a/11, McElligott, memorandum, 16 September 1931.

[180] Daly, *Industrial development and Irish national identity*, 177–8.

[181] *Irish Statesman*, 8 March 1930, 3.

[182] *Dáil debates*, vol. 34, 621 (3 April 1930); *Leader*, 16 February 1929, 53; *The Star*, 3 May 1930, 1.

[183] Fanning, *Independent Ireland*, 93; Lee, *Ireland 1912–1985*, 155.

[184] KDA, Fogarty MSS 33, 29-31/iv, Cosgrave to Fogarty, 17 July 1931.

[185] UCDA, McGilligan MSS, P35a/11, J.J. McElligott, memorandum, 9 September 1931.

[186] UCDA, McGilligan MSS, P35d/113(1–2), McGilligan to Joseph Walshe, 18 September 1931.

[187] UCDA, Fine Gael/Cumann na nGaedheal MSS, P39/Min/3(111), Meeting of the party, 5 November 1931.

[188] KDA, Fogarty MSS 33, 39–31/xiv, 40-31/xv, Cosgrave to Fogarty, 4, 11 December 1931.

[189] Oliver MacDonagh, 'Memoir', in Tom Dunne (ed.), Oliver MacDonagh, *Looking back: living and writing history* (Dublin, 2008), 84.

[190] *Irish Times*, 11 January 1932, 7.

[191] *Irish Independent*, 15 January 1932, 11.

[192] *Irish Times*, 15 January 1932, 7.

[193] *Leader*, 13 February 1932, 65.

[194] *Irish Times*, 30 January 1932, 10.

[195] Hanley, *The IRA*, 81; Meehan, *The Cosgrave party*, 176.

[196] Richard Sinnott, *Irish voters decide: voting behaviour in elections and referendums since 1918* (Manchester, 1995), 101–2.

[197] KDA, Fogarty MSS 33, 44–32/iv, Cosgrave to Fogarty 18 February 1932.

[198] McGarry, *Eoin O'Duffy*, 189.

[199] UCDA, Mulcahy MSS, P7/D/3(6), Mulcahy in conversation with Peadar McMahon, 19 August 1963.

[200] Brady, *Guardians of the Peace*, 169.

[201] KDA, Fogarty MSS 33, 45–32/v, Cosgrave to Fogarty, 29 February 1932; O'Halpin, *Defending Ireland*, 80.

[202] Munger, *Legitimacy of Opposition*, 11–13.

[203] Horgan, *Seán Lemass*, 65.

[204] Manning, *James Dillon*, 53.

[205] *Dáil debates*, vol. 41, 579 (27 April 1932).

[206] KDA, Fogarty MSS 33, 44–32/iv, Cosgrave to Fogarty, 18 February 1932.

7. LEADING THE OPPOSITION

[1] Deirdre McMahon, *Republicans and imperialists: Anglo-Irish relations in the 1930s* (New Haven and London, 1984), 81, 82, 91, 107.

[2] Deirdre McMahon, '"A transient apparition": British policy towards the de Valera government, 1932–5', *Irish Historical Studies* XXII (88) (September 1981), 331–61: 336–7. For discussion of the 'Economic War', see below.

[3] *Irish Press*, 14 January 1933, 2. De Valera later denied any knowledge of such an intrigue; *Dáil debates,* vol. 50, 2562 (2 March 1934).

[4] McMahon, *Republicans and imperialists*, 4.

[5] UCDA, FitzGerald MSS, P80/1111, Cosgrave to Hayes, 21 September 1932.

[6] *Irish Times*, 6 February 1932, 10.

[7] KDA, Fogarty MSS 33, 50–33/i, Cosgrave to Fogarty, 31 January 1933.

[8] NAI, MacDermot MSS, 1065/1/1, O'Higgins to MacDermot, 10 May 1927.

[9] McMahon, *Republicans and imperialists*, 102.

[10] Warner Moss, *Political parties in the Irish Free State* (New York and London, 1933), 192.

[11] UCDA, de Valera MSS, P150/2097, Newspaper cutting, 29 January 1933.

[12] *Dáil debates,* vol. 20, 1686 (16 August 1927).

[13] *Dáil debates*, vol. 76, 1052 (15 June 1939).

[14] Peter Mair, *The changing Irish party system: organisation, ideology and electoral competition* (London, 1987), 22.

[15] Foster, *W.B. Yeats: a life. II. The arch-poet*, 470.

[16] Jason Knirck, 'A cult of no personality: W.T. Cosgrave and the election of 1933', *Éire-Ireland* 47 (3 and 4) (fall/winter 2012), 64–90: 68–70, 81–3.

[17] *Irish Times*, 10 January 1933, 5.

[18] *Irish Independent*, 9 January 1933, 9.

[19] *Irish Times*, 4 January 1933, 7.

[20] UCDA, de Valera MSS, P150/2097, John Moynihan to de Valera, 21 January 1933.

[21] *Irish Independent*, 9 January 1933, 8.

[22] *Irish Times*, 12 January 1933, 7.

[23] *Irish Times*, 21 January 1933, 7.

[24] *Irish Times*, 20 January 1933, 7; 16 January 1933, 7.

[25] Meehan, *The Cosgrave party*, 207–8.

[26] *Irish Independent,* 24 January 1933, 9.

[27] KDA, Fogarty MSS 33, 50–33/i, Cosgrave to Fogarty, 31 January 1933.

[28] *Irish Times*, 21 January 1933, 8, editorial.

[29] Moss, *Political parties*, 193.

[30] *Irish Independent*, 6 January 1933, 8.

[31] Brian M. Walker (ed.), *Parliamentary election results in Ireland 1918–92* (Dublin 1992), 138–42; *Irish Times*, 31 January 1933, 8.

[32] McMahon, *British spies and Irish rebels*, 236.

[33] *Irish Times*, 23 January 1933, 7; *Weekly Irish Times*, 14 January 1933, 1.

[34] Brady, *Guardians of the peace*, 164.

[35] Dale Montgomery, '"Helping the Guards": illegal display and Blueshirt criminality, 1932–36', *Éire-Ireland* (Spring/Summer 2014), 22–43: 32.

[36] McGarry, *Eoin O'Duffy*, 186–8.

[37] Garret FitzGerald, *Ireland in the world: further reflections* (Dublin, 2005), 76.

[38] UCDA, Blythe MSS, P24/654, Blythe, marginal note, n.d..

[39] Mike Cronin, *The Blueshirts and Irish politics,* (Dublin, 1997), 129.

[40] Lee, *Ireland 1912–1985*, 181.

[41] John A. Murphy, *Ireland in the twentieth century* (Dublin, 1975), 82.

[42] *Irish Times*, 2 August 1933, 7; 23 August 1933, 6, editorial.

[43] *Dáil debates*, vol. 49, 1030 (1 August 1933).

[44] Maurice Manning, *The Blueshirts* (Dublin, 1970), 97.

[45] Manning, *James Dillon*, 79.

[46] *Irish Times*, 9 September 1933, 9–10.

[47] McGarry, *O'Duffy*, 222.

[48] UCDA, Cumann na nGaedheal/Fine Gael MSS, P39/Min/2(8), Fine Gael policy, 9 November 1933.

[49] *Irish Times*, 9 September 1933, 9.

[50] Regan, *Myth and the Irish state*, 92.

[51] *Irish Times*, 3 February 1955, 5; 15 February 1955, 5.

[52] Brian Maye, *Fine Gael 1932–1987: a general history with biographical sketches of its leading members* (Tallaght, 1993), 38.

[53] Manning, *Blueshirts*, 94.

[54] Cullen, Patrick J. Hogan, 297, 300.

[55] *Irish Independent,* 22 December 1933, 7.

[56] *Irish Times*, 30 April 1934, 7.

[57] Hanley, *The IRA*, 86–90.

[58] *Irish Times*, 11 December 1933, 7.

[59] Cronin, *Blueshirts*, 65.

[60] McGarry, *O'Duffy*, 267; Gomez Homen, cited in Dermot Keogh, *Ireland and Europe 1919–1948* (Dublin, 1989), 47.

[61] Cronin, *Blueshirts*, 98.

[62] For example, *Irish Independent*, 9 December 1933, 9.

[63] *Dáil debates*, vol. 50, 2121 (23 February 1934).

[64] *Weekly Irish Times*, 30 September 1933, 1; *Irish Times*, 8 January 1934, 8.

[65] *Dáil debates*, vol. 50, 2538–52 (2 March 1934).

[66] *Irish Times*, 3 May 1934, 10.

[67] *Dáil debates*, vol. 51, 1838–40 (18 April 1934).

[68] *Dáil debates*, vol. 50, 2383–4 (1 March 1934).

[69] Edward Harding, minute, 19 February 1934, quoting John Dulanty, *DIFP*, vol. IV, 281.

[70] Paul Bew, Ellen Hazelkorn, Henry Patterson, *The dynamics of Irish politics* (London, 1989), 52.

[71] *Irish Times*, 12 December 1933, 7.

[72] *Irish Independent*, 5 July 1934, 10.

[73] *Irish Times*, 2 July 1934, 7.

[74] Cronin, *Blueshirts*, 76.

[75] NAI, MacDermot MSS, 1065/2/4, Dillon to MacDermot, 25 September 1934.

[76] Manning, *Blueshirts*, 144; UCDA, Tierney MSS, LA 30/367(7), MacDermot to Tierney, 10 September 1934; *Irish Times*, 25 October 1934, 7.

[77] UCDA, Costello MSS, P190/330, Cosgrave to Costello, 14 September 1934.

[78] UCDA, Cumann na nGaedheal/Fine Gael MSS, P39/Min/2(67), Committee minutes, 20 September 1934.

[79] Cronin, *Blueshirts*, 198.

[80] KDA, Fogarty MSS 33, 60–35/ii, Cosgrave to Fogarty, 2 April 1935.

[81] NAI, MacDermot MSS, 1065/4/4, Tierney to MacDermot, 27 September 1934.

[82] UCDA, FitzGerald MSS, P80/1148(3), Hogan to Desmond FitzGerald, n.d. (late 1935).

[83] Mansergh, diary, 22 September, 22 October 1934, *Nationalism and independence*, 120–1, 122.

[84] Jackson, *Ireland 1798–1998*, 300.

[85] NAI, MacDermot MSS, 1065/2/5, Dillon to MacDermot, 1 October 1934.

[86] UCDA, Cumann na nGaedheal/Fine Gael MSS, P39/Min/4(16), Party meeting, 16 May 1934.

[87] *Leader*, 29 February 1936, 101.

[88] UCDA, Cumann na nGaedheal/Fine Gael MSS, P39/Min/2(145), Standing committee minutes, 13 October 1936.

[89] *Irish Times*, 10 October 1934, 7.

[90] Fearghal McGarry, *Irish politics and the Spanish Civil War* (Cork, 1999), 191.

[91] Kissane, *Explaining Irish democracy*, 167.

[92] Garvin, *1922*, 194.

[93] *Dáil debates*, vol. 41, 572 (27 April 1932).

[94] Regan, *Irish counter-revolution*, 356.

[95] George O'Brien, 'The budget', *Studies*, June 1925, 177–90: 190.

[96] J. Peter Neary and Cormac Ó Gráda, 'Protection, economic war and structural change: the 1930s in Ireland', *Irish Historical Studies*, XXVII (107) (May 1991), 250–66: 254.

[97] KDA, Fogarty MSS 33, 53–34/i; 4 May 1935, 62–35/iv, Cosgrave to Fogarty, 26 March 1934.

[98] McCracken, *Representative government*, 134.

[99] Bryan Cooper, *Irish Times*, 26 January 1924, 9.

[100] UCDA, Cumann na nGaedheal/Fine Gael MSS, P39/Min/2(115–6), Standing committee minutes, 1 October 1935.

[101] Minutes, 2 July 1936, UCDA, Cumann na nGaedheal/Fine Gael MSS, P39/Min/4(64).

[102] UCDA, Cumann na nGaedheal/Fine Gael MSS, P39/Min/2(85), Standing committee minutes, 17 January 1935.

[103] UCDA, Cumann na nGaedheal/Fine Gael MSS, P39/Min/2(97), Standing committee minutes, 28 March 1935.

[104] UCDA, MacEoin MSS, P151/783, Cosgrave to TDs, 16 October 1936.

[105] Manning, *James Dillon*, 110.

[106] UCDA, Cumann na nGaedheal/Fine Gael MSS, P39/Min/4(66–7), Minutes, party meeting, 11 November 1936.

[107] KDA, Fogarty MSS 33, 70–36, iv, Cosgrave to Fogarty, 26 September 1936.

[108] *Irish Times*, 15 June 1937, 6, editorial.

[109] *Leader*, 12 October 1935, 271; 26 October 1935, 319.

[110] UCDA, Costello MSS, P190/333, Unsigned letter to Cosgrave, 12 September 1935.

[111] *Irish Times*, 12 October 1935, 8, editorial.

[112] *Irish Times*, 16 July 1936, 8.

[113] UCDA, Mulcahy MSS, P7b/101(26–29), Mulcahy to Cosgrave, 24 December 1936.

[114] UCDA, Costello MSS, P190/315(1), Ard-fheis speech, 21 March 1935.

[115] *Dáil debates,* vol. 58, 1381 (25 July 1935).

[116] KDA, Fogarty MSS 33, 87–39/ii , Cosgrave to Fogarty, 27 February 1939.

[117] *Dáil debates*, vol. 61, 1389 (22 April 1936).

[118] *Dáil debates,* vol. 59, 2477 (11 December 1938); vol. 49, 1103 (2 August 1933); vol. 69, 3132 (13 January 1938).

[119] *Weekly Irish Times*, 12 November 1933, 1; *Dáil debates,* vol. 44, 1734 (27 October 1932). For a similar but earlier reference to MacEntee, see *Dáil debates 1921–1922, debate on the treaty*, 356 (9 January 1922).

[120] *Dáil debates*, vol. 66, 2066 (4 May 1937); vol. 75, 284 (29 March 1939).

[121] KDA, Fogarty MSS 33, 72–37/ii, Cosgrave to Fogarty, 26 March 1937.

[122] KDA, Fogarty MSS 33, 82–38/iv, Cosgrave to Fogarty, 26 September 1938.

[123] Cruise O'Brien, 'Ireland in international affairs', 115.

[124] Cian McMahon, 'Irish Free State newspapers and the Abyssinian crisis, 1935–6', *Irish Historical Studies* XXXVI, 143 (May 2009), 368–88: 371; *Irish Times*, 5 October 1935, 10.

[125] *Irish Times*, 8 October 1935, 7; 11 October 1935, 7; 14 October 1935, 13.

[126] UCDA, Tierney MSS, LA30/367(13), MacDermot to Michael Tierney, 6 October 1934.

[127] NAI, MacDermot MSS, 1065/6/1, O'Hegarty to MacDermot, 10 October 1935.

[128] KDA, Fogarty 33, 69–36/iii, 70–36/iv; 72–37/i, Cosgrave to Fogarty, 16, 26 September 1936; 26 March 1937; *Dáil debates*, vol. 64, 1197 (27 November 1936).

[129] *Irish Times*, 15 June 1937, 6, editorial.

[130] UCDA, Cumann na nGaedheal/Fine Gael MSS, P39/Min/2(152), Standing committee minutes, 21 December 1936.

[131] NAI, MacDermot MSS, 1065/8/1, Frank MacDermot to C.E. Callan, 12 April 1937.

[132] O'Sullivan, *Irish Free State and its senate*, 474.

[133] Lee, *Ireland 1912–85*, 210

[134] *Dáil debates*, vol. 69, 20 (21 July 1937).

[135] *Dáil debates*, vol. 54, 131–3, 138–40, vol. 53, 392–4, 397–9 (1 May, 14 June 1934).

[136] *Irish Times*, 11 June 1937, 6, editorial; *Leader*, 9 January 1937, 582.

[137] John Dulanty to Malcolm MacDonald, 26 August 1936, cited in McGarry, *Ireland and the Spanish Civil War*, 298, n. 112.

[138] Kissane, *Explaining Irish democracy*, 200.

[139] Cosgrave MSS, J.J. Walsh to Cosgrave, 25 May 1937.

[140] *Dáil debates*, vol. 68, 346–51 (14 June 1937). On the Irish version of the constitution, see Gerard Hogan, *The origins of the Irish constitution, 1928–1941* (Dublin, 2012), 359.

[141] *Irish Times*, 3 May 1937, 9.

[142] *Irish Times*, 29 May 1937, 11.

[143] Mansergh, diary, 28 June 1937, *Nationalism and independence*, 128.

[144] *Leader*, 3 July 1937, 534.

[145] *Irish Independent*, 25 June 1937, 8.

[146] Gallagher, *Irish elections 1922–44*, 176, 208.

[147] Canning, *British Policy*, 175.

[148] *Irish Independent*, 8 July 1937, 9; UCDA, Cumann na nGaedheal/Fine Gael MSS, P39/Min/2(158), Standing committee minutes, 12 August 1937.

[149] UCDA, FitzGerald MSS, P80/1132(2), Cosgrave to FitzGerald, 25 February 1938.

[150] KDA, Fogarty, MSS 33, 76–37/vi, Cosgrave to Fogarty, 21 October 1937.

[151] KDA, Fogarty MSS 33, 77–37/vii, Cosgrave to Fogarty, 15 November 1937.

[152] Ó Gráda, *Ireland: a new economic history*, 416.

[153] James Barr, *A line in the sand: Britain, France and the struggle that shaped the Middle East* (London, 2011), 196.

[154] *Dáil debates,* vol. 71, 48–49, 352–4 (27, 29 April 1938).

[155] *Irish Times*, 16 June 1938, 5.

[156] *Irish Times*, 14 June 1938, 8.

[157] *Irish Independent*, 8 June 1938, 12.

[158] KDA, Fogarty MSS 33, 80–38/ii; 81–38/iii, Cosgrave to Fogarty, 6 June, 19 July 1938.

[159] *Irish Times*, 29 June 1938, 8; 13 July 1937, 7.

160 UCDA, Cumann na nGaedheal/Fine Gael MSS, P39/Min/2(172), Standing committee minutes, 3 October 1938.

161 *Dáil debates*, vol. 77, 8–9, 119, 137 (2 September 1939); Donal Ó Drisceoil, 'Keeping the temperature down: domestic politics in Emergency Ireland', in Dermot Keogh and Mervyn O'Driscoll (eds), *Ireland in World War Two: neutrality and survival* (Cork, 2004), 173.

162 UCDA, Mulcahy MSS, P7b/106(119), Cosgrave to Daniel Binchy, 26 June 1943; KDA, Fogarty MSS, 33, 122–44/iii, Cosgrave to Fogarty, 4 February 1944.

163 NAI, D/T, S 14,213, Cosgrave to de Valera, 9, 16 July 1940, de Valera to Cosgrave, 13 July 1940. De Valera's reply required four drafts.

164 For example, UCDA, Mulcahy MSS, P7a/210, Cosgrave, cited in memorandum, 15 November 1940; UCDA, Mulcahy MSS, P7a/214, Mulcahy to de Valera, 24 December 1940.

165 UCDA, Mulcahy MSS, P7a/210, Mulcahy, memorandum, 30 May 1940.

166 *Leader*, 5 February 1944, 19.

167 *Dáil debates*, vol. 78, 1336 (3 January 1940); UCDA, Costello MSS, P190/313(2), ard-fheis speech, 20 February 1940.

168 *Dáil debates*, vol. 78, 1642 (4 January 1940).

169 UCDA, FitzGerald MSS, P80/1119(1, 3), Cosgrave, memorandum, 16 November 1940.

170 UCDA, Mulcahy MSS, P7a/221, Cosgrave to Mulcahy, 14 January 1941; UCDA, Mulcahy MSS, P7b/107(12), Cosgrave to the McGillicuddy, 3 July 1943.

171 Robert Fisk, *In time of war: Ireland, Ulster and the price of neutrality 1939–45* (London, 1983), 365, 381.

172 *Dáil debates*, vol. 78, 1329 (3 January 1940).

173 *Dáil debates*, vol. 85, 1673 (29 January 1942).

174 KDA, Fogarty MSS 33, 108–42/iii, Cosgrave to Fogarty, 16 March 1942.

175 *Weekly Irish Times*, 10 February 1940, 17.

176 *Dáil debates*, vol. 89, 2103–5 (15 April 1943).

177 UCDA, MacEoin MSS, P151/785, Cosgrave to Seán MacEoin, 1 February 1940.

178 *Dáil debates*, vol. 84, 1880–2 (17 July 1941).

179 *Dáil debates*, vol. 84, 1889 (17 July 1941).

180 KDA, Fogarty MSS 33, 103–41/vi, Cosgrave to Fogarty, 17 July 1941.

181 Manning, *James Dillon*, 175–6.

182 KDA, Fogarty MSS 33, 107–42/ii, Cosgrave to Fogarty, 20 February 1942, 3 September 1942; 112–42/vii.

183 *Leader*, 29 January 1944, 3.

184 *Dáil debates*, vol. 84, 1881 (17 July 1941). His obvious target was the Third French Republic.

185 KDA, Fogarty MSS 33, 96–40/iv, Cosgrave to Fogarty, 17 November 1940.

186 Cosgrave MSS, Granard to Cosgrave, 8 March 1943.

187 KDA, Fogarty MSS 33, 101–41/iv, Cosgrave to Fogarty, 24 May 1941.

188 UCDA, Cumann na nGaedheal/Fine Gael MSS, P39/Min/4(110–6), Minutes.

189 KDA, Fogarty MSS 33, 112–42/vii, Cosgrave to Fogarty, 3 September 1942.

190 UCDA, Cumann na nGaedheal/Fine Gael MSS, P39/Min/2(201), Standing committee minutes, 25 March 1943.

191 *Dáil debates*, vol. 85, 1675–6 (29 January 1942).

192 *Irish Times*, 1 July 1943, 3, editorial; UCDA, Tierney MSS, LA30/375, Hogan to Michael Tierney, 5 July 1943.

193 Michael Hayes, *Irish Times*, 14 June 1943, 2.

194 *Irish Independent*, 11 May 1943, 3.

[195] *Irish Times*, 5 June 1943, 1.

[196] Sinnott, *Irish voters decide*, 101.

[197] *Irish Times*, 19 June 1943, 5.

[198] Lee, *Ireland 1912–1985*, 240.

[199] UCDA, Mulcahy MSS, P7b107(12), Cosgrave to the McGillicuddy, 3 July 1943.

[200] UCDA, Mulcahy MSS, P7b/106(121), Cosgrave to Fr Eugene, Mount Argus, n.d. (late June/early July 1943?).

[201] *Leader*, 3 July 1943, 378; 17 July 1943, 407; 29 January 1944, 3.

[202] *Irish Press*, 11 November 1943, 3.

[203] Cosgrave MSS, Cosgrave to H. S. Guinness, 17 February 1944.

[204] *Dáil debates*, vol. 91, 1063, 1320–1, 2058–62 (22 October, 28 October, 11 November 1943).

[205] *Dáil debates,* vol. 92, 996–1003 (16 December 1943).

8. THE ELDER STATESMAN

[1] KDA, Fogarty MSS 33, 120–44/I, Cosgrave to Fogarty, 12 January 1944.

[2] *Leader*, 29 January 1944, 3.

[3] *Irish Independent*, 19 January 1944, 3.

[4] Cosgrave MSS, Cosgrave to Fr Eugene, Mount Argus, 29 January 1944.

[5] *Irish Independent*, 27 January 1944, 2; *Irish Times Pictorial*, 13 March 1948, 2.

[6] Cosgrave MSS, Maffey to Cosgrave, 22 January 1944.

[7] Cosgrave MSS, O'Sullivan to Cosgrave, 28 January 1944.

[8] Cosgrave MSS, Gearoid McGann to Cosgrave, 20 January 1944.

[9] UCDA, FitzGerald MSS, P80/1147(2), Cosgrave to FitzGerald, 9 February 1944.

[10] *Irish Press*, 26 January 1944, 1.

[11] Cosgrave MSS, Cosgrave to Michael Hayes, 3 February 1944.

[12] *Dáil debates*, vol. 87, 830 (2 June 1942).

[13] Cosgrave MSS, Cosgrave to Stephen Gwynn, 22 January 1944.

[14] *Irish Independent*, 28 January 1944, 2.

[15] *Leader*, 5 February 1944, 25.

[16] Risteárd Mulcahy, *My father the general: Richard Mulcahy and the military history of the Irish revolution* (Dublin, 2009), 201.

[17] *Irish Times*, 9 January 1946, 2; 6 February 1946, 3, editorial.

[18] Van Hoek, *People and places*, 31–33.

[19] Military service pensions application 49SP6746, 15, available at: www.militaryarchives.ie/collections/online-collections/military-service-pensions-collection.

[20] KDA, Fogarty MSS 33, 132–45/i, 135–45/iv, Cosgrave to Fogarty, 11 January, 5 December 1945.

[21] *Irish Times*, 12 May 1951, 7, editorial.

[22] *Irish Times*, 21 February 1948, 1.

[23] *Irish Independent*, 10 February 1945, 3; 27 May 1944, 2.

[24] *Irish Times*, 19 April 1961, 7A.

[25] Dolan, *Commemorating the Irish Civil War*, 107–10.

[26] UCDA, Hayes MSS, P53/222(112), Cosgrave to Padraic Colum, 18 March 1953.

[27] *Irish Times*, 4 December 1945, 5.

[28] *Irish Times*, 14 December 1953, 7, and subsequent correspondence.

[29] KDA, Fogarty MSS 33, undated file, Cosgrave to Fogarty, 30 November 1949.

30 Lennox Robinson, *Ireland's Abbey Theatre: a history, 1899–1951* (London, 1951), 126; *Irish Times*, 10 September 1957, 6.

31 UCDA, Hayes MSS, P53/267, 269, Cosgrave to Michael Hayes, 23 January 1954; to Cecil Lavery, 20 January 1958.

32 KDA, Fogarty MSS 33, 93–40/I; 94–40/ii; 132–45/I, Cosgrave to Fogarty, 22 February 1940; 6 April 1940; 11 January 1945.

33 UCDA, Hayes MSS, P53/217(4), Cosgrave to Sean Milroy, 20 April 1942.

34 Liam Cosgrave, 'Recollections', 10.

35 Van Hoek, *People and places*, 33.

36 Anthony Cronin, *Dead as doornails* (Dublin, 1980), 89.

37 *Irish Times*, 10 June 1965, 12.

38 *Irish Independent*, 17 November 1965, 18.

39 Fr Lucius McClean, *Sunday Independent*, 8 January 1967, 2.

40 KDA, Fogarty MSS 33, undated file, Cosgrave to Fogarty, 5 February 1952.

41 O'Connor, *Gogarty*, 302.

42 Kennedy, *Frank Duff*, 206, 215.

43 Murray, *Oracles of God*, 171.

44 *Irish Independent*, 17 June 1959, 10.

45 Lionel Fleming, *Head or Harp* (London, 1965), 89.

46 *Irish Times*, 3 November 1947, 4; 5 April 1950, 4.

47 *Irish Times*, 29 August 1958, 6.

48 Cronin, *Dead as doornails*, 12.

49 *Irish Independent*, 1 July 1963, 8; 20 November 1965, 12.

50 Cosgrave to Lemass, n.d., Cosgrave MSS, Lemass to Cosgrave, 23, 28 January 1963.

51 See Garvin, *Judging Lemass*, 187.

52 Cosgrave MSS, Beaverbrook to Cosgrave, 8 June 1963.

53 Kennedy, *Frank Duff*, 226.

54 *Irish Press*, 17 November 1965, 1.

55 *Dáil debates*, vol. 218, 1839 (17 November 1965).

56 *Irish Times*, 29 January 1955, 8; for Williams's authorship see Keogh, *The Vatican*, 125, 264.

57 Pride of place must be given to Nicholas Mansergh, *The Irish Free State*; Donal O'Sullivan, *The Irish Free State and its senate*; Terence de Vere White, *Kevin O'Higgins*; and J.L. McCracken, *Representative government in Ireland*.

58 Subsequently published as Francis MacManus (ed.), *The years of the great test, 1922–37* (Cork, 1967).

59 Éimear O'Connor to Michael Laffan, 13 October 2013.

60 *Dublin Opinion*, February 1944, 216.

61 Lee, *Ireland 1912–1985*, 173.

62 FitzGerald, *Ireland in the world*, 101; David Harkness, *The restless dominion: the Irish Free State and the British Commonwealth of Nations 1921–31* (London, 1969), 250.

Picture credits

4. DEFENDING THE TREATY

100	© RTÉ Stills Library; Cashman Collection
129	NAI, DÉ 1/3(182); courtesy of the National Archives of Ireland
130	NAI, DÉ 1/3(184); courtesy of the National Archives of Ireland
131	TCD MS 7814-105r; courtesy of the Board of Trinity College Dublin
132–3	NLI, IND_H_0101; courtesy of the National Library of Ireland
134–5	© British Pathé
136	Courtesy of John Weedy
137	© Hogan/Hulton Archive/Getty Images
138	NLI, PD 3064 TX (A); courtesy of the National Library of Ireland
139	NLI, EPH C87; courtesy of the National Library of Ireland
140	NLI, EPH B119; courtesy of the National Library of Ireland
141	NAI, D/T, S 1393; courtesy of the National Archives of Ireland
142–3	© RTÉ Stills Library; Cashman Collection
144–5	NAI, D/T, S 2817; courtesyof the National Archives of Ireland
146	© Hulton Archive/Getty Images
147	NAI, DT, 1/1/3, PG 93; courtesy of the National Archives of Ireland
148	NAI, DT, 1/1/3, PG 97; courtesy of the National Archives of Ireland
149	BNA, CO 739-6, page 1 of 6; courtesy of the British National Archives
150–1	NLI, INDH320; courtesy of the National Library of Ireland
152	NAI, D/T, S 1784 (1); courtesy of the National Archives of Ireland
153	NAI, DT, 1/1/3, PG 101; courtesy of the National Archives of Ireland
154	NAI D/T, S 8139(8); courtesy of the National Archives of Ireland
155	BNA, CO.739-7, page 1 of 5; courtesy of the British National Archives
156–7	CCCA, U271/A/47; courtesy of Cork City and County Archives
158	NAI, D/T, S 8142; courtesy of the National Archives of Ireland
159	Courtesy of John Weedy
160–1	© RTÉ Stills Library; Cashman Collection

5. BUILDING THE FREE STATE

162	Courtesy of Liam Cosgrave
213	Cosgrave MSS, Royal Irish Academy; courtesy of Liam Cosgrave and the RIA
214–15	NLI, PD 2159 TX (16) 40; courtesy of the National Library of Ireland
216	NLI, Ir 05 i 7; courtesy of the National Library of Ireland
217	NLI, LB 05 l 2; courtesy of the National Library of Ireland
218–19	NAI, D/T, S 4127; courtesy of the National Archives of Ireland
220	NLI, Gordon Brewster Collection, PD 2199 TX 425; courtesy of the National Library of Ireland
222–3	NLI, Brewster Collection, PD 2199 TX 115; courtesy of the National Library of Ireland
224	Courtesy of Liam Cosgrave
225	NAI, D/T, S 5111/1; courtesy of the National Archives of Ireland
226–7	Courtesy of Liam Cosgrave
228	NAI, G2/5, C.2/336; courtesy of the National Archives of Ireland; image of the mould courtesy of Colm Gallagher, with thanks to the Royal Mint; photo of the 1928 halfpenny courtesy of John Stafford-Langan
229	NAI, D/T, S 3678A; courtesy of the National Archives of Ireland
230	NAI, D/T, S 3678A; courtesy of the National Archives of Ireland
231	NAI, D/T, S 3678A; courtesy of the National Archives of Ireland
232	© Hulton Archive/Getty Images
233	© Punch Magazine Ltd
234	Courtesy of John Weedy
235	NAI, D/T, S 1834A; courtesy of the National Archives of Ireland
236	© Hulton-Deutsch Collection/Corbis
237	NLI, EPH E213; courtesy of the National Library of Ireland
238	NLI, HOG100; courtesy of the National Library of Ireland
239	Courtesy of Liam Cosgrave
240–1	Undated; courtesy of Liam Cosgrave

Opposite: Detail from cover of *Dublin Opinion*, Election Issue, February 1932, vol.10, no.120, showing Cosgrave, de Valera and Labour leader T.J. O'Connell on election platforms

Index